Colours of Money, Shades of Pride

We thank Xu Bing for writing Hong Kong University Press in his Square Word Calligraphy for the cover of this book. For further explanation, see p. iv.

To Jolanta

Colours of Money, Shades of Pride

HISTORICITIES AND MORAL POLITICS IN INDUSTRIAL CONFLICTS IN HONG KONG

FRED Y. L. CHIU

香港大學出版社
HONG KONG UNIVERSITY PRESS

Hong Kong University Press
14/F Hing Wai Centre
7 Tin Wan Praya Road
Aberdeen
Hong Kong

www.hkupress.org
(secure on-line ordering)

© Hong Kong University Press 2003

ISBN 962 209 625 5 (hardback)
ISBN 962 209 626 3 (paperback)

All rights reserved. No portion of this publication may be reproduced or transmitted in any form or by any means, electronic or mechanical, including photocopy, recording, or any information storage or retrieval system, without prior permission in writing from the publisher.

British Library Cataloguing-in-Publication Data
A catalogue record for this book is available from the British Library.

Printed and bound by Nordica Printing Co. Ltd., in Hong Kong, China.

Hong Kong University Press is honoured that Xu Bing, whose art explores the complex themes of language across cultures, has written the Press's name in his Square Word Calligraphy. This signals our commitment to cross-cultural thinking and the distinctive nature of our English-language books published in China.

"At first glance, Square Word Calligraphy appears to be nothing more unusual than Chinese characters, but in fact it is a new way of rendering English words in the format of a square so they resemble Chinese characters. Chinese viewers expect to be able to read Square Word Calligraphy but cannot. Western viewers, however are surprised to find they can read it. Delight erupts when meaning is unexpectedly revealed."
— Britta Erickson, *The Art of Xu Bing*

Contents

Preface	Colours of Money, Shades of Pride: An Artisan's Self-Representation	ix
Abbreviations		xix
Cast of Characters		xxiii
Map		xxvii
Chapter 1	Introduction	1
	Fieldwork as Personal Intellectual History	3
	Perceptive Basis for a Multi-Narrative Strategy	10
	Three Genres of Narrative	13
	The Practice of Alterative Ethnography and *Non-Foundational Social Analyses*	22
Chapter 2	Hong Kong and the Japan Watch Multinational: The Political Economy of Profit-Generating Machines on a Capitalist Periphery	29

Chapter 3	On Methodologies and Procedures	51
	Fixing the Physicality of Referents: The Artificial Time/Space Grid	51
	The Time/Space Frame	52
	Problems of Narratives and Signs	55
	The Impossibility of Objectivizing, Physicalizing and Naturalizing	57
	Pseudo-Solutions: From Musical Bars to the Collapse of Astronomical Decoupage	59
	From Hermeneutics to Dialogy	62
	The Relevance of What-Has-Been-Clarified for My Case	65
Chapter 4	The Ethnographic Narrative I: Before the Event (Day −35 to Day −2)	69
Chapter 5	The Ethnographic Narrative II: During the Event (Day −2 to Day +1)	133
Chapter 6	The Ethnographic Narrative III: After the Event (Day +1 to April 1987 and beyond)	245
Chapter 7	The Reflexive Narratives: Strategic Dialogues and Dialogical Strategies, Narratives of the Coming-into-Consciousness of Being Historical Agents	277
	The Awareness of an Encroachment of Rights: A Forced Learning Process	277
	The Making of a Collective Identity	295
	Ironies and What-ifs in the Making of Histories	310
	Regimes within Regimes, States over States	342

Chapter 8	Opening up, by Way of an Epilogue	359
	The Non-Existence of 'Industrial Solidarity' and the Reproduction of Everyday Livelihood	359
	Agents, Histories and Classes in Struggle	362
	The Geometry of the Construction and Sabotage of Workers' Solidarity	365
	Workers' 'Common Sense' and the Mapping of an Alternative Conception of the World	370
	The HK/JWM Glocal Dynamics Revisited	376
	To Win or Not to Win, That Is Not the Question	382
Appendix	Selected Reports from the Press — the Journalistic Construction of Reality as Discursive Practice	385
Works Cited		423

Preface

Colours of Money, Shades of Pride: An Artisan's Self-Representation

After many years of revision I now present my readers, the interlocutors of my lived experience, with narratives and analyses of an unprecedented sit-in, waged by some 300 female workers, in Hong Kong during the first two weeks of June 1986.

I have been urged to explain why it is proper that my account and analyses and the time/space framework involved and implied, be read and thought about. This request is both tempting and frightening, as it requires me to negotiate my presence as sales representative rather than producer, and to shift, in Goffman's terms, from 'backstage' to 'front-stage'.

It was Master Li, the carver of stone tea-serving trays at the 21 September 1999 earthquake epicentre of Pu-li, Taiwan, who opened my eyes to a whole new world, one in which his craft of transforming stone plates into tea-serving trays had transformed him into one of the master artisans of the area. During that life-enriching spring afternoon in his workshop/showroom, he reflected upon his trade and career and commented on the use-values and aesthetics of his craft, all the while pointing out his works and simultaneously serving tea to his guests. I observed a dignified human being whose skill and thought, body and mind, were united in perfect harmony. The experience revealed to me how artisans communicate through their wares as well as through their words.

Fancying myself as an artisan of some sort, that is, an independent producer in a craft that allows for some imagination and individuality, I hereby pluck up my courage and begin my show-and-tell.

The JWM incident involved more than 300 female workers and their rural families. The thirteen-day sit-in, according to official records, accounted for more than 50 percent of the total number of working days lost to strikes in Hong Kong that year. But what makes it significant to us is that the vocal public discourse which erupted from it continued for months, making it evident that 'social reality' is continually constructed and reconstructed from multiple perspectives in a strategic, interactive, discursive manner. This monograph has been produced by precisely such a process, and reflects and refracts it in both its form and content.

During the process, which occupied more than a year both prior to and after 'the event', the author played different roles, pursued different kinds of activities and obtained different kinds of information — as record-keeper, as participant-observer, as sociology-of-action practitioner and as oral-history co-constructor. The ethnographies generated from these activities were of a diverse nature and of uneven constitution. They were made possible, and constrained by, factors such as:

1. The roles I was playing, then and now;
2. The presumptions and assumptions embedded in the investigative strategies available to me; and
3. The methodological bias inherent in the research procedure and the extent to which it was understood and problematized.

The trajectory of my research engagement, in essence, has been away from established socio-scientific disciplines — a continual distancing of myself from standardized exercises of socio-typographical feature-sorting, historical-developmental model-fitting and economic-nomothetical law-finding. Along the way, it has been said that I have invented 'viruses' to subvert existing theories (Marshall Sahlins' remark), and that I have improvised methods of representation in constructing my 'experimental ethnography' (Jean Comaroff's characterization). The 'on-the-ground' battlefield situation makes me aware that, for better or for worse, the anthropologist's predicament is that the discrepancies in what he has observed do not remain in the 'materials' but become discrepancies in his very being. This, my point of arrival, has become clearer and clearer over the past sixteen years; but it was not clear when I first plunged into the JWM incident. On the contrary, the historical intricacies of this actual occurrence, coupled with the intellectual conundrum they invoked, demonstrated to me the imperative to unthink mainstream doctrines and take a path towards a point in many aspects coterminous with the various 'turns' — that is 'interpretive turn', 'linguistic turn' and 'cultural turn' — of post-modern thought. My act of trespassing, retrospectively perceived, also has somehow paralleled the act of 'post'-ing in its various applications (the post-industrial, the post-modern and the post-colonial) over the past two decades.

My intervention, therefore, is not a research project of labour history, nor an account of industrial relations. It certainly does not deal with issues of development, gender, social differentiation ... labour struggles in their conventional sense. What the project deems to be at stake is not the immediate (or remote) circumstantial conditions which can be seen to have 'caused' the industrial conflict; instead, it takes into consideration the overall politico-economical and ethico-cultural dimensions involved in over-determining and over-hegemonizing the commencement and the outcome of the dispute. As an ethnography of a strike and a critical theoretical analysis of the problematic of working-class solidarity, my account focuses on factory shop-floor politics and external politics and cultural politics as well, at a time when manufacturing and industrial activity was at its peak in Hong Kong.

Such an account, taking the interplay of social bodies and moral politics as its point of departure, should make a unique resource for labour historians, social movement practitioners, feminist advocates and others, as well as for academic sociologists and anthropologists. Drawing on a long tradition of non-foundational writings in Marxist and non-Marxist literature, and adopting discursive strategies of cultural studies, the richness of the work should be sufficient to persuade careful readers that a non-foundational approach can hold promise for the future of radical social analysis.

In re-articulating issues in ethnographic writings, labour relations researches and three-world theories, I use the tool of reflexive ethnography to expand the scopes of cultural studies and political-economic discourses. By problematizing the historicities and moral politics involved in societal negotiations and compromises, my various accounts lay bare the blind spots embedded in theories of flexible accumulation, core/periphery relations, and world system(s).

As the product of intensive ethnograph-based study, this book relies both on narrating the experience and on calling into question all foundational claims of narrational experience, that is, politics, cultures, labour relations, gender divisions, various social analytic categories, and so on. To be able to do this, I cannot homogenize the texts. The multi-genre presentations and reflexive mode of writings are meant to be read as a methodological demonstration, as well as an epistemological statement in their own right. They also purport to show the necessary correspondences between form and content, language and thought, and signification practices and their resulting products.

Intended as alterative — not alternative — to existing ethnographic practice, the book deliberately adopts a mode of presentation unfamiliar in conventional anthropological writings. By injecting in-depth narrative into it, I seek to enhance the constitution of ethnography in anthropology. Admittedly, intensive study of a culture has been a Chicago-anthropological tradition ever since the 1970s; but the presentation of in-depth narration has not been. I learned the importance of story-telling from Oscar Lewis while I was a prisoner-of-conscience and was translating his *Five families: Mexican case studies in the culture of poverty* into Chinese in jail in Taipei. What my later Chicago anthropological training brought home to me, unwittingly, was the convergence of cultural turn, linguistic turn, and interpretive turn into what I would call 'the narrative turn' in methodology. During the years of writing and revising the 'ethnographic' account, I benefitted by reading works from Kenneth Burke all the way to de Certeau. The work has been an extended working and reworking — that of a *bricoleur*, if you will. In sum, as far as the theoretical heritage of my research practice is concerned, I have not been a product of any particular academic institution or school of thought.

As the son of a suppressed left intellectual-literati of the 1930s, I was brought up in my mother's private library, where I had access to works of most of the early socialists (especially the 'Utopian Socialists' such as Fourier, Proudhon, and Saint-Simon) as well as socially-conscious literatures, both foreign and domestic. The works of Marx and Engels, for better or worse, were not available until I went overseas, as it was too dangerous even to mention their names during that era of 'white terror' in Taiwan. What influenced me most, in my youth, as I now recall, was the diversity of works, such as those of novelist Turgenev, social critic Lu Xun, radical philosopher Feuerbach and esthetician B. Crocé. This background, I guess, later gave me easy access to writers as different as Laclau, Volosinov, Touraine and Havel. In regard to discourses on radical political economy, this same basis has made me more a Polanyian than a Marxist, and has led me to configure my field research more akin to the *sociologie du travail* of Touraine, Crozier, and Bertaux; rather than to the industrial sociology of Burawoy and his disciples. As a self-conscious *narodnik* to this very minute, I am certainly very appreciative of what people like J. O'Connor, N. Long, A. Gorz, S. Marglin, E. P. Thompson, R. Williams, S. Hall, S. Terkel, R. Kothari, R. Guha, A. Nandy, M. Taussig, G. Spivak, B. Cohn, M. Sahlins, T. Turner and the Comaroff's have to say.

Since we all now know that the political is personal and the intellectual is practical and sensual, a few autobiographical notes are in order.

Soon after the death of my mother, I dropped out of high school, as a protest and rebellion. Within a couple of years, I had become an avant-garde music composer, a folk-song collector and a cultural activist. I ended up a 'left-leaning' political prisoner in 1968, while still a university freshman. In the 1970s, after being released from the military detention centre with neither civil rights nor private entitlements (such as resuming my college education), I became successful in international trade, specializing in promoting exports of small manufacturers. By the end of the 1970s, I had 'spent' all the money I'd made from trading in an experiment to operate a garment factory under 'reasonable' working conditions. I think I deserved to be broke, and was proud of it. In the early 1980s, I was an anthropology graduate student at the University of Chicago. Among other non-academic activities, I was a member of the steering committee of the anti-apartheid campaign on the campus. After being denied a research position at the Academia Sinica in Taipei and the possibility of doing fieldwork in Taiwan, I came to Hong Kong to do my fieldwork. In the spring of 1989 I went to Tiananmen Square as a young faculty member at the University of Hong Kong, to observe a social movement, a carnival and a massacre-in-the-making. From 1990, I then taught anthropology in Hong Kong and engaged in researching women workers' employment strategies and life histories, as well as the transformation of the social body in colonial/recolonized Hong Kong. I have been a frequent visitor to Eastern European countries and am familiar with the socio-political transformation in that part of the world over the past two decades.

With these notes you may be better able to see the extent to which my personal life experience has enabled and limited my intellectual horizons and my research perspective.

How do the spatial and temporal distances from my fieldwork site affect the understanding of my readers? It seems to me that both disparate territoriality and transforming temporal configuration have so far worked in favour of my precursory documentation and deconstruction. What would happen if there were substantial works available for us to understand how clumsy Japanese managerialism was during the heyday of worldwide 'Japanization', when my research was taking place? Did we really need a whole decade's economic slump to footnote what I found in concrete circumstances in the capitalist periphery of Hong Kong? Why can we not become alert to the way in which the 'economic miracles' in East Asia and elsewhere were fabricated — through double-dealing, corruption, cheating and bad-debt financing — by accounts of a time when the four 'little dragons' had yet to turn into four little 'snakes'? Surely my records of the multinational enclave of hyper-accumulation are demonstrative (as well as being heuristic) of the collusion of political expediency and speculative windfalls, as business-as-usual practices — with or without the recent Enron revelations?

If we look around, we realize that the rapid shrinking of the world of the 'global village' has made all human endeavours, both foreign and domestic, closer to our skins. What happens in the remote desert can easily be part and parcel of our everyday reality. The desperate resorting to blind managerial practice — both as ideology and technology, and in both public administration and 'personal' matters — will certainly make you and me 'redundant' and superfluous. Sooner or later we shall, one by one, fall prey to 'value-additive' manipulations in the name of overall (accumulative) 'efficiency'. An old saying has it that 'there is nothing new under the sun'. I want to add, 'There is nothing anachronistic under capitalism', nor about old dictatorial practices — the phenomena do actually recur! Yet, just as we have been reminded, by Stuart Hall, that there are no final guarantees for either Marxist ideology or socialist transformation, we know that there is no guarantee for managerial manipulation and dictatorial practices to prevail and claim victory either. The ebbing of unionism may not be as disastrous as it seems. After two decades, remembering the claims of Przeworski of the transformation of the 'proletariat into (a) class', I propose to 'de-classify out from the Proletariat' and focus on countless societal transformations and emerging subjects. The multiple takes of a single ethnographical intervention, even in its abbreviated reincarnation in this book, have made it amply evident that any eruption of moral indignation and quest for dignity among the masses invariably contributes to our hopes and aspirations for a better world. Mine is but one instance — a tale of the coming-into-subject of 300 individuals. The young women who appear in this book showed that, although the specific struggles may very well have been 'theirs', the politics and anxieties embedded in them are invariably 'ours'. We, as common livelihood-makers, have a genuine need for communication and consolation, knowing that similar predicaments may one day be imposed upon us, in our workplaces, on our families.

Today, I believe that it is even more imperative for all of us to scrutinize the historical practice of moral politics during the ascending phase of industrial capitalism, whether in Hong Kong or anywhere else. Facing a downward slope stretching out before us, we are forced, again, to transform our moral-political potential into concrete practices of moral economy. It is here where 'Colours of Money, Shades of Pride' matters.

I feel that the modality of 'my' workers and their struggles has made Hong Kong a more humane place; I am sure that their strivings and dedications transformed me into a better person to talk to, to listen to and to work with. It is upon this note that I invite you to share this experience of my transformation.

Having welcomed you, I nevertheless take this opportunity to issue a challenge: you are requested not only to live through the fully fleshed-out ethnography of 'our' workers, but also to come up with your own reading and rewriting of the account. If you fail, it must be my fault, for any reasonable ethnography should yield more information than the ethnographer herself /himself has been able to digest — in fact, that is a true measure of her/his craft.

In finalizing the prolonged ordeal of getting this book published, I have been sustained by the spiritual support of my mother, Lilian Dunn, who died at a young age. A friend and a comrade, she was a source of strength and inspiration. I am glad that I have been able to do what she would have liked to do if she had had the chance. As part of her flesh as well as of her intellectual dream, it is up to me to prove that her life as a mother and a woman, and all the possible and impossible dedications and sacrifices, were not in vain.

While I was enriching myself intellectually and politically, my daughters Yi-tzun and Shin-ho suffered a loss in their family life for which I cannot compensate, nor can I redeem the pain incurred to them after they were abducted by their mother's family. However, I hope that this book will present to them a father they were forbidden to know, and find the relief of discovering him a decent human being.

It would not have been possible to carry this project to completion without the immense patience, support and understanding of my wife Jolanta Skwarczynska. Every single page reflects her strength and boundless optimism. It is beyond my ability to express fully my gratitude — I can only dedicate this book to her as a faint understatement. Our boy, Benedict, must know how he makes our every day joyous, meaningful and hopeful; I hope he will also see that his parents tried hard to make the world a bit less unliveable for his future.

Because this book project has a long and complex 'archaeology' and 'genealogy', I have incurred numerous obligations and owe favours to a great number of individuals and institutions. I must apologize for not being able to reiterate all the names listed in the acknowledgements of my dissertation, especially the pseudonymous workers and their associates. Thanks, however, are also due to Judith Farquhar and Tani Barlow for their brave efforts in carrying out the 'mission impossible' of getting my original thousand-page manuscript appreciated and accepted by a publishing house in North America. I am also sorry that their students were forced to use photocopies of my chapters in their seminars.

After years of tedious back-and-forth in vain, fate endowed me with a Prometheus-spirited intellectual entrepreneur, Grant Evans, and an organic intellectual with remarkable vision, Meaghan Morris. It is due to them that this book acquired its second life. If readers like the book, they will also be appreciative of their courage and insight.

Ms Mina Cerny Kumar of Hong Kong University Press has been intrumental in working out the details of publication. Her enthusiasm and professionalism is superb.

Last but not least, it is John Thorne, whose patience, empathy, skill and hard work transformed my rather scholastic 'private property' into more readable 'public goods'. Whether it is, in fact, of some public good, is up to the judgement of you, my readers, and not for me to say.

Fred Y. L. Chiu
March 2003

Abbreviations

Press

CD	Central Daily
CP	Ching Pao Daily
EX	Express
HKCD	Hong Kong Commercial Daily
HKDN	Hong Kong Daily News
HKEJ	Hong Kong Economic Journal
HKS	Hong Kong Standard (in English)
HKT	Hong Kong Times
MP	Ming Pao
NEP	The New Evening Post
OD	Oriental Daily
SCMP	South China Morning Post (in English)
SPD	Sing Pao Daily
STJ	Sing Tao Jih Pao
STM	Sing Tao Man Pao (evening)
TKP	Ta Kung Pao
TT	Tin Tin Daily

WKY   Wah Kiu Yat Pao
WW   Wen Wei Pao

Organizations

AWR   Association for Workers' Rights
ASSC   Ashley Social Service Centre
CKRLS   Central Kwai Chung Resident and Labour Service
CFJP   Center for Justice and Peace
CLA   Christian Labour Association
CWA   Confederation of Worker's Association
FCSU   Federation of Civil Service Unions
FLU   Federation of Labour Unions
FTU   Federation of Hong Kong and Kowloon Trade Unions
GAAC   Government Agency Against Corruption
GCL   Global Confederation of Labourers
HKNRA   Hong Kong News Reporters' Association
HKTU   Hong Kong Teachers' Union
HKW   Hong Kong Wireless Television
HSHK   Humanist Society of Hong Kong (Woman's Right Committee)
JETCON   A Japanese multinational merged with JWM
JOUHK   Joint Organization of Unions (HK)
JCIULO   Joint Council of Independent Unions and Labour Organizations
JNCU   Japan Nationwide Council of Unions
JWM   Japan Watch Multinational
KLBC   Kai Lup Baptist Church
LB   Labour Bureau
LRA   Labour Relations Association
LRC   Labour and Residents Coalition
M/S B&T Beagos and Taylor (American public relations firm)
MC   McGee Centre
NYS   New Youth Society

OPBR	Organization for People's Basic Rights
PEL	Local watch factory bought by JWM
RMSA	Resignation Meritorious Service Award
SLCC	Shek Lai Community Centre
SSC	St. Stephen's Church
TWLSC	Tsuen Wan Labour Service Centre
UMELCO	(Building of the) Unofficial Members of the Executive Council and Legislative Council

Cast of Characters

Mr A	Mysterious contact person for JWM headquarters in Japan
Ah Lam	JWM third-floor worker
Amukas	Managing director of JWM head office in Japan
Ah Si	Protagonist of 'Ah Si Incident'
Ah Ton	Member of Labour and Resident Coalition (LRC); activist/self-proclaimed Trotskyite
Bai Sa-kuo	Editor of *Hong Kong Economic Journal* (HKEJ)
Banata	Vice-president, Japan Nationwide Council of Unions
Bao Yi-hai	Head of the LRC, a schoolteacher
Chan Mei-fon	JWM management spokeswoman; secretary of Beagos and Taylor (American public relations firm)
Chan, Peter	Reporter of *South China Morning Post* (SCMP)
Chen Siu-guan	JWM second-floor representative
Chen Yi-han	Public relations officer of the Japanese Consulate-General in Hong Kong

Chi-mei	JWM second-floor worker
Chichika	JWM Hong Kong shop-floor manager
Chien Fa-hin	JWM seventh-floor representative
Chien Fon-yi (Big Brother)	JWM second-floor representative
Chou Mei-Ying	Staff of Christian Labour Association (CLA)
Chu Chi-lin (Little Wife)	JWM second-floor representative
Chubiki	JWM Hong Kong managing director after sit-in
Chun Mai-ga	Officer of Labour Unions Registration Bureau
Dai-gau	JWM second-floor worker
Dai Fo-san	JWM second-floor worker
Dai Lin-wai	JWM seventh-floor workers' representative
Dai Yu-si	Head of pro-Taiwan Confederation of Workers' Associations (CWA)
Dou Wan-min	Female chairperson of LRC
Du, Leonado	Hong Kong Government Secretary for District Administration
Fan Si-lai	Volunteer teacher in 'oral communication skills'
Fan yu-lin	Reporter for *Central Daily*
Fu Kwon-sin	Staff of the Central Kwai Chung Residents and Labour Service (CKRLS)
Fukkako Kosho	Women's Rights Committee of the Humanist Society of Hong Kong
Gu Lai-hap	Staff of Tsuen Wan Labour Service Centre (TWLSC)
Gum Fu-yan	Female JWM line leader
Ha-lan	JWM third-floor worker
Ho-chie	JWM second-floor worker
Hon Lai-fon	JWM seventh-floor representative
Hu Hon-chi	JWM seventh-floor representative
Hsiao Chia	JWM second-floor worker
Hui Bei-kwang	Secretary of the Federation of Hong Kong and Kowloon Trade Unions

Cast of Characters

Kau-fu (Uncle)	JWM second-floor worker
Kusara	JWM Japanese shop-floor manager
Ku Han-yim	Chairman of Federation of Labour Unions (FLU)
Lam Tu-pi	JWM's attorney
Lam Yi-kai	CKLRS's part-time staff; social work intern
Lai-fon	JWM third-floor worker
Lao Kan-kai	Director of TWLSC; member of Executive Committee
Lee Siu-ching	Chairman of FCSU
Ley, Mobark	JWM's attorney
Li-pui	Author of letter to the editor of *Express* (EX)
Liang Li-an	Reporter for *Hong Kong Standard* (HKS); article writer
Lin Yi-chin	Chief of staff of CKRLS; district board member
Li Nai-kuan	Director of TWLSC
Lo Man-sa	Director of CLA
Lo Un-pu	JWM second-floor workers' representative
Lu Mei-chin	JETCON worker; supporter
Lu Shan	JWM factory manager
Dr Luk Sa-bien	Lecturer in the Management Department at the University of Hong Kong
Luk Ga-yip	Chairman of Hong Kong News Reporters' Association; chief of the City Desk at the HKS
Ma Po-kwan	anthropologist/field researcher
Ma Siu-yim	JWM second-floor worker
Mao Si-hai	the Labour Bureau's chief labour relations director
Minika	JWM Hong Kong junior management staff
Mo Ku-sin	JWM shop-floor production manager
Mui Len-shu	JWM second-floor worker

Ou Ho-chung	JWM business manager
Ou Yang-chung	Chairman of Hong Kong Teachers Union (HKTU)
Pei, Wendy	Reporter for *SCMP*
Po Lo-du	JWM most-hated foreman
Poon Ni-kwon	Director of TWLSC
Robinson, Mark	Director of the CFJP
Sa Mo-han	Mysterious middleman
Mrs Sheou	Woo Char-hwa's secretary
Shih Ding-yi	Labour organizer of CLA
Shita	JWM Hong Kong shop-floor manager
Sian Yun-chu	JETCON line leader
Sieu-pin	Member of LRC
Siu Fen-ni	JWM second-floor worker
Son Yan-min	Legislative Councillor, vice-president of FLU
Sisuno	JWM Hong Kong shop-floor manager
Smith, Warren	The Governor
Tosai	Deputy managing director of JWM Hong Kong
Tu Pi-sin	Director of Labour Relations of the Labour Bureau's Tsuen Wan branch
Father Wasini	Catholic priest
Wong Nieu-kwen	UMELCO member (industrialist)
Woo Char-hwa	JWM Hong Kong vice-general manager
Yang Lai-gau	TWLSC volunteer
Yen Chin-chih	TWLSC director/founding member; manager of government-subsidized youth centre
Yen Giu	Reporter for HKEJ
Yin-mei	JWM third-floor worker
Yin-yon	JWM second-floor worker
Yu-dan	JWM second-floor shop manager
Yue-mui	JWM second-floor worker

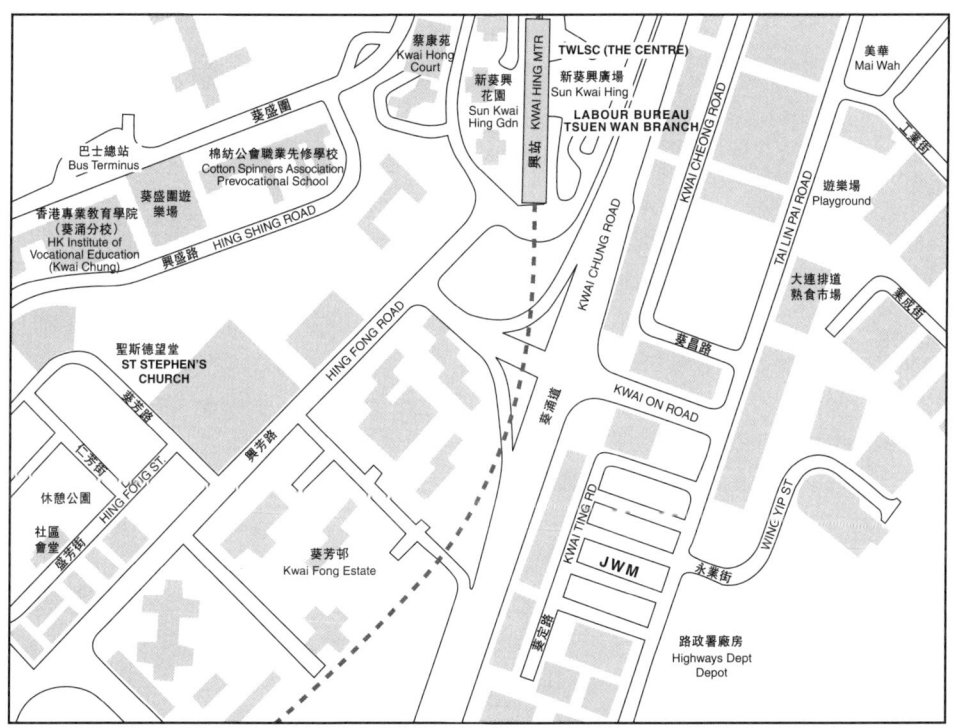

Japan Watch Multinational (JWM) and its vicinity

1 Introduction

During the first two weeks of June 1986, an unprecedented strike and sit-in broke out at the Japan Watch Multinational (JWM) in Hong Kong. It erupted spontaneously after thirty-six workers were fired on 31 May.

Or was it nineteen?

In the papers of 1 June, about two-thirds of the reports stated that thirty-six had been fired; the other third reported nineteen. By 4 June, some papers reported that seventeen more had been fired, bringing the total to thirty-six, but that only raised another question: Had they been fired on 31 May or later? And where did these conflicting reports come from anyway? Though I had been involved in the strike from the beginning, as a volunteer at the Tsuen Wan Labour Service Centre (hereafter, the Centre) and was an anthropology graduate student conducting research on factory work in Hong Kong, it was not until a series of interviews conducted long after the strike that I was able to solve the puzzle of the numbers.

By interviewing the journalists involved, I learned that those who had reported nineteen got their information from JWM management, while those who reported thirty-six got their number from the workers. Why the discrepancy? Some of the workers gave the following explanation.

Management had meticulously planned this 'wholesale slaughter'. At a carefully selected moment, with videotaping teams in tow, a tactical firing team began handing out dismissal envelopes on the seventh floor, where the workers were least organized. They planned on firing selected workers on the first, third, and sixth floors in sequence, finally ending on the second floor where the workers were best organized. To prevent the workers from reacting, the firing team attempted to expel the workers from each floor before proceeding to the next. However, one of the fired seventh-floor workers managed to wave her dismissal envelope in front of the momentarily open doors of the second floor. This action alerted the second-floor workers, who stood up, looked at each other, rushed up the staircase, occupied the 'office', and began their sit-in and strike.

Thus, the strike began before anyone on the second floor had actually been fired. So how did the workers determine how many were being fired? It turns out that one of them had found dismissal envelopes addressed to seventeen second-floor workers hidden in a usually locked conference room. Together with the nineteen already fired, that made thirty-six. Despite the fact that they had never formally been fired, some of these seventeen workers decided to leak the number 'thirty-six' to the press in order to demonstrate the full extent of the management's actions and thereby increase the sense of outrage and solidarity among the striking workers. Management first tried to cover up their actions by only admitting to firing nineteen, but eventually decided to admit to the total of thirty-six.

Much remains to be told about this incident — in which more than 300 female workers and their families, from the rural area of Pat Heung, were involved; and which accounted for more than 50 percent of the total annual working days lost to strikes in the enclave, according to the official record — but at the very least the journalistic version of it demonstrates that the 'basic facts' of the strike, as reported in the press, are anything but transparent. The 'fact' of the number of workers fired was the result of the interplay between strategic constructions of reality on the part of some workers and certain factions within the management. As an opening, this incident introduces both the central event which this book analyses — the

JWM strike — and, more importantly, my theoretical understanding: that social 'reality' is continually constructed and reconstructed from multiple perspectives in a strategic, interactive, discursive process. This understanding is reflected in both the form and content of this book.

I present three genres of narrative about the strike: selective summaries of press reports, my ethnographic description, and the workers' (and my own) reflexive consciousness as developed from later interviews. These three types of narrative are not three 'reflections' of a single 'reality', but are the very substance of that multiple and contradictory reality. The juxtaposition of these accounts is meant both to move the reader away from simplistic notions of linear history and to illustrate the importance of different forms of narrative in the process of social life. These three genres of narrative differ in both the positions from which they are constructed and the 'event' that they construct. A fuller explication of each, illuminating the theoretical issues involved, will follow. But let me begin with an introduction to my fieldwork itself.

Fieldwork as Personal Intellectual History

My research covered two time periods, September 1985 to June 1986 and September 1986 to May 1987. Each period involved two separate phases of inquiry.

The first phase

In the three months after my arrival in Hong Kong and before I had a chance to acquaint myself with the social context of work and employment, I carried out a series of sociological surveys. There were five major industrial districts — two on Hong Kong Island and three in Kowloon — and I initiated a first round of investigation in all five districts. With the surveys, abundant 'data' was collected, including data on social networks, wage histories, household budget accounts and family employment records. I was to use this extensive preliminary overview to locate and evaluate sites in which to carry out further intensive fieldwork. Yet these sociometric/human-geographic findings turned out not to be helpful for me to secure a social context for engaging the field. It was only in Kwai Tsing, Kowloon, that I managed to build up a relationship with the local labour service groups that was sound enough for an ongoing interaction. Hence, the information from these surveys can best be considered as sociologically-tailored 'data' — of the nature of a pilot study — with only minimal utility for my anthropological project.

The second phase

Beginning in the first week of December 1985, a major industrial dispute broke out in a famous multinational corporation's offshore manufacturing unit in Kwai Tsing. This dispute, between the management and 300 female operators, stretched over a period of three months and involved a settlement amounting to HK$5 million. Because of close contacts established with various local community and labour service organizations, I had the rare opportunity to carry out intensive participant observation among the workers during and after their various industrial actions. This experience readied me for a similar but more in-depth involvement with the JWM industrial dispute, mentioned above, that occurred sixteen weeks later.

In late April 1986, I was performing my usual duties as a volunteer at the joint office of Central Kwai Chung Labour and Residents Services (CKLRS) and the Tsuen Wan Labour Service Centre (TWLSC, the Centre) when calls came in from operatives working at JWM. These calls marked the beginning of a landmark conflict between JWM and the workers. This conflict, unprecedented in recent Hong Kong history, culminated in a record thirteen-day strike and sit-in at the factory. As a volunteer at the Centre, I observed the two-week sit-in and participated in almost all activities organized by the struggling workers. Working as a record-keeper for the Centre and workers, I obtained multiple sets of notes taken by various participants, in addition to my own personal ethnographic records. The strike ended on 13 June 1986, and I left Hong Kong at the end of the same month for my first report to my academic committee at the University of Chicago.

The third phase

In September 1986, I went back to Hong Kong with the idea of using the JWM strike as the major empirical focus of my fieldwork. I had originally planned to study the political culture of manufacturing production and reproduction in Hong Kong, with special emphasis on vertical and horizontal integration of the workforce. However, the situation on the ground dictated an alternative strategy. The multilayered crisis of an industrial dispute heightened the contradictions within various sites and presented unanticipated theoretico-ethnographic and politico-discursive challenges.

During my previous stay in Hong Kong I had lived through the crisis as an ethnographer and a somewhat 'gung-ho' unionist; but now I set out to perform a scholar's task. I began to collect every piece of published literature relating to the JWM case from nineteen newspapers, twelve periodicals, and five non-serial publications, as well as numerous internal communiques. In three months I managed to locate more than 300 separate pieces of printed material, from a diverse array of sources and political positions. What stunned me, as I gathered these accounts, was the degree to which the 'facts' not only contradicted each other in different written versions, but actually caused me to doubt whether they referred to the same 'event' I had experienced first-hand less than six months before! In the majority of cases, the materials simply denied the validity of my first-hand observations. It was virtually impossible to find a way to reconcile my personal records and memory with the published accounts at this 'factual' level.

The fourth phase

Faced with the above dilemma, I had to decide whether to give up the whole project or to dig further. I chose the latter and worked for six more months, carrying out intensive interviews with all the major actors involved in the 'making' of this particular 'history': militant unionists, strike leaders, participating workers, Labour Bureau officers, news reporters, union leaders from the region, public relations executives of famous multinational corporations, and business attachés of foreign countries. I did not interview JWM management or their legal advisers, partly owing to difficulties in reaching them and partly by choice.

The majority of interviewees gave me more than one interview, allowing me to clarify statements and make sense of what individuals understood to have happened. Second and subsequent interviews usually proceeded in a more involved, reflexive, conscious and intimate fashion than the first, as I engaged the actors in a process of recreating the 'event' and making history from their respective stances, at the same time enabling the interviewees to reflect upon any discrepancies that had surfaced and on contradictions emerging from the narratives of others. Interviewees were also encouraged to justify or criticize themselves or anyone else, if they so desired.

As interview records accumulated, a more panoramic view than I had previously imagined began to come into focus, expanding the geographic area, numbers of people, and time-span under consideration. Newly emerging constructions of the 'event' rendered it an increasingly multi-dimensional 'panorama'.

The above chronology of my fieldwork, albeit a simplified one, indicates that during different phases I pursued different kinds of activity and obtained different kinds of information; accordingly, the accounts generated are of a diverse nature. These accounts forced me to initiate alternative readings and to engage in differentiated discourses, seeking various definite 'answers' by asking concrete questions arising from features of the accounts themselves. The questions asked in different phases were dictated by:

1. The roles I was playing, then and now;
2. The presumptions and assumptions embedded in the investigative strategies I employed; and
3. The methodological bias inherent in any defined set of investigative procedures and the extent to which it was recognized and problematized.

In other words, how one positions oneself preconditions the questions one can ask and the questions one asks preconditions the answers given. To transcend this limitation one must cultivate one's reflexivity, in terms of the nature of one's gaze and the positioning of one's perspective. The multi-genre narrative strategy I propose is important, for it can make transparent the hidden, and sensitize and problematize issues of gazes, perspectives and horizons.

However, these methodological truisms were by no means clear to me while I was wrapped up in the investigation of the one 'thing' — a strike — on which people merely had different perspectives. In other words, it was not until I gave up the effort of maintaining the fiction that 'it's all just one world out there and culture is about interpreting it differently' that I became aware of what I had been doing all along.

The trajectory of my own personal intellectual history has been a series of detours — a continual distancing of myself from socio-topographical feature-sorting, from historical developmental model-fitting and from economic-nomothetical law-finding, all of which lead to a dead end. What rescued me from this dead end were the resistances and counter-resistances that I began to glimpse in the fourth-phase interviews. This dialectic journey of knowing, bumpy as it was, eventually gave me a totally new sense of direction, revealing a fluctuating, unique scenario.

I came to see that, in the first phase of my project, I had been like a prospector carefully saving whatever his panning turned up, hoping it would all turn out to be gold. However, I was far from satisfied with merely sifting through 'useful data' in search of socially significant features, as this strategy would not serve my purpose, which was to enter the lifeworld of the people in the field situation.

I understood that the rich documentation I had collected on the JWM case during the third phase might be envied by many historians. To them, discrepancies are inevitable and can always be explained away; stories can always be constructed to neatly fulfil the requirements of model-fitting and law-finding. The predicament for an anthropologist, however, is that the discrepancies within what he has himself observed are no longer of, or in, the 'materials', but are discrepancies in his very being. In effect, working against this predicament brought home to me the words and scholarly practice of Bernard Cohn and Greg Dening at a very basic and personal level (Cohn 1987; and Dening 1996).

The field in which I was working is a highly literate one. Written accounts of social process are constantly being constructed and reconstructed. Analytically, the accounts of the present investigation can be qualitatively differentiated according to:

1. The different social contexts to which they owe their existence;
2. The different forms they take as vehicles for information;
3. The different mediators through whom particular account-creating activities have been executed, including news reporters who showed up only once, and one who used her status as a unionist to infiltrate the strike line and monitor the workers for months for her boss, the chairman of the News Reporters' Association; and
4. The different ways and settings in which they have been generated, and the specific purpose or immediate political effect they are made to have.

Normally a certain amount of analytical deconstruction is required to make these determining features explicit. Only with such analysis can the role of differentially-positioned actors and their different assumptions, habits, and agendas be made clear. Despite the richness of the documentary record I collected in the first three phases of my project I could not see beyond the explicit content of records to the social processes by which they had been constructed. Hence my sense of contradiction.

Thus, during the last six months of my fieldwork, I spent hours talking, reviewing, discussing and reflecting with all the people involved in the making of a history which was only six months old, accumulating 200-plus hours of intensive, tape-recorded discourse and listening to, transcribing, comparing, double-checking and cross-checking the tapes. As this process progressed, new dimensions of the strike opened up.

In the process of retrospectively constructing a theorized history, my interviewees and I relived our lives as historical agents in an intense way. In doing so, we were able once again to transform the conditions of our existence, master them, and be transformed in relation to them. Past happenings were not only appropriated but interrogated. In addition, our presence in the intertextuality of 'now' and 'then' was closely scrutinized. Riding the vehicle of discourse, we shuttled once again through a time tunnel. As we progressed, we — mere nobodies to begin with — were mediated and transformed into significant historical actors, becoming conscious not only of how history had acted upon us, but also how we acted back upon it. The 'historicity' we thereby achieved provided us with empirical bases from which to call into doubt the bland cause-and-effect logic of the positivists, which tends to approach history as singular and total.

We further learned that an analysis of discursive position-making and position-taking in the thickness of concrete resistance and counter-resistance calls for an alternative mind-set. One must refuse to take the various agencies involved as having an *a priori* existence of a certain kind. One must refute the careless identification of 'functions' or chartering of 'needs' — concepts which have become habitual as the social-scientific world has attempted to suture the unsuturable: the social itself. In other words, what needs to be problematized are the statistical and nomothetic analyses that take individual actors as isomorphic units, and social scientific practices which leave the social relations of data collection and their consequences unquestioned.

Perhaps the thesis of 'the impossibility of the society' put forth by Laclau and Mouffe remains a novel idea, in some quarters, to this very day (Laclau and Mouffe 1985); but the time has come for it to become common-sense (i.e., good sense *à la* Gramsci 1989) for socially-conscientious minds to note that where there is an excess of meanings there is an excess of signs; where there is an excess of signifiers there is an excess of signifieds; where there is an excess of structures there is an excess of events; and, for that matter, where there is an excess of observers there is an excess of the observed.

These lessons, if pushed to their logical extreme, may actually lead to a total rejection of conventional sociological or ethnographic strategies and practices. Rather than reject anthropological research, however, it became more important to me that the hectic nineteen-month journey of my fieldwork had involved a double dialectic as well as a two-way process. As we worked, I was constantly transforming my research 'subject' (object!) and at the same time being transformed by 'it'. This double movement acting upon me transformed my presumed identity — from 'sociologist' to 'ethnographer' to 'historian' and then (for lack of a better term) to 'cultural critic'. During my transformation, the 'observed' also continued to escape the finitude of 'structure' and the discreteness of 'events'. Time and again the process of finding a way to identify myself overlapped with a process of finding a way to know the 'unknown'. This overlapping in effect completes what I mean by the dialectics of a double movement and two-way process. It is, I conclude, impossible to present the 'known' without involving the 'knowing', and vice versa. Since both the knowing and the known are plural, certain problems concerning the presentation of the narratives in this book must be addressed and resolved. At this moment, contrary to the 'need to break with both the positions of the "native" and the "objective" ' (Bourdieu 1990b, 27), I have found it imperative to engage both.

Perceptive Basis for a Multi-Narrative Strategy

In the final six months of my fieldwork I repeatedly talked and listened to over 100 people. My knowledge of the JWM case became a pool of perspectives and perceptions of remarkably diverse content. Gradually, I slipped into an alarming state — that of a JWM expert. I became alert that effort must be made to prevent myself from playing God — the Know-All somewhere above. It took self-restraint and self-reflexivity to keep on monitoring myself in various field situations. It was important not to deny or evade my subjecthood and positioning — on the contrary, it was important to make them explicit and visible and, consequently, more accountable.

During the interviews, I constantly struggled with myself about whether or not, and to what extent, to reveal myself and the knowledge I had accumulated. There was no ready-made formula except to learn through practice and mistakes.

Firstly, there is the relational (moral) dilemma one faces in the field: What responsibility does the information-taker have vis-à-vis the information-giver? What kind of reciprocity is involved? If the information you are going to get is deeply human and social, isn't it that everyone involved must be treated, first and foremost, as a human being engaged in a social relationship? If so, can one expect to be treated as a full human being if one fails honestly to reveal as much pertinent information as one knows? If you and your informant are on an unequal footing, how will this asymmetry affect the flow and quality of discourse? What kind of thing is he or she likely to say to you and what would you hope to expect from him/her? These are real questions, but their answers can be sought only in praxis, not in theory.

In my own research practice, I would make the first move by presenting to the interviewees the published materials I had collected in the form of a review, and ask for their comments. In most cases they listened carefully, with interest and curiosity, as if listening to some exciting story. As the discrepancies between journalists' versions and what the interviewees knew accumulated, they would begin to question, argue, deny and protest, sometimes vehemently. Quite often this would be a turning point in our relationship, leading to deeper engagement. Interviewees wanted to know more and clarify more and became, unavoidably, more responsive and responsible. Conversation became easier. At this stage I tried my best to keep my mouth shut for fear that any hint of subtle approval or disapproval would distort what might be revealed.

After this initial stage, the interviewee frequently inquired about the ethnographic records I had gathered. This information was used for comparison with what the interviewees themselves had experienced. Discussions tended to take the form of an ethnographic/historical reconstruction. I tried to keep my interventions to a minimum so as to let the interviewees' words and thoughts flow further. In the first interview, with very little encouragement and direction, this process usually lasted more than one hour.

In most of the cases, there was an interval of at least two weeks before a second interview. The purpose of this delay was to allow the interviewee to reflect on our conversation and to give me a chance to transcribe the tapes. This would enable the second interview to reach a higher discursive level. The 'cooling-off' had a positive effect; it gave the interviewees a chance to rethink what they had said and what they had experienced. Some of them even read through copies of journalists' accounts photocopied from my collection, and some of them used this period to consult with acquaintances who were involved. Many interviewees became even more active interlocutors during this period.

The second interview typically began with a brief recapitulation of what had happened during the first interview; new revelations sometimes burst out at this juncture. During this interview, I was aggressive and talkative. I interrogated the interviewees about the discrepancies in their previous interview, pushed for further justification of strong statements they may have made, and argued and reasoned regarding their judgements and choices. Through this approach, they were more convinced that I was not only interested in them and what they had to say, but also that I was at least as involved as they had been.

Subsequently — and especially when the interviewee held tightly to his or her version of events — I began to contribute information I had obtained from other sources or opposed parties. Heated debates, self-questioning and cross-questioning often resulted. Hidden theories and previously unacknowledged presumptions and assumptions were made explicit. The geographical framework expanded from the factory premises to the community at large, and then to the distant rural areas where most of the workers' leaders had their homes. Time horizons also expanded considerably, both backwards to the very beginning of the year of the events in question and even to several years before, and forward, right up to and including the present moment.

A new dimension of internal time/space unfolded as well. Against a background of breathtaking depth and breadth, the hidden properties of a cumulative sediment of existing social relations became readily discernible. Layers and layers of intermingled social connections and interconnectedness emerged. Various events, alignments and actions could be clearly seen and were at the same time constantly crystallized, dissolved, defined and redefined. All kinds of 'what if' questions, hypotheses and guesswork, both of the past and of the present, were made available for open scrutiny — they ceased to be 'counter-factual', 'un-factual' or even 'a-factual', and constituted what one might call the 'super-factual', in the sense that they existed at the very Centre of rationales for social action. This most significant dimension of the social-world-in-the-making described in this study will, I trust, emerge as affirming the practice of alternative ethnography — as exemplified by Crapanzano's *Waiting*; Kondo's *Crafting Selves*, Tsing's *In the Realm of the Diamond Queen* and Moeran's *Okubo Diary* (Crapanzano 1985; Kondo 1990; Tsing 1993; Moeran 1985).

Three Genres of Narrative

Press narrative

This kind of discourse involves the multi-subjective narratives of more than fifty journalists concerning the JWM strike. The salient features of these stories, if submitted to careful scrutiny, are by no means simple. They are accounts created in a similar fashion but reported by unevenly qualified narrators. The engagement and commitment of these narrators to the particular event varied, but it was usually tenuous. Though some journalists followed the event from beginning to end, most had very casual or sporadic encounters with the strike.

But to say that reporters' access to the event varied is not precise enough. There were at least two cases in which reporters were not there as journalists. They came as associates of their conservative professional associations, and used their press passes to spy on strike activities. These 'reporters' monitored levels of solidarity and amounts of material support pouring in from various directions. Their low-profile surveillance resulted in the production of a few highly sensational feature stories which accused some intervening groups of being 'Trotskyists'. I also gathered evidence that a few journalists were, consciously or unconsciously, used by the workers as couriers. These incidents make us aware of the danger of accepting whatever one can get from the field or from documents as 'data', without rigorous scrutiny or further qualification.

Generally speaking, this first genre of narrative consists of published accounts constructed by multiple subjects called journalists, for consumption by 'the public'. Neither journalists nor the public were subjectively aware of having any real interests in this particular event. But this apparent neutrality does not guarantee freedom from value judgement. Both reporters and readers positioned themselves as total outsiders, who cared only about the superficial and externals of an 'event' which they carelessly constructed (produced) and carelessly took for granted (consumed). To know is an active process; limited efforts yield a limited return, and limited questions can only find limited answers.

An effort to know must begin somewhere and the superficial and external is not a bad place to begin, so long as one is aware of its place and also of one's own whereabouts. However, the voluminous press narrative, for reasons of space, cannot constitute a separate chapter in this book. Instead, a sampling of social discourses from the journalistic world explicitly referred to in other genres of narrative are presented in the Appendix (see pp. 385–422).

Ethnographic narrative

Based upon the blow-by-blow notes I took during my fieldwork, an ethnography has been constructed. To execute this task, I had to be both inside and outside of what I claim to have observed. When I felt too much 'in', I would move 'out', and vice versa. I hoped such a not-always-comfortable ethnographic distance would allow me to maintain both my sense of reality and my academic stance. What worried me was that a close and emotional involvement in the strike might jeopardize my status as a researcher from overseas.

Having been both 'in' and 'out' of the JWM case results in a story different from the one the journalists told. Largely because of my inside position as a worker at the Centre, I detected a tremendous amount of time and space existing both between and inside those 'things' and 'events' — time and space absent in the journalists' accounts. The time/space configuration I faced was looser and more dispersed; at the same time, it was constituted by much denser and thicker content. Materials I gathered included my own notes, notes from two militant unionists who worked with the workers, and notes taken by different workers under various circumstances. Additional documents include working diaries, meeting minutes, announcements, news releases, songs and slogans, and photos and tape recordings of various occasions. These materials offered an 'empirical' basis from which I could construct an ethnographic description.

Through a somewhat comprehensive presentation, I try to give the reader a sense of the strike with all its diverse trajectories. However, I must make it clear at the outset that the moments I captured, like those a photographer records, were from the specific point and angle available to me. The on-the-spot decision of whether to 'click the shutter' and the later decision whether to make a 'print' from a particular 'negative', or even to 'enlarge' it, were all determined by my interests, as an ethnographer, in serving a particular mode of inquiry. Consequently, the temporal and spatial connectedness of this narrative is my own construct. Chapter 3, 'On Methodology and Procedures', gives a more detailed explanation of how I have constructed this space/time grid.

The purpose of my ethnography is to excavate a dense subterranean time/space for reflection and scrutiny. In my interviews with strike participants, I used the preliminary ethnographic narrative — which belonged to both myself and the interviewee and, in a sense, was jointly produced — as an empirical object for both of us to react to. These reactions flared spectacularly from time to time, at others constitutes flows of retrospective theorization and speculation. In the ethnographic narrative I also attempt to provide the present reader with an empirical basis sound enough to enable a deeper deconstruction, as well as to invite the identification of problems.

In the course of producing the ethnographic narrative, questions of a new sort constantly cropped up. The questions that emerged at this level were ones that the press reports did not allow, but were also conditioned by what had been made available. These questions concerned the *raison d'être* of categories that seemed to 'exist' and are the staple concerns of standard ethnography ('social structure' and 'culture' are examples), questions that circle around the notions of the 'function' of the entire 'event', seen as a whole with various 'parts'. Yet neither function nor event was easy to discern. An ethnographic operation required freezing processes into patterns, flattening diverse genres of narrative into a flat topographic representation, and fitting odd bits and pieces into a holistic picture analogous to a jigsaw puzzle. This is the work of an academic matchmaker, who tries to marry behaviour with the culture which supposedly underlies it, and attempts to pair event with structure, with the former supposedly parasitic on the latter. Understanding that these oppositions are but 'analogous expressions of the same misplaced concreteness' (Sahlins 1985, 156), we know that this social-scientific process can, at best, produce a mid-range hybrid of half-baked facts and models, and that the entities that emerge from it are but categories which are conventionally classified as social structure, cultural meaning, behavioural traits and value orientations.

During the inquiry I found that the question of industrial solidarity in the workplace was the wrong question to ask. My field information clearly indicated that the solidarity of the workers, especially among the struggling leaders, was not formed in the workplace, nor was it derived from working relations. Instead, the ethnographic account indicates the presence of a complicated process of transposing subtle socio-personal ties from rural domestic settlements to the urban production premises. The ties became meaningful in a situation of industrial conflict and were recognized by the parties involved only when they reflected upon it retrospectively.

Thus, I tried not to decipher the secret code of the 'rural-urban' continuum and its cultural significance with conventional categories of social structure, kinship ties, value involutions or behavioural survivals — staple concerns of the 'Chinese Anthropology' of a modernist persuasion. Although I did not yet have a comprehensive framework as an alternative to these conventional conceptualizations, I was quite sure that my work would not be an empiricist labour history, nor would it be akin to a structural-functional approach to workers' movements or social/societal movements (cf. Touraine 2000, 90–1; 2001, 34–5)

I now realize that the social ties mentioned above which were formed outside the workplace were not stable, nor were the roles and statuses of the people involved. These pre-existing relations-in-flux cannot be said to have provided a basis for industrial solidarity to emerge. It was not until the last phase of my fieldwork, when the group picked up the ethnographic account and subjected it to rigorous scrutiny, that these pre-existing relations really became comprehensible to me. It was in the process of re-examining the ethnographic record, both alone and with my interviewees, that I relearned what I had been doing all along — I had been quite irresponsible while I was indulged in my personal quest for an ethnography.

What was marvellous and exciting about doing fieldwork were the unexpected and unintended consequences of self-education. Since I was the document-creating agent, my transformation went hand in hand with the very process by which I handled and transformed whatever came to me. This was a process of being produced through production; the articulated subject's subjectivity becoming deeper the more he submerged himself in broader and broader contexts of multiple subjectivities. This is precisely the importance of the next type of narrative.

Reflexive narratives of worker consciousness

This sort of narrative led me into a much more subjective realm. Of course, one cannot deny or totally discount the existence of 'subjective' elements in the previous exercises. In the ethnographic narrative, although a new dimension of time/space became available and new questions emerged from both the density of the materials and from gaps and omissions in and among them, objective conditions and constraints — in socio-scientific terms — were invoked to account for them. These structures and functions were unable to explain, however, why such forces actually worked on the actors and actions involved.

The difficulties involved were more than technical and methodological. These 'structural' conditions and constraints invariably failed to account for anything concrete, because the categories employed were anything but actively constructed or theoretically generated by the narrators involved. The agents' own dynamic processes of discursive figuring were elided. This situation cannot be improved technically or methodologically in structural-functional ethnography because at the level of our second-genre narrative no clear agent exists. Rather, for this kind of social-science analysis, an agent becomes merely an 'individual' attached to a pre-existing framework. This particular 'individual' is taken either as a rural dweller, a female operative or an export-processing worker … etc., but never as an agent in the making of her own history.

I prefer to define 'agent' as one who mediates her/his own existence in relation to a constructed context. S/he must actively address her/himself rather than be passively interpellated (Althusser 1971; Laclau 1977, 81–198; Chiu 1995, 1–45). In giving meaning to the emergent conditions of her/his existence, an agent transforms those conditions to make her/himself a being who can be properly addressed. To exist is to act. And to act goes far beyond answering summons under a bestowed name — it is a constant process of creating an active self as well as participating in the construction of a responsive world of which the agent is a part. Without or prior to this mediation, an agent does not exist. In other words, only in and through an active discursive construction and praxiological interpellation can a transformation take place which also changes a passive, non-reflective being into an agent, an active and consciously acting 'subject'. The perspective from which the agent conceives the formation of her/his very 'agenthood' is crucial to this process.

Nevertheless, this agenthood can not be recognized or acknowledged except by those who are agents in the same sense. In other words, the agency of the workers was not possible for me to recognize or take into account in the second, ethnographic, genre precisely because I myself had not yet been transformed into an agent with respect to the situation in question. And it was not until I activated my own subjectivity and took action to re-mediate my existence vis-à-vis that of my interviewees that I was transformed into an agent for the situation and was able to appreciate their own particular agency.

If what has been said sounds tautological, it is. Precisely because this third genre of narrative reflexivity is circular, it is impossible to understand from the perspective of linear-logical thinking. During the process of generating this reflexive narrative I became aware of innumerable degrees of interpellation and agenthood, genres of mediation and reflexivity, forms of participation and senses of solidarity, types of action and collective existence. All these had been articulated through numerous involvements, including position-forming, position-taking and adjustments in orienting and aiming.

This process of articulation and its intricacies is demonstrated in Chapters 7 to 8, through various 'episodes' which became available as informants and I plunged critically into the thickness of the *lifeworld* discourses. In effect, every single 'episode' refracted a set of problems, together with their possible outcomes, into many more problems, all of which could be seen to challenge the conventional wisdom of social science. These new perceptions also revealed a very different sense of historicity and required an entirely new perspective on my part. Gazing upon this newly available vision, points in time and space anchored not only single events but also served as interfaces for the immensely fluid, discretional actions of multiple agents. Actions were taken according to each agent's situational position and perspective at a given point in time, and always involved possible alternatives, the perceptions and actions of other agents, and anticipations of the perceptions and actions of others.

To illustrate these inter/intra-subjective dimensions, the story I tell in the reflexive narrative is multi-stranded. Of course, no matter how much is told, it can only be a partial story. The reason I have tried hard to tell as much as possible is really to convey how small and limited our knowledge really is. Through the process I have described it has become impossible to provide a neat, straightforward, single-stranded story. Such a story would be more consistent with history as it is usually recounted; but I am more concerned here with the historicity of action and the multiplicity and complexity of the agents who make their own histories.

In this book I want to build a discursive relation with the reader. Making sense of a story like the one told here requires a particular form of engagement. I hope that readers will come up with their own questions, some of which may not be answerable. Knowledge is never complete, and therefore the act of understanding requires activity more than contemplation (Volosinov 1973, 1987). In real-life struggles for survival and decency, the problem is not how much information is out there for us to 'recognize', but rather how we are to understand and act — under the pressure of being constantly acted upon — given our limited knowledge.

The theoretical consequences of this insight are serious. Praxiologically speaking, I have called into question the notion of deeper structural properties — a set of functional prerequisites — which are latent and only need to be 'discovered' through a process of model-fitting, feature-sorting and law-finding by social-scientific experts. In its place I have insisted on grounding our narratives in a particular notion of the agent. Agents are people who act consciously. They do not exist prior to mediation through both action and discourse that transforms them into conscious historical subjects. If this is correct, how can we posit 'actors', 'functions' or even 'structures' that condition behaviour prior to the behaviour taking place and before the one who behaves comes into existence? These entities are possible, but only theoretically. They become plausible only through the operation of post hoc reasoning — one that employs an *a posteriori* exercise to do an *a priori* job.

In contrast, my presentation seeks to demonstrate where certain approaches to industrial social relations have gone wrong. I argue that 'class', for example, is simply a reification of active historical struggle. People working in an industrial setting do not automatically become members of a 'working class'. They must be involved in a dense and complicated oppositional social process. And if they (or rather, most of the time, only some of them) do become members of *a* working class (not *The* Working Class), they keep this status only through repeated reinforcement and only as the said social process (usually concrete struggle) that constitutes them as a class continues. To the extent that my material supports a theoretical claim, then, I would say that class exists while individual beings are interpellated and self-addressed, respectively and together, within a commonly shared context. Those who collectively construct a definite moral-political positioning and take up similar space in a political economy, taking action in solidarity, become a 'class'. At this moment, and only at this very moment, do we see the formation of workers into a working class. In our JWM strike case, 'class' was formed when the management carried out the 31 May 'slaughter' referred to at the beginning of this chapter, and this 'class' began to dissolve when some of the veteran workers' leaders decided to take their compensation and exit. In other words, a working class itself, as well as its consciousness, is produced and reproduced by its individual members, who share positions and actions in and through struggle. Therefore, a class theory outside an everyday-life context of conflict and compromise is a theory lacking in relevance — just another ahistorical and context-free mental exercise.

Nevertheless, I do not wish to suggest that no model — such as proletarianization, internal contradictions in a capitalist economy, or world crisis — can be right. What I am convinced of is that without accounting for or understanding the process in which the subjectivity of agents is formed, we will be left asking and failing to answer the same questions again and again. What is at stake is the mediation itself — the very materialization of a person into an agent, the making of individuals into socially meaningful subjects in socially significant actions. Existing theories that fail to address the problem involved in this construction amount to ungrounded speculation.

The Practice of Alterative Ethnography and Non-Foundational Social Analyses

As the product of intensive enthograph-based study, this book relies both on narrating the experience and calls into question all foundational claims of narrational experience — i.e., politics, cultures, labour relations, gender divisions, various social analytic categories, and so on. To be able to do this, I cannot homogenize the texts. The multi-genre presentations and reflexive mode of writings are meant to be read as a methodological demonstration as well as an epistemological statement in their own right. But they also purport to show the necessary correspondences: between form and content, between language and thought, and between signification practices and their resulting products.

An alterative ethnography — or an 'experimental ethnography' as Jean Camaroff calls it — is thus not a research project of labour history, nor an account of industrial relations. It certainly does not deal with issues of development, gender, or social differentiation ... labour struggles in their conventional sense. For what such a project deems to be at stake is not the immediate (or remote) circumstantial conditions which can be seen to have 'caused' the industrial conflict. Instead, this project takes into consideration the overall politico-economic and ethico-cultural dimensions involved in over-determining and over-hegemonizing the commencement and the outcome of the dispute. An alterative ethnography of a strike and a critical theoretical analysis of the problem of working class solidarity, my account focuses upon factory shop-floor politics and politics outside the factory, as well as cultural politics, at a time when manufacturing and industrial activity were at their peak in Hong Kong.

Such an account, taking the interplay of social bodies and moral politics as its point of departure, should be able to make a unique resource for labour historians, social movement practitioners, feminist advocates and others; as well as for academic sociologists and anthropologists. Drawing on a long tradition of non-foundational writings in Marxist and non-Marxist literature and adopting discursive strategies of cultural studies, the richness of the work should be able to persuade the careful reader that a non-foundational approach can hold promise for the future of radical social analysis.

In rethinking issues in ethnography writing, labour relation researches and the three world theories mentioned below, I use the tool of reflexive ethnography to expand the scopes of both cultural studies and political-economic discourses. By problematizing the historicities and moral politics involved in societal negotiations and compromises, my various accounts lay bare the blind spots embedded in theories of flexible accumulation, core/periphery relations, and world system(s). At the same time, these accounts provide me with rich and fluid spaces within which to substantiate the following enquiries.

(1) The investigation of hidden layers of social relations and interactions among workers, which set the basic tone and form a base for their solidarity and collective action in times of crises.

This part deals with subterranean time and space in physical terms, as well as with that which exists in various agents' minds. Physically, I have had to expand the time span to include periods both before and after the sit-ins. Spatially, I have had to ignore the confines of the factory premises and reach out to the workers' rural residential communities. With regard to subjective time and space, I try to grasp the overall meaning and significance of various terms of connection. For instance, I have had to account for the fact that the group of leaders addressed each other in joking, fictive kinship terms both long before and after the industrial action took place. Predicating upon the rural upbringing of the majority of these women operatives, issues of generational transmission of work ethic, values and various cultural forms (cf. Willis 1977) and dynamics of day-to-day practices and resistances (cf. de Certeau 1984) can be further problematized. In engaging the Thompsonian thesis of the 'making' of the working class, I open up the essentialized and impacted language of a working woman's 'world', a language which hangs somewhere in the limbo between 'kinship' and 'class'.

(2) The deconstruction of the structure of moral politics embedded in economic struggles.

I assess the impact of managerial manipulation of rewards — in our case, the 'privatization' of work benefits and related arbitrary differential treatments — upon the self-identification of the worker's social existence, as well as its effect on the construction of we/they relations. Special emphasis is placed on the morality of money-taking and money-giving. My case clearly indicates that it is not always true that the issue in dispute simply concerns the quantity of money. In this case it involved heated argumentation about 'what kind of money are we talking about?' With a value context which is by all means socially defined and culturally informed, money is never either purely transparent or colourless. Who gives what to whom for what? How is it done? When is it done? Who gets it and who doesn't? What is the justification for being treated differently and why? All these issues are at stake, not just how much money is involved.

To be able to understand these issues I look into the capitalist uses (politics) of manipulating social insecurity (cf. Marglin 1976), on the one hand, while on the other I highlight the significance of practices concerned with women's labour-returns (paid or unpaid) and their effect on sustaining livelihoods: certain practices lessen the necessity of the contribution of female labour power, thereby enabling struggles to be more concerned with moral issues.

(3) The analysis of discursive position-making, and the position-making of various agencies involved.

I do not take the various agencies involved as having *a priori* existence of any certain kind; neither do I posit functions or needs dictated by charters, but specify circumstances and conditions under which agencies appropriate specific signs and images to themselves. I also specify those circumstances and conditions under which agencies assign or superimpose particular signs and images on their adversaries. By so doing, I hope to make transparent the cultural dynamic inherent in specific strategy formations and its related ideological interpolations. This theme can best be demonstrated by our case, in which the cultural image of 'benevolent boss as benevolent king' became strategically available for both workers and management to appropriate and re-appropriate in their ideological war.

In a nutshell, the problematic of agenthood involves an appreciation of the ways ideologies, movements and subjectivities interact. Given the fluidity of the field site, it is important to be sensitive to the interactions between observer and observed. Only certain styles of writing are capable of conveying the reflexivities generated, which include the authors' own experience in coming to terms with the issues of praxis, narration, collective construction, humour, messiness and frustration. Here is precisely the place where questions of genre and narrative collide/collude with those of construction and self-criticism.

At a parallel yet different level the same principles apply with regard to the interplay of social bodies and moral politics. At this collective level in-depth analysis takes a form akin to the discourse analysis of cultural politics and the sociological intervention of new social movements (cf. Hall and Jacques 1983, 1989; Touraine, Wieviorka and Dubet 1987).

Following this line of inquiry, I learned that a 'cultural rationale' is not something existing *a priori* which has created and can therefore explain social actions. On the contrary, it is something created and reproduced and, therefore, to be explained (cf. Volosinov 1973). This theoretical orientation is in sharp contrast to some prevailing practices in sinology, which tend to reify various aspects of Confucian discourses and, in one way or another, press them into a thin base to support an explanation of 'economic miracles'. I recount the 'boss-as-king' phenomenon mentioned above to illustrate this.

At various points during the period of the workers' sit-in, their leadership actively sought to augment their bargaining power by appealing for support from their MNC's (multinational corporation's) overseas top management. They cabled directly to the managing director to solicit his personal attention, and then waited attentively for his intervention. At first glance, scholars may find this a manifestation of the Chinese worker's deeply-embedded 'sense of authority', as trickled down through thousands of years of Confucian teachings; others might take it as evidence of the 'false consciousness' of a nascent proletariat which isn't even aware of its own class position in a capitalist division of labour. These two positions, based upon radically different presumptions, actually share the same mixture of methodologies — a kind of hybrid exercise of socio-topographical feature-sorting, historico-developmental, model-fitting and economic-nomothetical law-finding.

An anthropological reading of the records of hundreds of hours of remarkably articulate discussions among the workers themselves, however, calls for an alternative approach. From the perspective of discourse analysis, I found that the workers carefully thought through, and consciously selected, their plan of action. They emphasized particular aspects of a conventional 'authoritative image' of the 'other' as a strategic act to serve their interests as they understood them. The workers' image of their top authority was meant to be imposed upon the managing director of the head office, who was actually their opponent — i.e., they did it to exert pressure upon an adversary, not because they believed in the image themselves. This transposition had multifaceted objectives: to add weight to their struggle and their self-importance, to ward off pressures from the local management, to boost morale among fellow workers, to create pretexts for seeking international support, to warn of a possible upgrading of action, to mobilize public opinion, and so on. The concrete operation of these tactics and the reactions they invited are too complicated to discuss in detail here. Couching the discourse entirely in the familiar Chinese moralistic idiom finally entangled the top management in it and confined the power of the image. Soon, both sides began to compete in borrowing from the same ideological arsenal, both to support arguments and to justify positions — waving their weapons under the shadow of the biggest statue, the most powerful hegemonic icon available: Confucius.

In other words, the 'cultural image' of the boss as benevolent king — a morally-sanctioned, socially-constructed image — became available for the adversaries to appropriate and re-appropriate in their ideological war. In this context, the image itself in reality turns out to be a rather empty, fluid one — like that of a cup, the contents of which change as different things are poured in and out.

It is precisely this contentless form that made it valuable and indispensable for both opponents. From the workers' point of view, once the MNC accepted the 'Confucian' image, it would be difficult for them (as well as for governmental agents, who could be made to carry the same image) to reduce or dismiss the event as a simple 'economic issue'. Whatever economic concessions the MNC made would reinforce the management's moral predicament. This in fact happened, when the JWM managing director came to Hong Kong and finally decided to sack the workers' leaders while simultaneously pacifying other striking workers.

Small as my ethnographic cases may be, under close scrutiny, they reveal much more complicated and dynamic processes than does present scholarship on industrial conflicts, sinology and labour history. I would suggest that no social action — or inaction — is comprehensible without taking into account the reasoning of those who are involved, which is invariably both economic and ideological, practical and cultural, utilitarian and moralistic, at the same time.

2 Hong Kong and the Japan Watch Multinational: The Political Economy of Profit-Generating Machines on a Capitalist Periphery

Hong Kong was formerly a British enclave at the mouth of the Pearl River. The island was occupied by the British in 1841, during the first Opium War (1839–42) between Britain and China. Its secession to Britain was ratified in the Treaty of Nanking (1842). Further territory (Kowloon) was added in 1860, and in 1898 the New Territories were added on a 99-year rent-free lease, by agreement between Britain and China.

The enclave comprises just 398 square miles, and in 1986 had a population of six million, including a 1.5 percent non-Chinese population. The population is largely concentrated in two conurbations, on either side of the harbour. In its general character, Hong Kong was Chinese, despite having been ruled by a British administration under British law.

Since 1843, the development of Hong Kong has been intimately connected with, and influenced by, the great continental society of China, although as a creation of mercantile capitalism in its most naked and brutal form, Hong Kong has always conducted 'business as usual', beginning with opium.

By the end of the eighteenth century, British merchants, in order to overcome the failure to create a market for goods of Western manufacture and to reclaim the silver they had paid for Chinese silk and tea, managed to create a demand for Indian opium among the Chinese population. By 1839 — just prior to the Chinese prohibition of the opium trade and the British occupation of Hong Kong — the amount of opium being pumped into China was increasing exponentially.

Ever since its days as the world's major opium market and as a bridgehead of capitalist penetration, Hong Kong's growth has always been in entrepôt trade.

After the defeat of the Japanese in 1945, and following the intensification of civil war in China, a flood of refugees entered the colony. Further events in China gave Hong Kong an industrial impetus. A number of Chinese entrepreneurs fled from the major industrial city of Shanghai, and the 1949 Revolution led to the creation of a nucleus of skilled workers and capitalists for the establishment of factories in Hong Kong. Then China's involvement in the Korean War in 1951, and the subsequent United Nations and US ban on trade with the People's Republic, sharply reduced Hong Kong's entrepôt commerce, forcing its businessmen to look elsewhere for earnings and its labour force to seek alternative means of subsistence. These businessmen took to manufacturing — both capital-intensive and labour-intensive.

The changing structure of postwar international capital interests resulted in shifting political relations and strategies of expropriation. A strange mix in Hong Kong, resulting from its unique history and location, made its transformation into a core offshore manufacturing outpost for international capitalism not only possible but imperative. In a span of twenty years, Hong Kong was transformed from a colonial entrepôt, dominated by its through trade with China, to a modern industrial colony and a major node in the international network of commodity markets. In the late 1940s, locally-manufactured products accounted for 15 percent of Hong Kong's exports. During the Vietnam War they exceeded 80 percent. By the end of the 1970s Hong Kong was, in spite of the small size of its population and the virtual non-existence of natural resources, among the world's top exporting areas. The value of its exports was greater than that of India in the 1980s and, after Japan, Hong Kong had the highest average per-capita income in Asia.

In 1986 the economy and systems of manufacture in Hong Kong exemplified virtually every type of what has been perceived as 'the' process of 'industrial evolution'. It included the most modern of factories, and a myriad domestic production systems. In December 1977, two-thirds of the 38,000 registered manufacturing establishments engaged fewer than ten persons; only forty plants employed 1,000 or more workers. Since then, Hong Kong's economy has been determined by its export earnings and has depended on the unhampered flexibility — in terms of both cost and mobility — of both capital and labour.

Hong Kong's workers were, at the time of the events with which this work is concerned, noted by multinationals for their dexterity, and were regarded as painstaking, docile and adaptive. They worked extremely long hours — an average of 56.1 hours/week (some 14,000 exceeded 105 hours/week in 1975). Children and females comprised a significant component of the workforce.

Hong Kong society has long been complex, fragmented, stratified and shifting. Among the working population there existed, in the 1980s, at least three different wage standards in three different districts, even within the same industries. There were also three politically antagonistic union systems, although none played significant roles in Hong Kong:

1. The pro-China *Federation of Labour Unions* (FLU), composed of seventy-two labour unions covering some 171,000 workers. Each union had two representatives, who attended biannual general meetings to elect standing committee members. The vice-chairman at the time claimed that the FLU was an independent organization, and that China provided only technical assistance. Financing came from rent and membership fees.
2. The pro-Taiwan *Confederation of Workers' Associations* (CWA), which had eighty-two labour unions covering 40,000 workers. The unions' representatives attended the annual convention and elected the executive board members, who were then responsible for the operation of the association's Executive Council. The CWA was affiliated with the International Confederation of Free Trade Unions. The Chief

Secretary at the time asserted that a certain relationship existed but that, basically, finances came from rent.
3. The 'independent' *Christian Labour Association* (CLA) and its allies among white-collar civil service unions. The CLA was composed of Christian organizations, which appointed representatives, who might be workers or others, to sit on its executive committee. The CLA was affiliated with the Hong Kong Christian Council. Funds mainly came from Christian sources. The Association regarded its labour activity as opposition to 'sins' within the social structure and within human nature.

The number of employee unions remained at about 240 for most of the period 1950–65. Total declared union membership in 1966 was roughly comparable with that of the early 1950s. Most unions were relatively small. During this period, the pro-China FLU group of unions achieved numerical dominance and moderated its confrontational posture towards employers. At this time the low level of union penetration among workers in the burgeoning manufacturing sectors of clothing, plastics, toys and electronics became acutely evident. Less than 10 percent of the 550,000 persons engaged in manufacturing during 1966 were union members.

A major new development within the union movement since the late 1960s had been the growth of independent white-collar unions, mainly in public administration but also in the fields of health, education and welfare. Between 1968 and 1983, the number of employee unions doubled. Conditions fostering unionization in the civil service included:
1. The government's official support for staff unionization;
2. The growth and changing occupational structure of the civil service; and
3. The system of staff relations within the civil service.

Generally, the overall stability in this highly unequal 'partial society' and 'partial economy' has been underwritten by increases in real wages. Until 1973, wages rose faster than the price of consumer goods, as the People's Republic of China supplied much of the food and other necessities at lower prices than those demanded in the international market in Hong Kong (Wong 1972, 29–57).

With such a subsidy from China (Arrighi 1973, 180–234), an investor in Hong Kong could expect to recoup two to three times the value of his investment within five years — a much higher rate of return than what could be earned from investment almost anywhere else. As a result, the socio-economic system of Hong Kong, an arena open for speculative capital from all over the world, was utterly permeated with the mentality of the 'fast buck'. All this was made possible by Hong Kong's only resource — labour. Indeed, the wellspring of Hong Kong could be tapped by any multinational, while Hong Kong's welfare was the responsibility of none of them — an extreme example of export manufacturing under what has been called the 'new international division of labour'.

As in some developing countries, international capital investment made Hong Kong a site for goods manufacture for the world market. The essential preconditions for this may be identified as follows:

1. A Chinese 'subsidy' in the form of cheap food (Lewis 1954, 39–91; Lewis 1958, 1–32; Wolpe 1972, 425–56; Mkandawire 1977, 27–43; Arrighi 1973, 180–234);
2. The high degree of division of labour in the production process, to the extent that most of the fragmented operations could be carried out with minimal levels of quickly-acquired skill (Frobel et al. 1978);
3. Techniques of transport and communication which lowered the cost of production and shipment to any place in the world;
4. The development of repressive labour control, in an infrastructure with attractive fiscal policies for international capital; and
5. A practically inexhaustible reservoir of disposable cheap labour, especially female, owing to the 'migrant' nature of the job engagement, itself made possible because active non-capitalist sectors could pick up and sustain themselves outside the 'capitalist labour market'.

In such an arrangement, productive processes in and for the world market were separated and compartmentalized at the local level. They were, at the same time, integrated — both vertically and horizontally — into the transnational operation of the individual companies. Thus, the domination exercised by the international monopoly sector over its various markets allowed it to absorb increasing labour costs in core countries by draining surplus from the peripheral local competitive sector. In the case of Hong Kong, the capacity to shift the production format actually served to transfer surplus to the international subcontractors upon whom it depended for survival, while at the same time minimizing loss resulting from the uncertainty of the market. In effect, this production format served as a buffer, absorbing possible loss and scale-economy nightmares caused by fluctuation in both the size of the production market and the size of the available labour supply.

This economy was the result of the interplay of political and social, as well as economic, forces in a specific cultural and political context. Understanding the division of labour in the modern world necessitates a series of particular questions about its form, degree and impact in different national and international contexts. That is to say, the historical constitution of a division of labour is the result of class, state and ideological relations. These relations are logically governed at the concrete level. This logic is in turn conditioned and informed by systems of meaning expressed in cultural and political terms.

The responsibility of an anthropologist is to highlight this logic both in concrete, operational and structural terms. Scholars of quasi-Marxist persuasion have generally stressed the role of non-capitalist relations of production in the reproduction of capitalism which, in turn, allows the persistence of these 'subordinate' modes of production (Long and Richardson 1978, 176–209). Anthropologists must analyse how processes internal to non-capitalist modes of production serve to further their own reproduction. Furthermore, anthropologists should also seek to demonstrate how social relations and cultural signs enter into and affect those labour processes that make the reproduction of a domestic system not only possible but necessary (Polanyi 1974).

Taking the labour process as my point of departure, I should point out that mercantilistic manoeuvring is the most analytically-significant aspect of the 'new' international division of labour. To wit: subcontracting and putting-out are phenomena which predate 'capitalism'. Neither is there anything new about the vertical/horizontal integration of manufacturing — it had simply never been carried out on a global scale. The integration of manufacturing became an issue and a problem precisely because isolation and compartmentalization of production were magnified to a critical level — horizontally in terms of task specialization and vertically in terms of hierarchical stratification. The globalization of the productive process is in actuality dramatized in a modern-day adoption of essentially mercantilist strategies of capital accumulation and valorization by post-Second World War capitalist concerns.

The direct appropriation of others' productivity in its realized form, as through subcontracting and putting-out, is a typical mercantilist strategy for appropriating native products, and in its modern form serves the same purpose of the accumulation and valorization of capital. International capitalists try to:

1. Substitute capital widening (i.e., an expansion of the size and availability of the labour force) for capital deepening (i.e., investment in new fixed capital cf. Lewis 1954), on a worldwide scale;
2. Exhaust and squeeze utility from worn-out fixed capital by extending its employment into third world countries and at the same time compensating inefficiency with intensity of work and cheap labour; and
3. Rely on the direct appropriation of others' productivity, appropriating labour power in its realized form, in order to perpetuate a thinly-disguised system of primitive accumulation, both to increase profit levels and to underwrite the reproduction of the capitalist world system.

This global system is predicated upon the structure of work relations with regard to external demand — a combination of Manchester capitalism, with all its authoritarianism in the work place (as pointed out by Hopkins (1971); and, for Hong Kong, by England and Rear (1975)) and the forms of late capitalist organization of work. It compels the labour force at peripheral manufacturing sites to achieve high levels of profitability and intensity of labour while forcing it to tolerate wage levels not much higher than those of the heyday of Manchester capitalism.

The perpetuation of this structure of work relations with regard to external demand in Hong Kong, as I see it, has been achieved through the result of collisions and collusions of interests. It is manifested by contradictions, which expose an opposition or disjunction of structural principles underlying contending social systems (Giddens 1979, 49–95). I suggest that one fruitful way of inquiring into Hong Kong's social formation — and, hence, into the articulation of global and local forces in the development of the global and peripheral capitalist production system — may be to look for the *contradictions* (Giddens 1979, 131–64) within local social practices instead of the *functions* they fulfil. I would argue that there exists a socially-created, historically-defined and culturally-informed domestic social system in Hong Kong, the structural principles of which systematically clash with those of multinational capitalism.

In light of the changing nature of Hong Kong society, it is important to emphasize that the issue at hand rests not so much upon the factual peculiarities of Hong Kong's social transformation but upon identifying the theoretically significant features of this transformation. Even at a general level, blatantly opposed viewpoints are characteristic of existing literature. For instance, Henry Smith (1966) characterized Hong Kong as 'John Stuart Mill's other island', while Eugene Cooper (1982, 25–31) described it as 'Karl Marx's other island'. As for Hong Kong's economic performance, Rabushka (1979) characterized it as a 'miracle' and Woronoff (1980), likewise, as a 'capitalist paradise'. These characterizations differ from the bleak depictions of the 'sweat-shop operations' and other nightmarish working conditions reminiscent of 'the darkest age of capitalism' offered by Hopkins (1971), England (1975), Cheval (1972), and Halliday (1974, 91–113), among others. Such opposing viewpoints reflect polemic differences, to be sure, not unlike the ones which divide proponents of modernization and dependency theories of development/ underdevelopment (MT and DT, respectively). It appears that, at the theoretical level, observers of Hong Kong society are guilty of their own subjective biases, and that these are built into their particular interpretations of the 'system'. Extreme utilitarian economists like Rabushka accent the positive aspects of capitalist accumulation in Hong Kong at the expense of the equally obvious consequences of such 'progress', namely the production and reproduction of an exploitative system of wage labour. On the other hand, 'radical' leftists like England and Rear are quick to point out the oppressive conditions of labour under the manufacturing process, although their understanding of the 'system' is one which is less Marxist than Western liberal, as is reflected in their emphasis on collective bargaining as the remedy for this social dilemma.

I suggest that, regardless of ideological persuasion, these and other observers of Hong Kong society have been unsuccessful in understanding the nature of socio-economic transformation precisely because, like the proponents of MT and DT, they fail to arrive at a satisfactory understanding of the internal dynamics of the system peculiar to the relations of production in Hong Kong, and fail to place these dynamics within the broader context of an international division of labour.

Perhaps the most plausible assessment of the Hong Kong system as it is referred to here is that it can be understood as an unstable equilibrium based upon a series of contradictions formed by elements both endogenous and exogenous. In this regard, Harris (1978) perhaps came closest to recognizing the existence of seemingly contradictory paradoxical aspects of Hong Kong society. He suggests five essential 'paradoxes':

1. Hong Kong was a colony without the conventional attributes of a colony;
2. Hong Kong was an open-ended economic entity, but not an open-ended society;
3. China appeared not to want Hong Kong but reluctant to relinquish claims to its sovereignty;

4. Hong Kong produced foreign exchange for China, but China did not control Hong Kong politically; and
5. Hong Kong had stability but an uncertain future.

Harris' dichotomies were somewhat superficial and simplistic, but they represented the state of the art of Hong Kong enquiries and their Eurocentric outlook. They represent a wholesale international transfer of categories, and of a disguised *realpolitik* embedded in confused sociological language, which in fact resembles that of MT and DT writers. I argue that our inability to understand the nature of contradictions within the system ultimately stems from a misinterpretation — on the part of both Marxists and non-Marxists alike — of certain fundamental theoretical issues related to modern capitalist social production and reproduction of the kind seen in Hong Kong.

In essence, my research seeks to de-dichotomize conventional micro/macro, quantitative/qualitative, distribution/production, synchronic/diachronic, ideological/practical, etc., bifurcations in social scientific methodology. To me, anthropology is *the* discipline capable of being sensitive to the internal dynamics of the local system at the concrete level of practice and, specifically, to the cultural-political logic which is manifest in every aspect of that practice. What the MT and DT formulations lack is a recognition and treatment of the endogenous mechanism and the cultural dimension which configures this mechanism.

I hold the following assumptions:

1. An anthropological inquiry into the concrete will reveal the nature of praxis in a definite set of 'economic rationales';
2. An anthropological reading of Marx will rediscover the cultural-political perspectives intrinsic to his argument; and
3. An anthropological review of the economists' polemics will expose the ethico-political values which circumscribe their 'universal' reasoning.

From this point of view, I shall consider the structuring of social processes of work in Hong Kong as obedience to the rules of a game which contending actors had to play. Within the limits of this game, the actors' strategies can be said to be rational, but we must understand that the game itself is a man-made construct and the result of numerous pre-existing contentions which are dependent on the cultural capacities and attitudes of the actors concerned (Crozier 1980).

The continuous working and reworking of the Hong Kong system is contingent upon the power relations and respective strategies of its two major contending actors: the Purchaser of Labour Power (POLP) and the Seller of Labour Power (SOLP). The contentions between them are predicated upon a number of major and minor contradictions in the form of simultaneous collisions and collusions of interests. The constitution of a division of labour in the historical sense is the result of a wide ensemble of relations — gender, class, state, cultural, ideological, and so on. These relations together are governed by a definite logic, at the concrete level, which concerns rationales of production operation, consumer orientation, specific motivation of definite actors, specific precepts about savings and investment, and so on. These particular logics are in turn conditioned and informed by a signifying process available in a particular setting in strictly cultural ways.

While capitalism has penetrated to the farthest corners of the globe, this penetration has been uneven, has occurred at different times, at different rates and in different forms. No matter the source of capitalist influence or how it entered into the picture, it did not simply descend from the sky onto a blank slate, but interacted with pre-existing cultural systems and social formations. In context-sensitive terms, the 'changeover' to wage labour greatly altered the ways of life and the meanings of work for formerly independent farmers and craftspeople. The concentration of people and material in one place — a labour force controlled under a single roof for repetitive production — created an entirely new perception of time, along with new work disciplines and tasks imposed upon the labourer from without (Thompson 1967, 56–97). Consequently, both subjective and objective aspects of the capitalist workplace define connections within the work process in general, and also signify the formation of worker consciousness. As a result, the boundaries between work and non-work, or between sub-categories of work, are drawn in different ways and on different terms. Both the concept and the value of work continue to change, depending on specific historical, technical, social and cultural contexts. The experience of work is thus an important socialization process for individuals — which, at the societal level, manifests itself as a process of cultural transformation.

In my Hong Kong case, I argue that it is not the world system in general that 'made' the situation of Hong Kong an exception or an aberration which existing paradigms have failed to account for. Rather, it is precisely the unique cultural/historical conjunction of Hong Kong's peculiar socio-economic formation that has made the permutations of the Hong Kong system not only possible but inevitable.

Taking this approach, I find that dynamics within the following perspectives have been salient and consequential. The reader is encouraged to keep them in mind while reading the narratives that follow (Chapters 4–7); we will revisit them in the concluding chapter.

The Size of the 'Production Market' and 'Available Labour Supply'

Adam Smith suggested that in any economy an upper limit is placed on the division of labour by the size of available markets in which the product can be sold (Fröbel 1980, 132). On the other hand, Babbage's theory was that an increased division of labour would permit the substitution of skilled labour power by less-skilled labour power, and hence the size of the available labour market also determined the extent of the division of labour (Fröbel 1980). Both these tendencies and processes exist in Hong Kong, and are opposing elements which determine the specific forms of the division of labour in Hong Kong. Smith's construction raises the problem of appropriating markets, while Babbage's theories highlight the appropriation of productivity. The central issue in Babbage's formulation concerns labour returns, the logic being to break tasks into components requiring lower and lower individual skill levels in order to facilitate activities of production and cut costs (Babbage 1986). Development of the division of labour in Hong Kong can be characterized as occurring at the intersection of these two tendencies.

The extent to which multinationals manage to appropriate the world market has direct bearing on the local availability of skills and labourers, and vice versa — and this is, to a large extent, culturally defined by prevailing cultural practices and conditioned by existing forms of social connectedness. The precise working-out of this contradiction is complex, for it does not exist in a vacuum; it can only be pinpointed at a specific time and space through in-depth field research.

De-skilling and Commoditization

In a labour process, two sets of relationships can be distinguished: that of people to their productive activities and that of people to their products (Giddens 1971). Alienation in both relations is integral to the expansion of the division of labour, and is inseparable from the capitalist division of labour. The simultaneous obscuring and securing of surplus value is characteristic of the labour process in capitalist modes (Burawoy 1979, 231–66). The productive scenario in Hong Kong manifests not only the collapse of the 'co-operation', 'manufacture' and 'machinofacture' stages discussed by Marx (Marx 1967) — suggesting that the stage theory might be invalid — but also presents the continued creation and recreation of 'modern manufacture' alongside 'modern domestic industry' (Marx 1967) as major productive activities. This is not in any way a 'historical survival', but rather a modern creation out of the confrontation of the specific needs of capitalist expansion and the special history of a culturally distinct society. Both the de-skilling of the labour force and the commoditizing of labour turn-outs are much less pronounced than one might reasonably have expected in Hong Kong manufacturing. In an attempt to explain this, Marx said that the global capitalist abuse of women and children in the ever-emerging capitalist periphery significantly delayed the reaching of the higher stage in periphery economies (Marx 1967). But this is clearly hindsight. To overcome this kind of teleological thinking and neo-evolutionary reasoning, I propose to look at the worker/productive-activity relationship, the worker/product relationship, and their related bearing on Hong Kong de-skilling and de-commoditization as structural contradictions which operate under both exogenous and endogenous cultural forces and constraints.

Two Types of Production and the Dual Character of an Article Arising from the Manner of Its Production

This can best be understood in Hong Kong as two distinct types of production — assembly-line production and transformational production. The former utilizes space as the major axis of co-ordination, and through a process of 'diachronization' combines various production processes into one ongoing process. The latter utilizes time as its major axis of transformation and through a process of 'synchronization' crystallizes segments of production into specific tasks. In assembly-line production the creation of new quality is central; it hinges upon the manipulation of 'things', and space enters the productive process as a productive element par excellence. In transformational production, the creation of new quantity is central; it hinges upon the manipulation of labour, and time enters the productive process as a productive element *par excellence*.

In most productive processes found in Hong Kong, both assembly-line production and transformational production are involved; they combine unevenly or fluidly, according to different production functions, input conditions and output requirements. Thus, the organization of production is a multi-dimensional problem-solving process. The putting-out and subcontracting systems dominating Hong Kong manufacturing can thus be understood as forms mediating these two types of production — forms which are conditioned by *the dialectics of time/space co-ordinations and contradictions*.

It is important to distinguish between these two types of production analytically in order to discern the rationales intrinsic to the dialectics of time and space involved. The transnational integration of Hong Kong manufacturing — both vertical and horizontal — constitutes a dialectic of time/space in production; time and space operate in terms of each other and also contravene one another (e.g., spatial constraints in Hong Kong result in multi-storied factories, within which production lines are broken into sections and placed on different floors, resulting in increases in the time element of production, as goods are moved vertically by cart, etc.) In such cases, time and space are not empty frames. Each bears its unique and specific cultural meaning while intersecting with the other in a practical context.

Organizational Strategies: 'Divide and Conquer' versus 'Concentrate and Control'

The dialectics intrinsic to the above two types of production — assembly-line and transformational — act upon the social relations of work to produce 'strategies' (in the genuine political sense) available to both the Purchaser of Labour Power (POLP) and the Seller of Labour Power (SOLP). In administrative language, one strategy is the politics of 'divide and conquer', the other is the politics of 'concentrate and control' (Watson 1980). The former seeks the development of minute divisions of labour, as reflected in the putting-out system; the latter strives to centralize organization by creating hierarchies, as manifested in the factory system. These diverse strategies are exemplified in my field of research.

In Hong Kong manufacturing, the continuing recreation of putting-out networks and peripherilization of production is the rule; that is, 'putting-out', etc., remains profitable in Hong Kong for unspecified, particular cultural reasons, and is not a fixed 'stage' of capitalist development which 'should have' already been 'passed through'. At this conjunction, conventional categories such as 'free market', 'perfect competition', 'economic man' and 'maximization' — categories typically assumed by orthodox economics — are inapplicable, and the much proclaimed 'universal laws' of the Europeans are unmasked as being native categories, rather than the analytical ones (Chakrabarty 2000, 3–23). Those categories were crystallized under a particular history within a particular culture. These sets of cultural categories run up against a series of strategies which are also values and cultural constructs which are non-Western and extra-capitalistic, and so the nature of the conjunction is altered. In Hong Kong, 'divide and conquer' as a strategy became relatively more profitable and therefore more appealing to multinational corporations in terms of global valorization and accumulation of capital. This is an instance epitomizing the cultural dimension that makes the permutation possible. Reflexively speaking, those 'rational economic rationales' promulgated by economists turn out to be nothing but inherent cultural constructs of the West (Chakrabarty 2000, 3–23).

Labour Engagement and Disengagement

Because a very large proportion of workers in Hong Kong are employed in small concerns which are extremely vulnerable to market fluctuations, it is strategically beneficial for the POLP to distance themselves from the SOLP and not to commit themselves too deeply. On the other hand, casual workers of all ages and both sexes (especially in booming manufacturing industries such as electronics, garments and plastic toys) must remain mobile and only minimally committed to any one job, in order to maintain steady employment and be able to bid up wages at times of peak demand (i.e., the 'ripple effect' of workers shopping around for marginal wage increments). In this sense, then, it is in the general interest of both Hong Kong's POLP and SOLP to develop and maintain a highly volatile labour force. However, both large and small firms seek to reduce turnover as much as possible, and try at least to keep on a core of experienced workers, even in bad times. At the same time, the refugee nature of the workforce makes the SOLP predisposed to trade off some degree of freedom for continuity of employment. Under these contradictions, I suggest that the putting-out system, capital widening (that is, the proliferation of a small-scale sector [cf. Lewis 1954; 1958]), and a so-called 'ambulatory labour [force]' (Sit and Ng 1980) are three elements of the particular complex solution that has been economically, socially, historically and culturally constituted in Hong Kong.

Buying and Selling Labour Power

In Hong Kong transactions between the POLP and the SOLP tend to take the form of buying and selling agreed amounts of labour, and not the power to labour over an agreed period of time; that is, the transaction is over the result of labour (labour power in its realized, concretized form) rather than over the potential of labour (labour power in its unrealized, abstract form). This reflects a set of cultural attitudes towards participation in the labour process. Of course, in the final analysis, all systems involve, in one way or another, the payment of wages — strictly or loosely, directly or indirectly — according to piece rates or subcontract rates, regardless of superficial variations of payment methods. By connecting labour performed directly to rewards, the POLP may hope to pay only for the labour which has been embodied in the merchandise and to instill in the labourer a built-in incentive for boosting productivity, thereby enlisting the labourer as a willing accomplice in his/her own exploitation. This logic at various points intersects with the survival logic of the SOLP. In a sense, the SOLP's refusal to be a 'labourer' (in a marked sense) while being exploited actually reinforces the POLP's mercantilist practices. However, I would suggest that the proliferation of the wage-according-to-result sector is actually in the service of the SOLP as a safety valve for frustrated ambitions, a supplement to wage earnings, a mitigation of the regimentation effects of market forces; as well as an embodiment of ties of kinship, common origin, etc. (in the sense that small-scale units often rely on such ties in employment). The flexibility that this system enjoys seems indispensable for the majority of workers, who set their long-term survival strategy rather defensively. The bottom line here is the sustenance and reproduction of material life, which in turn depends on internalizing the collective values of Hong Kong. Block (1973) suggests that the choice of long-term or short-term strategies is highly relevant in making economic and political decisions. I would emphasize, however, that the cultural dimension of buying and selling labour power, which gives rise to a complex of work ethics constitutive of the Hong Kong domestic system, is in collision (as well as in collusion) with global capitalism.

Informality in Economic Sector Relations

Insofar as Hong Kong is a partial society, it makes very little sense to analyse its economic sectors in terms of a formal/informal dichotomy. Rather, Hong Kong as a whole can be conceived as having experienced a sort of 'informal development' in the high seas of international capitalist speculation during the 1970s and 1980s. The seemingly distinguishable formal/informal elements in the economy are segments of vertical and horizontal chains of an international profit-realizing movement. Unavoidably, they fall into the global battle zones of the competitive sector/monopoly sector contention and constitute a local microcosm of it. This global perspective calls for inquiry into the internal mechanisms and organization variations in local non-capitalist economies, their feedback upon the capitalist mode of production, and thus the modification of the functions of both.

I believe such an inquiry may shed light on the nature of the collision and collusion of different forces. Politically, these include relations between the British and China, China and Taiwan, and Taiwan and Hong Kong. This is exemplified in the union movement in Hong Kong. There were two union systems controlled by two antagonistic political powers, China and Taiwan. Although British authority intentionally encouraged both so that they might cancel each other out, neither of the two was powerful, and neither really wanted to radicalize labour, or even believed in collective bargaining. Although the British authority was careful to prevent any amalgamation, the PRC never really supported the unions politically anyway, even in the heyday of the Cultural Revolution.

Constant Internal Movement and Overall Stability

Modern social theories — including those of Western bourgeois social scientists, third-world radicals, and orthodox Marxists — take 'social change' for granted. Developmentalists and dependency theorists only disagree with each other about the present direction of third-world social change, not about the change itself — its unilinear quality, what direction it should take, and so on. Their basic frame of reference is a highly functionalist co-operative model, together with a technologically deterministic approach. However, given the so-called 'peripheralization of the core' (identified by Burawoy 1983; Portes and Walton 1981; Sabel 1984; Sassen-Koob 1982) and the 'industrialization' of the colony (Hong Kong) and former colonies (Singapore, Taiwan and Korea), the ecological and geographical connotation of the core-periphery dichotomy must be abandoned. There are now cores in the periphery and peripheries in the core.

When people talk about 'internal re-colonization', 'revitalization of primitive accumulation', 're-mercantilization of capitalism', or 're-peripheralization', they are actually conveying ideas about two-way dynamics and reversibility, and acknowledging the existence of structural duality. They do not, however, demonstrate it.

In Hong Kong, one of the most compact and dynamic societies in the world, the actors' conflicts actually underwrite the society's ability to continue in a steady, stable state — a kind of Brownian movement. Assumptions made about this compact and dynamic society always miss the point, based as they are on teleological thinking and neo-evolutionary reasoning. In fact, there are profound cultural implications in the case of Hong Kong, because what emerges is the fact that fragmented fluidity contributes to consolidation, and the constant juggling of multiple forces contributes to the steady state of the systematic structure. We certainly see multiple forces involved in many societal contestations, along with the overall stability of Hong Kong as a system.

The Generality and/or Ethnicity of Knowledge Systems: Analytical Rationale vis-à-vis Native Rationale

Another perspective relevant to our empirical inquiry concerns how much of the cultural rationale underlying the process of production and reproduction in Hong Kong is 'Chinese' or, for that matter, 'Asian'. To answer this question, I suggest a two-tiered analysis: a theoretical analysis of the dialectics and contradictions embedded at the formal-logical level and an analysis of its manifestations as a system of praxis on the concrete historical level. On the purely logical level, the mechanisms and dynamics involved are not expected to be exclusive to Chinese 'Asian' categories, or to constitute a Chinese 'Asian' knowledge-system. On the praxis level, however, one might say that these mechanisms and dynamics are both Chinese and 'Asian'. However, a logical imperative does not imply historical necessity; neither does a historical imperative imply any logical necessity.

Take the question of Confucianism, for instance. Confucianism has not been a single entity over China's long history, but rather a complex of things that form a practical, cultural knowledge system collapsed together and signified over time. The polysemicity and multi-faceted nature of this 'school' makes me, a Chinese person, feel extremely uncomfortable in using it as an all-embracing term. To me, Confucianism in any specific phase of Chinese history was only one of the possibilities. What matters is not Confucianism or any specific branch of it *per se*, but rather its cultural signification. Given, however, the long historical engagement of Chinese society with this line of signification, Confucianism and Chineseness actually stamp upon each other — and much confusion has been the result. By the same token familialism, especially its patriarchal version, has been conflated with a 'Chinese' social conceitedness.

Social Body Constitution and Interventions of Existing Social Groups

The compactness and dynamism of the Hong Kong social formation is evident in almost every single social action. Generally, any sort of collective action will attract various social groups to get involved. These social groups spontaneously come to support one of the contesting parties. It is difficult for action-takers to refuse these offers. They can, at best, choose to rely on one party and to be ignored by its rivals. Such interventions become almost like a convention, under which the formation of a new social body becomes a 'communal' goal, the fate of which lies at the mercy — under the auspices — of its supporting agents.

Civic-Self Formation and Public Image Configuration

During the four decades after the Second World War, under the more relaxed postwar neo-colonial rule, many 'urban social organizations' (cf. Rowe 1984) in Hong Kong tested the political waters and gradually adopted open corporate identities. By competing for legitimacy in a new game, they shifted towards *Gesellschaft*-like associations. In the process, they created their respective 'constitutive other' — the 'public'. Within the confines of this newly-acquired sense of the 'public' a renewed civic self was constructed. Conversely, a parallel process was taking place, as a definable public image was constantly configured and reconfigured against a long-existing cultural nexus of societal connections, against an emerging commercial ethos, and in relation to various popular symbols. In this process a sense of 'public accountability' was established, both within and among particular group constituencies and between them and the public. I take this as the coming-to-age of a nascent public sphere that drives towards the formation of a genuine civil society.

Although the above process has been uneven among and within different types of social organization, I suggest that the extent to which these 'public' organizations manage to survive and reproduce themselves, in self-regulated fashion, is unprecedented in China's history (Chiu 1991, 2000, 2002).

Collective Action, Collective Consciousness and Collective Identification

As the book adopts a non-foundational analytical strategy, I do not presuppose actors, roles or functions prior to confronting the concrete field situation (cf. Przeworski 1989 and Chiu, in press). This enables me to appreciate the multiple constitutive dynamics involved in collective action, consciousness and identification. The fluidity of the field site constantly alerts me, as an observer as well as an intervenor, to note the interactive nature of agenthood, ideologies, movements and subjectivity. The tactics adopted by the management, and its various paid or unpaid agents, further clarify the (counter-) dynamics which aim to sabotage those constitutive mechanisms and processes.

In examining the JWM dispute, the above dimensions constantly mesh into one another. They are entangled with various justifications, contestations and compromises, in the perspectives of both management and workers. I hope to disentangle them by looking into concrete praxis.

JWM emerged as the world's biggest popular watch manufacturer two decades after the Second World War ended in Japan. In the 1970s, it began to subcontract part of its production to Hong Kong establishments, and in the early 1980s it established its own offshore production units in Hong Kong by annexing its subcontractors. Through these mergers workers were pulled together and moved to the premises in Kwai Tsing.

Within ten years, JWM's production capacity in Hong Kong redoubled. A new subcontracting network was built around JWM in Hong Kong and extended to South China, to utilize the cheap labour available there. At the same time, in order to alleviate the impact of the appreciating yen, JWM headquarters decided to give up manufacturing in Japan and relegate its entire production to its offshore units. In 1985, in a move to diversify and valorize capital, the JWM holding company decided to merge with JETCON and turn JWM-JETCON into the number-one computer printer/ accessories manufacturer in the world. It was at this conjunction that the workers' sit-in erupted in Hong Kong.

3 On Methodologies and Procedures

Fixing the Physicality of Referents: The Artificial Time/Space Grid

To use various incidents in our case to illuminate things cultural, social, political and economic, three genres of narrative have been set out to serve as referents. However, the physicality of these referents is not to be taken for granted, for they neither simply exist 'somewhere out there' nor exist merely as linguistic utterances. They are discursive artefacts, the cumulative hybrid of numerous 'events' and 'structures'. Events are structurally defined and structures are mentally formed out of events, but 'event' and 'structure', as parts of dialogical existence, are no more than things discursively perceived. The comprehensibility of each results from the overarching perceptual grids available to the narrator.

Within a sociolinguistic context, a referent — 'the sit-in' — is established, but only through a certain process. On the one hand, I have had to weed out supposedly 'irrelevant' elements from the desired referent, using the yardsticks derived from categorizations and their corollaries. It is a deliberate act, although underacknowledged, to make the physicality of the referent 'manageable' for a definite discursive exercise. Nevertheless, this process can be unconscious, taken care of 'automatically' by one's habitual, cultural, political or other 'blind spots'. However, this is a process in which various instances are used to verify or qualify some aspects of readily assumed formulations and, therefore, to reify the categories employed. The process of establishing a referent is, so to speak, both to cut the feet and to tailor the shoes. Precisely in this way we, as social scientists, have managed to 'think' our research 'objects' and refract back from them to figure out our own existence. Both empirical precision and logical rigour have to be sacrificed to fit various practical contingencies. Needless to say, this is an exercise at once teleological and tautological.

The problem for me is that referents and the categories thus established become taken for granted and are naturalized, objectivized, and de-problematized. They then assume the status of things-in-themselves, 'behaving' automatically. What has been forgotten are precisely those procedures that one adopts to conceptually fix the physicality of the desired referent and to 'empirically' define the referential-boundary of its operative category.

There is no easy way to get out of the existential predicaments of conceptualization and exposition. But one can make explicit the operations and circumstances in which the physicality of referents is fixed upon an artificial time/space grid.

The Time/Space Frame

To be fully aware of the operations and circumstances in which the establishment of a referent takes place, I begin with the time/space 'frame', in which both the referent and the category are taken to be situated. The fundamental problem in the journalistic formulation of this frame lies in the fact that the four 'Ws' — Who, What, Where, When — are customarily handled in the following fashion:

(1) Who, What, Where, and When are identified independently and separately. No inquiry is made as to mutually constitutive relationships among them. It is believed that an 'event' consists of the convergence and perfect overlap of these separate elements.

(2) One of the 'Ws' is often used to define others. The underlying presumption is that of a complete convergence of the four 'Ws' in an 'event'.

In narrative of this kind, the identification of places, times, entities and happenings is predicated upon the physically perceivable properties accessible to both the journalist and those interviewed. The resultant account is thus usually conditioned by chance. However, the time, place, entity and happening here are raw, in the sense that they are taken to exist *a priori* and 'preconceived' (prejudged), as unmediated existence. The problem involved is not so much whether there is or is not a 'physical' existence of time, space, entity or happening. This is precisely the kind of thinking which misplaces concreteness and results in positing bad questions. The real issue is: how can we, in a discursive operation, appropriate elements which are non-discursively generated and, at the same time, hope to use them to interfere with things discursively constructed to establish new arguments — a discursive existence *par excellence?* To simply rely on the 'pure and simple' physicality of those 'elements' is precisely to force the entry of things unmediated into a field of mediated operations to hybridize a typical empiro-positivistic product. Yet these non-discursively appropriated physicalities do not attach themselves to categories or enter into a discursive formation by themselves. They are assumed and put into operation by an agent who is caught up in a discursive operation. Nevertheless, this does not mean that those (assumed) physicalities will automatically adopt a discursive (dialogical) existence prior to the procedures of mediation that transform them into discursive elements. Things mediated and discursively established, therefore, have nothing in common with things which are appropriated and taken for granted simply as a function of some sort of pristine physicality ascribed to them.

Secondly, the non-discursive way of identifying 'sameness' is usually predicated upon physical criteria like propinquity, coterminality, concurrence or recurrence. However, propinquity, coterminality, concurrence or temporal recurrence do not mean the same thing in terms of place, entity or happening.

Propinquity, coterminality, concurrence or recurrence in terms of time may not have any cross-referentiality with the propinquity, coterminality, concurrence or recurrence in terms of place, entity or happening. Any one of the criteria identified in terms of any one of the 'Ws' pairing with any one, or more than one, of the others does not guarantee or prove any necessary interconnectedness between or among them. On the contrary, the more criteria are adopted the more possible combinations can result — the mathematical potential being 4 x 4 x 4 x 4 if four criteria are used, 4 x 4 x 4 x 4 x 4 if five criteria, 4 x 4 x 4 x 4 x 4 x 4 if six were adopted, etc.

Thirdly, in the case of concrete discursive operations, the problem is at once something more and something less than a mechanical mathematical formulation such as that suggested above. Most crucial to our concerns at this moment is to recognize that time, place, entity and happening are always mutually defined — they cannot be talked about in purely autonomous terms. A definite temporal referent must be established through the identification of relational times. The establishment of a definite spatial referent must be through the identification of relational places, and so on. This is a strategy which aims to use the concrete to reduce uncertainties and to enhance the exactness, or definiteness, of the referent. In mathematical terms, there must be two axes in a surface to decide a point in a two dimensional configuration, and there must be three axes to decide a point in a three-dimensional configuration. Generally stated: N axes are needed to decide a point in an N-dimensional configuration. The theoretical consequence of this is that there is absolutely no knowing whether a point has been fixed until we know the dimensions within which this point is supposed to be located. Here is precisely the kind of difficulty a social scientific discourse must confront, for there is no way to prejudge the dimensionality of things social. Understanding that it is not possible to exhaust, or even enumerate, the socially perceived dimensions that might be involved illuminates what Laclau meant by 'the impossibility of suturing the social' with a new light. It is always possible to subvert suturing the social by pointing out dimension(s) which have been left unaccounted for.

Fourthly, we must consider the nature of the 'axes' used to identify any of the 'Ws'. A number of markers can be used to identify things social in terms of the four 'Ws', but these markers are not of pure form. Each 'element' used is invariably a product of discourse — things dialogical — which is itself located in a definite matrix of four 'Ws' (implicit or explicit). These four 'Ws' are again products of concrete discourse and are anything but pure forms. In other words, all the 'Ws' (which are supposed to constitute nothing more than a referential frame, a formal scaffolding with no concrete existence) are eventfully defined and discursively constructed. The time-space frame which masquerades as a 'container' for things both concrete and discursively constructed is itself made of concrete and discursively constructed things. Why is there a tendency to deny this, to naturalize and objectivize, neutralize and transcendentalize, mystify time and space in all forms of narratives? To answer this question we first need to look into what a narrative is.

Problems of Narratives and Signs

A narrative fixes, sutures and flattens the multi-dimensional, polyvalent and fluid existence of the *lebenswelt*. Narratives make life fit for linguistic representation — usually in a linear, single-causal, two-dimensional and monovocal form. Technically speaking, utterance is a linear process *par excellence*. Sounds in temporal sequence are reproduced in writing with spatial sequence. This very formal constraint basically excludes the possibility of presenting synchronic and coterminous things by linguistic means, be they spoken or written.

A narrative is also a linguistic form which purports to represent things made known. Behind the veil of an epistemological ignorance, linguistic articulation in narrative form is used as a tool for assertion, and seldom as a means for multi-reflexive discourse. The narrative form tends to present its version of the world as *the* version, the only possible version. Even in everyday language, narratives usually evoke so general an overtone that they enable both the narrator and audience to escape from the concrete and the particular.

To be sure, the move to escape from the concrete and particular has its limits. However, at its logical extreme, this move makes 'form' the ultimate content. Consequently, reference is made only to those outside appearances that are most easily observed. Some everyday cases illustrate my point.

Sunday morning at the breakfast table Tom says: 'I want an egg.' Taken literally, he is making reference to something which never existed and never will. What is an egg? An egg is a discursive construct which exists only in the thoughts of particular language users. Tom will never be able to 'have his egg and eat it too!' It is because there is no such thing as 'an egg', existing outside of his thought and language, that he can eat for his breakfast. There are chicken eggs, duck eggs, ostrich eggs or even snake eggs, but never 'an egg'. All these eggs share but one thing in common — the egg-shape. We can infer from Tom's name that he is an English-speaking male. From there we may guess that people of this kind eat only chicken eggs for breakfast. And therefore, what Tom means by 'an egg' actually refers to a chicken egg and not to just any kind of egg-shaped object his language indicates. I would suggest that it is only after Tom's language has been subjected to a process of decomposition and recomposition that he can finally have something to eat. However, we still run the risk of giving him the wrong 'egg'. A chicken egg for breakfast involves cooking as well. However, we cannot be sure exactly how to cook it. The only other person in the world who knows how to do it 'right' may be Tom's wife; she may know that the only way he eats a chicken egg is after a one-minute boil. Now, this 'egg' as a discursive artefact becomes meaningful and applicable only to two persons, Tom and his wife.

'Has anybody seen my egg?' Tom's daughter Amy yells from upstairs. 'What egg?' her mother replies. 'The one I bought last night at Sears?' 'What? Egg from Sears?' 'Yes, the pink one.' 'Pink egg? Where did you put it?' 'In my drawer with all the underwear, ... but Bob played with it last night.' 'Oh, the egg, look for it in Bob's bed, but don't wake him yet.'

The egg they are yelling back and forth about turns out to be a plastic egg-shaped shell for the packing of stockings. This 'egg' is not even an egg-like substance, and can only be called egg-shaped at best. As a matter of fact, this 'egg' only came into Tom's family's discourse last night when Amy brought it home and showed it to Bob. And this 'egg' became a part of family discourse precisely because it is not a 'real' egg at all. This is a situation in which 'form' and shape are used to rape any tangible contents, and language is subjected to violent distortion and manipulation.

In the above cases we can identify processes by which a word is alienated further and further from a referent; from chicken egg to 'egg', to things egg-like, to things egg-shaped, and to things egg-likely-represented-and-symbolized. This is a process by which an outside appearance is taken as the ultimate form and the form is taken as the ultimate referent ... and the ultimate referent is taken as the ultimate label.

It is obvious that the process of signification of reality is a process of similar alienation. The conventionalization of signs in any linguistic community, in term of meaning and usage, loads signs with particularity and specificity, and at the same time rids them of any 'substance', lifting them to the plane of transcendence. The effect of universalizing a particular experience is invariably tantamount to iconicizing the sign and using it as a signal to usurp all the possible meanings (Volosinov 1973). The misconception involved is the assumption that generalizing the form and naturalizing the referent prove the existence of something.

The Impossibility of Objectivizing, Physicalizing and Naturalizing

To make a discursive artefact look like a non-discursive entity to prove its existence is impossible. Firstly, one cannot drain a temporal/spatial/entity/happening complex of its contents. Secondly, temporal/spatial formulations are predicated upon the concrete, and not the other way around. If you suck out the contents, the temporal/spatial formation must collapse.

Fixing physicality does not allow one to escape from the concrete and particular. On the contrary, to define the physicality of a discursive artefact is to connect it to as many concrete and particular things as possible; that is, to take into account as many axes as possible, not the other way around. Once a referent has been subjected to the misconceived process of 'generalization', its logical final destiny must converge towards greater uniformity, approaching some king of 'pure form'. This 'pure form' can exist only in the thoughts of a particular language user; something arbitrarily configured and self-represented. Typical examples of such 'pure constructs' are mathematical constructions: 'a point' does not occupy any surface, 'a line' does not occupy any area and 'a surface' does not occupy any space. In other words, a temporal/spatial referent, once subject to a process of generalization, must also be emptied of substance. This involves a project in which a temporal/spatial configuration as experiential referent is reduced to a relational referent, and a relational referent is further reduced to a 'pure' referent.

In the case of pure mathematics, configurations like 'point', 'line' and 'surface' become things which are 'good to think': acknowledged mental exercises in which these pure referents are able to operate only within the confines of an artificial, abstract system that does not project its own existence and the existence of its operative elements outside of its systemic confines, and cannot be used to make reference to elements outside of itself.

However, this is precisely not the case with regard to the act of 'physicalizing' time and space in social science:

(1) To 'physicalize' time and space is to deny that a temporal/spatial configuration exists only in the thoughts of a particular language user. It is to project the discursively-constructed time/space frame as a 'natural' and 'objective' existence; to force the 'pure referent' to operate outside of the confines of the artificial system in which it was constituted.

(2) The said time/space frame, once believed to be physical and objective, is perceived as being possible to operate universally in the 'natural' and the 'concrete'. This wishful thinking runs into a double impasse: on the one hand, a 'pure referent', being self-referential, can only be conceptual and counterfactual, which is anything but 'physical' or 'objective'; on the other hand, concrete things, which are said to exist physically and objectively, must owe their existence to a configuration of time and space which is anything but universal. Thus the cake is neither edible nor possible!

(3) Counterfactual things, contentless and approaching pure constructs (e.g., point, line, and surface in mathematics) are possible because they

exist only within their own discursive formation. To physicalize time and space is thus precisely the opposite: it is logically impossible to force a self-referential 'pure referent' to refer to the universe and use it as one wishes.

Configuring a referent in universal terms diminishes its referential power rather than enhancing it. The more general it sounds, the less it is capable of referring to anything concrete. In the case of physicalized time and space, the exercise of ridding the temporal/spatial referent of its contents and at the same time naturalizing and objectivizing it into a universal form is precisely to lose the referential function of a time/space configuration. It is self-destructive precisely because of its inherent logical incompatibility. On the one hand, if a time/space referent became an ultimate referent it should refer to nothing but itself. In this case it becomes absolutely useless. On the other hand, if this referent is to be useful, it must refer to at least one thing other than itself, and must therefore be something less (or more) than an ultimate referent.

Pseudo-Solutions: From Musical Bars to the Collapse of Astronomical Decoupage

Unfortunately, the above contradiction has seldom been adequately acknowledged. Conventionally, it is bypassed via a pseudo-solution: strategies have been adopted to make referents coincide with 'signs' from the physical world which are widely shared and taken for granted by both the narrator and his audience. This practice, when it is localized in a certain waterhole or termite mound, or at some tribal hero's birth or death date, configures a time/space grid which, however, we tend to think of as mythological and superstitious. If pushed to an extreme of generality and regularity, a sign derived from the moment of astronomical constellations will be sorted and labelled, and an ordinal numbering will be initiated and made to coincide with a birth/death date. We tend to think of this practice as historical and scientific. However, from the point of view of the present formulation, there is not a great deal of difference between the two. Be they mythological/superstitious or historical/scientific, both are acts that define the physicality of referents and artificialize time/space grids, thus enabling the configuration of narratives.

To artificialize time and space as a frame for operations of reference is to devise a grid to contain categories acquired through a process of physicality-fixing. To fix the physicality of referents is to transform 'the social' into 'society', enabling a linear, two-dimensional narration. In this move, units of time which function as 'billboards' must be erected so that 'events' can be displayed. Those units must be somewhat uniform, recurrent, and sequentially countable. They must be created, they are not given. The time unit must be arbitrarily demarcated and fissured *a priori*, but demarcating and fissuring time can only be artificial. Criteria adopted in fixing the unit must be exogenous to whatever might be put up against it: there is no relation between the 'billboard' and the possible posters which can be pinned on it.

The non-relation between time units and things to be hung on them can be configured in yet other terms. One remarkable symbol and tool for the demarcation of time has been the invention in the West of bars for musical notation. The space between two bars represents a fixed time-frame unit in which 'time' — notes and beats in musical terms — can take place. Each bar — the space between two bar strokes — as a time unit is uniform, homogeneous, isomorphic, recurrent, compatible and capable of being labelled sequentially. This space is supposedly empty, yet its total capacity *in posse* is pre-fixed. Thus, ironically, no measure is really empty. Any space between two bars (a measure), if empty or partially empty, must be be filled with a fixed amount of signs (pauses) to represent a negative existence (of sounds) in order to make up the prefixed total capacity. The space between two bar strokes is by definition the space (time) in which definite beats of sounds, or their progressively bifurcated parts, which add up to be exactly the total amount, are housed.

However, one most important presumption in such a notational/narrative system is that the bar strokes themselves do not occupy any space (time) and, for that matter, do not exist, in the precise terms set by this very narrative system. In other words, the non-existent status of the bar strokes indicates that (1) the bar stroke is an artificial device for marking out units and itself does not belong to any unit; (2) the bar strokes are used to define the physicality of the measures they confine, but they themselves are not defined in terms of their own physicality; (3) the bar stroke itself is therefore a kind of pure construct; (4) the bar strokes as markers represent the borders of the adjacent time units (measures) they confine, which, owing to the linear and sequential nature of this system of configuration, can be ordinalized and labelled sequentially for referential indexing, but the bar strokes themselves cannot.

Nevertheless, this indexing and numbering capacity becomes possible precisely because the measures the bars define are absolutely alienated from the bars that define them. In other words, the ordinalization of musical measures has absolutely nothing to do with what the measures may contain, and the referencing and indexing functions made possible by the measures are actually only available for referring and indexing the measures themselves and nothing else.

This example is precisely a situation in which an artificialized time/space grid is erected and superimposed upon happenings. The relationship (if any) between the grid and the happening can be described, at best, as coincidental. As a matter of fact, anybody who reads music knows that the measures and bar strokes are not part of the music. They are not to be taken as 'real' things, and have absolutely nothing to do with what music is or is not. Anybody who actually take the bars and bar strokes as physical existences will never be able to read music, not to mention play it. Similarly, anyone who takes the physicality of marks and the units they demarcate literally will only situate himself in a world alienated from the world which the notational/narrative system is supposed to represent (replicate).

Things of the nature of musical bars are bound to happen in a narrative which 'notates' and therefore represents a certain set of happenings — 'events' if you like. In this case, social conventions take the place of musical convention: the time/space demarcation assumes a form most usually made to coincide with astronomical cycles or with certain calendrical notations.

Given that a calendrical system has been created, for sheer convenience we usually it for the purpose of demarcation. Functioning like musical bar strokes, an artificialized time/space grid — using dates, weeks, months, years, decades, centuries — has been erected as a billboard to hang our memories on, and is used to reference and index happenings. Owing to the seeming generality and 'objectivity' of astronomical phenomena, we are trapped into uncritically taking these 'bar strokes' and 'measures' (date, week, month, year, and so on) for granted, and even believe they are objective, general, real, natural, omnipresent 'things in themselves'. The referencing and indexing made possible within this artificial system are mistaken to be an index of a 'natural' system, therefore available for the entire universe. For this reason, these demarcation marks which fissure time assume the status of seemingly communicable 'common denominators' for making reference in our everyday language. This habit puts us in an extremely vulnerable position and leaves us incapable of resisting an unavoidable confusion similar to that of one who takes musical measures and bars strokes 'for real'. In a nutshell: musical bars and bar strokes are not 'real' in a musical sense, and the time/space grid derived from astronomical decoupage is contentless; and therefore the temporal/spatial referents such a grid constitutes must also be 'meaningless', in a societal sense.

From Hermeneutics to Dialogy

Without being clearly aware of the problem exposed above, efforts which try to tackle the narrative predicament described earlier have, by and large, been in vain.

One admirable and notable effort has been the effort to revitalize the hermeneutic exercise in modern times. Much fascinating work has been done to decompose literary texts and 'social texts'. However, the deeper hermeneutics goes, the more it becomes involved in a circularity of hermeneutic decomposition which, unfortunately, renders what is said and done by the decipherer inconsequential. I would suggest that what literary hermeneutics has been working on are, by definition, 'reported speeches'

(Volosinov 1973). A hermeneutics on societal discourse will therefore be working on 'reported speeches' of a second, third or even fourth order. In Volosinovian terms, literary texts are speech within speech, utterance within utterance, and at the same time also speech about speech, utterance about utterance (ibid., 115). By the same token, social discourses taken as texts are speech within speech within speech, utterance within utterance within utterance; also speech about speech about speech, etc. In linguistic analytic terms, they are signs within signs, and at the same time signs that bear upon signs; in the context of discourse analysis, they are discourse about discourse, discourse that bears upon discourse and discourse about discourse. There is absolutely no way out; we simply circulate different orders of 'reported speeches', getting more and more deeply involved. What is left unproblematized is precisely the first-order living-world utterances and dialogue between the text that is perceived and the perceiver of the text — the codified and its decipherer.

Relying on this analysis, I suggest that a non-positivistico-empiricist confrontation with the problem must not try to get around the 'first-order living world', but must face it squarely.

Firstly, to escape circular tautological and teleological definitions, the existence of the decipherer and his positioning within intertextuality must be acknowledged and made explicit. Given the impossibility of transcendental objectivity in a world of dialogical existence, this is to argue for, not against, a sounder *operational* objectivity, as by exposing the hidden subjectivity involved we achieve a healthier and fairer inter-subjectivity. Since narrative can only be things represented in linear, single-direction and sequential fashion, to make explicit the involvement of the narrator is to take responsibility for the directionality therewith imposed.

Secondly, for the same reason, circumstances, processes and configurations of referencing, and especially those extremely 'formal' constructions like the act of time/space artificialization discussed above, must also be made explicit and properly represented. To make explicit the act of subjective appropriation behind a representation which would otherwise wear an objective disguise is to recover a space in which various intra-subjective, inter-subjective discourses can ensue. It is, so to speak, to invert the inverted, to make explicit the implicit, and thereby to make a clean breast of the whole process by which things have become convoluted.

Thirdly, to make explicit our very existence in the intertextuality of a narrative which we have been involved in making, we have to understand that acts that define the physicality of referents and artificialize time/space grids are the operational prerequisites which make our narrative possible.

To be responsible for the narrative of which we are the narrator is to illuminate these acts, but not to eliminate them. This is anything but a psychological or introversive undertaking, for the narrative predicaments with which we try to confront ourselves are logics of our human existence, not personal tragedies of any sort. I hope that I have made it clear that our existence therein is a dialogical one, not a psychological one. We construct a world in which we perceive, comprehend and act; we later represent it in a narrative; and we invite responses. It is only fair for the narrator to decompose and then re-compose the process in which this world was made available to him in the first place, and the process in which it is then remade and made available for his listener. It is by making explicit the unreality of the 'fake' parts that a narrator can claim responsibility for the things represented which were, at one point, taken as real by concrete agents and actors. This is precisely because fake things are only fake with reference to things which are not, i.e., the first-order living world.

An exercise aiming to 'de-naturalize' the not-so-obvious fictions which result from a narrator's quest for a coherent narrative, therefore, becomes indispensable. Doing so not only preserves the more genuine elements a narrative might incorporate but also makes them accessible to, as well as assessable by, the narrative-receiver who, invariably, is a participant in the dialogue the narrative aims to bring about.

In a narrative, 'events' are established through processes of discursive configuration. These processes take place in a certain time/space grid and hinge upon a set of referents. The time/space grid has to be created through a procedure of artificialization, as do the referents through a procedure of fixation. The same is true with regard to the 'structure(s)' to which the 'events' have been relegated. In other words, 'event' and 'structure' as such are wholly products of appropriated social interaction. The former is derived from happenings of the immediate sort, as determined by the circumstances of the discourse; the latter, from that of the more general kind, as determined by the whole aggregate of conditions perceived by a community of potential discourse participants. 'Event' and 'structure', as narrative artefacts are, so to speak, but moments in a continuous process of discursive configuration, which itself is but a moment in the continuous, overarching, creative process of social relations. To put it in yet another way, 'event' and 'structure' as things that we can discuss and apprehend cannot but be things of dialogical existence. Dialogical relations are socially organized and established and discursively represented. In this situation, things with partially (or even entirely) overlapping physicalities — whether in terms of time, space, entity or happening — do not necessarily or automatically relate in dialogical terms. The dialogical relationships between and among them have to be discursively configured and demonstrated. Things that do not 'talk' to each other or cannot be made to 'talk' to each other, therefore, are things that are irrelevant to the said discursive formation in common-sense terms. They are meaningless and lack relevance. On the other hand, things that do not collapse into each other in terms of their physicality are not necessarily discursively unrelated. Of course, to prove relationship is up to the narrator, who must provide evidence that they do take account of each other, address each other and/or even 'talk' to each other.

The Relevance of What-Has-Been-Clarified for My Case

Having said all this, I have finally reached the point where all the necessary preliminary clarifications are in place. A few words are still needed to address the particular necessity of these clarifications for my case.

Within each of my three clearly distinguished and marked narratives, particular times, places, entities and happenings are mutually and substantively defined and discursively constructed. The intra-narrative forms — the artificialized referential time/space grid and the physically-fixed categories — are defined by the definite 'contents' of each particular narrative. Each narrative, in other words, is constructed differentially in terms of the quality, density, thickness, depth and width of its concrete contents. As a corollary, the form — the referential grid and its categories — resulting therefrom cannot but be established differentially as well.

Now, the purpose of juxtaposing three narratives is to establish dialogues among them. Towards this end, I borrow the conventional calendrical marks of hour and date. For the journalistic narrative, relatively fewer of these calendrical 'billboards' are needed. For the ethnographic narrative, the number of these billboards increases, stretching (in temporal-sequential terms) from before the beginning of the journalistic narrative to after its end. This is to accommodate materials taken from my participant-observation and first-hand records. In the reflexive narrative, the numbers of these billboards again expand to house the results of hundreds of hours of intensive interviews.

Not only do the billboards increase greatly in number, but the 'posters' hung upon them vary greatly in terms of both quantity and quality. The spatial dimension, for example, expands from the journalistic narrative's factory premises to the ethnographic narrative's adjacent communities to the reflexive narrative's north Kowloon rural area and foreign multinational headquarters.

Now, all these three narratives are constructs and representations of what empirio-positivistic thinking would take as the *same* one-and-only 'event'. But it is not my purpose to continue maintaining the fiction that it is all just one world out there and culture, personality, world-view, ethos, etc., are only about interpreting it differently. It is also not my intention to play the game of 'misplaced concreteness' and provoke senseless debates over which version of the story is absolutely 'true' or simply relatively truer. Differences and diversities among different genres of narratives cannot be carelessly labelled as 'discrepancies'.

The only thing unreal in our narratives are the 'billboards', the date markers. In my use of the calendrical dates, holding them constant while at the same time denying their genuineness, I gain a free hand in seriously addressing the contents attached thereto. I hope that through a demonstration such as this, a discourse among different genres of narrative can be brought about to enable the illustration of points which escape conventional inquires.

The Ethnographic Narrative I: Before the Event (Day –35 to Day –2)

For eight months Ma Po-kwan had tried everything possible to get a factory job in order to carry out field research on shop-floor dynamics in Hong Kong. He shaved off his moustache, cut his hair, changed his eyeglasses and went on a diet — all to no avail. Friends remarked, 'You don't look like a worker and don't act Chinese.' But the real problem was that Ma was male. It was women that did the work in Hong Kong's electronic processing industries.

So Ma volunteered at the Central Kwai Chung Resident and Labour Service (CKRLS) and Tsuen Wan Labour Service Centre (TWLSC) and worked as a 'gung-ho' unionist.

DAY –35: 26 April 1986 (Saturday)

5:20 p.m. Thirty-odd women workers from the Japanese Watch Multinational (JWM) packed themselves round the long conference table at TWLSC. Without introducing themselves, they all began to speak. Finally an older worker, Hu Hon-chi, was elected to present their case. Hu had attended a workers' night school run by the New Youth Society, where district board member Lin Yi-chin had been a teacher, several years before.

As Lin's service group, CKRLS, shared the same office with TWLSC, Hu had persuaded her fellow workers to seek help there.

Since the beginning of March, there had been rumours of an imminent merger with another Japanese firm. Workers tried to get the management to clarify matters, but they refused. On 27 March, all the monthly-rated staff, including production line leaders and foremen/forewomen, had received handsome lump sum payments; but not the daily-rated workers, who looked to their immediate supervisors for an explanation. The answers received, if any, irritated and humiliated them.

The operatives first questioned the legitimacy of paying the money to the monthly-rated, and speculated that management had used their shares to buy off the monthly-rated workers. They then sent representatives to ask for help from the Government Agency Against Corruption (GAAC) and the Labour Bureau (LB). Neither could help and the workers gave up for a while.

Then came the Ah Si Incident.

Ah Si herself was asked to present this story. She had resigned for personal reasons at the end of April. It was standard practice for a worker who was resigning and had worked in the factory for more then five years to receive a 'Resignation Meritorious Service Award' (RMSA) equal to five to six days' wages per year of his/her service. However, when Ah Si handed in her resignation, Mo Ku-sin, the production manager, told her she should not expect any RMSA, as the old system had been modified.

This caused grave concern among all the workers because, if what Mo said was true, then:
1. Workers were being deprived of their due without being informed;
2. Although the money was not a big sum, its cancellation, coupled with all the recent minor changes in the workers' welfare scheme, constituted a real threat;
3. The upcoming merger was not beneficial to the operatives; and
4. The 'secret money' paid to all the non-operative staff magnified the unfairness of their treatment.

Co-workers on Ah Si's floor questioned their foreman about her treatment. He, however, denied any change in the overall welfare provisions and said that Ah Si did not get the money because her service was not 'outstanding'.

Ah Si burst into tears and was unable to continue her story. Another worker, Chen Siu-guan, took it up. Chen Siu-guan heard from a friend who worked in the office that a poster put up in 1981 concerning the RMSA had disappeared immediately after the first rumour of the factory's merger surfaced. She had warned her friends that the RMSA money was likely to be cancelled. The management, when questioned, confirmed the forthcoming merger, but denied any cancellation of welfare payments. Regarding the lump sum payment that monthly-rated staff had received (which amounted to two-thirds of a month's salary per year of service), the management first said it was a 'reserve fund' or 'provident fund', and later 'meritorious money'. A 'reserve fund' (public or private) or 'provident' payment for retirement or quitting was an idea which the Hong Kong government was resisting. No worker at JWM had ever heard of the factory having such a provision. The workers felt that, because of the merger, the management had simply paid their monthly-rated severance pay according to Hong Kong's Labour Ordinance, and deprived the daily-rated workers, some of whom had worked for more than ten years, of their due.

The Centre staff then introduced the Centre and explained relevant provisions of the Labour Ordinance, which, in this case, would not help these workers. If they wanted to fight, the Centre staff suggested that the workers organize themselves.

About half of the workers present volunteered to be co-ordinators, and it was decided that a workers' general meeting would be held on Monday, 28 April.

DAY –33: 28 April 1986 (Monday)

5:30 p.m. Around 180 workers met at the Kai-lup Baptist Church. Lin Yi-chin, Fu Kwon-sin, Gu Lai-hap and Ma representing the Centre, seated the co-ordinators on the podium and started the meeting. The co-ordinator chosen as moderator proved inefficient, so Ms Gu took charge. Index cards were distributed to the workers to collect information: name, age, address, telephone number, floor and production line, job title, date of employment, and current wage. Another co-ordinator, Lo Un-pu, was then chosen by the workers to present the JWM's workers' case. Gu then explained the legalities of their case and the defects in the labour law. Lin then suggested focusing on four factors:

1. The RMSA;
2. The 'mysterious money' paid to monthly-rated staff;
3. The contents of the 'provident fund' which the management had referred to; and
4. Possible modifications in the JWM welfare scheme after the imminent merger.

Ah Si then presented her case again and warned that her maltreatment reflected deep, crucial problems facing all JWM workers. She also spoke of the abuse she faced after she had refused to extend an internship in Japan so she could return to Hong Kong to get married.

Fu and Ma then assured the workers of their right to fight against unfair treatment.

Eleven representatives and leaders from different floors and lines were chosen. After a break, these Representatives (RPs) took charge of the meeting. A 'struggle fund' was decided upon. A total of 158 people signed up and donated HK$3,000 cash. The meeting then adjourned.

Lin, Gu, Fu and Ma returned to the Centre and assessed the meeting. While basically optimistic, past experience made them cautious.

DAY –32: 29 April 1986 (Tuesday)

5 p.m. After work, the eleven JWM RPs and twenty-two rank-and-file supporters came to the Centre to draft an open letter to the management, declaring that:

1. The internal instability at the factory had undermined the workers' security and efficiency;
2. Information on the imminent merger should be made available;
3. All workers should be paid a lump sum; and
4. All earlier benefits should be made available to all workers.

It was agreed that the letter would be signed by all the operatives the next day.

Chu Chi-lin and Chen Siu-guan, workers on the second floor, explained how they had been summoned to the office and told that the 'provident fund' was available only to the monthly-rated workers and had to be paid before the merger. This 'explanation' was not accepted and the manager was told that he could call the money whatever he liked, but no explanation could justify such discriminatory treatment.

After the workers left at around 10:00 p.m., the Centre workers assessed the situation. They noted:
1. A lack of communication between the RPs and the rank and file;
2. That some of the RPs lacked confidence in themselves and their workers' commitment;
3. That different floors had different strengths in terms of existing social ties, group sentiments and the will to fight; and
4. That the management might continue interviewing the workers' RPs individually, to divide them.

DAY −31: 30 April 1986 (Wednesday)

JWM RPs and supporters collected signatures for their open letter to the management.

DAY −30: 1 May 1986 (Thursday)

5:20 p.m. RPs and supporters packed the room at the Centre and reported on the day's events. Chen Siu-guan, representing the workers, handed the

JWM representatives spoke in the centennial memorial
meeting of May Day in Hong Kong on 1 May 1986

open letter, with 180 workers' signatures, to the management. The management again stated that the money was a 'provident fund', but Siu-guan insisted they should reply to all the workers and their RPs.

Later in the day, the management interviewed more RPs, changing the story and calling the money 'long service retirement awards'. Some RPs laughed at this, and said that management was being insincere and perhaps thought that the workers were fools.

At a meeting called later, all RPs and supporters agreed that there had to be collective action, or management would never take them seriously and the workers would become discouraged. The collective action should be fun and show their solidarity. They decided that all the workers on different floors would blow their whistles at the same time. In addition, a team was organized to publish an internal newsletter and leaflets.

7:30 p.m. Six workers went with three Centre volunteers to participate in a May Day rally organized by various labour organizations. JWM workers reported on their case and received a warm welcome. They also met workers from other factories who had fought for their cause with the help of the Centre.

DAY −29: 2 May 1986 (Friday)

10:00 a.m. During the morning break, workers from different floors gathered at the fifth-floor canteen and all blew their whistles at the same time. The noise affected everyone in the building. The management did not know how to respond. After enjoying the impact of their action, the workers went back to work.

At noon, the management posted a special notice on the canteen wall:

1. The factory is going to merge with JETCON but the exact date is not set. With regard to the future treatment of the workers, the present situation will be maintained. After the merger, workers' past duration of service will be acknowledged, calculated from the day they came into the service of the factory including those who came earlier at PEL [a local watch factory, had been bought by JWM].

2. The management does not intend to reduce benefits. The modifications in the number of New Year holidays and annual sick leave days were misunderstood by the workers. They were meant to produce better benefits for the workers. For instance, we changed the method of calculation of the 'full-attendance award' to using each week as a calculating unit. This way we actually increased wages six days a year for those who go without missing a single working day. And the reduction of New Year holidays has been compensated for by the annual raise in wages.

3. The so-called 'resignation award' is a 'long service payment'. Workers who have worked for the factory for five years will be paid on their resignation, but only under the condition that the said worker did not violate any regulations. In a normal situation resigning workers will be paid the award according to the following formula.
    a. Those having served the factory for five to seven years will be paid thirty-two days' base pay.
    b. Those having served the factory from eight to ten years will be paid forty-eight days' base pay.
    c. Those having served the factory for ten years and over will be paid sixty-four days' base pay.

Anyone objecting to the above calculations of long service pay should follow the provisions set by the Labour Ordinance.

5:20 p.m. About fifty JWM workers rushed to the Centre. They compiled the notes they had taken from the management's notice.

1. It had tried to shift the workers' attention away from the 'mysterious money'.
2. It had adopted the term 'long service payment' from the government.
3. The notice was obviously an effort, after the cancellation of the RMSA, to substitute the government-regulated minimum welfare standard for an existing, better one.

All agreed that, while the management had pretended to step back a little, it had in fact hardened its position.

It took Ma, Gu and Fu of the Centre almost an hour to calm the workers down. Finally, they decided to draft a letter in reply, and also a leaflet to expose the management's devious ways. A meeting and rally was planned for all the workers on 6 May (Tuesday).

DAY –26: 5 May 1986 (Monday)

5:20 p.m. After work, more than thirty workers arrived at the Centre to prepare for the next day's rally. While the RPs planned the agenda, the editing team and other workers drafted an open letter in reply to the management's announcement, asking for clarification and reiterating their objections.

Their first leaflet read:

> Expose cheating! The management has substituted a 'Long Service Payment' for the RMSA, as dictated by the Employment Ordinance. Our RMSA has been cancelled. 'Long Service Payment' implies that anyone who resigns on her own will not get a single cent. The payment only goes to older workers who have served long years and are 'dismissed without being given a reason'. We therefore strongly urge every one of you to come to our rally on Tuesday after work.
>
> Attached are the provisions of the 'Long Service Payment' listed in the current 'Employment Ordinance'.
>
> Long Service Payment:
>
> Starting from 1 January 1986, employees who have been dismissed by their employers for reasons other than summary dismissal, redundancy or voluntary resignation, and who have completed a number of continuous years of service with the employers, are eligible for Long Service Payment.
>
> The required number of years of service is related to the employee's age, and is as follows:
>
> | | Age | No. of years |
> |---|---|---|
> | Less than | 40 | 10 |
> | | 41 | 9 |
> | | 42 | 8 |
> | | 43 | 7 |
> | | 44 | 6 |
> | Not less than | 45 | 5 |

An employee who has fulfilled the qualifying years of service and who is forty years of age or above is entitled to a long service payment calculated at the rate of, in the case of a monthly-rated employee, two-thirds of her last full month's wages for every year of service. For daily-rated or piece-rated employees, the sum is calculated at the rate of eighteen days of wages for every year of service. An incomplete year of service at the time of dismissal will be calculated on a pro-rata basis. The sum of long service payment receivable cannot exceed the total amount of wages earned during the period of twelve months preceding dismissal.

An employee who is aged thirty-six years or more but less than forty years is only entitled to 75 percent of the amount calculated in the above manner, whereas an employee who is aged less than thirty-six years is only entitled to 50 percent of the amount.

DAY –25: 6 May 1986 (Tuesday)

At noon, the management posted another announcement on the canteen wall, explaining the number of days allowed for sick leave and the basis for calculating annual leave. The workers understood the announcement as an effort to cut back the JWM benefit scheme and make it equal to that of JETCON plants in Hong Kong.

5:20 p.m. About 100 workers attended the solidarity rally at the St. Stephen's Church third-floor meeting hall. Centre staffer Ms Gu spoke on the Long Service Payment (LSP), explaining the legal provisions available. She also gave a brief review of the history of the fight for a central provident fund, the government-capitalist resistance and the final watered-down version of the LSP. Next, an RP reported on events on different floors since the meeting of 28 April. Hon Lai-fon, RP from the seventh floor, urged the workers to act swiftly to curb the management's 'conspiracy'. The workers' response was enthusiastic, and teams were organized to work out strategies.

After the rally, RPs and volunteers went back to the Centre for a meeting. Dai Lin-wai spoke of her sister at the nearby JETCON factory. Her benefits were less than those at JWM. It was obvious that JWM benefits were to be lowered to match JETCON's. After an hour, most people agreed on the following points:

1. After the merger, the better welfare scheme at JWM would be replaced by JETCON's.
2. JETCON management would not maintain different benefit schemes at different work sites.

3. The worst scenario would be one where even the JETCON scheme would be reduced.
4. The merger would benefit the owners in many ways, so it was only reasonable to try to increase workers' benefits.
5. Workers of JWM and JETCON must get together. The two benefit schemes should be carefully compared, and efforts should be made to encourage JETCON workers to strive to win the JWM benefit scheme.
6. It was important to find out whether anyone at JETCON had been paid the same 'mysterious money', and if they had, to discover who and why.

The workers then unanimously decided to (a) demonstrate in front of the factory and (b) distribute leaflets to JETCON workers. They then made banners, slogans and placards, and drafted a leaflet — 'JETCON and JWM Joint Action' — with a cartoon showing a boat full of people on the high seas, implying that 'we are all in the same boat'. The leaflet urged JETCON workers to join their struggle.

DAY −24: 7 May 1986 (Wednesday)

The factory closed at 5:15 p.m., thirty minutes later than usual. Shortly before closing, management suddenly 'promoted' fifteen skilled workers to be 'assistant line leaders' (ALLs), who received HK$100 monthly subsidies. ALLs had to help line leaders keep accounts, supply materials, and arrange positions, in addition to sitting on the line like ordinary operatives. As ALLs were experienced workers, they were also frequently substituted for other workers where necessary. In workers' terms, they were 'do-all operatives' or 'almighty workers' — workers nevertheless. While line leaders supervised and policed workers, ALLs were chosen for skills in production procedures. ALLs were daily-rated, like all line workers, but line leaders were monthly-rated and were entitled to all staff benefits, including periodic banquets with office employees. Line leaders identified themselves with management.

Among the fifteen workers promoted to ALL, four were RPs, and none of them was happy about their appointment. The increased responsibility and workload was not worth $100/month. They saw it as an attempt by management to divide the workers and sow discord amongst them. There had never before been fifteen promotions at one time.

5:15 p.m. After work, about 150 workers lined up in front of the factory holding up banners and placards, blowing whistles and shouting slogans. JWM's Japanese managers and high-ranking administrators watched the workers carefully from the opposite side of the street.

After a fifteen-minute demonstration, the workers marched to the JETCON factory, closely followed by the management. Though JETCON closed at 6 p.m., the Japanese managerial staff and local foremen were on the street, having obviously been informed of the demonstration. JWM workers lined up in front of the factory gate holding the banner proclaiming 'JETCON and JWM joint action' and placards with a cartoon of two hands firmly held together. They blew their whistles and shouted slogans. When JETCON workers walked out, JWM workers approached them, handed out leaflets and tried to talk to them. At the same time, JETCON staff members and foremen also approached the JETCON workers and persuaded them to not take the leaflets and to go home. This confused and scared most JETCON workers. However, a few stopped and took leaflets. Suddenly there was a flash — a JETCON foreman was taking pictures of them. Irritated, the JWM workers surrounded him and forced him to take out the cartridge. The camera was empty. He explained that he had been told to use the flash to scare the workers. The workers, hearing this, laughed at him and let him go. By this time all the off-duty workers from JETCON had gone, and the JWM workers decided to disperse.

Back at the Centre, thirty-plus RPs and supporters held a meeting. They felt the demonstration had enhanced the workers' confidence, whilst the management really feared further action. Wishing to save the name and prestige of the company, they were extremely scared of the workers' solidarity. Workers wanted to use the opportunity to increase rank and file participation to strengthen solidarity. Actions suggested were: staring at the Japanese managers who appeared more often on the shop-floor recently;

complaining about the air-conditioning; and stretching, coughing or yawning all at once. However, they decided to temporarily withhold such actions. As the management was expected to call a meeting the next day, it was decided that meetings with RPs should be arranged at least twenty-four hours in advance and that all RPs should be present. The workers thought it was important for them to act on their own accord rather than on order. No decisions were to be made without discussion and approval at workers' meetings.

The editing group organized three teams to prepare a newsletter, and more materials to distribute at JETCON.

DAY –23: 8 May 1986 (Thursday)

At 7:00 a.m., the management summoned all foremen to a secret pre-work meeting. Foremen avoided all contact with workers that morning. Later, the management requested a meeting with the RPs. The RPs refused, telling the management of the 24-hour advance notice, and so the meeting was postponed to 9 May.

In the afternoon, foremen and supervisors on different floors summoned individual workers to the office for a 'talk' with management. The workers had not expected this. They were told that their RPs had deserted them, as requests by the management for meetings had been refused, leaving the management no choice but to approach individual workers. Management pressed each individual worker for information on what they wanted from the recent demonstration, and took notes.

The management worked hard the whole afternoon. Except for the workers from the second floor, who refused to talk individually, most workers told the management what they thought. Some third-floor workers were forced by their foremen to sign a document which looked similar to the recently-posted announcement. The body of the document was written in blue ballpoint but the last paragraph was written in pencil. The contents had something to do with a 'resignation award'.

5:00 p.m. Workers came to the Centre and took leaflets and booklets on labour laws published by the Centre to pass on to JETCON workers. When another JETCON foreman tried to take pictures, JWM workers called police headquarters to file a deposition. Fu Kuon-sin of the Centre first sent the workers home and then worked on the deposition with the police, telling them the workers were Centre volunteers legally distributing the Centre's educational materials.

In the evening, telephone calls from RPs and supporters from different JWM floors began to come in and continued to do so until 11:00 p.m. It was decided that the RPs should disavow any documents workers had signed, and should explain to their constituents the danger of talking to management privately and, especially, signing documents individually without collective consultation. The RPs all agreed that the pencilled-in paragraph on resignation awards was likely to be erased after signatures were secured. The RPs decided to use this instance to 'educate' their constituents and enhance discipline among them. To strengthen their own legitimacy as representatives, the RPs would secure signed authorizations from the rank-and-file workers and would remind their fellow workers not to believe any oral promise from management.

Workers who had been to JETCON to distribute leaflets called in to say that the foremen had tried to threaten them. One worker reported that she had got the impression that the JETCON workers were interested in the JWM struggle.

DAY –22: 9 May 1986 (Friday)

10:00 a.m. The management held a meeting with eleven RPs. There were fourteen management representatives, including Japanese managing director Tosai and two other unknown persons (one of them Japanese) and floor managers. The RPs were well prepared and acted on their own accord. Chu Chi-lin, a 24-year-old woman who lived in a northern New Territories village, did most of the talking. She denounced the management for bypassing the RPs and thus subverting their legitimacy and sowing discord among workers. She warned that if management kept on threatening workers they would be forced to take drastic action, and full responsibility for any consequences must be borne by management alone. She told the management to show good will and sincerity in negotiations and the workers' congress would agree not to take any action that day. The workers unanimously requested the management to pay daily-rated workers as they had paid the monthly-rated workers at the end of March.

For its part, the management denied that they had sent people to threaten workers, or that actions of the previous day had been designed to divide workers. They only wanted to 'help' the workers express their needs and resolve the dispute.

The management spent almost an hour explaining the nature of the payment to the monthly-rated workers. They did not like the workers calling it 'mysterious money'. They then repeated all the old stories. Once again, workers pointed out contradictions. Management representatives could not agree on how to deal with workers or the substance of talks, but they studiously avoided addressing the heart of the issue — why some employees were paid and others were not.

The vice-general manager, Woo Char-hwa, lectured the workers on 'outsiders' who were members of the 'black society' (underworld or 'mafia'). He, as a manager and older person, had to warn the workers of the dangers of getting mixed up with the underworld. Workers laughed at him or argued with him and tried to get the discussion back to the issue of the 'mysterious money'.

At this point, the extremely impatient managing director Tosai burst out, 'If you insist on talking about that money, there will be no more meetings.'

'If we don't talk about the money why should we spend our precious time here talking to you guys,' Chu Chi-lin sharply responded.

Tosai jumped up, banged his fist on the table and left the room. Other management representatives were nervous and embarrassed.

RPs left for the canteen to report to their fellow workers. The first official negotiating session between management and the workers had ended in disarray.

Around noon a woman worker from JETCON called Centre staff about the JWM case and JETCON, making it clear she did not want anybody to know of her visit. The staff arranged to meet her in a friend's office nearby.

In the afternoon, JWM vice-general manager Woo invited four of the most active RPs to his office for a 'chat'. He was extremely nice. In his 'private' capacity, he showed them part of a document with a formula indicating a lump sum of money to be calculated on an employee's basic salary: from five years at 6 percent, seven years at 7.5 percent, ten years 10 percent. Woo told the RPs that the money was the company's 'provident fund'. The RPs asked him to show them more of the document; he refused. Chen Siu-guan then asked him about her friend — a line leader, recently promoted, who had received a lump sum much larger than dictated by the formula. Woo answered that a few individual monthly-rated employees who had made remarkable contributions to the company were paid a larger sum. The RPs expressed their doubts and he stopped his persuasions. It seemed, the RPs told Centre staff, that he knew the workers would not believe him, and neither did he believe what he said.

5:00 p.m. After work, a second JWM 'propaganda team' went to JETCON to pass out booklets and the newsletter, *Tsuen Wan Workers*. At around 5:30 p.m., Fu met three women from JETCON. One, a line leader, wanted to know a lot about JWM, but talked very little about JETCON. Fu explained the general situation and urged them to offer more information for comparison. Fu learned that:

1. They had long known about the merger;
2. Nobody got any extra money;
3. Their existing welfare system seemed worse than that of JWM, although there had been no reductions; and
4. Because of what they had learned about the JWM struggle, some workers had refused to work overtime.

The women agreed to keep in contact and would try to collect concrete information about their welfare provisions.

Back at the Centre, JWM RPs and supporters came for an after-work meeting. RPs gave detailed reports on the morning meeting and the afternoon 'chat', and the 'propaganda team' reported on their action. Centre staff referred to the previous day's 'third-floor incident' and urged workers to strengthen discipline and solidarity on different floors and different lines. Fu said that JETCON workers also were thinking of doing something and some of them had stopped working overtime. JWM workers were overjoyed.

Finally, a decision was made to increase the number of RPs to keep watch on the fourteen members delegated by management. Three more RPs were recommended; Chien Fa-hin (sixth floor), Lo Un-pu (second floor) and Chien Fon-yi (second floor).

The editing team designed a leaflet, *Our Rights and Benefits — Newsletter No. 1*, for JWM and JETCON workers, which explained what had happened in JWM and emphasized the importance of exchanging information. There was also a slip attached for the JETCON workers to fill out and return to the Centre.

DAY –21: 10 May 1986 (Saturday)

10:00 a.m. Two policemen from the Intelligence Unit came to the Centre for information on the JWM dispute. They stayed for an hour and took notes on everything Fu told them.

In the afternoon, JWM management announced over the PA system that the intruding groups were troublemakers, and that the workers should be careful about these petty politicians who intervened for their own self-interest. Posters with a similar message were later put up on every floor, after which foremen and line leaders distributed a piece of paper to each worker. All workers were forced to write down their requests. Most copied points from their newsletter. The second-floor workers first refused to write anything, but later decided to comply and all of them wrote 'MONEY', in large letters.

The management then issued new regulations dictating that no worker was allowed to leave the premises or go down to the street during breaks. This created resentment. Another announcement told the workers that the money paid to the staff was a 'provident fund', paid because of the merger. Workers interrogated the foremen and line leaders who had earlier said it was a 'resignation award'. None of them could come up with a reasonable explanation.

In the evening seven workers from JETCON came to the Centre. Staff explained to them that, according to the law, if the merger caused losses for the worker, the company might have to pay them severance pay, or lay them off first before rehiring them.

DAY −20: 11 May 1986 (Sunday)

11 a.m. The Director of Labour Relations of the Tsuen Wan Branch of the Labour Bureau, Tu Pi-sin, dropped in for a chat about the JWM case. His office was very near the Centre, but this was the first time he had 'happened' to pass by. Tu requested that the Centre contact the JWM RPs so that he might have a talk with them. The Centre staff called some RPs to set up an appointment. As planned, the RPs all refused to talk, instead insisting that the Labour Bureau persuade the management to resume negotiations. A number of workers telephoned during the day to report that administrative personnel had telephoned them at home and had tried to persuade them to drop out of the workers' group. Chen Siu-guan reported that a boy, who refused to identify himself, had called her at 5:00 a.m. and had asked her many personal questions. This was seen as a concerted and organized effort by management to scare away workers. However, it was decided not to lodge a complaint with the police.

DAY −19: 12 May 1986 (Monday)

10:00 a.m. About thirty core leaders came to the Centre and held a meeting with staff. They were worried about the financial need of some workers to work overtime, and felt that something had to be done. All agreed that the calm in the factory resembled the quiet before the storm. This period had to be used to organize the rank-and-file workers, train 'second-line' leaders, build networks among the workers and issue newsletters.

To stabilize the workers' struggle, a process of institutionalization was needed. Some RPs and the Centre staff proposed the organization of a factory-based trade union. Centre staff would provide consultation on the legal and technical aspects of unionization. A vote was proposed and, with few abstentions, the proposal was approved. A total of twenty-one workers signed up as founders. It was decided to keep this decision strictly secret, to prevent any possibility of JWM management sabotage. Chien Fon-yi was elected to go to the government's Union Registration Bureau to inquire about procedures, and to the Christian Labour Association (CLA) to consult with the union specialist there.

The agenda for Tuesday's general meeting was set:
1. Reconfirm the workers' basic demands.
2. Analyse management's attitudes, tactics, weaknesses and possible actions.
3. Advise workers on how to react to unexpected situations and how to deal with foremen and line leaders on different occasions.
4. Explain the strategic significance of workers' refusing overtime and initiating slow-down action.
5. Hold small-group discussions for workers to express their thoughts and feelings.
6. Explain possible repercussions of the workers' actions in legal and practical terms.

6:00 p.m. Nine workers from JETCON came to the Centre with detailed information on their welfare provisions. Fu, Gu and Ma talked to them. Initial investigation revealed several things.
1. Those with perfect attendance during any week were given 1.5 days' 'full-attendance award' (FAA) — that is, six days' FAA per month. There was no provision for awards in case of resignation, but workers would be given a watch as a souvenir upon retirement and/or resignation.
2. Sick leave of one day per month was allowed; every extra day's leave would be deducted from the 1.5 days/week FAA — exactly what had been modified in the JWM case!

3. During May and June, the busy seasons, workers absent for less than three days would be eligible for a special $100 award.
4. There were no 'ALLs', and line leaders were not monthly-rated employees.

DAY –18: 13 May 1986 (Tuesday)

5:10 p.m. Workers and RPs reported that foremen and other staff with cameras were following the off-duty workers. Different groups called in for instructions. The Centre staff immediately arranged the Ashley Social Service Centre as an alternative site for the general meeting. The groups were instructed to disperse, lose their stalkers and then go to the new meeting site in thirty minutes, ensuring that they were not followed.

Soon after 6:00 p.m. workers began to arrive at the Ashley Centre, more excited than scared. Although they envisioned a conspiracy to victimize them, they were deeply insulted and firmly anti-management. It took the RPs and Centre staff some time to calm everybody down.

Dai Lin-wai spoke first, reporting the new harassment to boost workers' sense of indignation. Her talk was well received. Chu Chi-lin picked up the issue of management's suppression and terror tactics in analysing the management's basic attitude towards their struggle, remarking on the inexperience of the management and criticizing Tosai's bad manners and chauvinistic approach. Workers applauded loudly. Lo Un-pu then spoke on how to react in unexpected situations and how to deal with foremen and line leaders. Hon Lai-fon then emphasized the necessity to act collectively and with discipline. She urged those who were considering returning to work overtime to reconsider. She also proposed that workers take collective action on the shop-floor.

At this point, workers in the audience wanted to speak. They confirmed that a spontaneous but unco-ordinated slow-down had been taking place for a while, with little impact. However, given that experienced and skilled operatives were in daily control of all production on the floor while foremen and line leaders merely lazed around, there was potential for controlled slow-down.

RPs then led small-group discussions. Tales of insults and abuse poured out. Animosity between the shop-floor supervisory staff and operatives had deep roots. Cases showed that differences existed between different floors, production formats and production lines, but everywhere there was animosity between supervisors and workers.

Discussions had been planned for thirty minutes, but it was an hour before they ended. RPs took another thirty minutes to report their groups' reactions. Emotions were high, and Centre workers had to take over as moderators. The organization of a co-ordinated slow-down was proposed. People voted unanimously for quick action, but, fearful of being found out by management, they authorized RPs and Centre staff to plan the slow-down and to notify the workers only when they came to work.

Fu gave a brief talk on the legality of the workers' actions and reassured the workers that the police would not interfere in an industrial action. In private, some of the police had even expressed sympathy.

Although it was almost 10:00 p.m. when the general meeting adjourned, workers on the editing team returned to the Centre to work on the second issue of *Our Rights and Benefits*. The workers' demands were reiterated, management's deviousness was exposed and JETCON workers were urged to organize themselves and join the JWM workers. The leaflet ended with the slogan, 'Remember, solidarity is power!'

DAY –17: 14 May 1986 (Wednesday)

11:00 a.m. The Regional Director of Labour Relations in the Labour Bureau's Tsuen Wan Branch, Tu Pi-sin, called the Centre, requesting a 'talk' with the Centre staff and an interview with the JWM RPs, making it clear that he meant to intervene. Ms Gu Lai-hap (representing TWLSC) and Mr Fu Kwan-sin (representing CKRLS) went to the Bureau. In addition to Mr Tu, Ms Chau, of the Labour Relations Section, and Branch Manager Ms Lee, participated in the 'talk'. Gu and Fu elaborated on the JWM workers' three objections. Tu replied that after the previous week's chat he had talked to the JWM management, who agreed not to reduce benefits and the RMSA but refused to consider equal treatment for the daily-rated. According to the management, the lump sum they had paid the monthly staff was a 'provident fund', provided unilaterally by the company. After the merger the 'provident fund' would be modified and taken care of by a bank rather than by the company, which was why the management had had to pay off the staff. Since the company had only put aside funds for the monthly-rated staff, there was no payment for the daily-rated operatives.

At this point Chu, the RP, asked Tu whether he knew the story of the elderly cleaning ladies. He said he did not. Chu then told Tu that one of the cleaning ladies who understood Japanese had learned about the payment. She realized that the daily-rated had been discriminated against and went straight to the Japanese managing director. To quiet her, he agreed to pay her and the other four cleaning ladies their share, but insisted that the payment be kept secret. However, it immediately became common knowledge. When workers asked for an explanation, the management had tried to cover up.

Tu was obviously embarrassed and admitted that JWM management had not been sincere in its dealings with him, but had used him. Since he represented the government, it was hard for Tu to say any more. To hide his embarrassment, he requested the establishment of direct communication with the workers. He finally revealed that the Labour Bureau and management feared that the daily-rated workers would all resign once they were paid the money. Fu and Gu rebutted this excuse. Tu then rudely demanded to talk directly to the workers and hinted that it was the Centre's staff who were interfering. He stated that direct communication between the JWM management and the workers could reduce management's fear and lead to a resolution. Fu and Gu finally agreed to consult with the workers to see if they were willing to be interviewed by Labour Bureau officials.

Later, when Fu and Gu came back to the Centre and reported what had happened, they wished they had been more firm, but, as young people in their early twenties, it was hard for them to ask demanding questions of a middle-aged official.

5:20 p.m. After work, RPs and supporters came to the Centre with information from different floors. They found that on Monday evening many workers received calls from management warning them against participating in Tuesday's general meeting. A few workers were intimidated but most were irritated. It was now obvious that there was an informer among the workers and measures had to be taken to prevent further leaks. It was decided that discussions on strategy and planning would be the responsibility of RPs and selected members in closed-door meetings.

Chen Siu-guan reported that she had heard vice-general manager Woo mention that the 'mysterious money' amounted to two-thirds of a staff member's monthly salary, multiplied by the number of years they had served the company. She had asked further, seemingly irrelevant questions, and became convinced that Woo's claim was true. In other words, the 'mysterious money' equalled precisely the amount of severance payment that monthly-rated workers were entitled to. There was thus good reason to assume the 'mysterious money' was severance pay and the daily-rated workers had been discriminated against. For them, the amount should have been eighteen days' (two-thirds of a month's) wages per year.

Gu and Fu of the Centre reported on their talk with Tu. Ma Po-kwan analysed the role the Labour Bureau had played in past struggles. Lin Yi-chin, the District Board member, suggested that the JWM workers should deal with the Labour Bureau cautiously. With this in mind, it was decided to ask Tu to tell the JWM management to arrange the next negotiation session for Friday, 16 May.

After the workers had left, the Centre staff and volunteers held a meeting and concluded the following.

1. In the next negotiating session, management would propose to maintain, or even to increase, benefit provisions, because this would involve only verbal promises.
2. Management would insist that the 'mysterious money' was from the previous 'provident fund', which they had to pay because of the impending shift to bank management. Workers should push management to spell out how management had provided the money for the staff. If they said it had all been provided by management, the

workers should immediately request equal treatment. Should management reply that the staff themselves had contributed half, the workers should ask the management to pay them 50 percent of eighteen days per year.
3. Centre staff thought it unlikely that management had pocketed the operatives' share. Contrary to the workers' suspicions, there were structural constraints built into the Japanese multinational's constitution. Some of the workers believed that JWM, to 'save face', would give in if the workers threatened to make the dispute public. Whether this would work depended upon the local factory's autonomy and adaptability — qualities minimized in most Japanese corporations.
4. As far as the command structure of the local management was concerned, the usual high-middle-low formulation was too simplistic. It was suggested that there were at least five layers: highest (Japanese and male); high (Japanese and Chinese and male); middle-high (Japanese and Chinese and male); middle-low (Chinese and Japanese, some female); and low (strictly Chinese, mostly female), a racist and sexist asymmetry.

DAY –16: 15 May 1986 (Thursday)

6:00 p.m. Centre staff, accompanied by thirty JETCON workers, arrived at Shek Lai Community Centre. Fewer than ten JWM RPs were waiting for this first face-to-face contact. Hon Lai-fon thought that the workers were unsure of the JETCON people.

JETCON representatives first gave a briefing. The main points were: Some JETCON workers had got hold of the JWM workers' newsletters and had gone to their management, who responded that they would not reduce JETCON's existing welfare provisions. The imminent merger was for taxation purposes. In the present situation, it was absolutely impossible for management to lay them off and pay them any severance payment. What happened at JWM had absolutely nothing to do with JETCON.

Among the thirty JETCON workers, a number were Hakka-speaking women in their mid-thirties — Indonesian Chinese who had gone to China to study during the 1960s and had come to Hong Kong a few years previously. These women were outspoken and enthusiastic. They compared welfare schemes at JETCON and JWM, and their evidence confirmed that the JETCON welfare scheme was in general worse than JWM's. The two line leaders who had been visiting the Centre fell quiet. There was unease and mistrust between the JWM and JETCON workers and also between the JETCON line leaders and their operatives. The JETCON line leaders had come along because they, unlike the JWM line leaders, were daily-rated employees. Their secret war for monthly-rated status further complicated the situation.

One of the line leaders asked if JETCON or JWM would be the legal owner after the merger. There were wild guesses. Ma Po-kwan intervened to explain that it was of no importance who merged with whom: workers should not be treated like objects, and the real issue was welfare schemes. Workers should invert both JETCON's and JWM's strategy. In JETCON's case, the management said they would make no changes precisely because their welfare scheme already represented the lowest level. In the JWM case, the management said they would standardize the welfare scheme after the merger. Therefore, JWM workers should fight for the preservation of their existing welfare and their share of 'mysterious money', while JETCON workers should fight for a uniform welfare scheme which used the existing JWM scheme as its baseline.

Before the meeting adjourned, people agreed to work out ways to co-operate, but, given their different situations, they understood things differently. It occurred to the Centre staff that the JETCON workers just might want to be laid off in order to be eligible for their 'once-in-a-life time' severance payment.

DAY –15: 16 May 1986 (Friday)

10:00 a.m. Fourteen JWM workers' RPs arrived at the Labour Bureau with Gu and Fu. The management sent a six-member delegation: vice-general manager Woo Char-hwa; managers Ou Ho-chung, Mo Ku-sin and Lu Shan; and two Japanese who failed to introduce themselves. Managing director Tosai, who had walked out of the previous meeting, did not attend.

The meeting began without ceremony. Labour Bureau labour relations chief Tu Pi-sin assumed the role of moderator. He stated that the two factories planned to merge for tax considerations without substantial changes at either site. The dispute between management and the workers, as he saw it, amounted to a simple misunderstanding.

Woo followed Tu. 'The so-called "mysterious money" was a "provident fund" provided unilaterally by the management. Because of the imminent merger the fund would be administrated by a local bank instead of by management itself. Thus the sum accumulated before April had to be paid to the staff to enable a fresh start.'

One of the RPs interrupted, 'How come nobody in the factory ever learned of the existence of this "provident fund"?'

Woo replied that it was because the management had provided the fund unilaterally.

'How come there was no written provision in the staff's contracts about the existence of such a fund?' the RP asked again.

Woo answered, 'It was a new system which began in 1982 and therefore contracts did not contain its terms.'

Another RP protested, 'This is not true. People got "mysterious money" payments which amounted to much more than the four years' provident fund. They got different amounts according to the duration of their service at the company.'

Woo said, 'The fund was supposed to date back to 1970.'

Another question from the RPs was, 'How much was that supposed to pay?'

Woo said, 'It is a business secret, I'm not going to tell you. But the new system will be different, the provident fund will be provided by both the management and the employees. Therefore, we had to pay the staff.'

A few RPs asked at the same time, 'How come some of the employees were paid and some were not?'

Woo replied, 'Whether to provide this or not is a management decision. Labour has no right to request it ... it was the company's money ... we had the discretion ...'

Tu nervously interrupted Woo and tried to pacify the angry RPs. A break was called. When the meeting resumed, Chen Siu-guan asked, 'Why did the cleaning ladies — who as daily-rated employees, like line-operatives, were not paid — get their share after complaining to Tosai?'

Nobody from management seemed willing to answer. The two Japanese and Woo discussed in Japanese. Woo then discussed with his Chinese minor managers. Finally Ou Ho-chung spoke out, 'Originally there was no provision for the cleaning ladies, but the new system included them.'

'What new system? You mean the new system which took effect in 1982, as indicated by Mr Woo?' Chu Chi-lin jumped in.

The six members of management stared at each other. Again they discussed in Japanese. The RPs urged Ou to reply. He finally answered, 'After the merger the ranking of jobs will be different. According to the JETCON system the cleaning ladies will be included and that is why the management gave them the money'. But he obviously didn't believe it himself.

Chu pushed further, 'Why only the cleaning-ladies? Why didn't you pay your operatives? Who are the ones who produce everything? The ones who work like dogs and enable you, people in the administration, to lounge around and watch us all day?'

Ou, in a panic, defended himself, 'There was very little we could do. The money had to be approved by Japanese headquarters. The old cleaning lady who speaks Japanese complained to Mr Tosai so strongly that he got personally involved ...'

'What you mean is that because we didn't speak the language and didn't complain hard enough we didn't get money?'

Ou shrank back in his chair, silenced and dispirited. Woo tried to assert his 'authority' to rescue his junior colleague and save 'face' for the management. He burst out, 'There is nothing in your employment contracts about a provident fund.'

Hon Lai-fon then pointed out that there was nothing in the contracts of the monthly-rated either, and asked again why they had been paid but the daily-rated had not.

At this Woo again nearly lost his temper. 'You, you should not ask me such tricky questions, we … '

Now it was Ou who came to his superior's rescue, 'After the merger the new provident system dictates that rehired staff should work five years before being entitled to the full provident fund. The daily-rated will not be affected so they will not be paid. It doesn't mean that you have been treated worse than the staff … '

But he could not finish his sentence. The RPs could not contain their anger.

'We would rather be dismissed and paid!'

'It wouldn't matter if we were rehired and waited five years for the next provident fund, just pay us what we are entitled now!'

Since Ou's answer made management look even more ridiculous, Woo scolded him in front of everyone, but forgot he was speaking Cantonese, not Japanese. The other management representatives managed to stop him, but their conflicting lies lay bare. Hu Hon-chi then pointed out that her friend, who had worked in the office and had been dismissed early in the year, had been paid nothing.

At this point, Tu rescued the management and called a twenty-minute break. When the meeting resumed, he announced that Woo had telephoned the office and confirmed that what had been paid was 'provident fund'. He suggested that the meeting should temporarily drop the issue and discuss other problems. He then allowed Woo to again take the floor.

Woo announced that JWM management had decided to retain the RMSA. People who had served the company for more than two years would be eligible. Management would also observe the Labour Ordinance's provisions regarding 'Long Service Payments' for dismissed workers with over five years of service. Finally, the management, aware that the workers did not like the changes regarding sick days and annual leave, had decided to reinstate the original policies.

Woo's announcement, however, did not satisfy the RPs. Management was obviously trying to dwell on minor points. Hu Hon-chi accused management of trying to divide the workers. She denounced them for harassing, tailing and threatening the workers by calling their homes and individually 'interviewing' them. She warned management that if they tried to sabotage the RPs' status as the workers' elected representatives there would be no more negotiations, and any consequences would be the sole responsibility of management.

Woo denied that JWM management had ever instructed anyone to call workers' families or tail them. Such behaviour had been taken by individual foremen or staff and JWM management was not legally responsible. Hu, however, insisted that if the management could not discipline its own staff, they would be criminally liable. Arguments between the management's representatives and the RPs flared up once again.

A Labour Bureau clerk came in and whispered into Tu's ear. Tu stood up and literally shouted for an end to the quarrelling. He said that a messenger from JWM had arrived with a document to substantiate JWM's claim that the 'mysterious money' was a 'provident fund'. He requested a break, during which he had a closed-door talk with the management in his private office. When he emerged, Tu declared that the document would be shown only to the two Centre staff members, Ms Gu and Mr Fu, who could then report to the RPs. Gu and Fu were then invited into Tu's private office. One of management's representatives, Mo Ku-sin, held what he claimed was a tax form. Only two lines were visible, the rest being covered by black lines. These two lines showed: a duration of service up to ten years, and an amount of payment up to HK$40,000. The words 'provident fund' were typed, in parenthesis, after the figure.

Gu and Fu asked, 'That's all?'

Woo and Tu replied that it was, as the document was confidential, and no further information could be shown.

For a moment, Gu and Fu were almost overwhelmed by the existence of documented evidence. They became cautious, aware of the dangers of a hasty response. Gu asked Tu how one could be expected to judge a document's genuineness from only two lines. She insisted that she would be happy to persuade the RPs of the genuineness of the document if the whole document were shown to her.

'What's wrong with it? What is wrong with the parts we showed you?' The management and the Labour Bureau people said.

Gu turned even cooler, 'There may be nothing wrong with it but I don't know if everything is right with it either.'

After fifteen minutes of wrangling, a compromise was reached: Gu would describe what had happened in the private office and what she had seen, but she would refrain from any endorsement in her presentation. When she returned to the meeting, she gave the RPs an extremely 'objective' account of what had happened. A few RPs got the message from her apathetic neutrality and passive body language.

After Gu's presentation, Chu Chi-lin calmly responded that, because of past experience of being manipulated and cheated by ambiguous information, it was hard for them to believe the sudden emergence of 'evidence'. What they, as RPs, could do was to describe the situation to their constituents for them to judge.

The afternoon seemed a waste of time, but the workers made some small gains, such as the right to use the canteen telephone during breaks. Management agreed not to post announcements soliciting workers' opinions and to allow RPs to pass out questionnaires without the intervention of foremen or line leaders. Management, in return, obtained RPs' promise that workers would not engage in eccentric conduct during the period of negotiation. The next negotiating session was scheduled to be held on Thursday, 22 May.

The meeting adjourned at 1:30 p.m. The RPs returned to the factory and reported to their constituents at the 3:00 p.m. break.

5:20 p.m. After work, all the RPs and some thirty supporters arrived at the Centre to review the morning meeting. Some RPs told Fu and Gu that, before they had emerged from Tu's office, they had really been worried about the so-called 'evidence' but, when they saw Gu behaving like a 'wooden puppet', they relaxed. They imitated Gu's 'dummy look' and had everyone laughing. The Labour Bureau meeting later became an enjoyable subject for stories for the RPs.

The document showing HK$40,000 and ten years' duration of service was the focus of interest. Some figured that, assuming that the person who filed the tax document was a middle-level staff member and that his monthly salary was around HK$5,000, the amount of HK$40,000 actually indicated 6 percent of the annual salary paid over the past ten years. If this was accurate, then the money he received was actually his severance pay. In other words, the document itself might be real and reported a sum paid by management, but the words 'provident fund' had been typed in *post hoc*. This theory sounded plausible, as nobody in Hong Kong types their tax forms, and the form itself was not typed, with the exception of the words 'provident fund'. Everybody was delighted, like children who had discovered a hidden pot of candy. Some even planned to sue the management for forgery.

The meeting then assessed the negative impact of trivializing important issues and offering minor welfare provisions. A consensus was reached to forget about the latter and concentrate on the 'secret money'. Finally, the RPs were authorized to organize a more effective slow-down beginning immediately.

During the meeting, six representatives from JETCON dropped in to inquire about developments. Fu led them to another district member's office a few doors away. The situation at JETCON had changed little. There was much gossip, but nothing was organized. The six had come to the Centre on their own, and some of them were not even aware that fellow JETCON workers had stopped working overtime a week earlier. One of the most enthusiastic workers suggested that a letter should be drafted and signed by workers demanding that JETCON clarify the workers' welfare situation. Unfortunately, no one was willing to do this, and they had no idea of the numbers of people who would sign. Clearly, while these workers wanted gains, they were more concerned about possible losses. Fu was extremely discouraged and advised them not to take any action until they had a firmer grasp of the situation and were better organized. His argument got a lukewarm response. Before dispersing, they agreed to keep in touch. However, most of them declined to leave their names for the Centre's records.

DAY –14: 17 May 1986 (Saturday)

10:30 a.m. Vice-general manager Woo called Fu to inquire about the workers' response to JWM's proposals. Fu replied that the Centre did not yet know, that the RPs would be consulting with their constituents and that, if necessary, a general meeting would be called to facilitate further discussion among the rank and file. Woo asked Fu to inform him as soon as the Centre learned the workers' opinions. Next Tu Pi-sin called to ask if any decision had been reached by the JWM workers. Fu replied that the Centre knew of none, and asked why Tu was interested. Tu did not answer but simply mentioned that Woo had called him.

11:30 a.m. Tu called again. He said the management wanted to settle the dispute as soon as possible. He hoped that the workers would not interpret management's goodwill as a sign of weakness ... and so on. Finally, he asked again about the workers' attitude. Fu answered that, personally, he had noticed some dissatisfaction over the management's handling of the case. Like the Labour Bureau, there was only so much the Centre could do, as only the workers and their counterpart, the JWM management, could resolve the dispute.

12:30 p.m. Tu called again, this time admitting he was calling from the JWM office. He said he had spent the whole morning in the factory and had noticed the slack attitude of the workers. Management was angry and wanted to fire some workers but he had dissuaded them from doing so. Management requested an immediate meeting with the workers, instead of waiting until Thursday. The Centre staff replied that it was difficult to contact workers on weekends, and that since, by previous agreement, a meeting had to be called at least twenty-four hours in advance, the earliest possible date for another negotiating session would be Tuesday.

Immediately after this call, most RPs, who worked half a day on Saturday, rushed in. Management had betrayed its promises: foremen and line leaders had distributed a 'personal record' form to every worker on the line. One question was whether the worker planned to stay or quit after the merger. The majority of the workers refused to fill out the form but were warned that they would have to bear the consequences of refusing to co-operate. There were spontaneous 'wildcat' slowdowns all over the factory.

DAY −13: 18 May 1986 (Sunday)

Thirteen JWM RPs gave up their holiday and came to the Centre to prepare for the next day's general meeting and Tuesday's negotiating session.

The RPs insisted that management wanted to fire workers who had slowed down the work. They noticed that foremen and line leaders were watching the leaders. Workers were instructed to spy on the RPs and report to management. However, they all stated that they were not afraid of being fired, that there were enough people who supported equal treatment and the fight for workers' dignity.

The workers were now so restless that some collective action was needed. The leadership would either strike or organize a co-ordinated slowdown. If there were no action, the momentum would be lost and more 'wildcat' behaviour would ensue, and the influence and trustworthiness of the present workers' leadership would be discredited in the eyes of both workers and management. The Centre staff emphasized that any action had to be well organized. The RPs must strengthen their grasp of their constituents' common sentiments and propensities. The second-floor RPs said they could marshal at least 70 percent support, but those from the other floors could not put a figure on it. A decision was made to study possible actions.

Concerning the Tuesday negotiating session, the RPs decided to talk only about the 'mysterious money'. If management again insisted the money was a 'provident fund', they would request the same. They would not allow Tu to 'explain away' the issue or to talk on behalf of JWM management. In case no agreement was reached, they would request a higher-ranking official from the headquarters in Japan be sent to Hong Kong to negotiate. They would only talk to people authorized to make decisions for sums of over HK$1 million. They would attend negotiating sessions on request, but would not actively seek meetings, to show that they were not desperate. Tasks for the general meeting were assigned. RPs would draft an open letter to the management and collect signatures during the general meeting. A suggestion was made to set up a team to work on strategies for possible future meetings. Gu and Fu proposed electing 'second-line RPs' to work and be trained along with the RPs and to assume leadership if the present RPs were rendered helpless.

Finally, every RP was given a copy of government requirements for union constitutions and bylaws, along with a draft constitution and by-laws for the proposed JWM union. Chien Fon-yi, in charge of the technicalities of organizing an on-site union, emphasized the need for strict secrecy.

DAY –12: 19 May 1986 (Monday)

5:30 p.m. About 150 workers arrived at St. Stephen's Church third-floor meeting hall. Chu Chi-lin reported on Friday's meeting with the management.

The meeting proved beyond doubt that the daily-rated operatives had been discriminated against. Such differential treatment could not be justified in a Chinese context. If it was practised in Japan, the workers there must be deceived and cheated, or under constant threat from management, a situation that JWM management had tried to establish here. Chu concluded, 'So long as we bite the bullet and endure these temporary inconveniences our cause will surely prevail. Management cannot but give in to our rightful demands.' Once again, her talk was extremely well received by the audience.

Lo Un-pu emphasized that it was worker solidarity that would force management to take them seriously. The responsibility of every worker was to help build solidarity among all the workers.

Chen Siu-guan vividly described Friday's meeting, comically imitating the speechlessness of Woo Char-hwa and his later scolding of Ou Ho-chung. Everybody laughed.

In order to strengthen the image of the leadership, all RPs gave brief speeches, and then went down together to collect signatures for the open letter to management. The letter was simple and straightforward, expressing their dissatisfaction and demanding that all workers be paid.

Before the meeting adjourned, Ma Po-kwan presented the case of a similar labour dispute in a Hong Kong watch factory in 1981. He made special reference to the tactics the management had employed to destabilize the workers' solidarity and to sabotage the legitimacy and status of the worker's leadership. He also pointed out the dubious role of the Labour Bureau and the extent to which they were biased towards management – how they 'forgot' to tell the workers their legal rights or 'neglected' to inform them of necessary formal procedures. Almost all the workers requested a copy of Ma's source materials.

Finally, Fu explained to the workers that 'wildcat' slowdowns would not have the impact of collective action, which could show management that the workers were actually in control of production. The workers should invent their own ebb-and-flow style of production. The workers applauded this, saying it was really difficult and boring to work so slow all day long. They heard that the yield of some lines was down to 20 percent, but felt it would be more fun to manipulate the yield rather than just slow down. Some even felt that if a slow-down only meant low yield, then it was an insult to them as efficient workers. RPs and ALLs were authorized to co-ordinate the ebb-and-flow of individual line yields and total production turnover.

DAY −11: 20 May 1986 (Tuesday)

10:00 a.m. The negotiating session was held at the local Labour Bureau office. JWM management sent Ou Ho-chung, Mo Ku-sin, and two Japanese, Kusara and Shita. The workers' side was represented by the RPs. Tu Pi-sin and Ms Lee represented the Labour Bureau, and Gu and Fu represented the two labour service Centres. This time neither managing director Tosai nor vice-general manager Woo attended the meeting.

Tu began reporting on the previous meeting. Chen Siu-guan interrupted: since the meeting was between JWM workers' RPs and JWM management, both Labour Bureau and Labour Service Centre representatives, as observers, should keep as quiet as possible. Tu was embarrassed and stopped speaking.

Then Chu Chi-lin accused management of violating their promise in the previous negotiating session, thereby embarrassing the RPs and causing them to lose face, leading to spontaneous protests. Management should bear the responsibility and absorb subsequent costs and consequences. As management had violated agreements with the RPs, the RPs were no longer bound by their promises either.

Ou Ho-chung responded rudely that management was behaving properly. In the previous meeting, they had only asked the RPs to relay messages, which did not mean they should channel all communications through the RPs.

This issue was further muddled by Tu, 'Both sides should act according to what was agreed upon. If the management tried to consult the workers within the context of the agreement, they should be allowed to do so and be forgiven.'

Chien Fa-hin, a sixth-floor RP, spoke for the first time, saying that henceforth minutes should be taken in negotiating sessions and both sides should read and sign them. She continued, 'The company should send somebody in a position to make decisions. It is no use having people here simply talk and talk. Whatever is agreed upon in the meeting should not be overturned by higher management authority. If someone is not properly authorized he shouldn't be here, or he should go back to consult with his superior before he makes any wild promises.'

Mo Ku-sin, one of the most hated lower managers and a self-important tough, shouted back, 'The management has basically nothing to talk to you about. Our stance is firm and clear: no discussion and no compromise. Whoever is dissatisfied with the company might as well resign. We are really wasting time negotiating!'

At this point, Tu proposed a ten-minute cooling-off break. When the meeting resumed, the RPs said that, based on the principle of equal treatment, they wanted management to pay each daily-rated operative 6 percent of her annual wages, multiplied by the number of years of service, as their deserved 'provident payment', to be paid before the merger. The open letter, with about 200 workers' signatures, was presented to the management.

The Japanese manager Kusara responded. He said the issue of 'provident payment' was not on the day's agenda, and that he was instructed only to confirm the previous management proposal concerning sick leave and annual paid leave. He also mentioned that management had received complaints from workers who had been threatened and harassed by other workers. Finally, he said there were no instructions for further negotiation, but dissatisfied workers were 'welcome' to resign. The meeting ended in animosity.

Tu told Gu and Fu after the meeting that it would be difficult for local JWM management to make any modifications of the overall benefit system, which was basically designed by Japanese headquarters. Even the Labour Bureau's idea of setting up a provident fund for daily-rated workers after the merger had been rejected by Mo Ku-sin. However, the Labour Bureau believed the management would not fire workers unless they violated factory regulations, passed out leaflets during working hours or demonstrated on the street. Tu suggested the Centre persuade the workers, for their own good, not to upgrade their actions, as it could get them fired.

At the early-evening daily meeting of RPs, second-line leaders, supporters and Centre staff, Tu's comments became the hot topic. People even asked Fu and Gu to describe and imitate Tu's facial expressions, body language and tone when he revealed the secret 'tips'. Deeply mistrustful of all officials, they tended to try to explain everything in an inverse fashion. Different versions of the stories were constructed, with different interpretations of every word and act, and different underlying motives.

One theory was that the dispute had not been reported to the JWM Japanese head office. Therefore, no high-ranking Japanese presided over the meeting. Those attending were local low-ranking JWM personnel, used to deceive the workers. No wonder they said nothing, and simply sat there. Kusara was a part of the local middle management; the other Japanese also looked familiar; neither had been consulted or respected during negotiations. Furthermore, they threatened to fire 'troublemakers' because the local JWM management was really scared of publicizing the dispute, as JWM, a prestigious brand name, would 'lose face'. Covering up the conflict would be impossible once it was picked up by the press.

The workers decided to send a letter to the Japanese headquarters and address their grievances to the managing director. Twenty people volunteered to draft it.

> Dear Sir,
>
> We, 180 JWM (HK) workers who are discriminated against by the local management, are now bringing our grievance to your attention. On 16 May, a meeting was held at the Government Labour Bureau between the management and ourselves. Evidence was given in the meeting that a lump sum of money was paid to some of the employees of this factory. This fact was covered up, and those of us who did not receive the payment were cheated. We resent such discriminatory practices. They grossly violate the cultural norms of the Chinese, in which every co-worker should be treated equally. Management also unilaterally reduced our previous existing benefits. We tried many times to bring up the issue but were treated barbarously. The second meeting, held on 20 May, broke down, and we are now demanding an answer from your office regarding a possible solution. In case this telegram fails to facilitate your reply to the matter, we may have to use the mass media to attract your attention. Please reply by 9:00 a.m. Hong Kong time on 24 May to the following address: c/o Tsuen Wan Labour Service Centre.
>
> (Signed by 180 workers)
>
> 20 May 1986.

After the workers had left, the Centre staff had a meeting to assess the overall situation. Attention was focused on three aspects:
1. Long-term resistance;
2. Struggles at a basic and concrete level; and
3. Disparities and conflicts existing between Chinese cultural norms and standard Japanese management practices.

According to the Centre's past experience, the JWM management, like any other management, had its specific corporate culture. The typical Japanese factory regime, modelled after the postwar Japanese political regime, was understood to be extremely tenacious, and so the workers had to be ready for a sustained fight. The Centre staff hesitated to believe that a threat of 'losing face' would force management to submit.

In general, the short, relatively trouble-free history of Japanese multinationals operating overseas, together with the self-assurance and over-publicized 'Japanese-style management' success, may have rendered local management arrogant and overconfident. This had been true so far for JWM, whose vice-general manager, Woo Kar-wai, had been raised in Japan, and had a Japanese wife. Local management tended to overreact to workers' initiatives, possibly for several reasons. They might still believe in a wholesale transplantation of Japanese standard management practices to Hong Kong. The Japanese headquarters might not yet understand that the so-called 'East Asian' culture which Japan supposedly shared with its neighbours was, at best, only a partial reality. For whatever reasons, it seemed clear that JWM management was insensitive to workers' sentiments and incapable of considering them.

As efforts to communicate through dialogue had failed, further industrial action was imminent. Whether this would result in better understanding was uncertain — it might well render management even more defensive. Nevertheless, the workers now had little choice.

Day –10: 21 May 1986 (Wednesday)

In the morning, the Centre staff continued the previous night's soul-searching. The letter faxed to Japan seemed to reveal the following.
1. The rank and file wanted action to publicize the dispute through the mass media.
2. The workers' self-esteem had been hurt, and the different treatment concerning the 'mysterious money' was considered an insult. As Chinese, they would not stand for this.
3. Their feelings were partially provoked by the rude reactions from the local management. Asking for a top-management response could be

seen as an effort to heighten their self-importance, to apply pressure to local management, to avoid further insults, and to give warning and to legitimize actions they might take in the future.

4. No reference was made to either monthly-rated workers or daily-rated workers. The letter concerned the workforce as a whole, and denied the corporate definition of two categories of worker. The government's Labour Ordinance did adopt the terms 'daily-rated' and 'monthly-rated', but the workers' struggle was to deny government acknowledgement of corporate practices or strategies that resorted to structures facilitating 'divide-and-rule' policies. It was understood that a similar practice prevailed in Japan, where a small portion of 'cared-for' workers were well kept and extremely well treated, while the others — mostly female and operatives — were relegated to 'contract-worker' or 'temporary-hire' categories. The latter were hired on a daily basis, and theoretically 'fired' at the end of every working day, and so were not entitled to benefits of any sort.

Ma Po-kwan thought it necessary to understand the workers' sentiments in this multinational context. The Chinese say, 'Ice-sheets three feet thick take more than one cold day to form', so the workers' grudges and animosity must have deep roots.

In the afternoon, Tu invited Gu to his office for a talk. Management had informed him of the workers' slow-down. Tu suggested that they restore normal production so that he could consult with managing director Tosai and come up with a new proposal on Friday to resolve the dispute. He again asked to interview the workers' leaders himself. On the 'mysterious money', he told Gu that the 6 percent demanded by the workers was impossible. For the well-being of the workers, the Centre should persuade the workers to agree to a three-day cooling-off period, during which they should abstain from demonstrating, leafleting, or posting posters or banners.

5:20 p.m. At the after-work 'daily' meeting, RPs and responsible ALLs reported slow-downs on every production line, with the most co-ordinated action on the second floor. On the seventh floor there seemed to be no supervision — the foremen and line leaders let the workers do whatever they pleased. On the other floors slowdowns had not been organized but occurred anyway. The workers anticipated that an emergency meeting of the Japanese would take place after work. They were nervous and excited.

Gu reported her discussion with Tu. Most workers were not surprised to hear that management might fire them. To play for time, they agreed to a three-day cooling-off period. For one thing, the days conveniently responded with the three-day response-time to the letter sent to the head office. Wouldn't it be nice for management to get the impression that the three days were stipulated by the workers rather than the government agent! However, in accepting Tu's suggestion, two more conditions were proposed: Management should stop tailing workers and intimidating workers and their families. Tu's demand to interview workers was refused.

As for applying shop-floor pressure, they would maintain 50 percent of normal yield on every production line — for the present. This would show workers' solidarity and discipline the rank and file into giving up their individualistic 'guerrilla warfare'. Everybody agreed that worker discipline was necessary for any long-term resistance. Management and the workers' leadership competed for the workers' allegiance, and the leadership had to make it clear that the fight was not over a few cents, but to defend workers' dignity and to oppose all forms of brutality and discrimination.

Concerning procedural matters, no negotiations would be held without a direct reply from the Japanese headquarters. Communication between workers and the Centre was to be enhanced by assigning one person on each floor to telephone the Centre at least twice daily.

Day −9: 22 May 1986 (Wednesday)

In the morning, Gu informed Tu that the workers had refused to talk to him. In the afternoon Tu came to the Centre and accused Centre staff of writing the letter to the Japanese headquarters, something they should not have done during the cooling-off period. He did not mention how he learned of it. Obviously there had been a response from Japan. Tu avoided mentioning management. Centre staff said the letter was a good idea, and that it had been sent before the agreement was even suggested.

Tu was upset. He claimed the workers could never get the money they wanted. Gu replied that it was not for a labour service group to discourage workers' struggle for dignity and equal treatment. She emphasized that there was only so much that 'third parties' such as the Labour Bureau could do, and that it was not supposed to make decisions on either the management's or the workers' behalf. Tu then turned defensive, and said that the Labour Bureau tried to be neutral, and did not want to over-involve itself. He acknowledged the 'functional' and 'constructive' role labour groups could play.

At the 5:20 p.m. daily meeting, workers confirmed that the factory was quiet. All management personnel were busy, and none mentioned the 50 percent production decrease, but workers in the biggest production section — the second floor — were told not to come to work the next day. Management obviously knew that the second floor was the workers' stronghold and the base of their leadership.

After the JWM workers had left, fifteen JETCON workers arrived for a meeting with the Centre, eager to learn of the achievements of JWM workers. After being told that no concrete results had been achieved, they became very impatient. They were uninterested in the details, but complained that JWM workers had aroused them and then forgot about them. They refused to accept the explanation that the JWM workers had been too wrapped up in a difficult fight to communicate. They considered JWM workers 'selfish', and were glad they had not run the risk of betting on somebody else's battle. Ma tried to explain that nobody could fight another's battle, and suggested that JETCON workers were not fighting their own. A fight almost ensued between Ma and the JETCON woman leader who had originally contacted the Centre. The Centre was accused of favouring JWM workers. Sian Yun-chu, the JETCON line leader, commented that she should have realized the 'real' intentions of the labour groups.

At this point, Ma had to leave to prevent the meeting from ending in disarray.

Day −8: 23 May 1986 (Friday)

About thirty second-floor workers — RPs, supporters and second line leaders, mostly from the remote rural area of Pat Heung in the New Territories — arrived at the Centre around noon for further discussions. A working session was held to give a final touch to the union constitution, and twenty-one workers signed up as union founders. Chien Fon-yi and Lo Un-pu would go to the Registry of Trade Unions to hand in their official application and a copy of the constitution. A general meeting for all JWM workers would be called on Tuesday, 27 May, for the inaugural union meeting. Sister unions would be invited to send representatives. A committee to organize a press conference was formed.

In order to make the inauguration more lively, a skit was planned, in which aspects of management abuse would be dramatized, and possible suppressive measures that management might adopt in the future would be acted out, in order to ready the workers for crises to come. A workers' 'battle-hymn of solidarity' would also be written. All the workers at the Centre wanted to participate in planning the skit, and they were so noisy doing so that the Centre staff and RPs had to use another office.

Telephone calls from various floors at JWM reported that higher management staff and some Japanese were busy carrying business files around and rushing into taxis, leaving most of the workers sitting on the line chatting, without foremen or line leaders. It was obvious that management was preparing something. The second-floor RPs thought management would move against the workers' leadership and probably fire all RPs. To counter this, all the RPs should be listed as union founders and, later, as directors, as the Employment Ordinance made it unlawful to fire union directors for membership or activities in a trade union. Centre staff suggested extending the support base for the union, so the workers authorized them to contact all local labour organizations, trade unions, pressure groups, human rights groups and international NGOs and report back before the end of the week.

At 5:20 p.m., RPs and supporters from the other floors came for their daily meeting. They reported on the weird situation in the factory. They suspected a 'conspiracy' involving the firing of workers, especially the major 'troublemakers'. Workers competed to figure out who would be singled out. Being fired became a badge of honour. The workers decided that if anyone was dismissed, management would pay.

There were four possible scenarios of future developments:
1. Negotiations resumed and prolonged;
2. Negotiations deadlocked;
3. Negotiations concluded and money paid; and
4. Negotiations broken off, with management firing the 'troublemakers' and other workers.

Suggestions were made that plans be developed for each eventuality. In the event of the last scenario, every worker should be mobilized for either a sit-in or demonstration inside the factory, or for a demonstration on the street.

The Centre staff telephoned their closest associates for support. About ten groups were willing to sign an open declaration and send it to JWM Japan headquarters. This idea was well received, and the workers suggested sending it to the headquarters of the Japanese National Union of General Workers and to the ILO in Geneva as well.

It was 11:00 p.m. The workers had left. Lo Man-sa, the director of the Christian Labour Association, called to inquire about recent developments in the JWM dispute. Fu, characteristically polite and uncharacteristically cautious, answered every question in unnecessary detail, without volunteering any new information. He waited to be told the reason for the unusual late-night call. Lo finally explained that he had received a call from an unnamed acquaintance in a Japanese bank in Hong Kong, who had been asked by his boss to contact Lo to 'understand' the situation in JWM. Lo had not been involved, but he knew something about the case from his junior colleagues and from hearsay. This acquaintance, 'Mr A', insisted that Lo must know the organization and persons involved. He demanded that Lo do him a favour by finding out the facts. Lo had therefore called the Centre in the early evening, but had had only a short conversation with District Board member Lin Yi-chin, who did not know the details, so Lo had called back for more information. Fu replied that he would explain whatever he could. However, it did not take long for 'factual' questions to be answered. Lo finally volunteered that, shortly before he made this call, Mr A had called him again, this time making it clear that the JWM head office in Japan, through his Japanese boss here in Hong Kong, wanted Lo to play the role of middleman in the dispute. Mr A told Lo that he would be going out of town soon and so needed an answer as soon as possible. He said that two people had already been sent from Japan and were ready to talk with the workers. From Mr A's tone, Lo felt that there was some possibility of compensation for the 'mysterious payments', although not what the workers were demanding. As a veteran labour leader, Lo advised the workers to be patient and temporarily stop all unnecessary actions. Lo would consider seriously whether or not he wanted to get involved. As director of an established organization he had to consider the organization's reputation. If the workers were 'rational' and promised not to 'go to extremes', he would be more likely to get involved. Fu agreed to relay Lo's entire message to the JWM workers. However, everything would be decided by the workers' leaders, or through the workers' general meetings. The half-hour conversation ended in mutual assurances of closer contacts in the future.

A similar conversation took place on the TWLSC line. Yen Chin-chih, one of TWLSC's directors and the manager of a government-subsidized youth centre, spoke to Ms Gu, TWLSC's only employee. He explained that a Japanese banker in Hong Kong had got hold of one of his acquaintances, who did not want his identity revealed. This acquaintance said that the JWM management stood firm and would not pay the 'mysterious money' in full, although they might pay something. For the time being, it was important to prevent the workers 'from going too far'. He suggested that the Centre restrain them, if necessary, from confronting the management.

Yen also volunteered himself as a go-between for his friend and the workers, but Gu insisted the workers would not be willing to deal with Japanese top management through so many go-betweens and mysterious 'middlemen'. If Yen wished to help resolve the dispute, he should persuade the Japanese representatives to talk to the workers directly. Yen promised to work on it and get back to the workers the next day. For some reason, he had decided to intervene personally without going through the proper channels, by which instructions to the Centre's staff were made on the basis of resolutions passed by the board of directors.

Gu instinctively sensed something else was involved and became cautious, as Yen, although not her supervisor, was so eager that he almost ordered what she should or should not do. She told him only the minimum necessary.

Day −7: 24 May 1986 (Saturday)

Yen came to the Centre with 'proposals' from the 'middlemen' around noon. He said that since the company would not liquidate itself, no severance payment was required. The money management paid to the monthly-rated staff was due to the merger, and as there were no fixed criteria for calculating it — it depended upon individual performance — there was no basis for the workers to demand the same payment. Even if there was money to pay the workers, management feared that if JWM workers were paid, the workers at JETCON would demand the same. He thus felt that the chance of JWM workers getting any payment was almost nil. As the 'middlemen' had put it: even if there was some legitimacy to the workers' demands, they should put their case in such a way that management could be comfortably persuaded. In any case, the workers should give ample reasons to the representatives from Japan, and not create antipathy.

Yen's speech had elements of the language spoken by the Labour Bureau people, and reflected his limited perspective and wilful subjective wishes, perhaps as a result of his lack of knowledge of the events and his role vis-à-vis management. The Centre staff believed he thought he knew all that he needed to know and was confident of his personal influence on the future course of events.

What was pitiful, yet funny, was that the points Yen and the 'Japanese representative' made only served to demonstrate the discriminatory practices of the Japanese management, who superimposed a system on Hong Kong and looked for 'negative loopholes' in Hong Kong laws to defend themselves.

Gu decided that, as Yen was one of her Centre's directors, she must hide this conversation from the workers to save face for herself and her Centre, and felt that in future even fewer details should be forwarded to Yen, as the less he knew, the bolder he would be — he would make mistakes, and the more he made, the more vulnerable management would be. She would not, however, let him think the workers were ready to give in.

Immediately after Yen's call, vice-general manager Woo called. He was polite, and Gu could hardly believe it was the person she knew. Woo asked why the workers had exaggerated small things and had contacted the Japanese management. Gu replied that, since they had failed to receive any positive response from the local management, they had become impatient. Besides, management had said that changes had to be approved by JWM headquarters. The local management should not take it personally, they were not going to 'tell on' them — the workers were proud as individuals and as Chinese, and would never think of doing that. Woo said he knew the workers did not mean to hurt anybody, and neither did the management. The problem consisted of misunderstandings and a lack of communication. Woo then invited Gu to lunch, right away, to talk over the matter. This was unexpected, and Gu felt unprepared. She politely told him she was on duty in the office and could not leave. Woo then suggested a chat the next day with both Gu and Fu at 'the country club', and suggested she let the workers know, to avoid further misunderstandings. Gu accepted.

When Fu returned to the office, Gu informed him of the phone calls. Fu had some reservations about Sunday's 'country club' brunch, but Gu said she had already promised, and that by going they might be able to discover the hidden agenda. Fu agreed. 'There is nothing to lose as far as we ourselves are concerned, except to find out what the hell a "country club" is!'

Gu and Fu then worked out five guidelines for discussions:

1. Discuss the management's intentions but do not reveal those of the workers or Centre staff;
2. Approach Woo in a way that reduces management's readiness to dismiss workers;

3. Only mention the 6 percent payment if the situation is promising;
4. In the case of pressure to make a promise, remember the impact of management's decision to dismiss workers; and
5. Assess how management judges the strength of the workers.

Fu and Gu were uneasy that neither the workers nor their RPs would be present, and they became overcautious, worrying that workers might be fired. This could be their ultimate vulnerability, and they could be manipulated. Such predicaments had been frequently alluded to in staff internal education campaigns, but there was no simple formula, so Gu and Fu called a staff meeting. At the meeting a consensus was reached.

1. If prospects improved for reopening negotiations, the Centre would suggest that the workers raise their production yield in order to relax tensions and prevent firings.
2. Every situation and outcome should be analysed together with as many workers as possible. No Centre staff should make a decision of any sort without consulting the workers. If the workers requested guidance, all decisions should be made after sufficient discussion involving both the Centre and the workers.
3. The Centre staff did not represent the workers, but worked as a support staff and auxiliary force. No 'agency' role could be imposed on the Centre or Centre staff-related action. The Centre and its staff had to accept the decision of the workers' collective body.

5:20 p.m. Some thirty RPs and supporters came for the daily meeting. Yen's and Woo's telephone conversations were reported in detail. The workers concentrated on Woo's proposed 'country club' brunch, and most stated that they did not wish the Centre staff, especially Ms Gu, to go, as it was 'dangerous' to go to such a strange place and 'talk' to Woo and whomever he might invite — although they found it difficult to identify the 'danger' or possible negative aspects to the talk, they mistrusted the management and the persons involved. They felt it was not right for Centre staff, especially Ms Gu as a woman, to be dining with somebody they did not like. Their thoughtfulness was well taken by everybody in the Centre. Nevertheless, the Centre staff persuaded them of the utility of the brunch for opening up a side channel of communication and possibly creating new space for manoeuvring. Also, there was gossip concerning various 'scandals', and most workers believed that local management 'had dirt on them'. Now that the Japanese head office had been informed of the dispute, local staff would 'tinker with the pot' (i.e., explain away discrepancies to hide 'the dirt'). It was finally agreed that Gu and Fu should go to Sunday brunch to find out the nature of 'the dirt'.

11:00 p.m. The workers had left. The exhausted Centre staff held another meeting, to analyse and understand what had happened. In a meeting like this, Centre staff members not involved had to be extremely critical in interrogating those who were, to guard against self-deception. It was hypothesized that:

1. There were strong motives behind Woo's eagerness to have lunch as soon as possible.
2. If the 'tinkering-with-the-pot' theory proved false, Woo's action might be an act on behalf of the top Japanese management, as this day was the deadline the workers had posited for the Japanese headquarters' response.
3. If (2) above, then there had been a response from Japan.
4. If (2) and (3), there was reason to hope for a positive response.
5. Yen-the-busybody emphasized that some reconciliatory gesture should be made right away, as the 'middleman' was going out of town. Could this be interpreted as eagerness on the part of the 'middleman', or of the top management?
6. As all the above suggestions were hypothetical, it was decided that every major proposed negotiating response had first to be cleared through a workers' general meeting, so that it might be better analysed, and to show the solidarity and democratic practices of the workers' collective body;
7. If negotiations were proposed, the workers should insist that they be held in a 'neutral place'. The Labour Bureau office would be acceptable.

8. It was important to stick to principles and major issues, for it was likely that management and the Labour Bureau would try to sidetrack the dispute.

Day –6: 25 May 1986 (Sunday)

11:15 a.m. After Gu and Fu had been waiting for Woo at the Centre for nearly an hour, Woo called to say something had come up at the office, so, instead of the country club, Woo suggested a popular nearby restaurant. He spoke in a relaxed manner, as if they were all old friends.

Three men from JWM came to the noisy restaurant: Woo, Kusara and a Japanese stranger. Woo did not introduce his colleagues, and the impression was given that the stranger had recently arrived from Japan. To show the casual nature of the brunch, Gu and Fu picked up Ma who had just come by. He was not introduced either.

Woo said he needed to explain the JWM situation from the very beginning. In February that year there had been a complaint that the annual salary increment was too small, and old workers were dissatisfied because new workers received raises almost as large as themselves.

Things got worse after the Chinese New Year holidays. In April there had been the Ah Si 'incident', while Woo was on a trip to Europe and other higher management staff were not available either. Middle management's excuse — 'lack of outstanding criteria' — made things worse. In reality, workers who did not break factory rules should be considered 'outstanding' and entitled to RMSA upon resignation. When Woo returned from Europe in May, he learned of the complaints regarding the cancellation of RMSA, studied the situation and decided to release the money to Ah Si. To his surprise, this had a negative effect on the other workers, who felt that his action proved that 'if you don't fight you won't get anything'!

Woo kept on talking, intermittently eating *dim sum*. When the conversation turned to irrelevant chatting, the two Japanese sporadically threw out a few words in Cantonese. They knew the language, but they did not care about the discussion. Woo's story was too unsophisticated, even naive. Gu and Fu felt that he was not even seriously trying to convince them.

Conversation turned to the payment the management had made to the cleaning ladies. Woo said they were originally treated like the daily-rated. However, in the JETCON system, cleaning ladies qualified for the provident fund, so the JWM cleaning ladies were paid accordingly. As for the money paid to the monthly-rated workers in March, Woo remarked that it was for people who had worked for over three years to be paid when they left the company. People of different rank were paid, monthly, a fixed percentage of their respective annual salary by the company. The company administered the fund itself. This system had taken effect only a few years before. Because of the upcoming merger, the money had to be paid out to the staff to enable a fresh start. It was that simple!

Fu asked why there was no such provision for the operatives.

Woo replied that the company just did not save any funds for them, as their rate of turnover was too high — usually approaching 50 percent.

'What? Weren't those the *consequences*, not the cause?' Fu almost screamed, but he took a deep breath and asked if Woo thought would set up a similar scheme for them.

'Earlier no, but given recent events the company may be willing to consider the government's suggestion to set up a provident fund to substitute for the RMSA. But I don't see any possibility of the management accounting for workers' past years of service. Hong Kong management is independent of Japan. Here we have a different system.' He sounded like that he was reciting from a script.

Fu suggested that the Centre arrange for Woo to explain all this to the workers; but Woo said that there was no need to talk to the workers any more. To him, it was sufficient to talk to the two of them.

The tea was cold and the conversation tasteless. Gu had long since begun to chat with Ma, and Fu also no longer wanted to pretend he was listening. The lunch ended in an impasse.

2:30 p.m. The RPs arrived for a special meeting. What Woo had said made them angry. It proved that management had lied continuously during the negotiations. Description revealed the 'Japanese stranger' to be one of the lower management staff, named Minika — thus, everyone attending the lunch had belonged to local management. Either headquarters had faith in Woo and had authorized him to handle the case, or the lunch had been Woo's own initiative.

It seemed that something drastic must have happened in the factory between noon the day before and that morning — and that management, Japanese or local, were preparing a massacre.

But this had long been expected by the worker-leader's agenda. Teams went on working on drafts of their skit and the verses of their battle song. The agenda for Tuesday's general meeting was worked out and various jobs were assigned. After Chu Chi-lin discussed the overall strategy — with special reference to (1) the fair-treatment principle the workers were fighting for; (2) the 6 percent 'mysterious money'; and (3) the approaches that might be taken once the negotiations with management resumed — the lyrics of the song would be passed out. During the singing, slogans would be introduced. Then the skit would be performed. A suggestion was made to include something about how to act after management fired their colleagues in the drama.

Day −5: 26 May 1986 (Monday)

An open letter addressed to the JWM Japanese headquarters in support of the JWM workers' struggle was signed by nine organizations, including neighbourhood service groups, District Board members' offices, labour groups, social service agents and church groups.

Ms Gu called Yen Chin-chih around noon. He replied, hesitantly, that for technical reasons, contact with the middleman had not yet been made, but that, 'to make this kind of contact possible', the workers had to abstain from further airing their discontent.

The Centre staff and the workers discussed the previous day's 'lunch', speculating on various possible hidden agendas involved, and came up with conflicting theories. They hoped that negotiations with top management were at hand, and felt they would be to their advantage. On the other hand, it was understood that under-the-table manipulation (known in Hong Kong as 'swan-style' politics, in which apparent ease and grace contrasted with hurried underwater manipulations) was a typical Japanese management practice. The mobilization of interpersonal relations for corporate interests, as well as the employment of artificial 'privileged' communication channels, were standard practices in the postwar Japanese business' appropriation of social life. Such under-the-table deals had to be underwritten by successful disinformation campaigns, to sow discord inside the opposite camp.

It was easy to see that Yen might be used to suppress the workers on the day of their proposed deadline: Friday, 23 May. There was also a possibility of discord among the staff, or between the headquarters and the local management.

Centre staff believed that JWM management had probably decided to use people to play 'good guys' and 'bad guys' to disarm and divide the workers. Something had to be done to clarify the situation. They contacted Lo Man-sa of the CLA, but he could only provide the names of the two Japanese: Chichika and Sisuno. Lo was matter-of-fact. He said that he was not yet involved, but was making inquiries. However, he added that it would be tough for the workers to get any money from management, because it seemed to him that the JWM's company rules dictated that there be money for staff, but not for ordinary workers. The management was particularly reluctant to pay JWM workers for fear of inviting an uprising from JETCON workers.

It was clear to the Centre staff that Lo was not with the workers. As a veteran labour leader, Lo should have had something to say to boost morale. He was right about the mutual influences of events among the two corporate interests and the two sets of workers, but this was nothing new to the workers, who had realized weeks before the possibility that action taken by JETCON workers might be counterproductive for the JWM workers' struggle. Thus, a decision had been made to 'cool off' the connections between the two groups, with plans for a friendly labour group from outside the district to pick up the organizing drive of the JETCON workers, in order to share the work and to avoid suspicion. This latter never took place, for the JETCON workers had accused JWM workers of 'using' them, and had dropped out of sight.

While Gu was talking to Lo, Yen called to tell Fu that the 'middleman' had left for China. Any chance for the workers to negotiate with the Japanese was lost for the moment. Nevertheless, he again cautioned that the workers should exercise self-restraint.

Whether Yen had been used or not, one thing seemed certain: Headquarters had no intention of negotiating face to face. On the other hand, the workers felt the right decision was to refuse to talk to any middleperson and to insist on direct talks with the Japanese.

An emergency meeting was held at 2:00 p.m. Fu proposed that the letter to the Japanese union and the ILO be dispatched, and that the JWM union be announced at a general meeting of workers on the following day. Upon learning of the establishment of the union and the publicizing of the dispute, JWM management might (a) resume negotiations; (b) ignore what had happened so far; or (c) dismiss the workers' leaders and activists *en masse*. It was the last possibility that concerned the Centre the most, and they agreed that, should any workers be fired, the workers should demonstrate to demand their reinstatement.

After Fu and Ma had both pointed out that Woo had not been sincere at the previous day's lunch meeting with Fu and Gu, Gu reasoned that if high-ranking officials from the JWM head office were, in fact, sent, it would not necessarily be to negotiate with the workers — they might come to pressure local management either to settle early or to back up their reluctance to settle. The fact that no one had showed up so far probably meant that they would play the role of 'nice guys' and leave local management to play the role of executioner. At any rate, since the Centre could not sow discord between Japanese and local management, Gu suggested that the Centre and the workers forget about the complexities of JWM management and concentrate on formulating a multifaceted strategy of their own.

5:30 p.m. RPs and supporters arrived at the Centre. They said not one male management representative or foreman had been in the factory that day. Female line leaders stayed away from the production line. Nobody was supervising production, and the majority of workers were bored, working at less than half their usual speed. A few workers had seen Woo, Ou Ho-chung and Kusara in the factory, and said they looked much more relaxed than some days previously, especially Woo. The workers thought management was planning suppression. They came to the Centre to prepare for pre-emptive action and the next day's big show, and advised the Centre staff to ignore Yen. They wanted the Centre staff to tell Lo that:

1. The workers were eager for action, and that the Centre would not be able to hold them back;
2. They suspected communication problems within the management, and believed the Japanese lacked sincerity; and
3. The responsibility for any workers' action would fall on both headquarters and local management.

Day –4: 27 May 1986 (Tuesday)

The establishment of a premises union at JWM on 27 May 1986 (afternoon).

At around 11:00 a.m. Woo telephoned the Centre to ask Ms Gu about the workers' response to their conversation. Gu replied that the workers had scolded her for wasting time on such unconstructive talk. Woo then said that the workers had worked extremely slowly the day before. Gu replied it was because the workers were so discouraged. If the company could come up with a new proposal, the situation might improve. Woo replied that that was impossible, as there was no budget for any monetary compensation. He then said that official documents existed, but would be made available only by court order. Once the workers learned their contents, they would no longer be hired. Gu asked him what this meant, but he refused to explain. Instead, he said that, since the workers had been working so slowly, management had been forced to recruit new workers, who would come to work the next day.

Unexpectedly, Woo then asked Gu what kind of action the workers were planning to take. She answered that she could not tell anybody without authorization of the workers' body.

Finally, Woo suggested that it might be possible to pay workers their RMSA, but not any provident fund. Further negotiations could only concern the RMSA. He then referred to the open letter the workers had sent to Japan and asked when the press conference would be held. Gu declined to answer. Woo then remarked that if there were any public announcement, he would guess that the company would be forced to fire the workers involved. He then abruptly hung up.

After Woo's telephone call, three Centre members (Gu, Fu and Ma) of the newly established Emergency Committee were convinced that the union had to be set up during the afternoon general meeting. They contacted the worker-members of the Committee on each floor when they called in during lunch. Meanwhile, the Centre staff contacted bus companies and arranged possible meeting sites. At 1 p.m. it was decided that the inauguration would be held, and the licence plate numbers of three buses and the address of the Salvation Army's Meeting Hall were confirmed by the Centre.

At the Centre there was now frantic preparation: Telephone calls were made to news media and friendly organizations, banners were made, stage articles for the workers' drama were made, press releases were drafted, agendas and verses of the workers' battle song printed, portable loudspeakers borrowed, cameras and tape recorders readied.

At 4:00 p.m. the Centre staff divided into two groups. One would ride on the three buses to pick up the workers for the meeting, while the others went to the Salvation Army building to set up the meeting.

At 5:00 p.m. the buses parked across from the factory gate. A staff member stood by each bus; two or three JWM managers or foremen, both Japanese and Chinese, did the same. When the workers emerged from the factory gate the presence of the management personnel intimidated them, and there was some hesitation for about three minutes, but the RPs and supporters, with the help of Fu and Gu and their loudspeakers, successfully beckoned them onto the buses. The managers and foremen began to take pictures of the workers. The Centre had expected and prepared for this; their own 'shooting-squad' held up cameras and flashes to shoot back at the managers and foremen. Flashbulbs went off everywhere. Making faces at the company's cameras, the workers teased the managers and foremen, 'Why don't you make a face? Make a face, make a face!'

The three buses then left for the meeting place. Two cars from JWM followed them. At one point a woman appeared, who claimed that she had once worked at JWM, had learned about the dispute, was concerned and so wished to attend the workers' meeting. Centre staff refused her politely, and then set up a desk to register all participants.

6:15 p.m. The meeting finally began. Mui Len-shu, representing the RPs, reviewed the past month's developments. Next, Chu Chi-lin reiterated the workers' basic demands. She emphasized that to establish their own on-site union was an absolute necessity in achieving their goals. After her, Chien Fon-yi — 'big brother' — gave an inspiring talk on action in case the RPs were fired. She asked, 'Will you guys abandon us?'

Everybody shouted, 'No.'

'What will you do then?'

'We will fight our way through and get to the fifth floor to occupy the office.'

'Are you afraid?'

'No!'

'Don't forget to wave the big manila envelope (with dismissal orders and wage cheque) to show what has happened to you!'

'Yes!'

'Let's sing our battle-hymn!'

Everybody took out the sheet of paper they had got before entering the hall. The fourteen RPs led about 100 excited voices in singing loudly:

> JWM factory is in a dreadful state.
> We the workers will not easily yield.
> Fight against discrimination.
> In solidarity we must achieve our goal.
> Let us hold tight together and never leave.
> Pressures from bosses have no effect.
> Pooling our strength, together we are unafraid.
> Whatever task there is we do it with ease — so let's do it!

They repeated the song again and again, singing louder and louder. The faces became illuminated, flushed with eagerness and excitement. Some had tears in their eyes.

> JWM workers are not alone, unions and citizens are all behind us!
>
> We shall fight to reinstate our co-workers!
>
> Down with the suppression of union activities!

Hundreds of hands came up as the slogans echoed out.

As the songs and slogans continued, the RPs left their seats and joined their colleagues, and the stage was readied for the workers' skit.

Most of the actors in the skit were RPs and supporters. The most beloved and respected leaders — 'Big Brother' Chien Fon-yi, 'Little Wife' Chu Chi-lin and 'Wet Nurse' Lo Un-pu — played The General Manager, The Foreman and The Japanese. They walked onto the stage in a vain, swaggering manner. A few workers passed by. They shouted at them and stopped them. One threw a piece of money on the ground, as if to a beggar. A worker picked it up and threw it back. Everybody laughed. Chien, 'The General Manager', put her hand in her pocket and said, 'I have ten dollars in my pocket, it is up to me to give it to whom I please!' — but before she could finish she was fiercely scolded and pulled around the stage. Chu, 'The Foreman', acted out all the ways in which management abused the workers — she was rude and rough, smug and wilful, with a rampant thirst for power. After accusing workers of taking too long in the toilet and going too often, she turned to face The Japanese and The General Manager and immediately turned into a Pekinese, currying favour by wagging her tail, barking and licking her masters' hands. This was an improvisation, and people loved it. The show was on the verge of turning into a farce, and everybody was laughing. Then Gu and Fu, working backstage, urged 'the workers' to get on the stage, and an army of them did so. The management then took out a big envelope and handed it over to the workers. One of the workers was supposed to wave the envelope to show they had been fired, but she grabbed it and threw it on the floor. It then had to be handed back onto the stage, and there was more laughter. Those on the stage laughed so much that some almost fell. Some still tried to wave the envelope and perform the scene of occupying the office, but nobody cared about that any more. It was all just too much fun. The skit 'ended' in chaos.

After a twenty-minute break, the meeting resumed, to inaugurate the union. Hon Lai-fon reported on the organizing process, and told the workers that though it would still take a while for the government to formally recognize their union, it was important that every worker join right away to strengthen their solidarity. Sign-up sheets were passed among the workers, and ninety people signed. Those who did not have their identity cards with them promised to sign up later.

Next, Chou Mei-ying of the Christian Labour Association, who represented the guests and supporting labour organizations, read the open letter they had drafted and sent to JWM Japan headquarters' union, the Japan Nationwide Council of Unions and the ILO in Geneva. Mark Robinson of the Centre for Justice congratulated the workers in his perfect Cantonese.

The reporters were becoming impatient, so the Centre staff cut the meeting short. Fu briefly sketched the history of JWM's discriminatory practices, the breakdown of negotiations, and management's spying on workers' organizational activities. He reiterated the workers' three-point demand regarding the 'mysterious money': (1) the principle of fair and equal treatment; (2) the release of 6 percent per annum payment to the daily-rated; and (3) a peaceful solution through direct negotiations between workers and management.

The establishment of a premises union at JWM had been announced. It was almost dark when people left. On their way down the hill, Chou Mei-ying of CLA wanted to have a talk with the RPs. About fifty people went along with her to a small park. She mentioned something about unionized workers' strategy and strongly urged the workers not to take drastic action. But it was dark, the air was filled with mosquitoes and she fell short of elaborating her points.

Day –3: 28 May 1986 (Wednesday)

At 10:30 a.m. the telephone rang at the Centre. It was Woo. He told Gu that he had read in the papers that a union had been established at JWM. He wanted to know what that meant and what the workers were going to do. He also mentioned that the open letter had reached Japan. It was not clear to him what was meant by 'discrimination' and JWM management's 'divide-and-rule' management policy. The media attention made the Hong Kong management 'lose face'. Worse, they had been instructed to give an explanation to their Japanese superiors. Woo said that the head office had all the information about the Hong Kong factory, and once they intervened there was not much the Hong Kong management would be able to do. Now that the press had picked up the issue, Woo could only wait for instructions from Japan. Of course, he still hoped the dispute would not worsen and that the workers could be calmed down. Gu then asked if management's view of the situation had changed. Woo refused to answer. The conversation ended there.

After the phone call, Gu, Fu and Ma had a discussion. Ma believed the Japanese headquarters had tight control of their overseas branches. This fact had been intentionally blurred all along by the local management, but

Woo's revelation that the headquarters might take charge could mean that a 'killing' was in process and that Woo wanted to push the responsibility on to his superiors.

Gu and Fu were half-convinced by this. They suggested that the question of the Hong Kong management's 'losing face' might involve a complicated internal power struggle blurring management's perspective and hindering their ability to take drastic action. If so, there should still be room for manipulation. However, they agreed to prepare for the worst, and decided to inform the Union Registration Bureau of preliminary membership and push them to expedite registration. They then designed a leaflet entitled *Does It Pay to Join a Union?*, in which eight advantages of having a union were listed, and emphasizing the legitimacy of the union as the workers' collective body and its use in the struggle.

Chou Mei-ying of CLA called. She told Gu that she had received a phone call at home from an attorney working for JWM. She declined to name him, but said he wished CLA and its director Lo Man-sa would intervene as mediators, in which case anything would be open to negotiation. Even if management wished to dismiss some workers, he believed that he and Lo would be able to persuade them not to. She was told that the JWM management did not object to the workers' union, and felt that it might even help in labour-employer communication. When asked, the attorney had told her that he thought the workers should propose their own formula for a settlement and not wait for a management proposal. He assumed that after the merger the workers' accumulated length of service would be acknowledged and that there would be no change in their resignation award.

Finally, Chou said that Lo himself told her that he and the CLA would step in only on condition that the workers moderate their demands. If they insisted on fighting, then he and the CLA would not be involved.

Ms Gu, as was her manner, listened to Chou from beginning to end, making little or no interruption. She then politely promised to relay her message to the workers. The Centre, as a support group, had no choice but to stand behind the workers regardless of the course they chose.

After this discussion, Fu pointed out that, although management had approached CLA and Lo, yet Lo's preconditions were directed towards the workers. He thought it absurd. District Board member Lin Yi-chin said that, politically, an established group like CLA could not longer afford to lose. If the workers insisted on fighting until the end, CLA would be at risk. Ma pointed out that, if the workers gave up, there would be need for them to rely on outside assistance — 'You don't need a mediator to surrender!' The only reason the workers had accepted assistance was to facilitate their struggle with JWM management, not to court them, and there was no reason for them to suffer a setback to foster a courtship between establishments.

Gu insisted that the event should be reported to the workers in detail and a decision should be made only by them. After more than thirty telephone calls to RPs and regular supporters it was clear that the workers were capable of discerning the hypocrisies involved in the offer. They decided that they did not need this kind of assistance, but some were sophisticated enough to suggest that, while the present offer should be refused, Lo's offer as a go-between might turn out to be useful should the situation become desperate.

Day –2: 29 May 1986 (Thursday)

Centre staff met and reviewed the JWM situation from 10:00 a.m. until noon. They realized that what worried them most was the impatience and boredom of the workers. Reduced productivity hurt their dignity. On the shop-floor it is dreadful to be idle. 'A day drags along like a year!' A tell-tale sign was that workers were taking false sick leave. However, no 'cure-all' for this absenteeism was available. It was proposed to organize a group outing for the workers to practice co-ordination and co-operation, and to train second-line leaders. They also decided to strengthen organizing efforts and to set up a task force within the nascent union. Staff members decided to keep Lo Man-sa at arm's length for another week.

Around noon workers calling the Centre had little to say but complained of boredom. Most expressed disinterest in the planned outing.

At 3:10 p.m. a call came in from the second-floor RPs during their short break. They reported that management was again trying to play the trick of bypassing the RPs and dividing the workers.

Then, at 5:30 p.m., about fifty RPs and supporters rushed to the Centre with a questionnaire from management:

> Questionnaire
>
> 1. If the working conditions of the new company were the same or even better than your present ones, would you want to accept the proposal to work for the new company? Yes/No/Not sure yet
> 2. Comments
>
> Signature
>
> Return this questionnaire to the collection box before 9:00 a.m. on 31 May 1986.

Heated discussions ensued. In the first place the question was in the subjunctive mood — it might or might not represent the real situation. Secondly, there was nothing concrete — neither present working conditions nor future ones were spelled out. Thirdly, nothing had been proposed — workers were being asked to commit themselves to the unknown. Failure to respond positively could be taken as declining rehiring — the workers might be considered to have 'voluntarily resigned', and management would not even need to give them dismissal notices.

What was totally unacceptable to the workers was that this act constituted an outright insult to their newly formed collective body: management, as a legal person, was dealing with each worker as an individual. Done openly, it was a slap to every worker as a union member.

To counter the assault, the workers unanimously decided to hand over all forms to the fourteen RPs representing the collective body and request a meeting with management.

A four-page attachment came with the questionnaire, including a chart of welfare comparisons. A list of five points implied there would be welfare improvements after the merger. Another four-page attachment concerned the transfer of the company's various assets and the terms of re-employment. The language of the documents was polite, empty and abstract. It was obviously designed to justify the management's position rather than to convince the workers.

In the attached sheets accusations were made of internal and external incitement. A whole section concerned the 'mysterious money' — the document actually adopting this workers' term — but the arguments the management made only repeated previous clichés and served to further irritate the workers.

Under other circumstances these documents might have been perceived as goodwill shown by management, but at this particular historical moment the workers read them negatively. The workers and the management had become entangled in a process of reading-in and reading-out which, though unavoidable, only served to exacerbate existing tensions. Probably none of the workers or the Centre staff read through the whole set of documents thoroughly.

5　The Ethnographic Narrative II: During the Event (Day –2 to Day +1)

Day –2: 29 May 1986 (Thursday)

The situation was pressing. A letter to the Registrar of Trade Unions, informing him of the union's inaugural meeting, was drafted: 'Since at present there is a dispute between the production line workers and the management, we write to you in the hope that you will expedite the processing of our case as we fear that the management might sabotage our union and use excuses to dismiss those who are involved.' The letter was signed by the organizing committee of the union. Its purpose was to establish an official record of the *de facto* existence of the union and the workers' anticipation that management would sabotage their organizing effort.

The supporters also completed the previously designed leaflet, 'Does it Pay to Join a Union?', which explained the purpose of organizing a union and the necessity to keep secret its official establishment:

> In a Japanese-style patriarchal company like ours, the management is even more hostile towards any organizational efforts. It is therefore likely that sabotage will be attempted by the management to disrupt our organization before we are officially registered. Now that we have handed in our by-laws, you are strongly urged to join us to strengthen the union and reinforce our negotiations with the

management ... Only through collective action can we proceed to improve our working conditions.

While the supporters were working on the letter and leaflet, the RPs and Centre staff held an emergency meeting. The RPs reviewed the overall situation and surmised that management was either adopting delaying tactics to demoralize the workers or preparing an offensive. They had been much more relaxed and confident since the beginning of the week. There were rumours that temporary student-workers would be recruited for training, which never needed more than two or three weeks. There was still almost no supervision on the production lines and yield was unbelievably low.

Thus, the workers were prepared for the mass dismissal of workers and ensuing industrial action. What needed to be discussed were less drastic scenarios. It was decided:

1. The workers would negotiate only with Tosai or representatives from headquarters in Japan, and would not show eagerness.
2. The negotiating site would be a 'neutral' place.
3. The baseline would remain a 6 percent lump sum payment.
4. Whether to allow a representative from the Labour Bureau to join the negotiations would be decided later.

Day −1: 30 May 1986 (Friday)

Ma and Fu invited Gu, who was to report to TWLSC's board of directors around noontime, for morning *dim sum*. The three discussed the situation and made a few decisions:

1. Since the workers did not wish to involve middlemen, the Centre would stall Lo Man-sa for a week or two.
2. They would continue to push the Registrar for an early establishment of the union.
3. They would create opportunities to train second-line leaders.
4. Barring other developments, they would organize a weekend camp-out for 7–8 June and use the occasion to train the second-line leaders in organizational work.

5. They would try to persuade friends in the press to interview JWM management.

In the early evening Gu returned from her meeting exhausted. Five of her directors and one representative from CLA had attended the meeting. After she had briefed them on the JWM case, her immediate supervisor, Li Nai-kuan, told her to limit her role: She was TWLSC's only full-time, paid staff member; setting too high a goal would damage CLA's reputation. Yen Chin-chih, another TWLSC director who had failed to become a middleman, told Gu that this was an isolated workers' dispute and not a genuine workers' movement. She should merely persuade the workers to settle early. Lao Kan-kai, who worked for CLA and was also a TWLSC director, said he had heard that the JWM workers were encouraged to fight for self-esteem and dignity — an unrealistically high goal. 'There is nothing wrong with simply fighting for a monetary reward. We should not look down upon immediate material interests and force them to fight for the luxury of a noble cause.' On and on it went. Gu kept arguing. Finally ordered to follow a policy of pacifying the workers and downgrading their struggle, she replied, 'It is a militant unionist's responsibility to obey the collective decision of the workers and it is the right of a workers' service team to make on-the-spot decisions independently.'

Her story saddened everyone.

Day 1: 31 May 1986 (Saturday)

11:00 a.m. Fu Kwon-sin received a call from a Mr Lam Tu-pi, who introduced himself as an attorney with the international law firm M/S Mackinley who was calling in a private capacity. His law firm represented JWM management — which had decided to dismiss thirty-some workers that afternoon, for different reasons: some for negligence, some for demanding severance pay, some for refusal to co-operate with management — in short, for *misconduct*. Reasons would be given to each worker personally, and he could not comment in detail. In response to Fu's questions, he replied that his firm was authorized by both JWM local and Japanese managements, and that they handled various things in addition to the present dismissal of workers. He emphasized that JWM headquarters was not directly involved in the present matter.

Fu wondered whether the attorney and his information were genuine. Did he want him to inform the workers? Fu had a pressing appointment and there was no time to check on the attorney or to think through all the questions. Nevertheless, the Centre and the workers had to take the informant seriously. Fu briefed Gu — the only other person there — on the conversation. They assessed the situation and discussed possible responses to dismissals.

1. Because most of the production lines were located on the second floor, where most workers were concentrated and where leadership was strongest, the workers would sit in on the spot if management expelled the leaders.
2. Picket teams would be organized and dispatched to guard all other floors. They would register everyone coming through the premises, and frisk people for weapons brought in or factory property taken out, if necessary.
3. Second line representatives would be mobilized and placed in key areas to take over some responsibilities.
4. A public statement would be issued, demanding that management reinstate all dismissed workers and reopen negotiations, and stating that the sit-in would continue until these demands were met.
5. A telegram would be sent to JWM headquarters' management and union, and to other international labour organizations.
6. A sketch of the factory layout would be prepared, to guide collective action.

When Fu left the office, it was almost 12:00 noon. Gu was waiting by the phone for the daily lunchtime calls from each floor, which now had to be made from a public telephone on the street as, two weeks earlier, management had refused workers access to their telephone, but today the phone was unusually quiet. When Lam Yi-kai came in, after 1:30 p.m., for his afternoon shift as a social-work intern, Gu briefed him, and they began preparing banners, picket signs and megaphones. They both cancelled all appointments for the coming week, and requested people to come in to help.

Then Hon Lai-fon called: She had been fired and expelled from the factory. Gu told her to get back to the factory and back to her floor, as the RPs had decided that no workers would leave the factory, especially if management dismissed workers. Hon replied it was impossible to go back now, but Gu insisted. 'Do your best and notify other workers, urge them to go back if anybody comes down. I'm coming but don't wait for me ... go right away.'

Gu ran all the way. She saw Hon and a few workers sitting inside a factory van parked in the street, and led them back to the factory building. As they approached the gate, Chi-mei ran out. She told Gu and the others that all the workers were encircling the fifth-floor office.

Excitedly, Gu and Chi-mei rushed up to the fifth floor. Everybody was talking, but Hon and her friends hesitated, wondering whether all the workers knew what had happened. A few policemen arrived and pushed their way into the lift with Gu and Chi-mei. When it stopped at the fifth floor, hundreds of excited, noisy workers were crowding the doors. The policemen had to squeeze their way through to reach the corridor some five yards away. Following the police, Gu managed to reach the corridor gate and then, with the help of the workers guarding it, got into the office.

The first person Gu met inside the office was Chen Siu-guan, one of the most radical and active representatives, from the second floor. She came up to Gu with swollen eyes and told her that the management had fired tens of workers and forced them to leave. As they were alerted and rushed to the fifth-floor office, the women workers — herself included — were beaten up by the foremen. When Gu saw 'Big Brother' Chien Fon-yi among the RPs sitting on the floor angrily scolding the men around her, she became hysterical and told Chen Siu-guan and Chien Fon-yi to report to the police.

Women operatives occupied the fifth-floor office area and began a 13-day sit-in in JWM on 31 May 1986 (Day 1).

Local labour relations chief tried to intervene and defuse tensions on 31 May 1986 (Day 1).

Only after prolonged negotiation did the police inspector agree to send one of his female officers into the office to take depositions from the women workers.

The policewoman first got 'Big Brother' up and took her into the manager's office, denying entrance to Gu, as the deposition could be taken only from the people concerned. Through the big glass window, people saw her talk to 'Big Brother' with a serious face. Meanwhile, three other workers, who had been locked up by the foremen, were released from a small room, and they wanted to report their cases to the police as well.

During this chaos, Gu shouted to calm hundreds of workers crowded outside the office. Only then was Gu told that thirty-six workers, including every single RP, had been fired. The three RPs then spoke of how they had been locked in the small room after they had rushed into the office to reason with management.

Lam Yi-kai made his way through the crowd and handed his megaphone to Gu. An emergency meeting was called, and a consensus was reached that everyone would sit in until the thirty-six workers were reinstated.

Then a slogan was chanted, 'No reinstatement, no work; no reinstatement, nobody goes home; sit-in till victory!' In the shouting, the workers felt united, their morale greatly heightened. Somebody began the battle song, and it was sung again and again, together with the new slogan, louder and louder.

Meanwhile, workers were summoned by the female police officers to present their cases. The police inspector talked to Woo in his private office; nobody else was allowed in. To Gu's surprise, the workers with whom the policewoman talked were persuaded not to make cases against management!

Just then the production manager, Ou Ho-chung, came up to Gu and said that Woo wanted to talk to her. Gu agreed, but at first the workers did not; they thought it was 'dangerous', and that she might be 'bullied'. Gu, however, managed to convince them and promised to come out soon.

After Gu left, there was confusion. The workers outside began to question those who had met with the female police officer. Meanwhile, within the limited space between the office and a nearby meeting room, the quality of air was deteriorating. Fu Kwon-sin appeared and the workers cheered him. He immediately negotiated with the police and demanded that management restart the air-conditioner. He then went to the fourth floor, where the air was much better, and found a few male workers idling in the canteen, who told him the canteen/locker room would be closed after 5:00 p.m., when all the female workers went off duty. Fu went back to the fifth floor and suggested that the workers also occupy the fourth floor and use it as their base. Gu had just come out of Woo's office. She too realized that the air was suffocating and suggested that the workers go down to the fourth floor, but they refused, insisting that the office area should be sealed off and guarded as long as reasonable solutions were wanting. Fu suggested that the workers organize pickets to guard the office in turn. Those who were not on duty would stay on the fourth floor. The workers then agreed to move downstairs.

Just then, before anyone could move, workers from the first, third, sixth and seventh floors rushed up the stairs and pushed themselves onto the already crowded fifth floor. They had gone to the canteen/locker room after work and heard how their colleagues on different floors had been fired and mistreated, and how management had recorded their every move on video, following them all the way to the locker room. The workers felt insulted and humiliated, and had rushed up the stairs to the office floor to find their missing colleagues and 'get justice' from management. They now found 100 workers staging a sit-in.

With the arrival of workers from different floors the air quality worsened, but Gu got them downstairs to the fourth-floor canteen/locker room, leaving twenty workers guarding the office, to be relieved in an hour.

In the canteen, workers expelled all the remaining male staff and put guards at the doors. They encircled Gu, who began to speak in a low voice, forcing everyone to stay quiet to hear her. She said that Woo had been polite to her. He had asked about the situation with the workers outside. Gu had asked him what he had done to provoke them. Woo replied that workers had been dismissed, and asked what could be done in the present situation. 'He seemed friendly, or actually, scared,' Gu commented. 'I told him that it was easy: negotiate with the workers' representatives,' Gu continued, 'but he failed to respond to my answer. He also denied the air-conditioning was turned off. I told him that only made things worse. The workers were going to occupy the fourth floor as well. He said that, as a rule, the factory closed at five o'clock. I told him that if no negotiations were held with the workers, they would definitely stay. He again failed to respond. Obviously he was not in a position to give any definite answers. He must be frightened.'

The workers, delighted, shouted, 'Negotiate, negotiate, negotiate!'

Gu then reached the workers who had been interrogated by the policewoman, intending to push them to file formal complaints. Both Chen Siu-guan and Chien Fon-yi looked reluctant. Siu-guan said the police had coerced her into promising to drop the case. Gu could only keep quiet.

A few reporters and press photographers who had been by the Centre began to take photographs and ask questions, but management would not talk, so they turned to the workers. Most of them wanted to interview Gu and Fu, who declined, instead sending RPs to talk to them.

Now some 200 workers began to gather again on the fifth floor near the office. They chatted and sang their battle song, while their RPs talked to the reporters. Somebody brought snacks, drinks and balloons, and the area began to resemble a carnival site.

Ma Po-kwan had arrived at the factory about the same time as the reporters, but had waited outside for news teams from two television stations he had called. While he was waiting he talked to almost every worker he saw come down the stairs, most of whom were doing so to call their families to say they would not be home that night. Others came down for food or drink. Fewer than twenty people were going home, and some of these promised to return later that evening or the next day.

Since the workers were having a good time on the fifth floor, Gu and Fu came down to consult with Ma. Ma became angry when he learned that the assaulted workers would drop their cases, and insisted that a legal case be established in order to pre-empt management abuse. Fu and Gu agreed, returned to the office and managed to talk the workers into resubmitting their cases. The police inspector then sent out more female police, who talked to each worker individually and finally agreed to register their cases if they secured 'proof of injury' statements signed by officially recognized physicians. However, none of the workers agreed to go to a physician: As RPs, they were determined to remain in the factory. And so the matter was dropped.

While the police were 'firefighting' and the reporters dug up stories, Gu, Fu, and Ma continued their strategy meeting at the staircase by the street. They agreed that the workers should continue to sit in, to press management to negotiate. RPs should attend all meetings as the workers' sole representatives. In a sense, holding meetings with management would thus be an achievement in itself, as they would force management to recognize the workers' collective body and legitimize the authority of the RPs, amounting to a *de facto* negation of their dismissal. To minimize complications, the RPs should make only one demand at present: reinstatement of all dismissed workers. All action would be aimed at this single, clear goal.

Before details could be worked out, the Labour Bureau chief, Tu Pi-sin, arrived and the meeting had to be adjourned. Ma, still waiting for the television crews, left.

Tu headed straight for Gu and Fu, to gather information before entering the factory. Gu and Fu answered his questions in a straightforward manner. He was not a devious person — unlike his boss, chief labour relations officer Mao Si-hai — and sometimes was genuinely sympathetic to the workers' grievances and cause.

In the course of the conversation, Tu revealed that Woo had asked him to help solve the problem. Lam Yi-kai left Fu and Gu and went up to the canteen, where he informed the workers of Tu's imminent arrival. They worked out a reception: When Tu appeared, everyone cheered and applauded. Surprised and somewhat embarrassed, Tu greeted them hastily and then rushed to the office to talk to the management. The workers thus showed they knew why Tu was there, and that he should behave himself and not favour management.

When Tu emerged from the vice-general manager's office an hour and a half later, at 8:30 p.m., he announced that management had agreed to talks. The workers were delighted. A strategy session was called by Gu and

Fu with all the RPs, while Tu again disappeared into the manager's office. The RPs agreed that the goal of any talks should be reinstatement of all dismissed workers. Talks on other issues could follow.

When Tu again re-emerged after two more hours, a meeting was called for 10:30 p.m. in the fifth-floor conference room. There, fifteen RPs, Gu and Fu faced Woo, Tosai, Kusara, other lower-ranking management staff, and a big, bearded young Caucasian across a long table. Tu took his seat beside Gu and Fu, on the side of the workers.

Tu broke the ice by introducing the Caucasian man to the workers as management's attorney and head negotiator, Mobark Ley. Ley made no response, although people guessed, rightly, that he knew Cantonese. Tu volunteered to interpret and asked the workers what their demands were.

For a moment there was silence. Then, after a bit of eye communication, Chu Chi-lin, the outspoken 'Little Wife' from the second floor, spoke out. 'We demand the reinstatement of all the dismissed workers.' Without waiting for Tu to interpret, the fidgeting Ley began reading the papers in his hands. He recapitulated the dispute from management's perspective, sporadically stopping for Tu's translation. He said the management had decided to dismiss the workers because of low production. In addition, there was trouble on the shop-floor. The management represented the company and had every right to fire workers. They had put up with the workers' misconduct for a whole month. Nevertheless, the management kept an open mind — reinstatement would be considered on condition that normal productivity be resumed be restored. Ley insisted that the dismissals were by no means final. The company might reconsider. The workers should forget the 'misunderstandings' resulting from the company's upcoming merger. If normal productivity were restored, after a 'cooling-off period', the management would consider their demands.

Before he finished shuffling through all his papers, a question erupted from the opposite side, 'Since everyone's productivity was so low, why did management fire only thirty-six workers, not the whole factory?'

'Those fired were troublemakers,' Ley answered.

'What troublemakers? What do you mean by "put up with us"? What do you mean by "misconduct"?' the RPs shouted back.

Ley was so astonished that he forgot that he did not understand Cantonese.

'Little Wife' then spoke up, 'This is outright union-busting. A criminal discrimination against union members and their leaders. You guys know that every single worker you fired is either a union board director or initiator. Don't forget it is against the law!' Ley was, about to say something, but instead turned to Woo and, in a low voice, questioned him in English. Obviously, management had failed to inform him about the union. Trying to conceal his embarrassment, Woo said little in front of the workers. Ley became angry. Two management staff came up to explain something and calm him. Arguments ensued, and the meeting descended into chaos. Tu hurriedly raised his voice, 'We are taking a break. The meeting will resume in twenty minutes!' The management swarmed out with Mobark Ley, while the workers waiting outside pushed in to inquire excitedly about the meeting.

Day 2: 1 June 1986 (Sunday)

The meeting resumed after midnight, with Tu speaking first. Intending to build a better atmosphere, he explained that a 'cooling-off' period was standard procedure in a labour dispute. He then yielded the floor to Ley, who said that the 'misconduct' referred to the RPs' collecting of the questionnaires and forbidding the workers from handing them to the foreman. This interference with the internal affairs of the company could not be tolerated. Someone on the workers' side wanted to refute the accusation but was stopped by glances to communicate that the *gwailo* ('foreign ghost', the common slang term applied to 'Westerners' in Hong Kong, which can vary in nuance from the mere descriptive to humorous to semi-racist) lawyer should first be allowed to expose his ignorance. The tactic worked, as Ley again found himself trapped by the partial nature of the information management had given him. He was stunned to learn that

On 1 June 1986 (Day 2), the leaders lined up for chairing the general meeting on the fourth-floor canteen area where sit-in was staged.

the management had violated the agreement to respect the workers' representatives and to communicate with the workers only through them.

Chu Chi-lin then raised another issue for Ley's benefit, telling him about the animosity between management and workers. Ever since the merger decision, management had tried everything possible to reduce the workers' existing benefits and enhance control over them. The workers were defending themselves and resisting discrimination.

Tu jumped in when he heard the word discrimination. 'But the workers also agreed to resume normal productivity during the negotiation period ...' A multilateral debate began, and people argued over issues such as whether management or the workers had been responsible for the lower productivity over the past weeks.

It was Gu and Fu who halted the quarrel. When the meeting resumed, the floor went to Ley, who stated that the dismissal had nothing to do with the so-called 'union' that the workers claimed they had established, as the management was unaware of it. As a law-abiding, prestigious multinational corporation, the management would honour a government-sanctioned union once it had been made official, but this was not presently an issue. 'As chief negotiator,' said Ley, 'in response to the workers' demands, I propose the following conditions as terms to settle the present dispute. I present it orally now and my law firm will prepare a document for every individual worker to sign later.' Some workers then requested that he present the terms in writing, but since his draft was in English and there was no photocopy, a blackboard was brought in. Tu volunteered to translate the conditions on the blackboard. Four items were listed:

(1) Workers should resume normal productivity as soon as possible.
(2) There should be no demonstrations or disruptions.
(3) During negotiations, workers should not 'distort' and/or publicize the facts.
(4) The workers should wholeheartedly co-operate with their foremen and line leaders.

Mobark explained that as long as productivity was irregular, management could make no promises. In addition, no intervention in the company's internal affairs would be tolerated by outside pressure groups. Free of such pressures, the union might then be recognized. Japanese headquarters disliked having the dispute publicized by the media and resented public statements by local pressure groups. Negotiations would continue only on condition the workers co-operate with their superiors.

To this last managerial cliché, the workers turned a cold shoulder, and Gu and Fu had to encourage them to talk. The workers began to pick at the wording of the terms, questioning the meaning of every sentence, demanding further clarification, and arguing against Ley's rationalizations. Questions were raised in a disorderly fashion and answers were even less definite. Suspecting that the workers were enjoying this 'guerrilla warfare', which could trivialize and blur their goals, Gu called for a break, suggesting that the proposal be brought to the rank and file for consideration. Management, greatly relieved, immediately rushed out of the room.

It was 3 a.m. Twenty of the most enthusiastic workers lingered on the fifth floor, but some 100 had gone to sleep in the fourth-floor canteen. The RPs decided not to wake them, but consulted in the meeting room with the twenty supporters. As debates heated up, Tu came in. He wanted a private consultation with Gu and Fu. They went out to the staircase.

In a serious tone, Tu told Gu and Fu that 'neutral people like ourselves know well that to resolve the conflict, a cooling-off period must take place.' He said the management had agreed that responsibility for maintaining normal productivity fell on both the workers and themselves — however, they insisted that resumption of normal productivity was the condition for consideration of the workers' demands. They would instruct their staff to co-operate with the workers. He urged Gu and Fu to persuade the workers to accept these terms.

Gu and Fu were intrigued by Tu's eagerness. Gu commented later to Fu, 'There seems to be something more on his mind than just doing his job and putting out the fire!' Tu's sincerity and personal involvement had not offset the historical bad blood between militant unionists and their structural counterparts, the Labour Bureau officers.

The three returned to the meeting room and found that a consensus of sorts had been reached. Fu relayed Tu's suggestion. The RPs reacted by urging Fu and Gu to help work out the wording of a counteroffer.

The meeting with management resumed at almost 4.00 a.m. Some of the former management participants did not attend.

The workers' terms were six in number:
1. Normal productivity would be resumed, but both the management and the workers would be held responsible.
2. There would be no disruption during working hours, on condition that the management did not force the workers to do things against their will.
3. Neither the administration nor the workers should 'distort' facts.
4. The workers would co-operate with the management wholeheartedly, and vice versa. There was no need to single out foremen, leaders, and operatives, since animosity did not exist between them and the workers, but between the workers and the management.

5. Any settlement of disputes between the workers and the management should begin with management's respect for the status of the workers' representatives. The company must recognize them and negotiate through them.
6. There would be no arbitrary dismissal of workers during negotiations.

These points were put on the blackboard. Ley and the management people studied them and tried to clarify every detail. Woo, who had been sitting silently beside Ley the whole evening, tried to interrupt the meeting, but Ley ignored him and told the workers that the management now needed a closed-door meeting to decide whether the workers' proposals were acceptable.

At this point Woo finally burst out, 'No more meeting any more! This meeting has to be adjourned. It is 4:30 already!' The RPs wanted to continue until an agreement was reached, but Woo stood up, shouting, 'If you guys want to have a meeting, have it yourselves! I won't join. It is morning already! This is ridiculous!'

The meeting thus ended. Management promised it would resume on Monday at 9:15 a.m. Woo even promised the workers that they could stay as long as they wanted, or until an agreement was reached.

After the lawyer and management people left, the RPs and supporters decided to call a general meeting in the afternoon, to rally support. Centre staff were asked to notify all friendly groups and the press.

Five a.m. might be late, but the workers were too excited to feel tired. All they needed was fresh air. Down the stairs they went, pouring into the deserted street under the fading street-lights. It was too early for the morning paper or tea, so workers living in the neighbourhood took others home for a shower. At the factory gate, Gu, Fu, and five workers were stopped by the building doormen, as it was not yet 6:00 a.m. and people could only leave, not enter. They crowded into a company delivery van and took naps. Everyone had to prepare for another long day of struggle.

Ma Po-kwan, who had gone home around midnight, returned at 8 a.m. with copies of newspapers reporting the dispute — a total of twelve daily papers. He found Gu and Fu in the van and woke them up.

During breakfast, Fu and Gu briefed Ma on what had happened at the meeting. Ma did not like it. He pointed out the lack of Japanese headquarters representatives and the uncertainty about Ley's authority. He hoped that reinstatement was still possible but was worried no mention had been made of 'the money' — the issue they had been working on for months.

As an overall negotiating strategy, the three of them agreed that:
1. reinstatement of the dismissed would be the one and only demand;
2. restoration of productivity would take place step by step, as the responsibility of both the management and the workers;
3. money would not be mentioned until the dismissed had been reinstated;
4. industrial action would continue until an agreement was reached; and
5. the workers should watch for an injunction to force them off the premises.

In the fourth-floor canteen/locker room, most of the workers had awakened. They gathered at the long tables, eating breakfast brought in from the street and chatting among themselves. They were excited to see Gu, Fu and Ma in good spirits. They said that spending the night in the canteen was not too bad, except for the too cold air-conditioning. A few newspaper clippings were posted around the room. The atmosphere was easy. Some older female workers had returned home and come back with their babies — the factory had become a place for Sunday family outings!

Not until 11:00 a.m. had the RPs 'partied' enough with their colleagues to be ready for a meeting. They went up to the fifth floor, released the 'guards' from duty, and, together with the Centre staff, proceeded to discuss the agenda for the afternoon's general meeting. They would begin by condemning management's postponement of negotiations and unwillingness to reach a reasonable settlement, and brief everyone on the negotiations of the night before, reiterating their only demand and explaining the rationale behind their six-point counteroffer. They would then cite the contributions of each representative and hold a legal consultation session. Finally, they would pass a resolution for further action and organize a strike committee to plan continuing action in case negotiations broke down.

All of them knew it was unlikely that negotiations would resume before Monday. Management had turned timid, and were trying to buy time while awaiting instructions from the Japanese head office. Prolonged, difficult fights were anticipated, and another strategy meeting was proposed.

After a long discussion, consensus was reached:

1. Beginning on Monday, all workers would arrive to work on time and report to the fourth-floor strike committee without punching in their work cards.
2. Negotiations should resume as soon as possible and conclude before 10:30 a.m., when management might have a court injunction to expel the workers. If management refused to resume negotiation before 10:30 a.m., everyone should prepare for further action. Specific action would be decided by the strike committee which would inform the workers on the spot to avoid leaks.
3. The bottom line for negotiations was management's four points, but the workers should begin with their six points, giving in, if necessary, as negotiations progressed.
4. The 'secret money' would not be mentioned, but the workers would reserve their right to fight for it after the dispute concerning reinstatement had been settled.
5. If no settlement were reached on Monday, action would be upgraded by the following:
    a. Approach JETCON workers for a sympathy strike;
    b. Petition the legislative and executive branches of the government;
    c. Institute a local boycott of JWM watches;
    d. Request the head of Japanese headquarters to open direct talks; and/or
    e. Publicize the dispute, emphasizing the union-busting aspects.
6. Action should be taken not only to rally sympathetic local groups but also to build solidarity links with workers at the JWM Japan headquarters factory or at other premises.

7. Every condition or term suggested by management should be put in writing — a point particularly stressed by Ma.

It was about 2:00 p.m. when the RPs finished their meeting and returned to the canteen to brief the workers before the press and friendly groups arrived. Lin Yi-chin, the Kwai Chung District Board member and founder of CKLRS, arrived at the canteen. He stopped the RPs from calling the general meeting to consult with them immediately. He said Shih Ding-yi, CLA labour organizer, wanted to have a direct chat with the RPs as soon as possible. He thought it was imperative for him, a veteran labour organizer, to advise them. Lin replied that he was not in a position to promise anything — the decision had to be made by the workers and the representatives — but he would relay the message. The RPs first reacted negatively, saying they already knew what he was going to say: that he wanted them to give up their action. However, Shih was already down in the canteen and wanted to come up. Lin said that, under the circumstances, it would embarrass Shih and the Centre staff — especially Gu and Fu — if they did not talk with him. Gu and Fu said they too had no intention of forcing the RPs to do anything they did not want to do but, in the present delicate situation, the workers should not make more enemies. It seemed wiser to neutralize, rather than antagonize, people like Shih. The RPs accepted this, but decided that any discussion should be open to all friendly groups, not to Shih alone.

When the RPs, Lin, Gu and Fu went down to the canteen, reporters and representatives from various friendly groups were already there, and they and the workers applauded the RPs. The canteen had been decorated with coloured balloons and slogans such as 'Against discrimination of daily-rated workers! Against threats, surveillance on workers!' The fifteen RPs sat behind three long tables, facing a crowd of about 200. Behind them, a banner stretched across the hall — 'JWM Union General Meeting of Appeal — A Fight for Our Rights of Legal Collective Bargaining'.

The general meeting kicked off with everyone standing to sing the battle song. Then there was a recapitulation of the actions in the factory during the past twenty-four hours, followed by a report on different events and the workers' analysis of management's moves, with comments indicating the stupidity of management rationale and motives evoking laughter. The RPs emphasized that it was management which had adjourned the negotiation, and asked for the workers to be patient and persevering. They then read a prepared statement for the media.

Gu and Fu then took the floor. They praised Hon Lai-fon for managing to rush onto the second-floor shop-floor and alerting them; and Chu Chi-lin, for being the first to push through the management blockade to the fifth floor. Chien Fon-yi and Chen Siu-guan, who had been pushed to the floor by the foremen, were also mentioned so that all would hear of their courage and suffering. All were invited to speak to their fellow workers, who reacted enthusiastically.

Gu and Fu were then asked to talk. Gu emphasized the importance of being ready for action whenever necessary. She discouraged blind optimism and warned the workers that the battle might become more difficult. Fu, picking up where Gu left off, again stressed the importance of unity, 'In solidarity, we will be the victors — without it, we can go nowhere!' He had everyone shout the slogan three times.

Prior to voting, 'Big Brother' Chien Fon-yi officially presented the three-point resolution:
1. No reinstatement, no return home, no work.
2. Negotiate after the sit-in.
3. Both the management and the workers were responsible for productivity.

By a nearly unanimous show of hands, the resolution was passed.

Finally, representatives from the Centre for Justice and Peace, the Association for Workers' Rights, the Labour and Residents Coalition, the Organization for People's Basic Rights, the New Youth Society, TWLSC, CKLRS, and the CLA expressed their support and pledged their solidarity. Among them, Shih Ding-yi of CLA gave a long speech, trying hard to persuade the workers that he was on their side. Mark Robinson of the Centre for Justice and Peace and Father Wasini were appreciated for their excellent

Cantonese. Lin Yi-chin discussed the things he had learned about labour movements during his student years in England. He encouraged the workers to resist and to unite, and urged them to raise their struggle to a higher level and to fight for the dignity and decency of all working people by fighting for legislation to outlaw the current practice of arbitrary dismissals. Ma Po-kwan took the opportunity to point out how Hsiao Chia, who had been ill and had stayed home for a whole week, had also been fired for 'misconduct'. Laughter mixed with anger. Finally, everyone in the canteen stood up, held hands, and sang the workers' battle song again and again.

After the meeting, journalists rushed to conduct interviews, and the canteen became like a noisy, lively market. In the confusion Lin and Ma noticed Yen Chin-chih and Poon Ni-kwon, two TWLSC board members, having a serious talk with Gu Lai-hap, and it was obvious that they, as Gu's bosses, were trying to get her to agree to something, but that she kept refusing. At one point her voice became loud, and both Yen and Poon tried to quiet her with threatening gestures. In another corner, Shih Ding-yi of CLA had managed to get hold of a few RPs and was trying to sell them his ideas.

To break up Shih's intrusive lobbying and rescue Gu, Lin decided to call a consultation of all RPs and all representatives of friendly groups. The RPs were summoned to their 'secret meeting place': a bare space surrounded by lockers, with only one open, guarded entrance, on the right side of the canteen. About fifteen representatives from various groups were invited to the consultation. Lin insisted that the consultation proceed as the RPs had decided: It should satisfy Shih's request and at the same time — by including others — defeat his purpose. The discourse that resulted was thus general, with no one willing to show their intentions or interests. To avoid any possible provocation, neither Gu, Fu, nor the Centre staff in daily contact with the workers was present. As no decision had ever been made without consulting either Gu or Fu or both, the result was just a talking session.

In the canteen the workers continued to chat, while in the corner Gu, with a flushed face and tears in her eyes, kept her mouth tightly shut, staring at the wall, as Yen sat beside her, words pouring out of his mouth. Yen made it clear that the TWLSC board of executives had unanimously decided that Gu should advise the workers to give up their industrial action. He, on behalf of the board, ordered her to do so — insisting, in fact, that she was the only one capable of doing so, since the workers trusted her.

Gu replied that every decision had been made collectively by the RPs and their colleagues after extensive consultations.

Yen then screamed, 'Don't put it on the workers! You are the one resisting the suggestion.'

Gu raised her voice. 'So what if I don't agree with you guys? Are you going to fire me? Do whatever you wish. I am responsible to the workers and their struggles, not to your organization's name and reputation. Don't you know the proverb? "A general out on the battleground can refuse orders from the Emperor!"'

When Gu burst into tears, the workers, angry, rushed to console her. Some scolded Yen. 'How can you abuse our Gu like that? What kind of man are you?' At that moment Yen became one of the oppressors – in addition to management and the labour officers — that the workers most loved to hate.

The 'secret' meeting lasted for an hour and a half. When people emerged, Shih wore a grouchy face. However, he was not ready to give up and insisted on inviting all of the representatives of the support groups to a coffee shop, where he began lecturing them on his experience in labour disputes, concluding that prolonged struggles without compromise led to failure. 'If the workers decide to continue their sit-in and insist on their point, CLA and I are going to pull out. We are not risking our reputation for their wilful demands. CLA is too important to be jeopardized by failed disputes.'

At that point, Dou Wan-min, the female chairperson of the Labour and Residents Coalition (LRC) — a noted radical, perhaps Trotskyist, group — accused him of being defeatist, but Yen ignored her, insisting that 'Nothing, absolutely nothing, can be done now. If we don't give up, we are putting the workers at the risk of being fired!' Meanwhile, Gu and Fu sipped their coffee quietly — Yen had insisted on buying them coffee, but that did not mean they had to talk to him. In any case, it was more fun and less trouble to have Dou and Yen handle the arguments.

That evening about sixty women remained overnight at the factory, chatting, playing with the balloons, and joking with the security and police night watch. Like school kids at their first camp out, they were enjoying themselves. As they had to take shifts safeguarding the fifth-floor office, the fourth-floor canteen, and their 'secret meeting space', most of them slept for only three hours.

Day 3: 2 June 1986 (Monday)

As expected, management personnel were out in the streets before the factory buses arrived in the morning. They were there to 'persuade' the workers either to turn back or report to work. The pickets had to guard the street corners, as well as receive their colleagues and escort them to the canteen. Over the weekend, when most of the workers had remained in the factory, management had called their families to tell parents that their children might be 'missing' but, thanks to modern communications and the small size of Hong Kong, their threats failed totally. When they tried to force the workers to quit picketing the fifth floor, the workers simply refused.

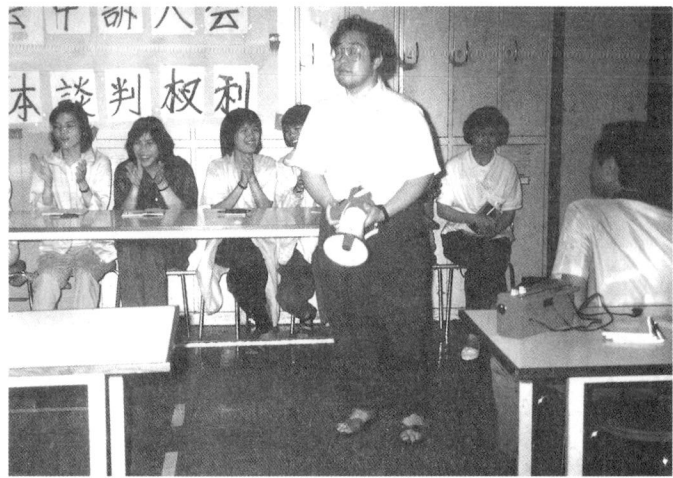

Guests and supporters spoke in the general meeting on 2 June 1986 (Day 3).

The negotiating meeting was not called until 9:45. a.m. Four persons represented the management: vice-general manager Woo Char-hwa; two Japanese, Tosai and Kusara; and one poker-faced stranger. After everyone had taken a seat, the stranger began talking, without introducing himself. He claimed to be the company's legal consultant, and tried to browbeat the RPs concerning the questionnaires, saying the questionnaires were one of the reasons that the management had fired them. It was necessary for the management to maintain discipline and keep production normal, and they had the administrative power to do so.

'We did not come to be lectured. If you care so much about lecturing, go somewhere else. We are here to negotiate a reinstatement,' responded Chu Chi-lin.

'There are some simple legal aspects that the attorney was trying to clarify first,' said Tu, the labour officer, 'putting out the fire' once again.

The stranger continued. 'The company has studied your counteroffers and reached some conclusions … It is the company's opinion that the new points raised by the workers show that the workers have failed to understand the company's position. Your demands basically hinder the management in executing its administrative power … before discussing reinstatement, the workers must first understand the reasons why they were fired … because they had engaged in sabotage … it is the management's main concern to maintain a normal, co-operative production … ' The words flowed like liturgies echoing in an empty chapel.

It thus became clear that management was not going to settle through negotiation, but was perhaps playing for time. As the lecture dragged on, people became impatient. Some were so irritated that they left the meeting or shouted back at the stranger. Fearing that unplanned moves might jeopardize their plans, Gu and Fu dispatched notes to urge the RPs to be patient. Other slips with various opinions then began to circulate, with the unexpected effect of lightening the atmosphere. The workers felt more comfortable, while management became more confused and worried. In a show of self-confidence, some of the RPs began loudly discussing things totally irrelevant to the meeting in Hakka, even as the management discussed among themselves in Japanese.

At 11:15, a.m. the stranger, ignored by everyone, was feeling insulted. Chu Chi-lin, sitting between Gu and Fu, jumped to his rescue! 'Is it that the company doesn't like the extra two points?' she asked the lawyer politely.

'Yes, you finally figured it out!' he replied excitedly.

'In that case, I, representing the workers, advise we give up. We fully accept the company's four points to reinstate the dismissed. It's a deal!'

'What?' exclaimed management. You could hear a pin drop.

'I, on behalf of the workers, officially accept the management's four points as final terms for reinstating the dismissed,' Chu repeated slowly and clearly. Woo pulled the lawyer to him and spoke into his ear. The latter listened, without nodding or shaking his head, and was obviously vexed. 'Don't you represent the company? And aren't you in the position to agree?' Chu advanced.

'I am authorized to negotiate ... We have to discuss ... ' The lawyer became less assertive.

'The four points are final, yes or no? Or are you guys going to add something on?'

'I'm not sure ... we have to discuss ... and see ... '

As Chu and the lawyer continued, Tu urged Woo to call a break. The workers refused. The tension mounted. Gu and Fu, who had been silent all day, stood and tried to calm everyone. They were forced to take up Tu's role as arbitrator and get both sides to agree to a ten-minute break. During the break, Gu, Fu, and the RPs learned from Tu that the lawyer was Lam Tu-pi, the man who had called on Saturday morning to inform them of the imminent dismissals. Amazing!

During the break, from across the hallway, people could see, through the glass windows, that intense debate was taking place inside the big office. An old, bald, Japanese-looking stranger was holding the telephone in one hand and waving the other, arguing with the three management delegates and the lawyer. His gestures and airs showed him to be one of the 'imperial emissaries' from Japanese headquarters.

The ten-minute break in fact lasted thirty minutes. When negotiations finally resumed, at 11:50 a.m., Lam had recovered his dignity. He spoke in a business-like manner, more softly than before, saying that management had decided to reinstate the dismissed workers according to the four points and to the terms proposed in the Saturday evening meeting. However, a few minor points needed clarification. Restoring normal productivity meant recovering 100 percent of previous yield within a reasonable period, and it would be the workers' responsibility to reach that goal. During working hours, no disturbances would be allowed: no demonstrations or disruptions of any sort, and certainly no slow-downs. The workers would not be allowed to invite 'third parties' to the factory premises. The company would say no more about retirement pay, as it had been explained over and over again. Further negotiations between the management and the workers would take place only under the condition that shop-floor productivity was normal. Neither the workers nor the management should 'distort facts' — therefore, the workers should release a statement to the press describing what had occurred at JWM as purely a 'misunderstanding', which had now been clarified, and would make no more accusations of discrimination or injustice. All the workers should pledge their 'full' co-operation with administrative personnel. Finally, a document delineating the terms just dictated would be officially drafted by the company's law firm, and every single worker involved in the dispute was to sign the document. This agreement would be a legal document, and the management would not hesitate to use its administrative power as the law granted.

Immediate objections were voiced by every single RP. All opposed the idea that each worker sign the document, as this would obviously disqualify them and sabotage unity. They also resented management's addition of new terms to the original four points. It was brutal to ask them to whitewash the situation for the corrupt management. Anyone who knew how the workers felt would have known that the terms were impossible, and they would surely break off negotiations without second thoughts. Gu and Fu were worried, for breaking off at that point was something the workers were not in a position to do. They consulted with the RPs next to them, especially with Chu, while others argued fiercely with the lawyer, who flatly denied that points had been added, insisting that the company considered a workers' statement clarifying their 'misunderstanding' as crucial; furthermore, the company wanted everyone to sign the document because it did not want to target only those who had been dismissed. His words only added to the workers' fury, and the situation became explosive. Chu stood up and requested a break, as the workers needed to discuss among themselves before replying.

Down to the fourth floor went all the workers' representatives. Some were so disheartened that they wanted to quit negotiation and upgrade their action. It took quite some time for Gu, Fu, Ma and Lin Yi-chin to get them all together for a strategy meeting in the locker room. After a lot of debate between the Centre staff and the RPs about the new conditions, the RPs finally, reluctantly, accepted that, to avoid risking further complications and uncertainties, they needed to achieve the goal of reinstatement. Ma suggested that the workers should request that management, and anyone else involved — the Labour Bureau, the Japanese Chamber of Commerce, etc. — sign the document as well. A committee for drafting the document was proposed, and management was to be responsible for any procrastination in arriving at a version acceptable to both sides. This would allow the workers to buy time and come up with a way to keep their dignity. All of these suggestions had to be kept secret until the end of the meeting.

While the RPs were having their meeting, the management was wrangling ferociously inside the general office. Through the windows one could see people arguing and shouting. The bald Japanese emissary, infuriated, was jumping up and down, his face purple, gesticulating excitedly to get his points across. As this went on and on, the workers became impatient. They finally pushed Tu into the office to urge them to resume the meeting. Tu was reluctant, but was convinced that there would be further problems if the dispute was not settled promptly. He went into the office three times and came out empty-handed. He confirmed that the fiery debate was being aggravated by incoming telecommunications and by opinions from the lower management.

It was almost 3:00 p.m. when the third round of the meeting finally began. Woo led his delegation in a relaxed manner. The lawyer, Lam, also seemed to have ready plans.

However, it was Tosai, the Japanese deputy general manager, who spoke. Tosai began by 'clarifying' the four points, claiming that the slowdown was the sole cause of the reduction in production, and that the workers were solely responsible. The management did not want a dispute, they wanted normal production restored. Therefore, the workers should come up with a date when this could be achieved. He continued to dwell on the issue, repeating his points a few times, until Woo cut in and said, 'The management will not tolerate the workers bringing in "third parties" and making trouble in the factory any more!' And he stopped abruptly.

Lam then explained the importance of the workers' statements to the media, and went on to repeat that all the workers involved in slowdown, stoppage, and the present sit-in were to sign the proposed agreement. Management would deal not only with those who had been dismissed, but with all the workers who had revolted.

'Yes, that's right. All of the workers revolted against management abuse. And fifteen of us represent them!' shouted Chen Siu-guan. The argument regarding the RPs' legitimacy then resumed — a topic so emotional that most of the RPs forgot what had been agreed upon in their strategy meeting. Personal grievances were aired by many to disprove the existence of any possible 'misunderstanding' on the part of the workers. Negotiations ground to a halt over trivial, inflammatory details.

All this time Fu, who had failed to predict this crisis, was phoning from the conference room to the fourth floor, and Gu was consulting with Chu, having yet to figure out the management's sudden hardening of its position. In the chaos, the lawyer was forced to drop its bomb before management had intended. He raised his voice in a tone of determination, 'No one should mention anything about the secret money, the so-called 6 percent lump sum, after the agreement is accepted.'

In the resulting explosion, no one could remember how the negotiations ended. Everything simply fell apart.

Down in the fourth-floor canteen, everyone was angry. Some picked up their placards and banners, ready to upgrade their industrial action. All they understood from Fu upstairs was that negotiations had broken off and that no further pursuit of the issue of the 'secret money' was allowed.

The Centre staff knew, however, that it was extremely dangerous at this point to allow spontaneous action. A general meeting was immediately called in the canteen, with Gu and Fu, each with a megaphone, moderating. The RPs took the floor and briefed the rank and file on the three sessions, emphasizing that, in order to keep the door to negotiations open, they had had to concede and offer to accept the management's four points in exchange for the reinstatement of the dismissed workers. They concluded that it was now time for everyone to express themselves and to come up with a decision to guide the struggle. After an analysis of the situation by Gu and Fu, people broke into small groups for discussion among themselves, and with their RPs and Centre staff. Everyone calmed down, and discussions proceeded. Meanwhile, Ma and Lin tried to determine how to conduct an effective poll.

When the general meeting resumed, after about an hour, Lin took the floor to help the workers come up with a polling proposal. In the discussion, many workers declared they would rather quit than give in to humiliating conditions. Some questioned the wisdom of setting reinstatement as their only immediate goal, leaving aside the issue of the 'secret money' — arguing that, as in past confrontations, it was not likely to be left out of any negotiating sessions. Though the amount of money involved was not much for the majority, the issue was a manifestation of the management's abuse and discrimination against the workers.

It was finally decided that the workers would vote either: (1) to *accept* the management's terms to have their colleagues reinstated; or (2) to *insist* on the original four points, i.e., their right to negotiate with the management on the discriminatory payment and to fight collectively for a just solution. This, of course, would mean persisting in the present struggle and setting up alternative mechanisms to advance their course.

The vote was conducted by secret ballot on small pieces of paper. Ma helped to clarify the proposal over his megaphone. Polling was orderly and resulted in a 155-to-6 victory for those insisting on the workers' stance. The workers were beside themselves with joy.

Just then, a news team from Hong Kong Wireless TV, the bigger of the two stations in Hong Kong, showed up at the canteen gate. As management refused to be interviewed, the news team went to get the story from the workers. They found not just a few storytellers but a whole troupe of performers. More than 100 young girls jumped onto tables to stretch banners, wave placards, shout slogans, and sing songs. Holding hands and swaying together, they were carried away. Standing up for themselves together made the young women feel taller and stronger.

The show continued long after the television crew was gone, subsiding only as nightfall approached. Lin instructed Fu to draft a news release to clarify the situation and the workers' position: an open announcement from the workers' collective body, which was to emphasize:

1. the management's broken promise;
2. the union-busting nature of the management's dismissal of the union leaders;
3. the workers' consistency in demanding reinstatement; and
4. the willingness of the workers to accept reinstatement on the four-point terms originally offered by the management.

Fu took pains to draft the announcement carefully. However, the announcement was never released.

Not everyone was in a festive mood. While all the above was taking place, Yen Chin-chih, the TWLSC director who had made Gu cry the previous day, was extremely restless. Having kept a rather low profile so far, he now began to lobby, through people from various supporting groups, for an invitation to Son Yan-min to help resolve the dispute. Son was a leader of the pro-China Federation of Labour Unions (FLU) and had been selected as a 'functional' member of the highest government legislative body (LEGCO) to represent the 'left' unions as a political force. He was balanced by a representative from the 'right', the much smaller pro-Taiwan Confederation of Workers' Association (CWA).

The FLU had been well-organized in the 1950s, but its popularity declined after the brutal suppression of the 1967 strikes by the Hong Kong colonial administration. Its power was further eroded after the Cultural Revolution in China. However, as the majority of workers were unorganized, the FLU's 170,000 members — although less than 5 percent of the total work force — still made it the largest labour organization in Hong Kong.

In 1986, after the signing of the Sino-British pact on the future of Hong Kong, the FLU's aims were amended as follows: 'To participate in social affairs, to strive for reasonable benefits, to enlarge patriotic unity and to enhance stability and prosperity.' To keep up recruitment, the FLU enhanced its welfare services. Son, a young salesman, was hand-picked at this time as the future star and sent to England for a year to 'study labour affairs'.

However, Son was no veteran of labour disputes, and had tried to stay away from them as much as possible. He felt more comfortable in meeting rooms — in the LEGCO Labour Consultation Committee, or in private corporation boardrooms — than on factory shop-floors.

As Son's background was well known to all the supporting groups, Yen's lobbying effort was by no means easy. He could not demonstrate the necessity of having Son around. However, because they wanted to be freed of Yen's constant nagging, and also because they did not want to disappoint him, the workers finally gave him a free hand to try to get Son involved, hoping that management might mistake Son as being sympathetic to their cause. Judging that Son would probably become involved one way or another, it seemed wise to have him appear as a visitor of the workers rather than as the guest-of-honour of the management. They urged Yen to call Son. After calling around for a long while, Yen rushed out and disappeared. The canteen then relaxed, and people began sharing food they had bought from street stalls. After 8:00 p.m., when most of the workers were chatting or taking naps, Yen arrived with Son and his female secretary. Gu and Fu gathered the workers together around the table to 'see' the member of LEGCO.

As a self-designated 'circus emcee', Yen introduced Son in colourful language. Son listened dully and then spoke in a well-modulated, lukewarm voice, repeatedly emphasizing that he came as a LEGCO member, not as the deputy chairman of the FLU. He wanted it to be clear that he would never have come to participate as a unionist. The purpose of his visit was to 'understand' the situation. As a LEGCO member, he would later try to 'reflect' the workers' opinion, but he had to be strictly aloof and neutral to do so.

Some of the workers began sporadically to respond. They had been caught by surprise and were unprepared. As the session continued, Son occasionally stopped speakers to inquire about minor details. Almost an hour passed. The consultation dragged along until the chief labour relations officer, Mao Si-hai, descended from the fifth floor to come to Son's rescue. He, the real circus emcee, smiled and introduced Son again, in language even more exaggerated and flattering. Son returned the favour by showering him with praises that gave everyone goose pimples. After this ritual, Mao invited Son upstairs to have a chat with the management.

When Son and Mao re-emerged, it was 11:00 p.m. Most of the workers were asleep but were awakened. Mao sat down facing the workers and raised his voice. 'The two persons in front of you are the highest two in Hong Kong, as far as workers' welfare goes. Don't worry, things will be settled in no time. Just depend on us … ' Son was disdainful of these remarks. He spoke rather rashly. He said that in the office upstairs he had been shown a company file from 1982 concerning the welfare schemes of monthly-rated and daily-rated employees. The monthly-rated were treated much better. According to Japanese custom, neither scheme had been openly announced, and no employees had ever learned the details of their welfare scheme. The schemes were determined at the company's discretion and were not discriminatory. When pressed, he replied that he did not remember all the details but admitted that there was some sort of provident fund for monthly-rated employees. What about the daily-rated? 'Well,' he began haltingly, 'Well, the company is going to merge and afterwards will consider the setting up of the kind of fund that you are all familiar with … '

Before he could finish, Mao slid in. 'The kind of public mutual fund we (the Labour Bureau) have been promoting recently for the benefit of all the workers in Hong Kong … It would be a kind of mutual fund provided by both the company and the workers, fifty-fifty. The company would manage it as custodian … '

There was a limit to the workers' politeness and tolerance. 'Mr Mao, we are interested in Mr Son's answer. Will you let him continue?'

Son suddenly lost his reserve and burst out, 'I am not obliged to answer any of your questions!' He then resumed his mask. 'You people want the dismissed reinstated, and it is still possible. What worries the company more is the conflict and friction between the administrative personnel and the workers. If reinstated, you must resume normal productivity and adopt a co-operative attitude. But you must understand that the 6 percent whatever-money-you-call-it never existed. It was simply never there!'

Son had finished, but much remained to be said. Mao, before picking up where Son had left off, praised him again, telling the workers that the LEGCO member had tremendous influence, and that the management would surely give him face. That was the best guarantee for solving the dispute. He expressed his 'personal disagreement' with the practice of keeping company welfare schemes secret, but said that different enterprises had their own designs, and it was not for anyone to judge. 'For instance, in your factory, most of the operatives who left the job, whether dismissed or resigned, were entitled to a "job-leaving gratuity". It is quite unique and nice. You think that since the monthly-rated got theirs, you should get yours. That is silly. You don't want to leave the job, right? As long as you stay, the amount due will increase accordingly, will it not?' He went on to reiterate management's points about the merger, and so on. 'They even expressed their willingness to set up a provident fund for the operatives, upon our advice.' He looked at Son and continued, 'They wouldn't want to make any public announcements under the present circumstances. It is because they fear that their friends might consider that they are giving in and that they have lost to the local workers. We workers should also sympathize with the management. They are often trapped in a dilemma. They are human beings, too. Now there are some psychological problems. For instance, after such a confrontation, your line leaders and foremen might really be scared ... ' The workers laughed and Mao did too. He continued, 'They are afraid that it will be difficult for them to be in charge any more ... their confidence is shattered.' The workers laughed again, but this time, in solidarity with Son's poker-face, Mao did not. Instead, he turned to Son and stretched out his hand. 'Mr Son offered his guarantee to the management that you will be co-operative. You must not let Mr Son down. The company gives face to Mr Son. You workers should also give Mr Son face.' As he finished, he stood up. 'It's midnight already! Don't worry about a thing!' He virtually lifted Son up and pushed him all the way down the stairs.

Day 4: 3 June 1986 (Tuesday)

Mao truly deserved to be at the top of his profession. He was a magician. Misrepresenting the case with perfect composure, he had completely convinced Son. Even the workers were confused by the unlikely story, but there was nothing they could do about it. All the references were there, but were systematically distorted. But it was late, and people were too tired to care.

Some time after 1:00 a.m. Woo and Po Lo-du, the gigantic foreman, followed by four young males, came down with Polaroid cameras, telling the pickets they were going to take pictures. In the canteen, they took pictures of the lockers, the window frame, and the banners on the wall. Gu and Fu and some of the workers woke up and followed the six-person team upstairs, where they continued taking pictures of everything, including the members of the picket team sleeping in the corridor. This irritated the workers. Some of those whose pictures were taken were young women wearing shorts. This constituted harassment, and they complained. The men went into the office without responding. The workers then asked Fu to get the photos back. Fu went into the office but was unsuccessful. The workers went to the police, who had been stationed in the factory since the sit-in. The policeman did not want to bother, but finally promised to get the pictures back. However, he came out without the photos and told the workers to forget about it. The workers insisted. He went in again. Once more, he came out empty-handed, but assured the workers that the pictures were only of bodies and legs, no faces. To his surprise, this made it worse. Neither the workers nor Woo and his men would back down. The policeman then reported to headquarters by radio.

In ten minutes, a tall Caucasian commander, followed by twenty-some police of the special anti-riot unit, dashed into the corridor only to find the atmosphere quite calm. He interrogated the workers, took their depositions, and then rushed out with his armed brigade like a cyclone, leaving tremendous animosity and ill will between the workers and the management.

At 8:00 a.m., Ma Po-kwan arrived with the workers who had gone home for the evening. When he learned from Gu and Fu that, contrary to Lin's urging, no news release had been dispatched, he angrily showed them a few newspapers with stories on the sit-in based on management sources and biased against the workers.

According to the papers, the management spokeswoman, Chan Mei-fon, had declared that the dispute was due to a misunderstanding by the JWM daily-rated workers concerning the merger, and that the fifteen RP's had taken the company's questionnaires and forbidden their fellow workers from contacting their foremen. Nineteen workers had been dismissed for repeatedly defying the management's fair and reasonable request, but their dismissal did not change management's willingness to rehire all JWM employees. Tosai had stated that rumours had worsened the misunderstanding, and advised the workers to resume production and not to worry, as they would be rehired under better welfare conditions.

Ms Chan had also referred to an announcement posted by the management the day before, which had declared that it was to be a normal working day, that the recent slow-down would not be allowed, and that workers would be dismissed if it continued. She commented that if negotiations were successful, management would not execute the terms of the announcement, but if the workers persisted, the troublemakers would all be fired. She further explained that the management had not acknowledged the status of the RPs because they wanted every worker to understand the conditions for reinstatement and sign the agreement.

What was this reported announcement? Neither Ma nor Gu nor Fu knew of it! They went up to the fifth floor and finally managed to locate a handwritten sheet of paper among piles of posters. The management had expected that it would go unnoticed by the workers but would serve to support their case in the media.

―――――

Ma insisted on a strategy meeting. Most of the RPs were still sleeping or were having breakfast, so Ma, Gu and Fu held their discussion without them. They agreed that Son and Mao had not improved the situation, and then agreed on three points:
1. Not to give in to the management's postponement tactics;
2. To protect the fifteen RPs, insisting that all documents be signed by them alone; and
3. To clarify public announcements made by the management.

They analysed possible scenarios. Management could secure an injunction order from the court — Mao had actually hinted this the previous night. Other situations were imagined and countermeasures proposed. Ma emphasized the importance of establishing a 'normal' working schedule for the sitting-in workers to strengthen their endurance. They should also begin to think of ways to end the sit-in and claim victory. He suggested that the agreement and its conditions, no matter how ridiculous, could be accepted, provided it was co-signed by Mao, Son, and the Japanese consul-general.

Ma then proposed a general meeting. Some of the RPs had now joined them, and volunteered to speak. Chu Chi-lin wanted to lead the discussion of the essence of the management's proposal: to accept the four points on condition that they give up further pursuit of 'the money'. Chien Fa-hin agreed to analyse what Son and Mao had said. Lo Un-pu wanted to refute the management's version of the firing of the workers. Together RPs agreed to mention the rumour that management already had an injunction order and might fire everyone if the sit-in continued. After these presentations, opinions from the rank and file would be solicited, and a binding poll would be conducted.

Before the meeting plan could be properly worked out, Gu and Fu were 'invited' a fourth time by Mao to go to the fifth floor to 'chat' with management. This time they went.

By now the canteen was bustling with activity. Reporters and members of various labour and social organizations were chatting. People sensed that something crucial was imminent.

When Gu and Fu came down fifteen minutes later, they immediately gathered all supporters from various organizations. Gu explained that Mao had wanted Fu and herself to meet with management, but they had refused, so he now wanted every group with representatives present to have a chat with management to help resolve the deadlock. Most of these supporters were from local grassroots groups sensitive about transgressing the subjectivity and rights of the workers, who shared a distaste for the working style of the labour officers and big union heads, their technocratic approach, and their proclamations of being the workers' proxies. A consensus was reached — none of them would talk to the management. Instead, they suggested that management have direct talks with the workers and their representatives.

Gu and Fu took the message and soon returned: Management wanted them to reconsider. They took Ma aside and told him that Mao had suggested that management would want at least to talk with him, because 'it seemed that the workers believed in him'. Fu had been astonished and had tried to protect Ma, a visitor from a foreign country, by saying that he was only there to observe, but Mao had screamed that he 'observed' with a loudspeaker by his side all the time!

Ma took this 'invitation' as a warning: The Hong Kong government had been known to expel activists. He felt threatened, but he immediately took the issue to the workers and other groups. During the discussion, some of the group representatives had changed their minds and were about to accept the invitation. He opposed them, on the grounds that no real militant unionist would talk to management without workers present. It was then suggested that management should come down to talk with the supporting unionists in the presence of the workers. Gu and Fu took this suggestion upstairs but came down a few minutes later without a reply, although they had noticed foremen running about on the fifth floor and intense discussions taking place inside the office.

While everyone was guessing what was happening upstairs, Mao came rushing straight towards Ma. Ma stood up and clapped his hands, 'Mr Mao is coming to listen to us. Let's welcome him!'

In response, people rushed towards them, surrounded them and sat down — so swiftly that Ma found himself sitting down next to Mao. Before he could even figure out the introductions, vivid, bitter stories of the workers' factory life began to pour out, and the canteen hall echoed with sobbing from various corners. There were endless stories of abuse, disparagement and oppression by loitering managers and foremen, by chauvinistic males, by the enforcement of 'scientific' management. Chen Siu-guan told the story of their Singaporean production manager, who had devised a bell to discipline the workers' bladders. The whole floor was supposed to urinate twice in the morning and twice in the afternoon, when the bell was rung. 'Once I was wet through to my feet ... ' She could not finish her story. Weeping hysterically, she jumped up, dashed out of the hall and down the stairs.

The spontaneous outpouring had been unexpected. Ma commented, 'An ice-sheet three feet thick takes more than one day to form.'

Mao nodded reluctantly and replied that there certainly were some serious managerial problems. Unwittingly, a sigh — so light as almost not to be heard at all — rose from Son's female secretary — 'Those poor little girls!'

Together, Gu and some workers ran down the stairs to comfort Siu-guan. Those who remained continued to volunteer their personal ordeals to whoever was close by — sobbing, whimpering, and patting each other on the back. Pent-up fury was washed away with tears in a collective catharsis. Mao, superfluous, was smart enough to sneak out quickly without people noticing.

Ma Po-kwan stood outside the canteen gate, too emotionally involved to keep the distance necessary for academic observation. Mao ran into him with a sense of relief. Taking Ma as a like-minded student of industrial sociology, Mao initiated a conversation that could only take place between members of the technocratic élite. 'What matters is fairness more than gain! Isn't it?' Politely and professionally, Ma picked up the topic, commenting on the Japanese-style discretionary manipulation of employees' welfare and suggesting that there were deep roots to the workers' grudges. Mao nodded, but had no more time for scholarly discussion. He ran up the stairs to talk to the management.

Mao reappeared about 2:00 p.m. with two lawyers, followed by Woo Char-hwa, Sisuno, Mo Ku-sin, and most of the administrative staff. They approached Fu and Gu, who were sitting at one of the long tables. The Chinese lawyer, Lam Tu-pi, told Gu and Fu that the company was 'inviting' them to leave the factory premises right away, and that there would be no negotiations with the workers until they did so. Lam was being diplomatic, but Mobark Ley, the Caucasian lawyer, held a set of legal documents. Gu asked whether management was applying an injunction to expel them, but Lam replied, 'No, you are invited to leave to enable us to resume negotiations.' The several policemen in the canteen gathered by the gate, holding their walkie-talkies in 'talk' position to communicate with headquarters. The plain-clothes ones, who had been expressing personal sympathy with the rank and file that whole morning, now refrained from talking with the workers.

Fu told Lam that they would first have to consult with the workers, but Lam insisted that it was not necessary. The dispute was the company's internal business and outsiders had to leave.

As the exchange continued, the workers came up to the first-line tables. Increasingly, male staff gathered by the gate, opposite the workers and less than two metres away. Tension mounted.

All Lam had to say was no and again no, even refusing Gu's request to gather her personal belongings. At this, the workers advanced one step, encircling Gu and Fu and holding them tight. They shouted, 'Don't go! Don't leave us! Let them expel all of us!'

'Such a sentimental Cantonese movie!' said Woo sarcastically.

Po Lo-du added, 'Don't you want to keep them overnight again?'

The obvious sexual reference pushed the confrontation to an explosive point, and management had to step back from the canteen gate, while Mao jumped in to calm the workers. Chen Siu-guan screamed and rushed forward at Po Lo-du, but Mao held her back.

'Don't pretend you are innocent young girls,' Po said, pouring oil on the fire. Only then did those on the management side, including Woo, scold Po and order him upstairs.

The quasi expulsion exercise thus fell apart, sabotaged not by the workers but by management themselves. Bitter weeping and acrimonious curses sporadically lashed through the canteen as Siu-guan was consoled by her co-workers. The management did not know what to do, but stood by the gate, as they had been instructed not to give in.

The two parties were deadlocked. Fu grabbed a loudspeaker and jumped on a table. He looked at each worker and spoke clearly. 'Do you believe in yourselves? Do you know what you are fighting for?'

'Yes,' the workers replied.

'You have been fighting all along, efficiently and proudly, haven't you?'

'Yes!' they shouted.

'You will keep fighting, right?'

'Yes!'

'Keep on fighting with or without me and Gu around, right?'

'Yes!' The reply was much weaker this time.

'Be sure that you are not dismissed on grounds of being led by outsiders, and be sure all the gung-ho unionists aren't slandered as imposing their will on you. You have never been used and will never be used by anyone. We all have great confidence in you. Do you have even greater confidence in yourselves?'

'Yes!' The response was loud again.

'We will back you, and we will be available at any moment. Let us show them our unity by not being afraid of physical separation. Let's show them how well every one of you can fight, right?'

'Right!'

'Come cheerfully to see us off and get on with the negotiations. You must win!'

On the fifth floor, the RPs sat waiting for the meeting, but then management changed its mind and decided it should be held on the fourth floor, in front of all the workers. The workers suspected they would be expelled from the fifth floor and at first refused, but settled on the fourth-floor canteen, while the picket team watched the fifth-floor office. The RPs were forced to sit facing the management with their backs to the workers, an arrangement designed to create an atmosphere of alienation among the workers and to intimidate them.

The management team included the two lawyers, Woo, three Japanese, Mao and Tu from the Labour Bureau, and Son Yan-min's female secretary. Mao volunteered to moderate the meeting.

The meeting began with the workers asking about management's four points, which they had already accepted. Lam replied that recent radio broadcasts biased against the management demonstrated that the workers were still distorting the facts. Regarding the request that all workers sign the agreement, he said that it was not just the thirty-six dismissed workers who were involved, but all of them; hence, all the workers should sign, to guarantee their future co-operation.

Suddenly Mao stood up and left the canteen, without explanation. Tu took over as moderator.

The workers questioned how management could justify firing the thirty-six workers. Lam repeated that it was their prerogative and revealed a new point: Those who had been fired had refused to acknowledge that the daily-rated welfare scheme had nothing to do with that of the monthly-rated.

'You mean those who had been given the letter of dismissal?' asked Chu Chi-lin.

'Yes,' replied Lam.

'How about those of us who were not given letters of dismissal?' she asked.

'People who were not given a letter of dismissal, legally speaking, were not dismissed,' Lam asserted.

'The management just reneged on its word yesterday and imposed extra terms on us. "Legally speaking" doesn't mean much to them, does it?' Chu continued. 'Yes, there were disparities between the monthly-rated and ourselves. They strolled about with folded hands, chatting and eating snakes while we worked like machines, prohibited even from going to the toilet. Who is going to accept this kind of discrimination?'

Tu replied, 'The management admits there is room for improvement.'

'What about our reinstatement?'

The Japanese-speaking management team then discussed among themselves in Japanese, without answering. Lam picked another topic.

'About the long-service gratuities, there is some need for clarification. Those who have worked for five to seven years will be paid thirty-two days' wages upon leaving; eight to ten years, forty-eight days; and over ten years, sixty-four days. This was set up in 1982. You don't know of it because only high-level management can read the document. The company's policy is not to publicize it.'

'Are you sure that the scheme didn't exist before '82?' asked Hon Lai-fon, who had been working for more than ten years.

Again the lawyers and management conferred without responding.

'How high is the "high-level management?"' asked Hu Hon-chi, another veteran of over ten years.

'Assistant manager and above,' Lam answered.

'Are you kidding? We were told of the scheme before the factory moved to these premises by someone lower than assistant manager. You'd better do your homework before instructing us.' Hu and Hon joined forces.

Once again the management spoke among themselves in Japanese. Then Woo burst out, 'You guys are talking about these discrepancies only to create a pretext. What you really are up to is the so-called "mysterious money".'

'Yes, you are right. The monthly-rated get it and we also deserve it,' countered most of the RPs.

Lam, angry and shamed, shouted, 'If you don't believe my words, no more negotiations. You want to talk, you'd better believe me!'

In a hierarchical society like Hong Kong, such conduct violates the propriety that accompanies high status. It was self-debasing for a general manager and an attorney to jump on the workers, and it provoked a reaction. Jumping out from the workers' row was the emotional Siu-guan, who pointed her finger at Woo and screamed, 'You fire me, you fire me, right? Just pay me the wages and the legal compensation you owe me, and I'll never see you guys again!'

Woo, with a cunning smile, coldly murmured, 'Sure we will! Don't you worry about that!'

It was becoming a dogfight. The workers watching the fifth-floor office rushed into the canteen, but before they could talk to their representatives, a member of management also rushed in and whispered in Woo's ear. Woo nodded, and then loudly announced that the factory gate would be locked that night at seven o'clock. 'Tomorrow will be a normal working day. The thirty-six workers need not come back. The others who do not come to work will be considered to have resigned. The seventeen of the thirty-six who have not received their dismissal envelopes will be officially notified of their dismissal before seven o'clock.'

To his disappointment, his announcement surprised no one. Some foremen came down and began calling the names of those who were to go upstairs for their dismissal envelopes.

Just then Mao Si-hai dashed through the gate and stopped one of the foremen. He turned to Woo and began to argue with him and the Japanese in English. Lam and Ley then stood up, turned to the workers behind them, and urged those dismissed to go upstairs for their notices and the others to come to work the next day. 'If you don't want to lose your jobs!'

Mao, who had been trying to silence the lawyers, suddenly faced the workers. 'We shall adjourn for one hour!' He pushed the management team out and up the stairs.

Back in the joint office of TWLSC and CKLRS, Gu, Fu, and the other expelled support-group personnel discussed countermeasures. They had learned from their journalist friends that management was going to hold a press conference in an hour, and when Chien Fon-yi called to report the further dismissals, they decided to hold their own, at the Labour Relations Association (LRA) in Kowloon at 8:00 p.m. Fon-yi was told to send a few RPs.

More than twenty reporters were waiting at the LRA when Gu and the workers arrived. Five RPs spoke, emphasizing that management had once again broken their word and had fired RPs during negotiations, thus suppressing their newly-formed union. At one point a stranger suddenly jumped up and interrogated the workers. No one knew who he was, or what paper, if any, he represented. After this unexpected episode, an announcement concerning union-busting and the disregard of the workers' right to collective bargaining, signed by twelve local labour organizations, was read out. The CLA had not signed the document, although it had sent a representative to 'observe' the press conference.

Negotiations resumed at about 8:30 p.m. Only Mao spoke, saying he hoped the dispute would be resolved peacefully to everyone's satisfaction. He agreed that the welfare of the daily-rated workers should be looked into, but said the workers should resume production as soon as possible. There would be a 'gentlemen's agreement' between the two sides later, which would include provisions for 'long-term service payment' amounting to two-thirds of a month's wages — eighteen days' wages — per year, although those who had worked for fewer than two years would get only seven days' wages. Anyone 'voluntarily resigning' could take her wage compensation for annual leave right away and come back to collect the long-term service payment later.

Because it had been a long day and because the workers felt they had won, the meeting turned into something like a tea party, with the workers joking and playing with the Japanese lower management. No one cared about the terms of the negotiations any more.

At that very moment, in the fifth-floor inner office, a news conference was taking place. The top five in management, with their Japanese headquarters envoys, were being directed and coached by 'experts' from the biggest American public relations firm, Beagos and Tayler, which they had hired the previous day as crisis-management specialists. Ms Chan Mei-fon had been sent to handle all publicity. Some of the points which were made became available to the workers only when they appeared in the newspapers the next morning.

When Gu got back to the factory from the LRA with the five RPs it was almost 10 p.m. She stayed on the fourth-floor staircase to avoid harassment from the newly-hired private security guards (JWM paid rent on the factory rooms and offices, but not the staircase). From there she could hear the raised voices of Chen Siu-guan and Lo Un-pu. Lo angrily reprimanded Chen for disregarding the agreed-upon format and her lack of discipline during negotiations; Chen objected that she, an elected representative, had as much a right as anyone to speak her mind. Their conflict attracted the workers' attention, and the other RPs tried hard to stop it. The situation was rather chaotic.

During this confusion the pro-China 'left' labour leader, Son Yan-min, arrived with his female secretary, went directly to the canteen and conducted a 'direct public opinion survey' among the workers. No security guards raised an eyebrow at this. They were obviously not unwelcome. After a few minutes Hsiao Chia, the picket team leader, ran from the canteen to the staircase, grabbed Gu and urged her to get hold of all the RPs and send them to the canteen, telling her the workers were 'talking about everyone quitting and accepting monetary compensation. The workers have not heard what had happened at the negotiation table, and the representatives have not bothered to tell them; we must get the representatives back inside.'

Gu ran down the stairs and tried to persuade those she ran into to go back to the canteen. Some, including representatives, did so, but at least the same number continued to descend. When Gu returned to the fourth-floor staircase, Son and his secretary had already left the canteen and had gone up to the fifth floor to talk to the management.

Hsiao Chia complained about the disorganization and the RPs' lack of communication with the workers. She insisted that a representatives' self-examination meeting be held immediately. In the meeting she made a fierce critique, and suggested that the RPs meet more frequently and that their meetings include some non-representatives to serve as liaison with the workers. Her suggestions were adopted. The core members of the picket teams would preside at the meeting, and be responsible for transmitting information back and forth, if necessary, with the rank and file. However, there was neither a discussion of the management's pay-to-sack proposal nor of Son's all-embracing one-stroke solution — pay on resignation.

Day 5: 4 June 1986 (Wednesday)

Early in the morning, before the factory buses arrived, the picket team was divided into small brigades. Around 7:30 a.m. they went downstairs to watch their fellow workers alight from the buses. Using portable loudspeakers,

Women Worker's representatives petitioned in front of UMELCO in Central on 4 June 1986 (Day 5).

TV anchors and reporters of various presses covered the petition on 4 June 1986 (Day 5).

they guided their colleagues to the canteen. Most workers who had gone home for the night returned by bus. They were told there would be no more negotiations that day, and that management had agreed to let them wait on the fourth and fifth floors. There was no need to punch in or to go to the shop-floor. They were also advised to keep cool and not to argue among themselves. Everything was well co-ordinated by Chi-mei and Hsiao Chia. Chen Siu-guan was enthusiastic and was excitedly bossing people around.

Meanwhile, an extended representatives' meeting took place on the roof-top. Fu briefed them on management statements of the previous night which had been printed in the newspapers that morning, but before he had the chance to finish the RPs stopped him and said to forget about trivial matters. Unconvinced, he reported that some newspapers said the company wished to 'rehire' the sacked workers later, but had to sack seventeen more now. Laughter was the response. He insisted on reading out a headline which stated that the dispute would soon be settled since there had been genuine 'direct' talks between the workers and the administration. The workers scolded him this time. Gu reported the Son formula: that everyone quit with a payment of twelve days' wages. Lo Un-pu called Son crazy, and others agreed: Son had never been on their side. He only thought of money, but the workers were fighting for reinstatement. Neglectful and ignorant of the workers' main goal, what he proposed just sowed discord among workers, whether intended or not.

Then Chi-mei rushed in to urge the representatives to go down to the canteen for a general meeting/rally. The foremen and line leaders had come down to try to split the workers and get them to work, but they had held hands and sung their battle-song until the foremen and leaders gave up and left. Everyone laughed after they had gone.

Chi-mei, who, because of her good human relations and hard work, had been in charge of logistics, was urged to take charge of discipline and order, and to moderate the general meeting in the absence of Gu, Fu, and the other militant volunteers.

The rally was reported to the Centre as having been successful. Three resolutions were passed.

1. The thirty-six dismissed must be reinstated.
2. The 6 percent back pay (the so-called 'mysterious' money) must be included in any overall settlement.
3. Their union must be able to operate and to exercise the right to collective bargaining after a settlement was reached.

The workers denounced the management for its lack of sincerity in dealing with them. In the announcement, the Japanese administrative style was challenged. Finally, there were calls to resume contact with JETCON workers and for a renewed push to complete union registration.

At the meeting, the workers discussed Tosai's claim to the press of the previous night: that all dismissal letters had been passed on to the Labour Bureau by JWM management, and that it was for the Labour Bureau to forward them to the individual workers. However, neither the Labour Bureau nor the management had commented on the matter. Something was fishy! Tosai had also told the reporters that injunction orders would be applied to workers who 'interrupted or hindered production'.

In response, the meeting agreed to the following measures:
1. At least twenty workers to sit-in at the factory no matter what happened;
2. About fifty workers to stage demonstrations at UMELCO, to appeal for public sympathy;
3. A special team of ten pickets to be stationed at the gate to watch the management and respond to whatever might happen;
4. A third-front elected leadership of more than twenty to
    (a) assist the representatives and second-line leaders,
    (b) familiarize themselves with all tasks, and
    (c) get ready to assume leadership in case the first- and second-front leaders were incapacitated or expelled.
5. In case of an injunction order, the workers would wait for instructions: no one was to go home on their own initiative.

As the workers held their meeting, Gu and Fu went back to the Centre to consult with Ma about Lo Man-sa, the head of the CLA, who had called the Director of CKLRS, Kwai Chung District Board Member Lin Yi-chin, when he learned that Son Yan-min was involved in the dispute. Lo had requested an invitation to 'give a hand' and talk to the workers. Lin said he would relay the message and let the workers decide. Lo had called Lin again the previous night and again that morning to ask when he could come. Lin had called the Centre and wanted Gu, Fu and Ma to think it through and call him back.

After some discussion, the three of them decided that Son's intervention was dangerous. He was inexperienced, wilful, and stubborn. Worse, as a LEGCO member and figurehead of the FLU, he had one foot in the Hong Kong British administration and the other in the Chinese shadow power, and to serve the interests of either, or both, he had to be a hard-line champion of 'stability and prosperity' in Hong Kong. In addition, bad blood had been brewing between him and Lo, as Son had refused to help Lo become a consultant labour representative for the 'Basic Law', and the brief honeymoon between the 'independent' CLA and the FLU had ended after that. The FLU was once again ready to attempt to consolidate power and monopolize labour organizing, in support of the regime-to-be and its capitalist allies. Given this situation, Lo had to be careful about Son's moves: It was easy to understand his eagerness to get involved. Over the past decades, the FLU had not organized workers at all; it had been the 'independent' unionists and their religious-group backers who had led labour activism in Hong Kong. Among them, Lo had emerged as a popular leader, representing the 'prudent' strategists, who now concentrated on augmenting their influence in the face of the renewed onslaught by the Chinese-backed FLU — another reason why Lo was so eager.

Given the struggle for leadership between these 'superpowers', the Centre activists could only hope to balance them out. By maintaining an equilibrium between them, the small local groups might still find room to manoeuvre.

Lo arrived at the factory just before 2:00 p.m. and was greeted warmly by the workers on the fourth floor. He claimed to be on the workers' side: They should fight both for dignity — to reinstate their colleagues — and for the money they had been denied. Amidst cheering and applause, he left for the fifth floor to push the management to resume negotiations.

Time passed and the workers became impatient. Some workers thought management was delaying because they had learned of the planned demonstration in front of UMELCO, whose weekly meetings usually adjourned around 5:00 p.m. This concern was brought to the Centre, and it was decided that some workers would proceed to UMELCO and meet Lin Yi-chin there.

The 'negotiating' session was not called until 3:35 p.m. Mobark Ley waited until the RPs had sat down and become quiet before announcing that the meeting had to adjourn at 4:30 p.m., as the factory would shut its doors then and use injunction orders, if necessary, to expel all workers until the next morning. He then made the same offer as the previous night: Anyone who wanted to quit would be paid fifteen days' wages plus seven days.

The RPs created an uproar. Some accused management of going back on their word by firing workers during negotiations. Some asked if the space in front of the lift belonged to the factory. Was it covered by the injunction order? Ley had nothing to say. He advised the dismissed thirty-six workers not to return the next day, as the management was going to post their names and announce their official dismissal.

'Why don't you carve our names on the factory walls!' Chu Chi-lin replied.

Everyone laughed, including management. The local Labour Bureau chief, Tu, stood up to suggest resuming negotiations the next morning at 11:00 a.m., but there were objections, mostly from management.

At this point Chien Fon-yi sneaked out of the meeting room and went down to the street with Chi-mei to report to the Centre. Ma instructed

Chien to rush directly to UMELCO. In case there was a communication breakdown, she was to report to Lin and Fu in person to facilitate the beginning of the demonstration.

Lin was already on the square, near the colonial-style UMELCO Hall. He called the Centre, and Ma told him what he had learned from Chien Fon-yi a few minutes earlier. Lin was not surprised. He said that now the workers could make an issue out of the management's arbitrary behaviour; the management had promised Son, the FLU vice-president and UMELCO member, that they would not evict the workers before the negotiation was concluded. What they had just done was a public slap in the face.

Fu and about forty workers soon showed up at the square. Lin immediately consulted with Fu and decided on a change in strategy. Instead of appealing to UMELCO, Hong Kong's 'parliament', they would approach Son Yan-min, who had been hand-picked for UMELCO by the colonial authority to be the 'functional' representative of Labour. Having involved himself in the dispute, he could make a major political gain if he succeeded in 'putting out the fire'. This would entail political risks, since risk always accompanies gain — as idealized in the *laissez-faire* economy of Hong Kong — but it was only fair to ask him to iron out the problem created by the management.

Inside the UMELCO building, Lin, as a Kwai Tsing District Board member, requested an emergency consultation with Son. Son wore an extremely long face. He listened to Lin concerning the most recent developments at the factory. Lin urged him to call JWM management and halt the expulsion. Son was not sure what to do, but promised to relay the results of his telephone call to the workers.

Outside, the workers were lined up in front of the building waving their banners, and reporters came forward to cover the story. Ho-chie, a second-floor worker, spoke for her colleagues. Easygoing and outspoken, she made an ideal interviewee. The demonstration was reported in all the papers the next morning, and both television stations showed the workers making a spectacular display of singing and shouting slogans.

When Son emerged, the demonstration caught him by surprise. He refused to discuss any details with Lin, but informed him that he had called both the Labour Bureau and the management, and that the latter had agreed not to expel the sit-in workers, so everyone should 'go home' and stop putting on 'shows'. He told reporters that it was normal for both sides to swing back and forth in their decisions, and it was important for both parties to remain level-headed in seeking solutions. He then left, avoiding further questions. The workers also dispersed, some for home and a few to the Centre with Fu.

At the Centre, some twenty female workers from JETCON, all daily operatives, had arrived to demand a closed-door meeting with Gu. They had come to inquire about the strike and sit-in at JWM and to report changes at JETCON, where there were meetings taking place between managers and foremen almost every day. Every department called meetings with workers, who were warned not to 'make any trouble'. The workers claimed there were policies to lay off old workers, to minimize trouble and hold back all severance payments.

Gu asked them what they were going to do, but they replied that there was nothing they could do. They were desperate and disappointed, but they did not want to fight for themselves, and some began complaining that the JWM workers had tried to 'use' them, and that the JWM workers were fighting only for themselves and had discarded them after they had outlasted their use! Though extremely irritated, Gu tried not to hurt anyone's feelings, and adjourned the meeting.

A heated debate was ignited by Lin Yi-chin's report of the JWM sit-in to a Joint Council of Independent Unions and Labour Organizations (JCIULO) meeting. Lin suggested that the leaders of independent unions, like the Federation of Civil Service Unions (FCSU), initiate a first-hand investigation of the situation. Shih Ding-yi, the labour organizer of the

CLA, strongly objected to the idea and tried hard to prevent other parties from getting involved, but in doing so he actually strengthened their interest.

'There is no use arguing. Why don't you guys just go to the factory premises to have a look?' Lin suggested, cutting short the debate. His suggestion was accepted, the meeting was adjourned, and about fifteen people went with him to the factory. Shih Ding-yi refused to go.

At the factory, fewer than 100 workers had stayed overnight. They found it highly encouraging that representatives of so many labour groups had come to visit. They told their stories and their thoughts on the struggle, and various unionists promised to relay them to their own rank and file. Before leaving at about 9:00 p.m., they held hands with the workers and repeatedly sang their battle hymn. Lee Siu-ching, chairman of the FCSU, stayed on.

At about this time, Lo Man-sa called Lin Yi-chin from the hotel room of 'a very important person from JWM's Japanese headquarters', who had just arrived. He was trying to negotiate with him on the workers' behalf, but he could not say anything more. He urged the workers in the factory to refrain from taking any action, even from singing. It was obvious that Shih Ding-yi had informed him that the unionists had decided to visit the factory. Sensing intricate dealings, Lin replied, 'Why don't you come in and try to convince the workers yourself?' Lo, after some discussion on the other end of the line, agreed to come.

When Lo stepped out of the elevator on the fourth floor of the factory, however, he froze. Before him was 'Big Mouth' Ah-ton, a rare self-proclaimed Trotskyite, who had arrived with other activists from the Labour and Residents Coalition (LRC). Although the workers urged Lo to report what had happened at the hotel, he was extremely reluctant to say anything. Hemming and hawing, he merely said that it was tough to negotiate with the Japanese top management, who were the ones standing fast against the workers' demands. 'Big Mouth' simply could not keep himself from capitalizing on this opportunity, and began to blast the so-called unionists who 'pretended' to represent the workers but were practising 'secret diplomacy'. He was so excited that no one, not even Lin, could stop him.

To avoid embarrassment and to learn what had happened, Lin invited Lo to 'go out for a coffee'. Lee Siu-ching joined them. They gathered on the staircase until midnight, and left only when they learned that the gates were closed and no one was allowed in.

Day 6: 5 June 1986 (Thursday)

At 9 a.m., some 100 workers gathered on the fourth-floor canteen to hold their general meeting. Those who had not attended the UMELCO demonstration demanded a detailed report of the event. Ho-chie, whose pictures were in almost every newspaper, told the story vividly and comically, and canteen filled with laughter. Afterwards, the RPs reported the reasons for the breakdown in negotiations. A poll led to decisions:
1. to demand for reinstatement; and, if that failed,
2. to fight for *en masse* dismissal compensation;
3. to insist on the workers' right to organize and to oppose any persecution for doing so; and
4. to demand negotiations and peaceful solutions.

An evening of 'celebrating the JWM 20,000-hour /person sit-in' on 5 June 1986 (Day 6).

The meeting ended before 11:00 a.m. Although people waited and waited, no negotiation session was called.

At 1:30 p.m. Lo Man-sa appeared with Mao Si-hai, Tu Pi-sin and his deputy, Ms Lee, to request a briefing. Mao first praised Lo for his efforts at negotiating with management, again emphasizing his skills and persuasive power. He then 'advised the workers to trust him — and the Labour Bureau — but not anyone else'.

Lo explained that the dispute was a matter of misunderstandings caused by badly-handled minor discrepancies. He had clarified with management that the dispute had not been instigated by the thirty-six dismissed, nor by any third party. It was simply a matter of inexperience, on both sides, in dealing with disagreements.

He then analysed the overall situation, advising the workers to ask themselves, 'What kind of trump cards do we have, if any, in our possession?' What would be better: to stay in a hostile working environment or to take the compensation and leave? He said the workers should not have taken action during the negotiations. At present, it was useless for them to meet with the management. Instead, he would mediate between the two parties. The workers must take no further action, and must avoid irritating the management. 'You guys should understand that the management will not pay you the 6 percent that you have requested. If you keep on insisting, it will only make the confrontation worse. And ... ' (Tu Pi-sin tried to interrupt here, but Lo simply talked over him) ' ...what is important is to keep the dialogue going.'

In response to this didacticism, the playful Ho-chie raised her hand to speak. When she was acknowledged, she stood up with both hands behind her back like an elementary school student and voiced sheepishly, 'But all we want is to come to work at the factory and be able to talk!' The workers burst out laughing. Upon that note, the honourable guests stood up and said they had to rush across the harbour to 'negotiate' for them. A loud 'goodbye' was the response.

At the Centre, Gu, Fu and Ma were having a discussion. They had received a call from Lin, who had learned from Lo Man-sa that a top-management team from Japanese headquarters, of at least four members, was in Hong Kong. Lo had given the impression that they refused to even to compromise, and that Lo and the thirty-six workers would inevitably be fired, but with generous compensation. The Japanese top management wished to retain the other workers, but would not give them the 6 percent lump sum, though smaller sums would be given to those who remained. Lo wanted to augment compensation for both groups, and hoped that the Centre would co-operate to calm the workers during negotiations. Lin suggested that the Centre discuss the matter and make a decision as soon as possible.

During the discussion, Chu Chi-lin called to report the details of the session with Lo and the other labour officials. She then asked, 'Since the CLA is working with the Labour Bureau and the Japanese bosses, can't we also augment our support from overseas?' Her question reminded Ma of his acquaintance in Japan, Mr Banata, vice-president of the Japan Nationwide Council of Unions (JNCU). After a brief discussion, it was decided to contact Banata.

Fu now proposed that a rally be held in the factory to raise morale and prepare the workers for the approaching showdown. Gu hesitated, then seconded him. Ma opposed the idea: He did not like having another 'political' gathering under the present circumstances, when neither Gu nor Fu could be present. However, he did realize the value of solidarity with other unions, and he thought the workers needed to relax and enjoy themselves. In the end, the three worked out something more along the lines of a party than a meeting — an evening of 'celebrating the JWM twenty thousand person/hours sit-in'. Gu and Lam Yi-kai went shopping for party goods, and Fu and Ma invited all 'friendly' groups to join in.

When night fell, party goods were brought to the workers' canteen. Soon everyone was involved in preparations. New banners were made, the room was decorated with paper ribbons and balloons, and a portable music system was installed. The celebration turned out to be a great success. Led by Lee Siu-ching, chairman of the Federation of Civil Service Unions

(FCSU), about twenty leaders from various civil service unions, local labour services, youth clubs, church outreaches, and worker/resident coalition groups came with warm regards, drinks, and talent shows. One boy even brought a bouquet of flowers.

Everyone was having a good time when Lo Man-sa called from JETCON and complained to the workers' leaders, blaming them for the 'action' and warning them that management was greatly irritated. He said that it caused great damage to negotiations. He was also discontented with Lee Siu-ching, formerly his ally, over the party. Obviously, local factory management had reported the celebration to their superiors, who were meeting with Lo at JETCON, where they used this piece of information to exert pressure on Lo. The leaders explained that there was no action, they were merely entertaining themselves, but Lo almost shouted, 'Why do you get all the "third parties" involved in your entertainment? That is what is called "action".' The conversation stopped short of a quarrel, as the leaders abruptly ended the party.

As Lee Siu-ching and other unionists were leaving, Gu, Fu, and Bao Yi-hai (the head of the Labour and Residents Coalition, a schoolteacher by profession) were on their way in. Bao, after hours of inconclusive discussion with Gu and Fu at the Centre, insisted on presenting his arguments directly to the workers. It took a while for them to get most of the RPs, who were cleaning up the canteen, up to the rooftop.

Bao had brought a 'resolution' passed by his group: an 'Analysis of the Overall Situation of the Confrontation and Available Counteracting Measures'. In their view, 'the Hong Kong workers' struggle as manifested in the JWM strike' was entering a crucial conjunction, and 'the outcome of this important battle' concerned not only JWM workers' immediate gain or loss, but constituted a part of Hong Kong workers' overall struggle. Based on their analysis, it was suggested that the strikers move to the street and demonstrate outside the Japanese consulate till their demands were met.

Bao was surprised when his group's position failed to impress the workers. This was partially a result of his pushiness. With no history of working together with workers or of building mutual trust, his task was difficult. Fu got into a heated debate with him, and in an hour they were both exhausted.

Near midnight, Fu and the RPs agreed that workers should demand the right to participate in the negotiations between Lo Man-sa and management. Otherwise, Bao declared, 'the workers should go to the meeting site and stage a demonstration there.' It was finally suggested that an emergency meeting be held in the morning.

The RPs then rushed down to the canteen for the night. Finally, they had a chance to rest.

Day 7: 6 June 1986 (Friday)

A little after 8:00 a.m., all fifteen workers' RPs arrived at the Centre. Gu, Fu, Lin and Bao had to stand to make room for them. After a briefing, Bao suggested that the RPs go to where negotiations were taking place between Lo Man-sa and the Japanese top management. It was extremely dangerous to have the 'union establishment' act as the self-proclaimed representative of the workers. Information from his journalist-friends confirmed that four Japanese, including JWM's managing director, legal advisor, and 'labour union experts', had flown in a few days previously. The RPs had to be present at the negotiations, and if they were refused entrance, they should sit in at the meeting site. When Fu challenged the last point, Lin intervened and suggested leaving the option open.

Lin made a phone call to Lo's residence to ask if they could participate. Lo replied that he had to consult with the management first. When he called back, he said that the management would not hold any negotiations. As far as he could tell, there was no possibility for the thirty-six dismissed workers to be reinstated. However, compensation had been suggested, and he would come to the Centre to inform them of the details.

Before Lin had finished relaying Lo's message, Chu Chi-lin and her allies interrupted him. 'What details! You don't need details to fire workers!' It was obvious that management was postponing a peaceful solution and denying collective bargaining. The management had invoked new conditions; when the workers accepted them, they backed off. They could only conclude that the management totally lacked sincerity. Bao agreed.

He assured them that, given the postwar history of Japanese management union-busting, their aim was to destroy the union. To defend their right to organize, industrial action had to be upgraded.

A consensus had already been reached to call a general meeting when Lo walked in. Immediately, a show of light-heartedness was put on, and the discussion descended into trivial chatting. Lin went to greet Lo, who was confused by the unlikely atmosphere.

'Ready for dim sum? Let's go before we starve!' shouted Fu. Gu echoed him. They hid their notes and, with the RPs, ran out of the office.

Lo, however, was also crafty, and he responded, 'Right, let's go for dim sum. I haven't had any breakfast either. It's on me. Let's go, let's go!' Gu and Fu's scheme to continue the meeting and avoid Lo was thus defeated but, as the Chinese proverb has it, 'Newborn calves fear not the tiger.' They were not ready to give up, either.

Everyone walked to the restaurant. As they ate, the environment rendered serious discussion impossible, but Lo decided to do his best. He sat with the workers, persisting in presenting his message over the hustle-and-bustle of the noisy restaurant.

'What about those who were not fired but are unwilling to stay?' asked one of the workers.

'Well, you can always resign. The management proposed that those who resign will get something: Those with over two years of service may get twenty-some days' wages. It would increase with the duration of service. You all know that!'

'What about our union? If everybody leaves, who's going to run our union?' asked another worker.

'We should not mention the union at present. If we do, the management may target the thirty-six dismissed even more. They will be even more reluctant to make concessions.'

Lo found it difficult to respond satisfactorily to all the questions. Finally, Gu intervened, not to rescue Lo, but because she believed that the discussion would end in trivial details and jeopardize morale. She thought of what Ma had repeatedly said, 'Every proposal from the management, no matter what, must be put down in black and white, to prevent them from evading and denying. Why don't you go get the proposal written down? It would greatly facilitate the workers' decision-making,' Gu suggested.

'Yes, why don't we go get the proposal in writing?' responded Hon Lai-fon. Chen Siu-guan, the easily-excited representative from the second floor, agreed, and the two of them stood up to leave with Lo.

'No. Only one person should go with Mr Lo,' Gu shouted. She had intended to get rid of Lo and to stop trivial talk, but she disliked the idea of workers going along with Lo to the management. In response, Lo stood up and left, and Chen and Hon followed, leaving the others uneasy.

It was almost 10:30 a.m. when Gu, Fu, Lin, and the five remaining RPs returned to the Centre. The RPs then headed back to the factory to bring their colleagues to the afternoon meeting in the third-floor meeting hall of St. Stephen's Church. They were surprised to find that a few members of the 'Unions of Metalworkers' — controlled by the pro-China FLU — had been on the fourth floor since 9:00 a.m., chatting with the workers. The picket team guarding the factory said that the two RPs, Hon Lai-fon and Chen Siu-guan, were still in the fifth-floor office. In order to prevent any alarm, the RPs decided to sneak the workers out in small groups and leave the picket teams guarding the canteen and the fifth-floor office.

At about 1:00 p.m., about 100 workers arrived at St. Stephen's Church. They were asked to sit in small groups for briefing by their respective leaders and to discuss possible action. Then the RPs were called on stage, and the general meeting began. After a bit of morale-boosting by the leading RPs, Fu and Gu decided to say something before the workers broke into small groups again to work out their action plans.

Fu analysed the overall situation from the point of view of a workers' collective, and then called for the workers to speak out openly. 'Only when there is sufficient public debate can a well-rounded strategy be formed. Only after all of you speak your mind can you best be served,' Fu concluded.

Ma found this too abstract. He hopped on the stage, and after a few words with Gu, took over the microphone. He wanted to tell some stories of other important labour struggles and use them to reflect upon the current moment. Before he could begin, however, the door of the meeting hall, although guarded by pickets, suddenly slammed shut. Gu jumped on the stage and pulled Ma down. 'They tried to dash in, you get down ... don't know what they want.' Ma didn't know who 'they' were, but he knew he was not supposed to be caught 'inciting' the workers. As a foreigner doing research, he might very well be expelled.

On the stage, Gu gestured to quiet the workers. In a low, calm, clear voice, she said, 'People of the management and the Labour Bureau suddenly appeared and tried to push their way in. Our meeting has to be adjourned for the time being. Everyone stay. I'll be back to inform you as soon as possible.' On her way back to the door, she told Ma and other representatives from friendly groups to stay. But Gu could not get out — the doors were pressed shut by the pickets outside, who were refusing the outsiders entry to the meeting hall. 'No one except the workers are allowed!'

'Why, I'm with you,' protested Lo Man-sa.

'No, no one but the workers themselves.'

Hearing Lo's voice, Gu pounded on the doors and shouted to the pickets on the other side. While Gu calmed Lo down, Fu and Lin were trying to appease the unexpected intruders: the head of the FLU, Son Yan-min; his female secretary; the head of Labour Relations section of the Central Labour Bureau, Mao Si-hai; the Regional Labour Bureau Director, Tu Pi-sin; and his secretary, Ms Lee; and three unknown men, introduced as unionists by Chen Siu-guan and Hon Lai-fon, who were with the group. This strange mix of people complained that it was not fair to exclude them from helping the workers. The Centre staff explained that the workers were having a general meeting, and that they themselves were there because they had borrowed the meeting site. This explanation was rejected, and Gu and Fu were requested to ask the workers if they could join the meeting. Gu and Fu went to consult with the RPs, who compromised: The meeting was not open to others, but since the guests had come in good faith, the meeting would adjourn to let the RPs consult with the 'guests'. The closed-door workers' general meeting would then resume.

The RPs, the nine intruding 'guests', Chen Siu-guan, Hon Lai-fon, Lin Yi-chin, Gu and Fu, met in a seminar room around a large table. Mao Si-hai, with a beaming smile, spoke. 'Although the negotiations with the management have stalemated for days, thanks to Mr Son's, Mr Lo's and others' persistence, a turning point has been reached. A new proposal has been forwarded by the company. Of course, it should be decided on by the workers after discussion. However, before you get into the details, I would like to tell you that I personally told the management that they are the ones responsible for the dispute. I told them that it was not good to have so big a disparity between the monthly-rated and the daily-rated. On the other hand, you must understand that there is a lot of pressure on the management and staff. Were it not for the tremendous efforts of Mr Son and Mr Lo, the situation might have exploded.' Pulling out a piece of paper he tried to convince the RPs point by point, 'The thirty-six will be paid severance pay in full. They can even "voluntarily" resign and not be considered fired. For those who are willing to stay and work for the new company, a twenty-day wage bonus will be awarded on 1 July.' On and on he went, as those who had come with him nodded their heads, and tried to be as cheerful as possible.

Lo then spoke. 'As an independent unionist, I would urge the workers who don't have to go to stay as long as possible, to strengthen your newly-formed union. Frankly speaking, I don't think we have failed at all. There is still plenty of room to improve whatever welfare there is to come. In the final analysis, if we refuse the management proposal what else can we do? I know, you will say: Go out to the street, protest and demonstrate. But pushing to the extreme will invite management to resort to expelling everyone. Please do think it over. Regarding the thirty-six of you who were dismissed, we will try to persuade the management to hire you back later. Although not everyone will be rehired; at least some will.'

'How do we know those who want to stay won't be abused again?' questioned a few RPs.

With unusual eagerness, Mao, Lo and Son responded, 'No written repentance pledging not to commit the same offence again is required; it was a rumour that you'll be forced to admit that it was your fault, or to renounce yourselves or your representatives; we guarantee that there will be no retaliation, or forced confessions.'

The RPs Chu Chi-lin and Chien Fon-yi countered, 'Which of the management suggested that? Does that mean the management don't need to admit their faults? Whose fault was it, anyway?'

Alert to the sensitivity of the issue, Son took the floor. 'I told the Japanese top management that their management was at fault, and I made a few criticisms. The Japanese also realized that there are loopholes. They are definitely willing to improve their ways. But as far as I'm concerned, I would say the workers have achieved much. What we need to do is to consolidate our gains. If we lose sight of what we have achieved and instead insist on fighting mindlessly, we may be the losers, for it is not likely that anything better will come out.'

As Son repeated himself, the meeting disintegrated into small groups. Soon the other unionists joined the discussion about accepting the money and the great moral victory. The structure of discourse was so channelled that no reference was made to the management's proposal by either the intruders or the workers and their allies, and the identifiable positions of people were blurred. The stage now, so to speak, was in total control of the 'intruders'. Reacting to them were Chen Siu-guan and Hon Lai-fon, who had gone with Lo in the morning and had come back with him and the others. At one point, Chen began to joke with one of the unionists who sat beside her and said, 'When we get the thing over with, how about taking pictures with us?'

Meanwhile, the workers waiting in the meeting hall were bored. Their small group discussions fell apart. When Gu entered, they all went up to her. Some complained about the long wait, others inquired what was going on 'in the small closed room'. Gu asked them to be patient. Suddenly, Hu Hon-chi rushed in. She was a representative from the seventh floor and had served the company for more than ten years. Without consulting Gu, she began to gather together some of the workers. When Gu asked her what was going on, she replied, 'I'm getting the thirty-six dismissed to join the consultation.'

'What?!' This time it was the cool-headed Gu who lost her temper.

'We decided to have all of the dismissed get together to decide what to do,' Hu answered.

'Who are "we"?'

'We, those who are in the seminar room.'

Obviously, things had escalated out of hand.

After consulting with Ma, who had remained in the hall, Gu went to the seminar room for about ten minutes. When she came back, she gathered those who had been dismissed, but were not RPs, into the seminar room. The best she could do was to get the workers to meet among themselves. No one, except those thirty-six, were allowed to remain in the seminar room.

There was no knowing how the thirty-six got along in their discussion. After a few minutes, they sent five RPs out to invite Gu and Fu to join them. When Gu and Fu refused, they almost begged. They even asked Lo and Mao to convince them. 'Gu and Fu have always been a part of us. They have to be present at our discussion.' Oddly, neither Lo nor Mao could refuse the workers, and they unwillingly pushed Gu and Fu into the room.

Peering through the windows, one could sense the high emotions in the small, packed room. As Fu talked, most of the workers kept their heads down. When Gu talked, almost everyone began weeping. Thirty minutes later, Fu, Gu, and the workers emerged. In addition to the 'guests', who were still waiting, a documentary movie team had arrived. None of the workers was in the mood to say anything. They went to the washroom to freshen up and went straight to the meeting hall. Gu and Fu went with them and came out with Ma and the other supporters. Then the meeting hall doors were closed, and were guarded by the picket team. The workers' general meeting resumed and they were on their own.

Out in the receptionist area, the 'guests', the supporters, and the film team of more than twenty people waited. An hour passed; the atmosphere was heavy. No one said anything. After almost an hour and a half, someone said a poll would take place in a few minutes. At this news, the 'guests' were relieved, but the supporters were depressed.

Sitting by Ma on the floor, Fu murmured in a hoarse voice, 'All gone, everything's gone.'

'Cheer up, there's still something we can do,' Ma responded.

'No, there's nothing more. It is their careers and their money. How can we make them lose their jobs and jeopardize their already difficult livelihood?' replied Fu, as tears rolled down his cheeks.

In an extremely friendly manner, the 'guests' brought out drinks and offered them to everyone. Bao Yi-hai, straightforward and unsociable as always, refused every offer. Meanwhile, the film team, not knowing who had called them, were setting up their apparatus.

Missing from the scene were Lo and Gu. Lo had asked Gu for a private conversation, and Gu could not refuse, partly because her Centre was subsidized by the CLA, where Lo was the director. They stood and talked by the downstairs entrance. Lo said he had been shut up by the management, who had questioned his representation, as the workers had continued their 'action' even as he was negotiating. It was, as she might imagine, extremely frustrating. When he had talked to JWM's highest official the previous night, he was told that the thirty-six dismissed must go, although they would be compensated. More importantly, he agreed to consider the setting-up of a mutual fund for the daily-rated after the merger. 'Of course, the final choice is up to the workers,' Lo stressed. 'They may or may not accept the offer. If they don't, we have no alternative but to assist them and keep on fighting. However, to be frank, I don't see any hope for a better solution.' Under the circumstances, he thought it wise to accept the offer and retain as many workers as possible, to preserve morale and to keep the union alive. He defended his negotiations with the management, telling Gu, 'There's nothing secretive about our negotiations at all. The reason for not having the workers go along was technical. Although others may misinterpret it, I think you understand. In high-level negotiations, one must act professionally. I had to play various roles and put on various faces. Not only acting aggressively but sometimes also playing it soft. In some occasions, I may even have to beg a little bit. It is for the workers' benefit. Do you think that the workers will ever be willing or able to do the same thing?'

Gu said nothing, but kept her head down and took notes.

'Of course, I did not mention the union,' Lo continued. 'It was precisely the future of their union that was on my mind. That was why I fought for those who might stay as much as for those who had to go. It is crucial to keep workers for the future development of the union. The worst choice is to resign *en masse*. It is easy to be extreme. In that case, no one but the workers would be the total losers. There are more things to gain if the workers stay. There will be nothing left if they decide to quit.'

As Gu did not respond, Lo, somewhat irritated, again shifted gears. 'Of course, if the workers refuse to accept the offer, if they try to upgrade their action, the offer would be forfeited. On the contrary, if things are resolved smoothly, there will be at least eleven or twelve among the thirty-six whom the management will consider rehiring. You should understand that the reputation of the CLA and your group are at stake, if we keep on fighting a losing battle. It is impossible to reinstate the dismissed, because the management are under great pressure not to do so. The Japanese business community, both in Hong Kong and in Japan, are pressing the local people as well as the Japanese headquarters not to give in. What is worse, the greatest resistance comes from local middle management. They will do anything to prevent reinstatement.'

At this point a Catholic priest came down to remind Gu that the time for leaving the meeting hall had long passed. Gu ran up the stairs. About twenty 'guests' and supporters were in the third-floor reception area, and Gu shouted to them, 'The whole thing has dragged on so long that the church will never allow us to use their meeting hall any more. All of you better apologize to the priest in person!' She then ran to the meeting hall and told the picket guards to tell the moderators to conclude the meeting as soon as possible, as the church wanted the hall. Immediately, people moved towards the entrance to the hallway. The atmosphere was so tense that people could hear their own heartbeats.

Suddenly, the doors of the meeting hall swung wide. Led by Chu

Chi-lin and her close associates, the workers rushed out. 'The meeting will resume tomorrow morning, when the decision will be made,' announced Chu.

'Did you cast ballots?'

'Yes, we did, but we decided not to count the votes.'

'What?' 'Why?' 'What?' Mao, Son, Lo, and other 'guests' shouted.

'We decided to nullify the poll. It was simply not possible for us to make a reasonable choice under such stress. And it is not fair to force us. We are not going to do it. We need more time to think.' Chu said decisively.

'What? How could you do that? Who is the one who made the decision?' Mao screamed in fury. The despairing Son said, 'It is not right, even illegal. You should not infringe upon the workers' rights.' His secretary and three fellow unionists echoed his sentiments. Lo, disappointed, said nothing.

So the meeting ended. People dispersed, some in anger, some profoundly perplexed.

The workers had left. After tidying up the meeting hall for the priest, and repeatedly apologizing, Gu, Fu, Lin, and Ma went down to the street. They were amazed by the outcome — although none really knew what had happened.

Lin and Gu went off to the factory, while Ma and Fu returned to the Centre to find 'Big Brother' Chien Fon-yi and Chi-mei waiting to brief them. There had been much debate before the individual polling on whether: (1) to accept the compensation and leave; (2) to continue working for the company and keep on struggling for their welfare; or (3) to quit *en masse*.

Why had they refused to count the ballots?

'Well, the poll was pushed by a few and was put together in great haste and under tremendous pressure. None of us [meaning the core leadership around Chu Chi-lin] felt comfortable with the formulation. At the same time, not everyone who was entitled to vote was present. We simply need more time to think. We didn't think it was fair to be pushed into making a decision by outsiders.'

Listening to this, Ma was amazed. The workers had faced one of the greatest organizational conundrums in collective action, yet had managed to get out of the trap by simply relying on their intuition!

'Did you know that there was a film team in the hallway?' Fu asked.

'No, we didn't know. But we did sense something fishy about the whole business. It was supposedly the workers' general meeting, wasn't it? Who invited all the "guests" over?' Chien Fon-yi asked.

'No one. They simply showed up,' replied Ma. 'This morning's English press, *The South China Mornig Post*, reported that Son Yan-min has pulled out from mediation in the JWM dispute. He was said to have quit after the workers had been incited by the Centre to demonstrate outside UMELCO. People close to him told the press that he was not happy with the way the Centre had been handling the dispute. In addition, both he and the Labour Bureau accused the Centre of inexperience and of persuading the workers to escalate their action. Mao Si-hai also complained that the workers should have approached the Labour Bureau earlier, before the dispute had got out of hand.'

'What? Approached them earlier? What did they do to us when we went for help two months ago?' screamed the hot-tempered 'Big Brother' before Ma could finish.

'That's not important,' Fu stopped her. 'What's crucial is why both Son and Mao and the other "unionists" were here this afternoon. In the first place, Son was jealous of Lo and wanted to quit. Now he returned because he thought he should be around to share the credit when the dispute was peacefully resolved, right? They, including bureau chief Mao and Japanese top management, thought they had managed to subdue the workers. That explains everything, including the mysterious filming team, right? The whole thing was a set-up.'

'Right, precisely!' echoed Chi-mei, the picket team leader. 'Hsiao Chia told me that, when she was guarding the canteen, those self-proclaimed "unionists" tried to convince her and the other workers. They told her that they themselves had suffered by participating in union activities when they were young, and they would not want to see us risk the same. They advised us to adopt a moderate approach ... '

'I also saw Hu Hon-chi talk to two of them at length on the fifth floor,' echoed Chien. 'I couldn't tell what they were up to, but once I showed up, the conversation stopped abruptly.'

While those at the Centre tried to find the missing pieces of the puzzle, Gu and Lin went up to the fourth-floor staircase in the factory. They were told that Son and his secretary had followed the workers back to the factory, unsuccessfully pressing the RPs to count the ballots and warning them that they were breaking the law. He then tried to talk to the rank and file. He finally left with a long face. An informal meeting was then held in the canteen, as some workers demanded to know why the RPs had decided not to count the ballots.

Meanwhile, there was the sound of quarrelling from the stairs as some workers left. They wanted to return home for the night, after a whole week's absence, and would return early the next morning.

Chen Siu-guan came to the staircase to talk privately with Gu. On the rooftop, Chen told her that she was under pressure from her boyfriend to stop her involvement. Her family had problems with both her and her boyfriend. Worse, she was in bad shape financially, and complained that there were no funds to support the workers' action. 'How do you expect us to go on when we lack rice in the pot?' Gu finally promised to do her best to find a remedy. Chen, not quite satisfied, went home.

Gu was told to contact the Centre, and so went down the street to a public phone. The Centre briefed her on what they had come to understand, and Ma explained the importance of not having a ballot with a one-of-three-choices formula, 'The mathematical consequences of such an exercise can only divide the workers.' Fu and Gu then agreed to raise funds and loan Chen Siu-guan HK$1,000. As Gu was about to review the possibility of a conflict of interest among the workers, Lee Siu-ching told her that representatives from fourteen unions were on their way to the factory to visit them, and suggested drafting an announcement condemning management union-busting activities. Gu agreed. Drafting the announcement and getting it signed by the fourteen union representatives, however, would take too long, and so the contents were relayed to the press by telephone.

There were about fifty workers still on the fourth floor when Lee and his fourteen colleagues walked in. The short discussion between them was business-like and down-to-earth. 'The independent unions will begin raising funds for the JWM women workers' struggle tomorrow morning!' Lee promised, as they left after midnight.

Day 8: 7 June 1986 (Saturday)

At 7:00 a.m. Gu woke up on the top-floor staircase, where she had spent the night with the core leaders. They urged her to go to the Centre and telephone the workers who had gone home for a 10 a.m. general meeting. Gu found Fu at the Centre, sleeping on a bench. From their telephone calls, they learned that most of the workers had already left for the factory. Curiously enough, even after a week the factory bus was still running.

Gu and Fu reached the factory around 10 a.m. only to be told that the workers' general meeting had already adjourned. Some 100 workers had cast ballots on whether to accept the management's proposal as a total package — seventy-three had voted to reject and the rest had abstained. Fu, who had been quite pessimistic, was surprised. Before the vote, Chu Chi-lin had given a passionate speech, moving some to tears. In addition, a few of the rank and file had criticized the RPs and the thirty-six dismissed workers for meeting among themselves the day before without the rank and file, warning that such splitting of the workers' collective must not recur.

At 11:00 a.m. management called the RPs to the fifth floor and asked for their decision. Chu Chi-lin replied that the rank and file had rejected the package. She then suggested the resumption of negotiations for the reinstatement of the thirty-six workers, to continue until a final agreement. The management, represented by the local Hong Kong staff, was unprepared, and repeatedly emphasized the previous day's proposal. The only piece of new information they presented in the hour-long meeting was that the managing director of the JWM Japan head office was now personally involved and would like to address the workers at 4:00 p.m.

The core leaders believed it to their advantage to confront the top-echelon management of JWM. After the meeting they informed Gu of the 4 p.m. address. Gu returned to the Centre and called vice-president Banata of the Japan Nationwide Council of Unions (JNCU). Banata said that he and his colleagues had visited JWM headquarters management, who had denied any knowledge of labour disputes in their overseas units but promised to look into it. With regard to the union at JWM headquarters, Banata told Gu to 'forget about it. It is not the same breed of animal and we are not on speaking terms.' Under these circumstances, JNCU would boycott JWM products and publicize the issue. Banata suggested that Gu give the news to the international wire services, as 'it might get back to the Japanese news media sooner that way.' Finally, he promised to cable JNCU's official statement to the Hong Kong JWM branch and urge them to keep good faith and reach a peaceful settlement with the Hong Kong workers.

Ma found all this less encouraging than the others. It confirmed his worst fear: that the JWM union in Japan was a so-called 'yellow union' — a typical Japanese management-run union. Nevertheless, he said nothing, even emphasizing the bright side and urging the Centre staff to reveal the Japanese friends' positive action to the workers. He also urged them to release the news of the prospective Japanese action to the local media. 'The most important result of international networking is to reinforce solidarity, usually in symbolic terms,' he explained.

Mao Si-hai showed up in the canteen. Aware of the mindset of the workers, he approached Chu Chi-lin directly and demanded a private 'chat', but Chu wanted to speak publicly. They ended up talking in a corner. It was a funny conversation: While Mao spoke quietly and tried to get Chu to lower her voice, Chu tried to infuriate Mao into raising his.

Mao pressed Chu to release the ballots cast by the workers the day before; he knew they had not been destroyed, and who had them. Chu tried to play innocent, but failed. Mao warned her that it was illegal to keep ballots without counting them and announcing the result. Chu replied that the ballots were the workers' private property; and anyone who tried to take them was committing the offence of misappropriation. Mao charged that the morning vote had been unbelievably fake. Chu replied that workers would not cast votes simply to please those who spied on them. 'Whether the Labour Bureau, or for that matter, you, Mr Mao, believe in it or not has absolutely nothing to do with the workers' autonomy. The workers have the right to vote as many times as they want and to decide on their actions.'

As Chu's voice grew louder and louder, more and more workers approached Mao and Chu. Mao finally dropped the conversation abruptly and left for the fifth-floor office.

At 1:30 p.m., all fifteen RPs were summoned to the fifth-floor meeting room. Waiting were the two lawyers, Son Yan-min, Lo Man-sa, Mao Si-hai, Tu Pi-sin, and Mrs Lee from the Labour Bureau, together with two Japanese management representatives, Tosai and Kusara. There was a conspicuous lack of local mid-rank management.

The attorney, Mobark Ley, spoke with his customary authoritative air. 'The JWM management's offer, as made known to all of you yesterday, is final. No change is to be made in any form. The reason for the dismissals was their [the workers'] personal misbehaviour. They broke the factory rules. Even then, the management has decided to compensate them. They will be paid up to an amount of their respective severance pay upon dismissal. You must appreciate the lenient nature of such treatment. There has never been any issue of discrimination whatsoever in JWM's long history. It was, and still is, standard management practice to hire staff and workers on a monthly-pay and daily-pay basis, respectively. This has absolutely nothing to do with any kind of discriminatory practice. Regardless of this, the management plans to establish a mutual fund for the daily-waged. It is the top management's resolution to act in good faith and to initiate reforms. Yesterday's offer will be strictly followed without any discount. You, as workers' representatives, are asked to inform all the workers of the concrete offer. Beginning at 5:00 p.m. today, and tomorrow from 7:00 a.m. to 12:00 noon, the workers are instructed to come up to the management to identify their intentions and to sign themselves up.'

Ley's voice echoed emptily in the silent meeting room. Minutes passed. Finally Mao broke the ice by suddenly beginning to apologize for the RPs. He asserted that both sides were sincere, but that there was some communication breakdown, and the best way to bridge it was to have the workers speak their minds. He said that now the RPs were in an embarrassing situation, and that some sort of conflict of interest might exist between the thirty-six dismissed and the general rank and file. After a lengthy, idiosyncratic review of the dispute, he concluded that the time had come for all the workers to speak for themselves. Finally, he stressed that the previous day's ballots had to be made public. Only then would the free choice of the workers be vindicated.

Demagoguery was what the RPs heard in this wonderful campaign for the workers' individual rights and freedom. 'Thank you for respecting the workers' decision,' 'Big Brother' Chien Fon-yi answered in a tone similar to that of Mobark Ley. 'Just for your information, a resolution was formally adopted by the workers to reject the management package. And it was final!'

'It is impossible for the foremen and leaders to work with the thirty-six dismissed. The management must stick to its guns,' Kusara commented, while the RPs laughed at 'Big Brother's' mocking tone. They then laughed even harder, as 'gun' means penis in local slang. The meeting had to be adjourned.

When the meeting resumed fifteen minutes later, Hong Kong branch managing director Tosai asked the RPs whether there was any precondition for their suggested resumption of production. The RPs simply answered, 'No', ignoring the ambiguity of 'resume production'. Tosai did not clarify, but read a prepared question, 'What do you intend to do in the negotiations afterwards, since you insist on keeping the dialogue open?'

'We can correct a lot of unreasonable practices on the shop-floor, improve the working environment and welfare provisions and inquire into why there should be differential treatment between the daily-waged and the monthly-paid.'

'You mean the 6 percent?' Tosai was obviously dissatisfied with the evasive answers.

'Yes, including the problem of the "mysterious money".'

Tosai looked at his notes. A third question, 'Does this mean that you don't intend to quit your jobs at all?'

'No, we don't.'

'What did you vote for, or rather, vote against?'

'We voted to reject the management package.'

After these answers, Tosai adjourned the meeting.

Ten minutes after the RPs had returned to the canteen, Son and Lo came down. Sullenly and dispiritedly, they strolled towards Chu Chi-lin.

'There's nothing we can do to help any more, we might as well just leave …' Son grumbled.

'You are welcome, don't worry. Bye!' was the reply.

Chu was eager to see Son and Lo off because she had just got a message from the Centre that about forty unionists from twenty-two organizations, led by Lee Siu-ching and five local district board members, were on their way to the factory. When she was sure that Son and Lo had left the premises, she led the RPs down to receive the supporters. However, the first few people she saw by the entrance, negotiating with some uniformed guards, were reporters who had come for a management press conference at 3:00 p.m. at the second-floor 'press centre'. The guards were denying them entrance, claiming that 'outsiders' was not allowed to go upstairs without the management's written permission. Ready to stage a public relations coup, the RPs began to chat with the reporters and argue with the guards.

At that moment, a big red banner appeared, followed by marchers with placards, and the guards took up a defensive stance, as if confronting a dangerous enemy. Leading the marchers was the president of the Federation of Civil Service Unions, Lee Siu-ching, with Gu and Fu. Catching sight of the banners and the marching brigade, hurrahs erupted among the RPs, and some ran forward to welcome the marchers. Reporters with cameras also ran towards the marching band.

Seeing the guards defending the entrance, Lee stopped the march and went to greet them. The marshal of the guards, recognizing Lee as a famous and popular independent union leader and member of the government's Labour Consultative Committee, also stepped forward. Lee told him that they came peacefully to support the women workers. He understood that the guards were hired by JWM to protect the factory premises, that he respected their duty and had absolutely no intention of making their job difficult. In a few minutes, it was agreed that, since the parking lot by the gate did not belong to JWM, the rally would be held there, on the ground floor inside the gate.

Although by now the management had notified the guards to let the press in, some of the reporters preferred to cover the rally, while others went along with the RPs to the fourth floor to bring the workers down to join in. However, once the RPs went up the stairs they were stopped by members of management, who meant 'to have another session with all the RPs'. The RPs were aware of the news conference at 3:00 p.m. and also knew that the management was aware of the workers' rally at the same time, so it was clear that the session was to divert the workers' forces; but, to avoid further complications, Chu and her associates decided to go along and leave the others to mobilize for the rally.

When they arrived, the fifth-floor meeting room was empty. Chu and her group were about to leave when Kusara rushed up to invite them in and persuade them to wait 'for just a few seconds'. The wait turned out to be longer. Kusara finally returned and, knowing that he did not have the right to demand the presence of all RPs, read slowly from a prepared draft:

1. The management did not accept the suggestion of 'resuming production' before a final settlement was reached.
2. The management had no new proposals.
3. The managing director of the Japanese head office, Mr Amukas, was in Hong Kong. He felt bad about the situation and would like to have a 'chat' with the workers. He would listen to their grievances at 4 p.m. in the canteen.
4. Fearing the workers still had no clear idea of the management offer,

200 copies of the announcement which had been posted earlier outside the office would be passed out to all workers before 4 p.m.

As there was no need to respond — Kusara was but a messenger — Chu and the others left after he had finished. When they arrived at the parking lot, they found some 50 visiting unionists lined up on one side and about 100 women workers lined up opposite, all holding banners and placards. People cheered when Lee announced that various unions had raised HK$5,000 to support their 'working sisters' and then handed the cheque over to the RPs. The workers sang their battle song, the guests sang 'We Shall Overcome', and the workers posed for photo sessions for the twenty-odd reporters. Meanwhile, the leaders were being interviewed by the press. In the carnival atmosphere the workers were disappointed only that the TV crews had not come — if they had, it would have been one of the best shows staged by Hong Kong workers on television for years.

It was now almost 4:30 p.m., and the management tried to get the workers back to the fourth-floor canteen. The visitors finally left and the workers went up. In the canteen, Tosai introduced a smiling middle-aged Japanese man to them. '... Our managing director, Mr Amukas, who has come all the way from Japan to attend to our workers and their difficulties ... '

Amukas nodded and then stopped smiling. Without speaking, he gazed at the workers like a general inspecting his troops, while the canteen turned silent. Then, smiling once again, he spoke, and Tosai interpreted.

'I made a special trip to Hong Kong to look at your situation. I hope that you will be able to get back to your jobs as soon as possible and serve the company. I know you are good workers. I also appreciate that, even in this serious dispute, you have always resorted to peaceful means and have never acted destructively. I regret that extremely hostile relationships were established between the thirty-six of you and the managing staff. The management had no choice but to ask the thirty-six to leave. It isn't appropriate and I feel sorry, and that is why we decided to compensate you in terms as favourable as possible. Please understand it is due to the lack of mutual trust that we cannot keep you working together. Maybe, some time later, you will return and be welcome. In case there are others who are not dismissed but do not feel comfortable staying, we will also offer compensation upon your resignation. For those of you who decide to stay, awards will be made available after the merger. All the terms are specified in the notice we have copied for you. You may raise any questions you have or air your complaints before making a final decision. I'm here to listen, for I assure you that, both among the overseas offshore units and at our headquarters in Japan, with more than 15,000 workers, there has never been a dispute like this before ... '

'How did it come about that the management decided to dismiss thirty-six of us? Were there any legitimate reasons?' asked one RP.

'Well, one of the reasons for dismissal this time was the production slowdown, which has taken place since the middle of May. Your delivery schedule was bottlenecked. As a matter of fact, your management did think of withdrawing the dismissal at one point ... '

'There was absolutely no slowdown on the third floor, and yet ten workers there were fired. Is that because they are involved in organizing our trade union?' another RP asked.

'No, it is not true that the management dismissed them for their union activities. I didn't know a union was being organized. The dismissal decision had nothing to do with it. In Japan, we also have unions. The relation between our union and management is extremely cordial.'

'Why did you only mention that middle management does not trust the workers and not that the workers cannot trust the management? Some workers who were ill and took sick leave during the period were also fired. Isn't it true that, were it not for our organizing a union, these people would not have been dismissed?' voiced a third RP.

'It was no big deal to have workers organize a union. Why didn't you consult with the management nicely?'

'You said that you had to fire the thirty-six because of production slowdown. Don't you know that there were 200 workers who didn't work normally? Concerning the slowdown, we were all responsible. Why didn't you fire us all?' It was a voice from the far corner.

'It was because the thirty-six were the core figures. We should not blame the other hundred-plus workers. About the organization of unions, let's talk about it later.' Amukas replied, feeling the heat.

'Why were workers also fired on shop-floors where there were no slowdowns? Isn't it contradictory to what you have just claimed?' pressed a third-floor RP.

'Well, about such details ... I ... I am not clear ... '

Tosai intervened. 'It isn't simply the slowdown, it's also because some of you disobeyed orders. It was because of the questionnaire which you turned in to your RPs instead of to your foremen and leaders.'

'It was precisely because of the mistrust the workers had vis-à-vis their foremen and leaders. Having been abused by them, they had no one to rely on but their own elected representatives' said Chu Chi-lin.

'But it is the management's wish to communicate with its workers,' replied Amukas, who obviously did not like being surrogated.

'Is this why the management sent its staff to tail us every evening after work, and called us at home to threaten and harass us? That's communication, I guess!'

Amukas was rather embarrassed by 'Big Brother's' jeering comments. 'It was quite unfortunate that such mistakes took place. I felt very bad when I learned about it. I just hope that from now on the workers' relationship with us will gradually improve, especially since you have already begun to speak your minds ... '

'Yes, our minds are that we want to resume our jobs,' a few voices were raised spontaneously.

Amukas hesitated, but chose not to evade the issue. 'Well, there's absolutely no problem for over a hundred of you. What is hard is the problem of mistrust with regard to the thirty-six. There is no solution to that. Of course, money is not everything. But mutual trust is of utmost importance if people are to work together.' He hesitated. 'We only hope that we will be able to compensate them as favourably as possible.'

'How about dismissing us all and compensating us since you're not willing to reinstate the thirty-six?' the workers demanded, almost in unison. *That* can of worms was now open.

Tosai became nervous and grabbed Amukas to whisper into his ear. All the workers, with a tacit understanding, fell silent. As they watched Tosai whispering to Amukas in an alien tongue, the tension grew.

Amukas seemed neither to appreciate Tosai's information nor to agree with him, but he tried to conceal his impatience and waited for him to finish. Then he turned to the workers.

'To lay off workers, or for that matter to pay them severance pay after the lay-off, involves complicated legal provisions in accordance with existing labour regulations and laws in Hong Kong. The JWM company is not prepared to get involved in all those complications. It is, of course, possible for me to help those who want to reapply after the merger. There's a Chinese expression, "The pull of one hair may affect the whole body." We are in so delicate a situation that anything which happens to a small part may have serious impact on the whole. The decisions we make here may have a grave impact on other companies in Hong Kong. They're all concerned with the outcome and its possible repercussions … '

'What we mean is this: The Hong Kong management had the guts to dismiss the thirty-six of us *en masse*. You might ask them as well to dismiss all of us and pay the severance claims,' Chu said.

'The situation of over a hundred of you is quite different from the thirty-six. Those thirty-six were already dismissed. They had no choice, and therefore I decided to compensate them. Should some of you who were not dismissed choose not to stay, that is something different. It's not possible for all of you to quit and demand compensation of eighteen days per year served.'

It was quite clear that Amukas had got the workers' point, and had presented his bottom line; but the workers had tried to turn the argument around once again. Finding himself on the defensive, he raised his voice, 'Well, if the dispute is peacefully resolved, then there will be a chance.' He stood up. 'Thank you for your suggestions. I'll study them carefully.' Then he and Tosai left the canteen.

Most of the workers felt the meeting had advanced their cause. A few, however, seemed to have something else in mind, and felt that Amukas had been treated too harshly.

It was time for dinner, and the workers wandered out to get some food. Some went home. Hsiao Chia was worried, and went down to consult Gu and Fu in the parking lot. She pointed out that the next day, Sunday, the factory bus would not run, and she feared some workers might stay home. After a week, the workers' numbers were now dwindling day by day, and there was a free-ride sentiment creeping in. It was thus decided to hold a self-examination meeting, to include both the RPs and volunteer supporters.

At 8:00 p.m., on the rooftop, the session opened. Both RPs and non-RP supporters agreed that recently, especially in general meetings, there had been signs of disintegration among both rank and file and RPs — indeed, in the present session, some of the fifteen RPs were absent — in particular, Hon Lai-fon and Chen Siu-guan, who had actually taken naps during the morning meeting. Some RPs suspected that some workers would rather listen to the management than to them; others doubted that the RPs, as a body, were steadfast enough. It was evident that there were serious communication problems. Some blamed this on the management strategy of perpetual postponement; others considered it a consequence of the workers' lack of initiative. Having failed at heavy-handed suppression, management was now tempting some of the workers with material gains.

Hsiao Chia proposed three major tasks:

1. To take the initiative in every aspect of the struggle — the workers must set the terms and the stage for the management, not the other way around;
2. To expand the picket team in response to management's hiring of extra guards; and
3. To regiment members into specific task forces. A press task force was especially necessary, to counter management's public relations work.

Gu then pointed out that some RPs lacked patience under stress in dealing with the rank and file. They tended to forget to relay information and to instruct the workers rather than to invite their responses. She quickly added that this was quite understandable, as the RPs needed support and assistance, and she endorsed the idea of setting up various task forces to work with the RPs.

Fu then analysed the total alignment of the antagonist forces. He placed JWM management in the Centre — under constant pressure from Japanese headquarters; from both high- and middle-level Japanese staff; and from Japanese and other foreign enterprises in Hong Kong, through their chambers of commerce. Amukas had hinted at this. If this was correct, the workers had to consider extending their actions beyond the factory premises. They might distribute leaflets in the industrial zone and solicit workers' sympathy, stage a boycott of JWM products, or petition the government or the Japanese consul-general.

However, Fu insisted that before any such actions could be taken, the task forces had to be organized and ready to operate. He proposed task forces for:

1. fund-raising from supporting unions, organizations and workers;
2. public relations, receiving guests and press releases;
3. record-keeping (including meeting minutes, news clippings, banners and slogans) and propaganda leaflets;
4. soliciting complaints from the rank and file, including those raised against other workers;
5. picketing and discipline — to guard the factory round the clock, and prepare for the imposition of injunction orders brought against the workers; and
6. studying possibilities for further action.

Fu's proposals were discussed and accepted. Finally, a working schedule for the following day was decided upon.

1. Another extended RP meeting would be held at 10:00 a.m., to substantiate the proposals.

2. Negotiations would be held with management, in a meeting to last not more than one hour, followed by a meeting of RPs to review the situation and report to the rank and file.
3. A workers' general meeting would be held between 4:00 p.m. and 6:00 p.m., to inform them of recent developments and to solicit suggestions for action.
4. Preparations would be made to receive visitors from various unions and support groups and to hold a press conference in the evening.
5. An extended RP consultation would be held at 8:00 p.m.

Day 9: 8 June 1986 (Sunday)

Before the scheduled 10:00 a.m. extended RP consultation, Gu and Fu met to review the pattern of interaction between the RPs and the rank and file. They agreed that the logistics at the factory were well taken care of by the picket team. Every morning incoming workers were taken to the factory by bus and led by picket team members to the canteen, where they waited, sometimes with their children, while their representatives negotiated. Lunch was brought in daily. The serious problems concerned internal rivalry among the RPs and their failure to communicate with the rank and file. Every morning they consulted with Gu and Fu, but they had stopped conferring with their colleagues. No proper briefings were made after negotiations or at the end of the day.

In the consultation which followed, sentiments similar to those of Gu and Fu were expressed by the supporters. The more outspoken ones were those who had formerly been less involved. Hsiao Chia, for one, commented that a 'glass wall' had existed between the RPs and the rank and file for a while before the leadership took note of it. Worse, according to Kau-fu, was that the RPs did not seem to have confidence in the workers. They suspected the rank and file might become irresolute if told of complications. Ironically, some of the RPs themselves were wavering, so that some workers could not help but feel that Amukas might be more sincere and straightforward than they were! Hsiao Chia called for genuine mutual understanding between the RPs and the rank and file — the RPs had to understand the workers' stance and the workers had to understand the pressures on the RPs. They had to support each other and struggle together.

Chi-mei then explained that she was among the rank and file who had been working for less than two years, who expected no compensation if they quit or were fired, and thus were not fighting for personal gain, but were protesting against unfairness. They could not swallow the abuse of having their leaders fired. They wanted to expose the 'suppression' of local labourers by foreign capital enterprises.

Yue-mui, who never spoke in public, warned the leadership, including Gu and Fu, that it was devastating to the workers' morale for the RPs and the thirty-six dismissed to have closed-door consultations with 'intruders'.

Mui Len-shu, who had kept the ballots cast in the church, then confirmed that 50 percent of the workers had chosen to 'resign voluntarily'. This, according to her, was because they felt ignored.

At this moment, Lo Un-pu, the beloved 'Wet Nurse' of the second floor, mentioned Chen Siu-guan's and Hon Lai-fon's napping during the negotiations the morning before, showing their 'non-co-operation' with the rest of the RPs. She also reminded everyone of the faulty 'pick-one-out-of-three' polling format, which would bring out individual preferences rather than define a collective stance. 'What they tried to do was to put the interest of the dismissed before that of the workers,' Lo concluded. 'That was why Chu Chi-lin and others decided that the thirty-six of us should not be allowed to vote on the issue.'

The participants of the consultation agreed upon the following guidelines for future action:
1. To fight for collective dignity, not personal gain;
2. To work for a rapid resolution and avoid being 'dragged along' by management;
3. To be aware of public pressures exerted by government and foreign interests; and
4. If the struggle for reinstatement failed, to resign *en masse* and fight for severance pay for all.

To sustain the struggle, a 'third line' of personnel was elected, to work with the 'second line' RPs, assist them, assume their responsibilities in an emergency, and remain as the backbone of the union. No matter what happened, the workers decided that their union must be kept alive.

It was almost noon when the consultation adjourned. Some of the workers went down to the street for lunch, but most were present by 2:00 p.m. for the scheduled meeting with the management. Somehow nothing had happened, and they could only wait.

———————

At 4:15 p.m., Amukas, Mobark Ley, and Tosai arrived, accompanied by Mao Si-hai, Tu Pi-sin and Ms Lee, all from the Labour Bureau. The RPs sat at the front, with the rank and file behind them, for the meeting — or, rather, audience. Mao stood to play his role as emcee-interpreter-peacemaker.

'What is your counteroffer? Please spell it out concisely and precisely,' he asked, looking at the RPs.

'We request that all the dismissed workers be reinstated or all of us be dismissed and paid severance.'

Mao hesitated to interpret this to Amukas. Tosai jumped to whisper into Amukas' ear, but before he had a chance to finish, Amukas stood to speak. Mao interpreted.

'It was really my greatest pleasure to meet and listen to you. I appreciate very much the things you told me yesterday. I was surprised to know of the dispute between you and management, and it was the first time that I learned that you are organizing your union. I have investigated our internal problems and promise to improve things after the merger.

'From my investigations, I realize communication between you and the management has broken down. I feel sorry for that. Frankly, I would like to keep the thirty-six dismissed workers. However, because of the lack of trust between the workers and their line leaders/foremen, it is not possible for them to work together any more. There would be too many problems in the future. There is no alternative. That is why I have decided to compensate the thirty-six as generously as possible. I believe that yesterday, after all of you had aired your grievances, the misunderstanding was clarified. My offer would apply only to the thirty-six of you who were dismissed. Of course, I will also improve things here for those of you who stay. I know that you resent the dismissal, but you must understand the circumstances the thirty-six face are rather embarrassing. If we hire them, there will be strong repercussions from the line leaders and foremen. The management is in a difficult situation. It was the management here which dismissed them in the first place, and I decided to compensate them according to the labour regulations. We didn't dismiss the rest of you and, of course, we are not liable to make any severance payment.'

'You said that there are mental barriers between the thirty-six and their administrators. The same exists between all of us and our administrators,' complained a rank-and-file worker, as pieces of paper with comments and opinions moved from hand to hand among the RPs.

'Big Brother' Chien Fon-yi said, 'You compensate thirty-six of us because you feel we weren't to blame for what happened. However, those of us who were not dismissed were as much mistreated and abused as the thirty-six were. You force them to stay only to make them suffer more. And they were even less to blame!'

Lo Un-pu echoed, 'The administrative staff who incited the conflict were not only unpunished, they were actually rewarded with a lump sum. There can't be anything more unfair than this!'

'Right, right, it's unfair ... it's discrimination against us ... ' repeated the workers. 'We demand a fairer proposal.'

Amukas simply reiterated what he had said, 'There cannot and will not be any fairer offer. Furthermore, the company needs every available worker to resume production. Absolutely no one will be fired later.' But the workers continued to press him.

Amukas finally pleaded, 'There is tremendous mistrust. Working relations on the shop-floor have become impossible. It would be nice if we could keep those fired and resume production. We don't know a better way to resolve the dispute. We have done what we could. You must understand, we are not even obliged by law to compensate the thirty-six. It is the goodwill of the company. We consider them victims. Over one hundred of you are not,' he concluded.

The note-passing among the RPs began to subside as the topic turned to union-busting. Amukas, instead of denying it, lamented, 'Were it not for the fact that the thirty-six dismissal notices have been delivered, we might still keep you. You know — "Spilt water cannot be recovered", as you Chinese say!'

At this point, a consensus seemed to have been reached among some of the RPs. Through eye communication, Chu Chi-lin was pressured to speak on everybody's behalf. She, who had never hesitated before, was surprisingly reluctant to talk. Lo Un-pu shot in instead.

'There are solutions and alternatives if you are willing to look for them. As far as the workers as a collective are concerned, what we are fighting for is fairness and justice. I propose, on behalf of the thirty-six dismissed, that we receive less compensation, but that those who quit get equal treatment. How about fifteen days a year for everybody?'

This was a bombshell. It disturbed the management, the rank and file, the representatives. Although most of the rank and file appreciated the sacrifice Lo Un-pu proposed, not all those who had been dismissed agreed to it. Avoiding a direct challenge to the proposal, Hon Lai-fon instead told Amukas that most of the thirty-six were willing to stay, as they had 'wrongly' been identified as 'troublemakers'. Hu Hon-chi suggested that every individual worker 'pour out her heart'.

Mao Si-hai was suddenly excited. 'Those of you who never speak out, speak out! Pour out your hearts to Mr Amukas and to all of us!' He stood up and called to the workers.

A few workers responded. Others tried to stop them, and there was a quarrel between those who wanted to communicate directly with the top management and those who wanted to maintain the session for collective bargaining, with the rank and file behaving in a disciplined manner. Oil was added to the fire by Mao, his associates and the management. There was chaos when, suddenly, a few voices began singing the battle hymn;

others joined in, and it became louder and louder — but there were intermittent jeers, and the meeting disintegrated. Management and the Labour Bureau representatives left for the fifth floor, unleashing more squabbles among the workers.

A few minutes later Dai-gau, a picket team member, rushed down from the fifth floor to Chi-mei, the picket team leader, and whispered in her ear; Chi-mei then whispered to Chu Chi-lin; and Chu, without saying anything, ran all the way up the stairs with Dai-gau following her. A few minutes later, Dai-gau dashed back down and yelled to Chi-mei that Hon Lai-fon had gone to Woo Char-hwa to negotiate her share of the compensation. Chu was trying to stop her, and they were quarrelling inside the office, surrounded by more than ten people from management and the Labour Bureau. Chu was 'fighting with her back to the wall'. Alarmed, Chi-mei ran up the stairs, followed by twenty workers.

In the general office, Chu was telling Hon, 'You were already fired and expelled from the factory premises when we were alerted of the dismissal. So please understand that were it not for the actions of your colleagues you would not be eligible for anything.'

'But I'm the one fired! I'm the one who lost my job. If I hadn't dashed to the second floor, none of you would know what had happened,' Hon replied, and looked to Mao and Woo for support. Mao and Woo, with more management staff, then stood to protect Hon's 'individual right', and escorted her into the inner office to sign up for 'voluntary resignation' and receive her compensation cheque. Woo repeatedly declared that 'cheques are ready for everyone!'

In the meantime, down in the canteen, another fierce quarrel erupted between Hu Hon-chi, one of the oldest workers and an RP from the seventh floor; and Sieu-pin, a member of the Labour and Residents Coalition, a worker herself, who had come to support the sit-in the week before. Sieu-pin tried to persuade Hu of the importance of solidarity, but Hu screamed back, 'Why should I sacrifice for everybody? What was there for me in my fight all these days? Why should Chu Chi-lin and the others dictate that the thirty-six of us should not vote? Why should we bow to the rank and file and why can't we make decisions for ourselves? Why not allow everybody to speak out and make their own choice?'

'Because, as Chu convinced all thirty-six of you, those of you who were fired were "rescued" by the collective action. You owe whatever compensation you receive to them.'

'No, I owe them nothing. I can even say they owe us. They're not entitled to ask us to sacrifice any more!'

'What? They owe you?'

'Yes, they owe us their jobs. They'll be able to work here and with better welfare provisions. Who are you to lecture me? You are not a JWM worker. Your coming to help only make us workers suffer ... ' Sieu-pin was shocked by the personal attack, and fell quiet.

Hu dashed up to the fifth floor and ran into the office to sign up. Chi-mei and her group were just on their way out. The two exchanged nasty, bitter looks.

Out in the parking lot, Fu and Gu were informed of the disputes. They understood the contradiction caused by the voluntary lowering of compensation, but it was hard for them to judge the extent of the workers' disunity, or to know what kind of action was needed. They suggested an extended consultation the next morning, followed by a general meeting. They went back to the Centre to find that Ma had left and Bao Yi-hai was sitting in for him. The three of them discussed the situation. Bao insisted that it was a result of the workers' loss of initiative, and that action had to be upgraded.

Day 10: 9 June 1986 (Monday)

In the morning, Ma got to the Centre before 7:00 a.m. He wanted to consult with Gu and Fu and warn them of the changing tone of the press. Something had to be done to counteract the efforts of management (through its PR firm) and the Labour Bureau (mainly the two-faced Mao), who were systematically distorting the image of the sit-in. Everyone had been so wrapped up in crisis-handling that they had neglected the press reports.

A report on 8 June in the *Ming Pao*, contained Mao Si-hai's claim that many 'external elements' were intervening in the JWM dispute, turning it into a non-labour issue; and he accused them of blocking a compromise on various occasions. In addition to this accusation, Ma worried about the distortion of leaving JWM's law firm and PR firm, and the friendly FLU and CLA, out of the 'external elements' — the so-called 'third party' — which term was meant to denote only the Centre and other grassroots worker support groups. The report went on to cite Amukas as saying that those fired had had slack working attitudes, and to repeat management's announcement that Monday would be a normal working day, when the workers would resume production.

Even more amazing was a feature story in the *SCMP* (Appendix I, Day 10), in which the dispute at JWM was said to offer a good opportunity for fresh co-operation between the 'left-wing' unions and independent unionists to intervene and resolve the dispute peacefully, as soon as possible, so that they might then accumulate political capital and strengthen overall union leadership of labour!

Ma ran into Gu and Fu near the Centre. Together, they decided to call a press conference in the afternoon to rebut Mao's slander. However, they were now most concerned about the internal crisis among the workers. Gu and Fu thus took the lift to the factory's roof, and Ma was told to go back to the Centre to inform the press and to man the telephone.

On the rooftop, thirty or more workers were waiting for the extended consultation. Chi-mei began by reporting that few workers had reported to work and that production lines were still idle on every floor. However, fewer workers had joined the sit-in.

Some workers from the second floor then reported that they had received phone calls from Chen Siu-guan, who had been absent since Saturday morning. She told her colleagues that they were fighting a losing war and advised them to report to work as soon as possible. 'A tramp, a slut, a good-for-nothing!' were the comments from every corner. To those present, it was unforgivable of Siu-guan to change her position. They pitied her short-sightedness and selfishness, as her compensation was among the smallest; but harder to swallow were her attempts to persuade her colleagues on management's behalf.

Interestingly enough, people were much less hostile towards Hon Lai-fon and Hu Hon-chi, despite the fierce arguments of the previous night. They understood that they had betrayed the workers' collective, but they also recognized that, as they had worked for more than ten years, they were getting lump sums which could change their lives. And they had not asked their colleagues to switch sides. They were wrong only in choosing the wrong time and in acting openly, consequently undermining the collective.

Most of the workers, then, were prepared to see some of their colleagues break and, as a result, the collective as a whole did not seem to have been hit hard by the 'dropouts', or traumatized by the enemy's strategy to sow discord. They were practical enough to seek ways to isolate any future incidents and minimize damage.

Gu was asked to comment on the legal status of the dispute. She concluded that existing laws could neither help nor harm the workers. She then suggested that further action should be planned as practically as possible.

Many questions were raised. As the consultation had been intended for self-criticism, Fu suggested that everyone think about counteroffers, the chances of winning, time limits, whether workers should resign *en masse* immediately, reasons for the present chaos, what would happen when the thirty-six left, and finally, whether the workers would give in if offered substantial concessions.

The practicalities of real-world struggles set limits to workers' philosophizing discourse concerning uncertainties. Talking was simply not enough — they had to 'do something' to feel good about themselves — and it did not take long for the workers on the rooftop to demand 'something to do' instead of 'wasting saliva'. '... There are many preparations for the press conference this afternoon and our actions tomorrow ...,' Gu was saying, when she was stopped by the workers' cheers. They longed for action.

Task forces were set up and people volunteered. Fu was assigned to draft an announcement to refute Mao at the press conference and to compile a list of supporting organizations; Ma was to call friendly groups in Japan, and also boost local support; Gu was to help plan demonstrations in front of the Japanese consulate the next day; Chu Chi-lin volunteered to take charge of the production of leaflets, banners and slogans. The workers then rushed down to the canteen where preparations for the demonstration were already in progress.

Around noon, different task forces gathered to brief each other. Fu's draft response to Mao was accepted, with a few minor changes. Then all concentrated on the demonstration. Gu declared that it should have three targets: the Japanese capitalists' suppression of manual workers, JWM management's discrimination against union activists, and the practice of arbitrary dismissal. A detailed schedule was proposed. A protest letter would be delivered to the Japanese consul by RPs. Everything should proceed in an orderly and peaceful manner to win support from the general public. A representative would be elected to deal with the media. Chu suggested that leaflets explaining the workers' struggle and calling for a boycott on JWM products be designed, and aimed at JETCON production unit. Finally, a few people were chosen to report to the rank and file before the press conference.

Now Chu Chi-lin insisted it was time for new leaders to emerge. She volunteered to stay in the factory to 'sit-in' by herself, using the opportunity to design leaflets, while others went to St. Stephen's Church for the general meeting and press conference.

The workers arrived at St. Stephen's about 2:00 p.m. Ha-lan, with Lo Un-pu's assistance, began the meeting with a report on the status quo. Then Yin-mei analysed the situation and Ah Lam assisted, after which Gu explained the legal status of the dispute. Finally, Lai-fon and Chien Fa-hin proposed actions for the next day. Then the workers were organized into six discussion groups of about fifteen workers each, with each led by two RPs. Discussions went well, and those who were usually quiet began to talk.

Well after 3:00 p.m., over a dozen reporters arrived. Lee Siu-ching also came, bearing a message of support from thirty-four unions. The general meeting was therefore temporarily adjourned, and the workers came together again for the press conference. Lee was invited to sit on the stage.

Without hesitation, the four workers' spokeswomen criticized labour relations chief Mao Si-hai's slander, stressing that the workers had never changed their position — it was management that had constantly shifted its stance. The workers persisted in their demand for reinstatement, while the management continued to play dirty. Answering reporters' questions, the spokeswomen reiterated that the main goal of the struggle was to challenge the suppression of their rights and the infringement of their benefits, and so they demanded the reinstatement of those who had been arbitrarily dismissed. Any difficulties between administrative personnel and reinstated workers would depend on both sides, not on the workers alone. If management refused their demands, the workers would upgrade their actions, convince the public of the rightness of their cause and appeal for support. The fact that management was willing to discuss money missed the point: Dignity and fairness were also involved. The fight was to secure the lawful welfare of the so-called 'daily-waged' and to ensure that they would no longer be abused or discriminated against; and the recent stalemate was caused by management's attempt to discuss only money and not reinstatement. The thirty-six had not been fired for 'misbehaviour' but because they spoke for their colleagues. Amukas had openly admitted, during negotiations, that local management's dismissal of the thirty-six had been a mistake. This was why the workers resented being blamed by the Labour Bureau, who knew the truth and yet made statements to the contrary. They mistakenly thought that, as long as they sided with the management, solutions would be reached; but solutions were not attainable precisely because they ignored workers' opinions, disregarded their dignity, and ignored basic principles of fairness and justice. Therefore, the 120 workers who had been fighting all along continued to insist that they were not acting for personal gain. It was explained that there had always been a tremendous welfare disparity between themselves and the administrative staff, and that it was the present, overt abuse of the lump sum payment which had ignited long existing discontent.

Near the end of the press conference, Lee Siu-ching announced that thirty-four unions, mostly of civil servants closely associated with his confederation, had declared their support for the JWM workers' fight against arbitrary dismissal as a tactic of union-busting. Fu then clarified the Centre's role, emphasizing that the support groups offered assistance and consultation only, and that every single decision was made by, and only by, the workers.

As it was too early for the reporters to go to JWM for the daily news release at 5:00 p.m., the majority of them stayed after the press conference adjourned to hear the results of the workers' meeting. They were invited to wait in the reception area with Lee, who became a popular interviewee. Lee told them there were signs of disunity among labour groups and unions that supported the workers — mainly those affiliated with the Federation of Civil Service Unions. He said it was disappointing that other big labour organizations had shied away this time, and that perhaps they did so because the leaders of those organizations were trapped in the dilemma of also being government-appointed council members. He then announced that funds had been raised to support the sit-in by his affiliates, and called for more unions to join them.

The general meeting adjourned about 4:30 p.m., and the reporters and supporters were called into the meeting hall. On the stage, a blackboard showed the result of the workers' poll: Seventy-five insisted on the original demand, with thirteen against. Four spokeswomen announced the passing of the resolution for a continuous sit-in, and then announced the plan to petition the Japanese consulate and demonstrate there the next day. Finally, the rank and file were advised to go home and prepare for the next morning's show of force. Leaders and supporters were expected to return to the factory to sit through the night.

Day 11: 10 June 1986 (Tuesday)

Over one hundred workers came early and reported to their respective action teams before 9:00 a.m. The atmosphere was festive — most workers had brought drinks, snacks and lunch, and some had brought young children and babies.

Groups met in the canteen. Their leaders emphasized discipline: They were not a mob and would not disturb public order; their goal was to win sympathy from the general public. As banners and placards were allocated to each team, people were put in charge.

Before setting out, the workers voted to accept the petition to the Japanese consul-general, which protested (1) the union-busting tactics employed by JWM management, and (2) the discrimination against, and exploitation of, local workers. The petition then further reiterated their demands.

At 10:00 a.m. the workers were ready to leave. Chu Chi-lin had again volunteered to stay at the factory to maintain the sit-in, understanding that the rank and file wanted a piece of the action. She was confident that nothing would happen to her, although she would be alone at the factory.

Police?/Japanese? surveillance on the street demonstration from the opposite multi-storeyed car park on 10 June 1986 (Day 11).

The workers handed in the protest letter, by the door of
the Japanese consulate on 10 June 1986 (Day 11).

Workers demonstrated in front of the Japanese consulate
on 10 June 1986 (Day 11).

At 11:00 a.m. the demonstrators arrived at the Japanese consulate in the Bank of America Building. Many reporters were waiting. The workers lined up along the sidewalk, spread the banners, held up their placards, and slipped into their JWM uniforms to pose for photos.

When Lee Siu-ching arrived, he learned that the building's security guards had refused entry to the workers. He consulted with Gu and Fu and decided to go up to the consulate, on the twenty-fifth floor, with three RPs, to arrange for the delivery of the letter. The four were received by one of the consuls. Lee negotiated for about half an hour with the consul, who insisted that, owing to the limited space and the tight security set-up of the banks in the same building, they would rather send people down to receive the letter. However, the workers intended the opposite, and the negotiation stalemated.

Back at street level, more media teams, including both Chinese- and English-language TV stations had arrived. To appeal to English speakers, friends from support groups had helped the workers make banners and placards in English. Lo Un-pu, the elected spokesperson, was bombarded with questions, and Lee Siu-ching again became the most popular interviewee. He explained again that the reason the mediators failed to arrange a settlement was because they failed to understand that the workers were fighting for rights and dignity, and not only for monetary reward.

When Lo announced the consul's refusal, the demonstrators all jumped up from the sidewalk where they had been sitting and began to wave banners, sing protest songs and shout slogans. More and more passers-by stopped and watched, some coming up to inquire into the matter. More uniformed police also appeared, and as many, if not more, plain-clothes men from the police intelligence unit. It did not take long for the consulate to learn that their truculent approach had not worked to their advantage. People were sent down to negotiate, but it took an hour for the cautious consulate personnel to suggest that twenty workers come up to deliver the petition. Lee persuaded the workers to accept the offer. The twenty RPs went upstairs, where Lo Un-pu handed the letter to the public relations director of the Japanese consul-general. The ritual was thus completed; workers cheered and flashbulbs flashed. Lo told the reporters that the workers would be sitting by the sidewalk waiting for a reply, and would stay overnight if necessary.

Around 1:00 p.m. Ma rushed to the demonstration with a big stack of newspapers, which he showed to Gu, Fu and the major leaders before giving them away to the rank and file. He pointed out that the workers' press conference had attained the expected result.

One of the newspapers reported that Mao, on one occasion, had stated that neither the management nor the workers were to blame, and that the dispute was a result of 'lack of proper communication'. Yet he also asserted that it had already developed into a 'social incident'. He suggested that it would make foreign enterprises more 'watchful' and less willing to invest, hurting the Hong Kong economy. In conclusion, he claimed that even the Labour Bureau had something to learn from the event. He would use the lesson to discuss improving management in foreign companies to avoid similar incidents in the future. Stripping aside the rhetoric, Mao was making a conscious effort to connect the JWM workers' struggle to a threat of divestment by multinationals. It was amazing that the first such threatening statement came, not from a foreign business interest, but from a government agency — the Labour Bureau!

Elsewhere, the management had announced that, of the 120 striking workers, 27 had reported to work, and that 8 of the 36 dismissed workers — including 4 RPs — had accepted the management's compensation offer. The compensation ranged from several thousand — to more than HK$20,000. Furthermore, another twenty-five workers were interested in accepting compensation. In response, however, the demonstrating workers insisted that the figure was grossly exaggerated and that there had been no resumption of production.

Nevertheless, neither Ma nor Gu nor Fu could dismiss the significance of the announcement, as they knew that the true number was likely to increase over time. It was obvious that the management was practising the 'normalize production' strategy to break the strike. During lunch, the three of them reviewed the situation and reached the understanding that the sit-in was ending. The workers' leadership should be aware of this and plan a smooth and dignified way to 'step down the stairs' while they could still influence the majority. They agreed that decisions had to be made by Chu Chi-lin and her core group before it was too late.

Ma suggested that the workers should not merely wait by the sidewalk, which was boring and exhausting; after consultation, the workers suggested marching to the Bureau of Union Registration a few blocks away. While they realized that this would achieve no substantial result, the workers would get some activity and the media might also report on their inquiry into the legal status of their union — a rallying point for the workers. This suggestion was enthusiastically received and only a few workers were left to watch their banners and placards. They expected few supporters to visit them before the working day was over. However, Lee Siu-ching arrived unexpectedly soon after most of the demonstrators had left. He was disappointed to find no reporters around. He had brought with him a letter of protest signed by thirty-four unions, which he delivered to the consulate.

Almost as many police as workers went to the Union Registration Bureau. The workers stayed outside while their representatives went in to demand that the bureau chief protect union activists' rights, as the labour law dictated. Less than ten minutes later, they came out with the message that there was no evidence that the JWM management had fired the thirty-six for union activity. 'The reason stated in the JWM dismissal notice was "low productivity". Therefore, the Bureau does not consider they broke the Union Protection Ordinance ... ' This, of course, gave the workers another opportunity to jeer the authorities and protest. On their way back to the Japanese consulate, they marched in high spirits, waving placards and banners and catching the attention of many white-collar workers as they came out of their offices in the busiest district of Hong Kong.

Back at the consulate, the workers found enthusiastic supporters visiting them, some with snacks. Among them was Bao Yi-hai, about whom the workers were ambivalent. Bao began lobbying them to sit in overnight 'since the consulate had turned a deaf ear to workers' demands'. Some workers decided to go home after dark, others to return to the factory, but a few agreed to stay overnight on the sidewalk. No matter what his intention, Bao's behaviour, as usual, brought some disturbance.

Another visitor was a member of the Centre's executive committee, Lao Kan-kai, who came not to support the workers but to summon Gu for an 'emergency directors' meeting'. In order not to irritate the workers, Gu told Lo Un-pu that she had some 'personal' matter to attend to and left. 'I'll be back at the factory as soon as possible, say 10 p.m. Wait for me.'

When night fell, Lo and the core leaders left for the factory. Bao went along to pick up some sleeping bags for the overnight sit-in.

At CLA headquarters, Gu was under pressure and was again playing her 'silent' game. She kept her mouth shut and head bowed and took detailed notes, hoping to get the whole thing over as soon as possible and go back to the factory and the 'real struggle'. There were eight directors in the meeting. In addition, Lo Man-sa, director of the CLA, which partially funded the Centre, kept coming and leaving, showing that, busy as he was, he cared about the issue but would not dictate terms or intervene.

Without pretence, the executive director announced that the meeting had been called to 'straighten out the stance of the Centre' with regard to the JWM dispute. Since the dispute had yet to be resolved, it was not appropriate to review the way Gu had dealt with it; but it was imperative to assess the position the Centre had taken thus far. Following this, there were multiple analyses of the entire dispute. There were different viewpoints concerning the current action, and the issue of 'loss of face' for the Centre was brought up. It was wrong to upgrade the struggle and magnify the conflict between the Japanese and the Chinese, as it was meaningless to ask a foreign government to intrude into the affairs of a multinational enterprise. Someone should be held responsible for using the Centre's name to sign open letters and documents, even if the contents were acceptable. Lo casually commented, 'The CLA and I will surely clarify that there's no such thing as Japanese capital oppressing Hong Kong workers. The workers' slogans are exaggerated.'

Finally, Gu was reminded that there were pro-Trotskyite elements trying to use the dispute to their advantage, and the Centre must adopt measures to oust them.

In the factory canteen, Chu Chi-lin was disappointed to find that Gu could not come and, instead, that Bao had accompanied Lo Un-pu and Fu. On the way to the factory staircase, which was not covered by the injunction, Fu was puzzled to learn from a newspaper that Amukas had accused the workers of 'no-show' at a scheduled 2:00 p.m. meeting the day before. What meeting? Fu ran up to the fifth-floor office and looked among piles of announcements on the bulletin board. One read:

> 8 June 1986
>
> Attention all workers. The following is the result of meetings between the management and representatives: Management has exchanged many opinions with the representatives this afternoon and the atmosphere was extremely harmonious. The company hopes to resolve the dispute in a peaceful manner and expects your renewed proposals. For this reason, the negotiations have been postponed to 2:00 p.m. tomorrow. The company wishes to find a way to satisfy everybody. We again welcome everyone — either as individuals or in small groups — to express yourselves. You may telephone the management before 10:00 p.m. tonight and from 7:25 a.m. to 2:00 p.m. tomorrow or send them a note.

Of course, an announcement like this was meant to be read by some workers and neglected by others! It was part of the overall war of nerves and publicity, designed to discredit the workers and, if possible, to disrupt their general meeting and press conference, which had been scheduled for the same time.

Gu arrived on the factory staircase only after 11:00 p.m. and saw Chu, who complained of tiredness. Gu knew there were crucial things to discuss which could not be discussed with Bao around. When he and other supporters left around midnight, Chu, Fu and Gu finally managed to talk.

Chu told Gu and Fu that, since early morning, Mao Si-hai had been consulting with the management. He was ecstatic at finding Chu alone guarding the canteen and talked to her from 11:00 a.m. to 7:00 p.m., stopping sometimes to 'make some phone calls' upstairs. He had wanted Chu to be 'flexible'. He was frank, funny, even self-ridiculing. 'No matter what kind

of role we play, we know it's not forever, right? And no matter what position we take, we are after all reasonable and practical people!' The thrust of his argument had been fourfold:
1. The splits among the rank and file weakened their power.
2. The demonstration in front of the Japanese consulate had been the last peaceful resort available to the workers.
3. Since they only intended a peaceful protest — even Amukas expressed his admiration of the workers' resolution not to initiate violence — the only option left was to find a way to save face.
4. As there were still 80 to 100 workers in the hard-core, the strike could drag on for some time, a purposeless contest of egos damaging to all parties.

'It doesn't make sense, does it?' Chu stopped to comment.

Then she continued; every time Mao went up 'to telephone', he brought back bits of news. First, he told Chu that management would hold a press conference, where Amukas would dismiss the workers' protest at the Japanese consulate by claiming that no Japanese government pressure would be applied to private business disputes, either in principle or in practice, so that the Japanese consulate could only ignore the workers' demonstration. The second time he came back down he told Chu that Amukas would announce that, among the 217 women workers, 28 had resigned and 89 had reported to work; and that, among the 36 dismissed, 16 had agreed to accept compensation.

'But it was not true that the factory had resumed production,' Fu said. 'Well, I asked the same question, but Mao said it was not important so long as "normalization of production" was announced and workers were paid to stay home!' Chu answered.

After Mao's third trip upstairs, the news was that management would fire those workers who had not reported for work if they failed to show up in the next two days, as the company had already lost half a million Hong Kong dollars.

'Finally Mao said, "You guys are quite satisfied, aren't you?" A joke typical of him, don't you think?', Chu said.

Before leaving for an official dinner Mao had been extremely warm and personal, inquiring about individual workers' personal and familial situations and showing concern about their well-being and future. In response to Chu's claim that a decision had to be made by consensus, Mao urged Chu to call him that night. He gave her his home phone number. 'You must call me no matter how late. Call me at my house. I'm sure you will make the right choice, with your wisdom and care for the others.'

The situation was ironic, as Mao had pre-empted Gu and Fu in talking to Chu about accepting the inevitable. It was embarrassing, but undeniable, that this was the first time — but perhaps not the last — that Fu and Gu agreed with Mao.

'But what about the union?' Fu and Gu asked. This was *the* question.

'Actually Mao assured me that Amukas will pledge openly that the company will respect the union. And Mao personally suggested that we should keep as many workers as possible to continue our fledgling union.'

'Such a crook!' jeered Gu and Fu — but they could not help but admire Mao's craftiness.

It was almost 2 a.m. when Chu called Mao at his home and told him that the workers would be willing to consider being more flexible. Mao immediately told her to come to Amukas' hotel suite at 11:00 a.m. the next morning 'together with some of your closest pals, if you like, and we'll study some details.'

It was evident that it had all been anticipated.

Day 12: 11 June 1986 (Wednesday)

When Bao Yi-hai returned to the Japanese consulate with sleeping bags and blankets, it was 1:00 a.m. With him was Yang Lai-gau, a male volunteer at the Centre and a workers' leader in an earlier electronic multinational dispute. Two of the four workers there had already gone to sleep, but the four of them who were awake sat close together and talked until dawn. About 8:30 a.m., three RPs from the factory arrived to fetch their colleagues, bringing breakfast with them. Bao opposed returning to the factory, but he had to give up, as he had to leave for work. As the workers took down the banners and placards, a few reporters arrived. The only plain-clothes policeman around was glad to see some action. He reported the conclusion of the demonstration through his walkie-talkie. 'Good luck to you guys!' he said. The workers left.

Back in the factory, Chu, Gu and Fu greeted the sixty workers who had returned to continue the sit-in and work on new banners and leaflets. Some brought home-made glutinous rice dumplings, as that particular day was the Dragon Boat Festival. The delicacies reinforced social ties among colleagues and led to homesickness and other more complicated emotions. The sharing of the dumplings constituted ritual commensalism, and brought a precious, precarious sense of 'oneness'. The yearly festival commemorates a famous early poet's difficult struggle.

What Chu, Gu and Fu wanted least was for the hotel suite appointment to turn into an 'extramarital' negotiating session. Chu requested, and Mao promised, that the 'contact' be strictly unofficial and therefore nothing but a private talk. Mao actually suggested that the reason for the arrangement was precisely to avoid the presence of local management. 'Only Amukas will be present, and I will act as an interpreter, nobody else!' he stressed.

Chu wanted to keep herself completely uncommitted, so that in case of a breakdown, no political repercussions would result. She and her closest associates decided that no other RPs would go with her, that those who went would be associates with no recognized position, and that neither Gu nor Fu would go, to avoid 'putting all the eggs in one basket'. They also decided Mao was not trustworthy, even as an interpreter, so they called Lin Yi-chin in the morning and asked him to interpret for them. Surprisingly, he was available. He promised to meet them in the hotel lobby.

Before Chu and her three confederates set off for the hotel, one worker handed her two dumplings. 'Give these to Amukas to show him the graceful bearing of the Chinese,' he said.

'Don't you think he might take it as flattery?' somebody objected.

'Not with me!' replied Chu. 'Besides, it will be fun to see how he accepts ... it might help relax the atmosphere ...!' Before she left, she advised the workers to halt their preparation of banners and placards.

Amukas, too, was conscious of the private nature of the contact. He kept his promise that nobody else would be there, and consulted Mao on how to make the meeting as relaxed as possible.

When Chu presented Amukas with the dumplings, he immediately reached for the telephone and ordered drinks and delicacies for everybody. Over tea and coffee, he inquired about his visitors' families. To complete this warming-up ritual he volunteered his personal experience, telling the workers that, though now the CEO of the world's biggest watch manufacturer, he understood perfectly why the workers were fighting, as he had been an enthusiast when he was young. 'Even something of a radical, if you like,' he continued. 'Demonstrations and marches are not unknown to me.'

Then Amukas got down to business. 'I apologize for the unnecessary firing of workers. This kind of thing has never happened at JWM before. Serious mistakes were committed by your local superiors.' He looked at Mao and nodded, 'We have decided to have Mr Mao and his department run management courses for them to improve their communication skills.' Mao nodded back and Amukas continued. 'This kind of miscommunication and misunderstanding will be minimized. However, "spilled water cannot be recovered". I'm personally sorry for every one of you who has lost the opportunity to continue to contribute to us. It is a big loss for us. We know all of you are good workers and nice girls. I also appreciate your non-violent approach. But what can I do? I have a board of directors to report to and public stockholders to answer to. I can only compensate you as generously as possible ... I know you are not after money, but it is a way for us to express our regret ... ' He spoke like a grandfather to grandchildren rather than as an employer to employees. 'If you think there is still something to be improved in compensation, as long as it is not excessive, I have the authority.'

'For example, say, you request a doubling of your compensation for annual leave you failed to take,' suggested Mao, as he knew this would not amount to anything astronomical.

'No, that isn't necessary.' Rejecting him was the righteous Chu. Mao had once again ignored their moral stance and acted to demean them in front of a foreigner and a male. As Lin interpreted, the four workers gave Mao a dirty look.

There was little left to discuss, for none of the workers intended to dwell on the details. 'Instruct your inferiors to prepare a written proposal. I'll relay your words to my colleagues. Everything will be decided by the workers' collective alone,' Chu said to Amukas, and gave Mao another nasty look.

'Will you kindly consider that this may be the only way out for both the management and the workers? Unfortunately, the dispute has been so badly publicized that it doesn't leave us many alternatives. There is a lot of pressure from various corners,' Amukas stressed.

'Yes, we'll think about it, but I won't take a single penny of compensation from JWM,' replied Chu, and stood up to leave.

'I'll instruct our office to prepare a comprehensive proposal and make it available to you before dark. I'll also instruct the factory to withdraw the injunction order tonight,' added Amukas as he stood up and walked towards the door to see the workers and Lin off. 'We must have a final meeting tomorrow. Don't misunderstand us. Our major consideration is how management will treat those who stay on.'

'And the union. Money and compensation for those of us fired is of no consequence. Were we not prepared for personal loss, we could not have fought and insisted until now.' Chu threw the ball into Amukas' court at the very last moment.

'We will certainly not allow for any more management mistakes. We have no problem with your union at all ... ' Amukas pledged eagerly.

'I will assume you're sincere. Whether I'm right is for the rank and file to judge. The first test is what you propose tonight. We'll study it carefully and have a general meeting tomorrow. Goodbye.'

Out of the suite in the Shangri-la Hotel went the four workers and Lin.

'Why don't you go home, greet your parents and have a decent meal? It's the Dragon Boat Festival anyway and you have been away from home for almost two weeks', suggested Lin. 'Come back tomorrow morning and we will discuss our baseline against the proposal. I'll notify the Centre and your colleagues in the factory.'

Chu and her associates were persuaded, and hopped on the train for their homes in the rural area of Pat Heung.

At the factory canteen, about sixty workers were still sitting in. They had been chatting with Gu and Fu, trying to get complicated sentiments off their chests.

'In the very beginning, we felt everybody was in solidarity, but now some think it is important to get the money.'

'It was rather boring before the strike and now we are exhausted. Some said that we asked for it ourselves. Isn't it cruel to make such a statement?'

'I think they are totally different from us. We can't communicate, can't understand each other. Of course, some who participated in the first place finally dropped out. They told themselves that it wasn't worth it. If we insist, we will end up losing everything, including the jobs. It isn't nice, but some people do have to worry about it. But it isn't fair to the outside supporters, who have even less reason to be involved! It's okay for one to quietly drop out or even accept the money, but one should never work against the workers' collective. Some adopt a wait-and-see attitude ... you might say they are the free-riders ... well, there will always be people like that. It's rather disappointing to know people who took the money and ran. I was real mad about it. What the heck are we struggling for if they simply surrender?'

'These twelve days of sit-in were quite an experience. It wasn't bad at all. No work, air-conditioning, slept well, ate well (laugh). The only thing is we might not be paid for it!'

'Forget about those who only offered lip service and never came to sit in.'

'Real friendship only shows itself in adversity. After all the encounters you feel you understand life and people much better.'

'Your wisdom won't be enhanced if you never confront bad experiences. For example, the sixteen who took the money and ran — you didn't know what they really were before they did that, did you?'

Conversation halted when Lin showed up. He briefed the rank and file about their hotel suite contact. The strikers knew Chu really meant it when she said her concern was for the future of the remaining workers and their union. They were also sure that besides Chu, there were other leaders who would reject the management's money. They would not let themselves, and the workers, down.

Lin finally persuaded them to go home for the festival. Bitter-sweet, they were convinced that it was a good fight and promised to be a lifelong memory!

Day 13: 12 June 1986 (Thursday)

About 9:00 a.m., with about 100 supporters and RPs in the fourth-floor canteen, Gu and Fu walked in with a management proposal which had been delivered to the Centre the previous evening. With security gone, the doorman had greeted them with unusual courtesy.

During the discussion, differences emerged between those who had been fired and those who had not. While they consented to conclude their month-long struggle, the ones who were to stay insisted that all the workers should retain their right to be reinstated later or, according to the management's formulation, they should be eligible to be rehired after three months, since they had not been dismissed but had only been asked to 'resign voluntarily'. They insisted on this, even though none of the thirty-six would ever reapply. Those who were fired, i.e., the leaders *sui generis*, emphasized that the management should pledge to:
1. respect their union;
2. establish a provident fund for the operatives within six months; and
3. convert all the operatives from daily-rated to monthly-paid status.

The Ethnographic Narrative II

On 12 June 1986 (Day 13), leaders and supporters got together and cheered themselves after a three-month-long 'good-fight'.

Their counterproposal was agreed upon and given to the RPs for the afternoon negotiation. They then went down to the street to have lunch, while Gu and Fu rushed back to the Centre to relay the message to all supporters.

At the Centre, Ma insisted that some sort of final general gathering should be convened to explain to all the worker participants about the conclusion of their collective action. He felt the worst possible thing would be for a collective action to end and vanish without a trace — victory was only victory when it was claimed. In situations when victory is only partial, the winner tends to be the one who proclaims it. Ma thus argued for a collective action to consolidate the workers as a collective will and pre-empt the management in proclaiming the winner. Gu and Fu agreed, and proposed having those who remained host a farewell party for the thirty-six. Fu, motivated by a mischievous playfulness, suggested inviting Amukas 'to see how he would take it!' Ma warned of the danger, but reluctantly agreed, assuming that the worst had already happened, and that there was nothing more to lose.

At 2:00 p.m. sharp, the ten remaining RPs were invited to the fifth-floor conference room for the final negotiating session. Son Yan-min and Lo Man-sa, who had not been present since the St. Stephen's polling five days previously, were there, smiling broadly, having obviously been invited to witness the finale. Sophisticated politicians, they behaved with grace, lightening the atmosphere with witty remarks. Beside them the Labour Bureau people, led by Mao Si-hai, were surprisingly subdued. Amukas, relaxed and casual, greeted the RPs one by one. With a hint of condescension, he said, 'I sincerely give up the claim of winner, but I'm not prepared to be challenged.' The large, mysterious bald Japanese labour expert, who had always been jumping on his colleagues, was also smiling. Despite the hosts' disavowal, there was almost an atmosphere of celebration.

Amukas began by praising all 'his' workers, referring to the 'peaceful ways' they had expressed their discontent, without damaging factory property. He felt sorry for those who had to go but would convince the local management to rehire them after the merger. If those who had 'voluntarily resigned' had financial difficulties, the company was ready to consider further compensation 'so long as they would try to convince their co-workers to stay ... '

Chu Chi-lin spoke for the workers. She said the leaders, who had been fired, were concerned that some of the rank and file might run into difficulties if they agreed to settle on the present terms. What was important was their fate. Money alone was not enough. The workers requested that Amukas, representing the JWM management, pledge openly to respect their union, establish a provident fund within six months and turn all the operatives into monthly-paid employees.

Amukas, relieved, promised to make the union pledge to the press. In addition to supervising the setting up of a workers' provident fund, he would come back in three months to monitor the situation himself. Finally, he would 'try his best' to improve 'his' workers' welfare and see what the board of directors could do to turn all the workforce into monthly wage-earners. 'It is a deal.' He stood up and reached his hand out to Chu, as dozens of flashbulbs went off from the dozens of reporters who had dashed in, just in time, for the historic handshake, and Son's, Woo's, Mao's and Tu's shining smiles.

'Our union has decided to have a farewell party for those who have to go tomorrow. You, Managing Director, are also invited as our guest.' Chu extended her invitation as the handshake was 'frozen' for the photographers.

Amukas was embarrassed on hearing the translation, but recovered quickly. 'No, no, no! I was going to suggest a banquet for those of you who are leaving. Everyone here is invited, including our friends from the press. What was the name of the restaurant? Somebody go check it out, quick!'

There was a disagreement over who would be host. Perhaps because neither Gu nor Fu were around, or because the significance of being host was not grasped by the RPs; or because they were overwhelmed by the management, the Labour Bureau and the press — it turned out that Amukas would host the 'banquet'.

Gu and Fu were angry when told of this public relations *coup*, and their first reaction was to suggest that the workers should decline the invitation. They felt the workers should have a chance to recoup their dignity. Ma was also disheartened, but he felt that each of the thirty-six should attend the banquet, even those who had taken the money and left earlier, if possible, so as to turn it into a workers' celebration. A no-show by the workers would seem like they had 'chickened out' and the banquet would be an occasion for the management to claim 'victory'.

A consensus was reached, and Gu and Fu rushed to the factory to take care of the 'pull-out'. However, they found that the workers were not eager to leave. They lingered and chatted to each other. The sit-in site, charged with the tension and uncertainty of the immediate past, had become a place of nostalgia. It was past 5:00 p.m. by the time Gu and Fu managed to pull everybody away from their 'battleground'. They had been affected as well, and they remained silent as they made their way to the Labour Relations Association to brief friendly unions on the settlement.

The consultation at the LRA had been called to co-ordinate continuing support for JWM workers' anti-union-busting struggle. Gu and Fu gave them a detailed presentation, and there were a few questions. People were concerned about the future status of the JWM union. Given that the Labour Bureau had tried to push a tripartite consultation and the management had claimed to establish a board of workers' representatives, they worried that the union would sooner or later be incapacitated. To prevent such a bleak eventuality, suggestions were made to strengthen the union's new leadership. The participants in the meeting also pledged to help the dismissed thirty-six find new jobs, and to go on monitoring the JWM situation.

Before the consultation adjourned, the chairman of the Joint Organization of Unions, Hong Kong, Chapter (JOUHK), handed out a copy of a telegram sent by the Global Confederation of Labourers' (GCL) Geneva headquarters to JWM in solidarity with the JWM workers. There were other solidarity messages from the Asia-Pacific Young Workers, Young Catholic Workers and October Forum. As these documents were being passed around, people sat glumly, wondering whether all the encouraging words had simply come too late, or if the sit-in had ended too soon.

After the consultation, Gu and Fu said goodbye and headed home.

6 The Ethnographic Narrative III: After the Event (Day +1 to April 1987 and beyond)

Day +1: 13 June 1986 (Friday)

Gu and Fu called JWM from the Centre at 10:00 a.m. and learned that there was no work for the weekend. Production would resume on Monday. Management undoubtedly wanted to distance itself from the memory of the sit-in, but the Centre's job was to keep the memory and its spirit alive — the struggle was not over.

Through a teleconference, the workers' leaders agreed to the designing of a thank-you card in the union's name to be mailed to their supporters. Eighteen supporters — nine of the thirty-six dismissed and nine of the second- and third-line leaders — agreed to form a core team to continue union organizing, and proposed 'underground' activity. They suggested the Centre 'do homework' for them to figure out how to:
1. renew contact with JETCON workers;
2. set up training courses for union staff;
3. establish overseas connections; and
4. learn from their own struggles.

Gu and Fu were eager to work on these difficult tasks, as they reflected the workers' initiative. A meeting was set for Sunday afternoon, 15 June.

In evaluating recent developments, Gu and Fu noticed that everyone present at the last 'negotiation' had been invited to the dinner except Lee Siu-ching, who was not a favourite with the JWM management or with Amukas. Fu called Chu about it, and Chu told him the workers did not forget people who supported them. They would invite him to the farewell dinner. Fu immediately called Lee, who was obviously pleased, at first. However, once he learned that Amukas had usurped the role of host, he declined, saying that it was not appropriate for him to be present, as he had to avoid embarrassing JWM management and 'other unionists'. He would thus keep both his image and position intact. Lee's political sensitivity alerted Fu and Gu, who then decided that none of the Centre personnel should attend.

At the banquet, as the leaders later reported, people appeared outwardly comfortable, yet remained alienated. The expensive restaurant was not comfortable for the workers. Although they told the press that it was being held at their initiative, as their own farewell party, the next day's paper suggested that it had been proposed by Amukas, to express his gratitude to officers and union leaders, as well as to show his leniency towards the workers.

Day +2: 14 June 1986 (Saturday)

Around noon, Gu and Fu came into the Centre to prepare for the next day's consultation with the core team. They discussed the spirit of the workers, who had just been through an ordeal. They considered that, ever since the late 1960s, the union as a social institution had been discredited in Hong Kong. The defeat of the ultra-left uprising and the subsequent government defamation campaign had left unions in a shambles. Thus, recruitment would be difficult. Four other factors would add to the difficulty:
1. Lack of tradition in establishing premises (on-site) unions in Hong Kong;
2. Divisions within existing union federations, and their political alignments with China, Taiwan and the Hong Kong colonial rulers, made them political appendages rather than genuine social forces;

3. Inability of a new union to provide the consumer discounts and co-operative conveniences which well-established unions provided; and, finally,
4. Lack of clear victory in the struggle.

Under these circumstances, the feelings of the core members would be crucial to their future potential in mobilizing the workers.

The eighteen core members believed that the following questions had to be asked:
1. How does one understand one's relation to a union?
2. How could the results of the sit-in be evaluated?
3. How could the leaders assess the workers' relations to various governmental and non-governmental institutions and social groups?
4. What were the objectives of the union, and how could they be achieved?
5. What help was needed from the Centre and other 'outsiders'?

Training seminars for union staff were proposed, including courses on the history of the labour movement in Hong Kong, organizational skills, labour laws and related regulations, administrative routines and functions of the union, and interpersonal relations and interview techniques. On his arrival at the Centre, Ma volunteered to conduct a course in Japanese-style management.

As Lin Yi-chin walked in with a stack of newspapers, the discussion temporarily adjourned. All of the papers gave important space to the demonstrations of the day before at the Japanese consulate by Hong Kong's biggest union — the Professional Teachers Union. Members of the union and of three other educational bodies had sent a letter via the consulate to the Japanese prime minister, Mr Yasuhiro Nakasone, protesting the distortion of the facts of the Sino-Japanese War in history textbooks — a serious and emotional issue for millions — just one day after the JWM demonstration.

The four at the Centre had the same question: Was it possible that the Japanese consulate knew of the plans for the demonstration, and so forced JWM management to settle its dispute and avoid the convergence of the two issues? The Hong Kong government may also have had a hand in it.

This had occurred to others. Someone from the *Hong Kong Standard* called to interview Fu, asking him if he thought the textbook controversy had any bearing on the 'surprise' concession made by the JWM management. Fu denied any surprise concession, but said that, in his opinion, the company had been under pressure from the Japanese consul-general. He concluded, 'In retrospect, going to the Japanese consulate may have helped' the workers to get better compensation.

While Fu was talking, Lin, Gu and Ma were getting angry over another newspaper item which credited the banquet to the JWM management, and the accompanying picture captioned 'JWM strike ends happily, dismissed workers are no longer disgruntled'.

Day +3: 15 June 1986 (Sunday)

At 3:00 p.m., fifteen of the eighteen core team members came to the Centre. To Gu and Fu's surprise, the mood of the leaders was low and their expectations bleak. Conversation was personal and focused on people's feelings towards each other. Acquaintances had built comrade-like bonds, in the process learning to get along and work with each other. They had learned to discern the 'true face' of the management and to appreciate the strength and commitment of their colleagues, and believed they would benefit from these experiences and would be better prepared to solve future difficulties. However, the leaders who had been forced to resign, such as Chu Chi-lin, Chien Fon-yi and Lo Un-pu, felt betrayed. They had been hit by the 'traitors' among them. They were hurt, and it would take time to heal the wounds. There were rumours about them, and some were worried about finding jobs in the same neighbourhood.

However, almost everyone agreed that 'it was worth it'; it had been 'a good fight' and they had had, for the first time, the chance to 'live up to themselves'. But afterwards would come both dreams and nightmares.

The RPs admitted that, at the end, they had lost the public-relations war. Outsiders, relying on a biased press, thought the workers were the losers. Yet they had surprised everyone, including the Labour Bureau and the chauvinist management, by holding out for weeks. However, divisions had developed within the leadership, and the rank and file were not to blame. The RPs were responsible for the breakdown in communications between themselves and the average worker. The attempt by some RPs to keep unfavourable news to themselves was precisely what created suspicion between themselves and the workers. If the RPs were ready to sacrifice, so were the average workers. Was it not a struggle for everyone's justice and dignity?

Of course, the middlemen who negotiated with the management on the workers' behalf — without having been authorized by them to do so — had delayed their action and suffocated their initiatives. Yet those RPs who had co-operated with the middlemen had made their plan workable. The leadership from the sixth and seventh floors were volunteers who had worked at JWM the longest and had the most at stake, while those from the second floor were selected by popular nomination; and this partially explained why the former were the first to co-operate with the middlemen.

Concerning the future of the union, 'Big Brother' Chien Fon-yi remarked negatively that in Hong Kong it was unrealistic to think that workers could beat capitalists. Companies might lose a million dollars and still be healthy, but a worker who fought for justice and dignity would find herself out of a job.

As the exchange among the fifteen drew to an end, Fu tried to put the struggle in a better light. He told his fellow fighters that they had achieved a few firsts in Hong Kong's labour history: the first group of women workers to stage a peaceful factory sit-in for thirteen days, the first group of Hong Kong workers to expose the self-defeating traits of a Japanese-styled industrial control scheme, the first to establish an on-site union in an electronics production unit and to force the Japanese management to pledge to respect its future existence. Lastly, they were among the first to put pressure on management to set up a provident fund for production-line operatives.

As Fu was about to finish, obviously having encouraged most of the workers, Bao Yi-hai pushed his way into the office. He questioned 'attending a humiliating banquet hosted by the Japanese oppressor' and followed with a lecture on 'self-respect'. His talk only served to alienate him further from the group. Gu stopped him and adjourned the meeting.

It was Ma, again, who brought in the newspapers (Appendix, Day +3). The *Hong Kong Standard's* coverage of the JWM sit-in was divided into three feature stories, one of which was an elaborate synthesis/analysis of the sit-in by Liang Li-an. The authors of the other two stories were not recognized. It was amazing that the newspaper that had covered the JWM case the least should print so many stories. Centre staff guessed that somebody with a motive had been working behind the scenes.

In addition, the *Hong Kong Daily News* had published an extensive interview with Amukas; the *Ta Kung Pao* had run an article on the changing strategy of Japanese investors; and the *Central Daily* published a story critical of the JWM management, the Labour Bureau and the unions.

Judging from this unusual after-event coverage and the *post hoc* reasoning from different angles, the Centre staff agreed that:
1. the event was over but the issue was still alive;
2. the JWM sit-in was a genuine historic event which manifested transformations in Hong Kong's economy and society; and
3. it had been a 'test-case' that would be carefully studied by labour, management and government.

Day +4: 16 June 1986 (Monday)

On this, the first day of restored production, the new union directors — the core team members who remained at JWM — came to the Centre after work to report that the factory was quiet. Although some workers who had withdrawn from the sit-in earlier seemed uneasy towards the others – indeed, it was reported that one such worker from the second floor had been crying, though no one was sure why — management pretended that nothing had happened. Some line leaders even bought popsicles for their workers at the afternoon break.

However, there were some dissenting voices. A worker had apparently complained that she had been pressured to go along with the sit-in. Two workers from the second floor were transferred to work on the microscope — a job nobody liked, even with a $5-a-day subsidy — for at least two months. This was a long time for work which hurt the eyes, but it was announced that it was necessary to improve shipment of products back to Japan.

After a briefing and exchange of information, an informal union board meeting was held. Most of the core members thought it would be difficult to organize the union, given that management was trying to further divide the workers and, especially, their leadership. They expected that only the workers who had persisted until the end would join. Some suggested that they should forget about the seventh floor. They suspected that the seventh-people would report their organizing activities to the management. Some worried that if more people were transferred to different work units, they would quit, thus weakening the union. Most of them sensed that the working atmosphere would grow more uneasy, and that there would be fewer and fewer people to talk to.

Before the meeting adjourned, the workers were told that a training course for union staff would be held every Wednesday, from 5:30 p.m. to 7:00 p.m.

After the workers left, Gu and Fu checked all the newspapers of the day. They found a letter in the *Express* from the Organization for Peoples' Basic Rights (OPBR) about the JWM case, which urged the government to amend the labour laws to protect workers' rights to organize unions.

Day +5: 17 June 1986 (Tuesday)

Another day of full-page coverage of the JWM sit-in, this time in the pro-Chinese, rather pro-management *Ming Pao*. The coverage was divided into several parts, with no authors identified (Appendix, Day +5). Taken together, they consisted of another conscious effort to establish a historical account of the JWM case, if not to rewrite (or write off) history! Although multiple voices were quoted, they were monologically presented. Why does a newspaper strive to proclaim omniscience, narrate and explain history, to account for everything?

However, perhaps to provide a more 'balanced report', there was an 'inconsistent' side column, which reported that a strike mediator had suggested to the Labour Department that an executive officer, instead of a receptionist, should interview workers who sought assistance, so that disputes did not get 'out of control'. The author confirmed that only after the JWM workers had been turned down by the Labour Bureau clerk did they turn to local labour groups for help (Appendix, Day +5). In the same vein, a feature story in the *Central Daily* (Appendix, Day +5) claimed that a by-product of the JWM strike was that the Labour Bureau had learned from the JWM case and had suggested that management in Hong Kong establish labour-management consultative committees to help resolve disputes — although there was strong resistance to this scheme from both the 'right' confederation of unions and the 'neutral/independent' factions. Lo Man-sa, representing the latter, had emphasized that the dispute was a labour issue and not a nationalistic conflict between Japanese and Chinese (Appendix, Day +5).

A third paper, *Wah Kiu Yat Po* (Appendix, Day +5), reported the persistent difficulties in organizing trade unions. Hui Bei-kwang, the secretary of the Federation of Hong Kong and Kowloon Trade Unions (a 'neutral' federation), said that unionization in Hong Kong was difficult. Chief Labour Officer Mao Si-hai claimed that lack of communication was the main cause of conflict and discord. Dr Luk Sa-bien, lecturer in the Management Department of the University of Hong Kong, suggested that Hong Kong 'follow Britain's example of setting up a third-party organization to help workers who wish to set up trade unions reach an agreement with their employers and reduce confrontations.' (Appendix, Day +5).

Day +7: 19 June 1986 (Thursday)

Directors of the new JWM union came to the Centre after work. Joking, laughing and excited, they watched slides taken during the sit-in. After supper, they returned to sort out the bookkeeping of their existing funds. Told of the 'Trotskyist' stories, they felt progressively frustrated. They were quite sure that the stories were all exaggerations, and they were insulted.

'They really don't believe simple workers like us can counter the management's tricks.' They concluded, 'You can never trust those who make their living in tampering with words for illicit purposes.'

Although the workers were disgusted by the games of intellectuals and politicians, they were practical enough to realize that they would need to better equip themselves to counterattack those who attacked them. They needed to be trained in organizing. Accordingly, they identified seven areas of major concern and drafted a their own programme.

Day +8: 20 June 1986 (Friday)

The eighteen core members arrived at the Centre just before 7:00 p.m. for a dinner organized by the Board of Directors of TWLSC, but too late to consult with Gu about possible developments during the banquet. Instead, they rushed to the restaurant in the next building for the appointment.

They had, in fact, met first in a cafeteria after work and had intentionally come late to avoid discussion with Gu. They did not doubt that the banquet was the occasion for a showdown between Gu and her 'bosses'. They had been told that the banquet was to express thanks to the workers for their $20,000 donation — the result of a collection among the workers to show their appreciation for Gu's work — and to have a chance to become mutually acquainted. To the workers, this clearly meant there would be a review of the sit-in and, very likely, a criticism session aimed at their beloved Gu. Their only motive for coming was to defend her. To do this effectively, they had planned in advance to avoid embarrassing or inconveniencing her, so that she could act naturally. The workers could then act on their own initiative to protect her. As they knew there would be two tables, they had decided that the original leaders who had been dismissed would sit with the directors and do the talking. They would push Gu to the other table, with younger, second- and third-line leaders, where they could all enjoy the meal and lighten the atmosphere by avoiding serious discussion.

As a result of their seating strategy, the dinner turned out to be a success for the workers and a total disaster for TWLSC board of directors. While people at the second table were having fun, the hosts at the first table were lectured by Chu Chi-lin, Lo Un-pu, Chien Fon-yi, Hsiao Chia and Ho-chie. They told the directors that the sit-in had ended too hastily and had caught the workers unprepared. Before going to the Japanese consulate, the workers' morale had been greatly heightened by their general meeting. Various task forces had been organized, and everybody was ready to work on leaflets, placards and other projects, not only for use at the Japanese consulate but also for a local boycott of JWM products in Hong Kong, and there had been plans for a sit-in at the Japanese consulate, or a sleep-in in front of it. However, the quarrels that ensued during the demonstration were discouraging and disappointing, and when the workers went to the factory the next day they were told to give up making leaflets and placards and to just sit back and watch. It then seemed as if any possible solution was at the mercy of Amukas' unpredictable will. The decision for this passivity had not been discussed or made by the rank and file. Caught by surprise by this line of argument, the directors failed to respond to the workers. They did not agree, but there was little they could say to those who were, in fact, the clients they were supposed to serve. In fact, they resented having paid to be lectured by them.

Gu figured out the workers' tactic halfway through the dinner. She was thus spared a massive 'public trial' this time. However, Gu's time came when the workers had left. (All of the grudges were to culminate in Gu's dismissal from TWLSC six months later — an act which caused a controversy which led to the closure of TWLSC. Gu was then hired by CKLRS, where she continued organizing the local workers.)

―――――

A reader's letter in the *SCMP*, signed by a Japanese woman, Fukkako, who represented the Women's Rights Committee of the Humanist Society of Hong Kong, supported the JWM workers' struggle against discrimination and being labelled 'troublemakers'. She gave Hong Kong citizens an example of a 'typical Japanese discriminatory practice': A big bookstore chain in

Japan dictated that 'women with an interest in philosophy, art, psychology, law, or modern art, or who take part in welfare associations, or have boyfriends who teach at a university, or any other similar condition, should not be hired.' The reason: 'These types of women are potential troublemakers.'

Day +9: 21 June 1986 (Saturday)

Gu and Fu went to the Labour Relations Association to attend a meeting, called by the groups which had supported the JWM workers, to consider the past and the future of their workers' collective and its significance for a Hong Kong independent union movement.

At the meeting, Lee Siu-ching reviewed his personal involvement. He admitted that it was the first time that he had personally intervened in a labour dispute in the private manufacturing sector. His reason was that management was allegedly dismissing workers for union activities and the workers had requested assistance. Lee agreed that the workers had persisted because their dignity was at stake. He also felt that management must have been aware of the planned boycott, and revealed that the governor of Hong Kong had given instructions to inform the Japanese consulate that the authorities would stand behind foreign investors. The officials were aware that industrial disputes could ignite anti-Japanese sentiment.

As the head of the Federation of Public Service Unions, Lee had been under considerable government pressure. He recalled that some people had questioned the appropriateness of the involvement of a civil service union in the dispute. Finally, he emphasized that he was convinced that the workers had independently distinguished between different opinions.

Some workers criticized the outside help. There had been a lack of co-ordination among the various groups, and this lack of 'tacit understanding' led most of them to be careful only to offer assistance and never to usurp the workers' leadership, never to bargain with the business establishment on the workers' behalf, never to try to 'put out the fire' or to play the role of arbitrator.

In concluding, participants agreed that it would be difficult for the JWM union to survive in the present overall political atmosphere. However, it was important for existing groups to build solidarity among themselves and to strengthen links.

Press reports included a letter in the *Express* signed by 'Old Hong Kong Li-pui', who accused the workers of disturbing the stability of Hong Kong and scaring away foreign investors, and called for co-operation between the workers and management to maintain Hong Kong's 'stability and prosperity'.

In the *Central Daily*'s 'Marching towards 1997' column, a commentary by Fan Yu-lin, entitled 'Concerning the Trotskyites', asserted that it was wrong to brand all people who work with Trotskyites as Trotskyites, as 'only those who have formally pledged allegiance to the party' could be so considered, and random use of the label only served to exaggerate their power.

Day +10: 22 June 1986 (Sunday)

The *Sing Pao Daily* featured an article which, despite a certain amount of apparently pro-labour rhetoric lauding 'heroic' sacrifices by 'vanguards', also pointed out that 'Hong Kong society does not tolerate militant labour movements' and wound up by warning that 'pushing too hard can only hurt the movement' (Appendix, Day +10).

Day +15: 27 June 1986 (Friday)

An article by 'Shan' in the *Wah Kiu Yat Pao* (Appendix, Day +15) quoted one of the dismissed RPs as saying that, although she had no regrets, she might 'not have favoured using such radical means' if she had to wage the struggle again, as 'in a strike, whatever the outcome, the workers themselves are always the ones who suffer most'. But she said the strike had changed her life, that she could not previously have imagined that she would meet with officers of the company, officials of the Labour Department or reporters. Before the strike her life had been concerned with going to the cinema, shopping and playing mahjong. Now she felt that life had been meaningless. After the strike she had become a volunteer at the Centre, and had also volunteered to help collect signatures against the building of the Daya Bay nuclear plant near Hong Kong.

Concerning the strike itself, the RP affirmed that, although she had gained valuable information from certain labour groups, all decisions were made by the workers themselves and that there were no 'Trotskyists' involved. The final decision to end the strike came about, according to her, because, although the RPs themselves were not in pressing financial difficulties, some of the workers were, and so it was decided to bring the strike to an end.

Day +16: 28 June 1986 (Saturday)

In the evening the TWLSC held a special directors' meeting to review the role TWLSC had played in the JWM dispute. Gu was asked to be present. Lo Man-sa, head of the CLA, also showed up.

It was emphasized that the review was to be impersonal and business-like. The first task was to review when each 'third party' involved in the strike became involved. This led the discussion to become a debate on principles vis-à-vis the practices of intervention in labour disputes. There were different opinions among the directors concerning intervention at JWM, ranging from the positive one held by Gu's immediate supervisor Li Nai-kuan to the critical and resentful position of Yen Chin-chih. In between were Poon Ni-kwan, Lao Kan-kai, and others. Lo Man-sa avoided taking sides. After three hours the meeting concluded that 'class struggle' should not be waged in the production unit, as the workers should not be made to sacrifice for a cause to which they did not necessarily subscribe.

Day +18: 30 June 1986 (Monday)

An article by Chan Kwok-lam in the *Central Daily* (Appendix, Day +18) reported that a woman involved in the strike denied that there had been an manipulation of the workers by outside forces, and that no 'Trotskyists' had been involved beyond the single appearance of a young member of the Revolutionary Marxist League at the factory staircase and that of an elderly man from the *October Review* 'who gave a letter with donations to the workers' when they went to petition the Japanese consulate. Neither appeared again, nor were they contacted by the workers.

> In the course of negotiations, the workers said that Fu Kwon-sin, an executive of CKLRS, and Gu Lai-hap, an executive of TWLSC, were served with an injunction order by the employer and forbidden entry to the factory. At the negotiating table, the workers 'fought alone'. Nevertheless, they encountered some labour association representatives who were not invited by them. These representatives stood firm behind the management and tried to persuade the workers to give up their demands. If one claims that there were outsiders intervening and manipulating the workers, they were surely not from the groups supporting the workers, but from those called in by the management.

Another worker was reported as saying that the strike had been ended because some of the workers were in financial difficulties, but the workers did not admit defeat, and that the struggle had taught workers 'that they had the strength to fight for their rights on their own'.

Chan ended his article in the following manner:

> However, had Mr Amukas ever pondered on the question: Why is it always the workers who are the ones sacrificed? We tried to contact Woo Char-hwa, director of JWM in Hong Kong, and Mao Si-hai, the Chief Labour Relations Officer, concerning the question of why there were labour association representatives not invited by the workers at the negotiating table, but they were unavailable for comment.

Day +20: 2 July 1986 (Wednesday)

The Hong Kong *Economic Journal*, the only Chinese-language newspaper not yet covering the JWM dispute, published a long article: 'A general assessment of the JWM dispute', by Bai Sa-kuo. It accused the *Express* of 'confounding right and wrong' in its 12 June article, and criticized various other media reports. The author particularly criticized Mao Si-hai's claim of the 'changing nature' of the dispute and his accusation concerning 'third parties'. Bai described Mao and the Labour Bureau as the most active 'third party', and went on to expose his attempts to play the role of a 'multi-headed snake'. He also pointed out that Wong Nieu-kwen, a local industrialist and the powerful appointed chairman of UMELCO, had constantly urged the JWM management to tighten its grip, suggesting that JWM dismiss one worker every day to intimidate the workers. Bai was amazed that public opinion never accused the foreign industrialists of pressing JWM management to refuse to reinstate the thirty-six workers. The only groups who did this were some small social groups and international labour organizations — including some in Japan — who spoke out for justice. These groups did play a positive role in resolving the stalemate.

Finally, the author praised Amukas for his awareness and his recognition of the workers' 'natural tendency' to strive for better welfare and working conditions. This praise, however, merely served to introduce the author's grand finale. He concluded:

> There are many reasons why Japan has become an industrial giant. Healthy industrial relations are indispensable in achieving such success. The ways in which Amukas handled the JWM dispute were remarkably rational, sensitive and flexible. Amukas' ways provide many lessons for mean Hong Kong officials with narrow vision and for those Chinese capitalists who remained backward and conservative. High-handed measures will not adequately resolve disputes and conflicts between the workers and their employers. Never to return are the days when workers worked without complaint, under hardships and criticism, and remained loyal in their service, like faithful house pets.

Day +21: 3 July 1986 (Thursday)

Various newspapers reported a labour dispute at a newly established PC board factory, the result of the management's attempt to 'reform' the wage and welfare systems. Twenty-five workers staged a sit-in on the premises and six representatives were sent to UMELCO to contact their boss, UMELCO Chairman Wong Nieu-kwen, who refused to talk to them. The workers then sought assistance from the Labour Bureau. After four hours of negotiation, the twenty-five workers agreed to 'resign' and take the factory's offer of a specially-arranged severance payment.

Day +22: 4 July 1986 (Friday)

The volunteer union directors came to the Centre after work. Together with Gu and Fu, they discussed issues concerning the role of local non-union labour organizations, relations between on-site unions and trade unions, labour movement strategies and orientation, and the legislation of more progressive labour laws. They also approved the arrangement of a six-session course for union staff starting 9 June.

The Hong Kong *Economic Journal* published an article by Son Yen-min entitled 'Labour problems in Hong Kong's future economic development', in which Son made reference to the JWM dispute. He criticized 'obsolete' modes of management: a patriarchal style of operating, refusal to communicate directly with the workers, discouragement of union organization, and union-busting practices. He also criticized employers for viewing worker's welfare as charity rather than as a lawful right.

Day +25: 7 July 1986 (Monday)

At a social workers' association meeting, Yen Chin-chih, representing TWLSC, was interviewed for a radio broadcast. Yen told the interviewer that the only paid staffperson at TWLSC had refused to obey a decision of the TWLSC board and had violated TWLSC's policies. This had complicated and prolonged the JWM issue. He also criticized Lee Siu-ching for failing to fully understand the facts before jumping in.

Day +27: 9 July 1986 (Wednesday)

At 5:30 p.m. Fan Si-lai, a veteran woman social worker and volunteer at the workers' night school, lectured on oral communication skills at the first class for JWM union staff. The twelve workers who participated enjoyed themselves.

Day +28 10 July 1986 (Thursday)

Twelve anxious JWM union directors arrived at the Centre. They had learned that, during July's rush, most workers had been asking to work overtime. As work pressure mounted, the attitudes of the line leaders and foremen improved. Wages had been paid for the whole sit-in period, and a special bonus was given on the day of the merger. Although some of the second-floor workers had been transferred to the seventh floor, only a few workers resigned. The management had made an announcement:
1. There would be a factory-sponsored outing to a holiday resort in China for JWM employees on 13 and 14 August. The management would pay $250 of the $300 cost for each worker. Chi-mei had been asked to represent the workers and to co-ordinate with line leaders.
2. The management instructed each line leader and foreman to have a daily 'chat' with his workers from 7:55 to 8:00.
3. The whole factory would have a week-long break, during which workers would be paid half wages.

The union directors felt the management was systematically trying to buy off the workers. Some of the old workers felt that management had treated the workers better since the sit-in. Newcomers were amazed by 'extra' benefits. At the same time, management was attempting to minimize any possible conflict between operatives and their immediate supervisors, and some staff had begun to persuade workers not to join the union. There were rumours that management at JETCON was pushing a management-initiated union — a Japanese-style 'yellow' union — to pre-empt any organizing effort by the workers.

At this point, Gu and Fu interrupted to report that sources from the Labour Union Registration Bureau had said that JWM management lawyers had approached the Bureau and requested access to the new name list of union directors, claiming they needed it to compare with the previous name list that they had acquired. The Bureau denied the request because it was illegal to release it. Under the present circumstances, it would certainly have been dangerous to do so. Later, other law firms tried to acquire the list. Then the Bureau received inquiries about the possibility of registering another union under the same name as the JWM workers' union. These requests were also turned down.

Ma was of the opinion that JWM management was trying to establish some sort of joint consultative committee (JCC), a three-sided consultation.

Finally, the second-floor union directors confirmed that two unknown Japanese were assigned to the second floor to supervise the local male foremen and female line leaders. They worked hard and forced local management to work hard, and were resented by local staff, who could no longer fool around. Some of the workers were glad that the 'running dogs' could no longer 'watch us work with folded arms', but others felt it only made local staff press them to work harder. In any case, this was not an effort to localize management, as Amukas had claimed in his press interview.

To counter the management's 'sabotage conspiracy', Gu, Fu and the directors came up with countermeasures: enrol new workers in the union; share experience with JETCON workers; organize social activities; hold union meeting to elect new directors; and set up a task force to ensure recognition of the union.

―――――

A feature article entitled 'Different views on the JWM labour dispute', by Yen Giu, appeared in the *Hong Kong Economic Journal*. The author, briefly reviewing the history of the dispute and emphasizing the differential treatment of the monthly-rated administrators and the daily-rated operatives, pointed out how management had exploited this to force the monthly-rated to take management's side. With no job security, workers could be dismissed arbitrarily at any time. It was thus impossible to organize an on-site union in Hong Kong. Although the author wondered how long the JWM union could last after the major organizers had been fired, he was positive about the achievements of the JWM workers. At the least, the JWM workers had put into question the habitually arrogant management attitude that 'those women could never do us any harm!' The ambiguous attitude and scandalous behaviour of the 'established unionists' in the struggle was shameful. They had not supported the smaller labour organizations, and had allowed the press to call them 'third parties' and 'Trotskyists'. Throughout, the Hong Kong news media had produced 'yellow journalism'. It was now time for the media to take a good look at itself.

Day +33: 15 July 1986 (Tuesday)

Twelve union directors came to the Centre to work on different projects. They decided to use the Centre's mailing address as the union's official address.

The programmes task force proposed two sports teams: volleyball and badminton. They would use the union's name to book space in the community gymnasium at least once a week. They proposed to write to TV and radio stations, movie studios and the Hong Kong Observatory to arrange tours for the workers. They also planned a debating contest to improve their public speaking ability.

The teams working on union organization contacted the Labour Union Registration Bureau to push for licensing, and initiated communication with unions and labour organizations both locally and abroad, as well as with JETCON workers.

Day +34: 16 July 1986 (Wednesday)

Lee Siu-ching's second training course, on interpersonal relations and organization, was well received.

Day +39: 21 July 1986 (Monday)

A feature article appeared in the *Central Daily* under the heading 'Involved in labour disputes as mediators; status of labour organizations not recognized; organizers tried to secure right to negotiate'. The writer complained that there was no law ensuring the recognition of labour unions by management. As a consequence, in eight of ten cases, labour organizations were expelled from the negotiating table and individual workers were left alone to face management and their legal assistants. Currently, the FLU was fighting to secure recognition of rights to negotiate for its seventy-plus associates, while smaller groups, such as TWLSC, were constantly prevented by court injunctions from entering the negotiations. However, Yen Chin-chih, the TWLSC director who had tried to force Gu to quit, said that labour groups should not necessarily fight for the right to negotiate. Due to lack of manpower, small local groups could only play supplementary roles and should avoid getting involved in major disputes, which they should leave to the established unions.

In another article, appearing in the *Hong Kong Economic Journal* under the heading 'During JWM dispute labour groups encouraged workers to take radical action; Labour Bureau negligent from the beginning', the deputy commissioner of the Labour Bureau was quoted as saying that the Bureau acted as moderator, not judge, in dispute cases. Chief Labour Officer Mao Si-hai commented that, in the JWM case, the local labour groups failed to advise workers to approach the Bureau for mediation, and instead urged the workers to take radical action, which delayed resolution of the conflict. He claimed that it was only his personal intervention which had led to a settlement. Lee Siu-ching was quoted as saying that the workers had felt it necessary to protect their dignity, and therefore had intentionally delayed an overall settlement. He denied that labour groups had made decisions on the workers' behalf, and said the aims of labour unions were different from those of government departments, and should not behave in the same way. Son Yan-min declared that the role of the Labour Bureau was not to judge right or wrong, but to mediate, although, according to the Labour Ordinance, it was not to force either management or workers to accept its mediation. Finally, Mao Si-hai confirmed that the Labour Bureau was one of the JWM mediators. He criticized local labour groups: 'Their purpose was to protect the interests of one side and, consequently, they could not be effective. There was some negligence on the Bureau's part in the earlier stages, but once the central bureau stepped in, it found that the workers were already reliant on local labour groups.'

Day +41: 23 July 1986 (Wednesday)

A third class, on establishing sound leadership, was held for the union directors at the Centre. Most of the directors came, and suggested the schedule be changed, as some foremen and line leaders were suspicious of the workers who refused to work overtime every Wednesday.

Day +43: 25 July 1986 (Friday)

Prior to the long break, the JWM workers planned a trip to Beijing — a plan initiated by the dismissed leaders (Chu Chi-lin, Lo Un-pu, Hsiao Chia, Chien Fa-hin and Chien Fon-yi), all Hakka speakers from Pat Heung, who were not under pressure to find work immediately. Most of them had at first refused the compensation from JWM but, at the last moment, after Woo had persuaded Chu that 'if they refuse, it will only benefit JWM and nobody will even know about it, not to mention appreciate it', Chu decided that all of them should take the money. Yet, still uneasy about accepting 'this kind' of money, which had come 'unjustly', they felt it should be squandered. This sentiment justified the trip. (Later reports were that the trip had been pleasant. New friendships had been built based on those 'good hard times', and comradeship had been renewed).

Day +54: 5 August 1986 (Tuesday)

JWM union directors came to the Centre to plan their union's official inauguration, on 25 August, at St. Stephen's Church. Tasks for the next three weeks were:
1. to invite all the union leaders, support groups and media personnel who had been involved;
2. to publish union by-laws in a small booklet for distribution among the workers;
3. to recruit members;
4. to prepare financial reports; and
5. to organize a weekend camping trip as a pre-inauguration activity.

The union would emphasize welfare and communication services. In doing so, the union would educate the rank and file, secure legal status for negotiation rights and counter the management's efforts to establish a joint-consultative committee (JCC).

One overall union director and one overall deputy director would be elected, for one-year terms. Under them would be five task forces: Co-operation and Communication, Welfare and Financing, Rights and Benefits, Self-education and Study Projects, and Publications and Public Relations — each with its own director and deputy director.

Day +62 & +63: 13–14 August 1986 (Wednesday–Thursday)

These two days had been set for the JWM management-sponsored outing. Although entitled to a $250 subsidy, not a single daily-rated worker participated. Such activity 'was not their game'; it had been designed by the management, who thought of themselves as 'high class' and 'expensive'.

Day +64: 15 August 1986 (Friday)

A long article appeared in a popular monthly entitled 'Different views on the JWM industrial dispute', by Luk Ga-yip, the long-serving chairman of the Hong Kong News Reporter's Association (HKNRA), who had reported on the JWM strike for the *Standard*. Luk began by confessing that he had once intervened in the JWM dispute, on the management's side: On 7 June, he had received Lee Siu-ching's call to support the workers. He had declined, saying that HKNRA usually 'was neutral on socio-political issues'. On 9 June he had gone to the workers' meeting as an observer; and the next day he attended a management press conference and, afterwards, had had a talk with Amukas. Amukas suspected that Lee Siu-ching had incited the workers to act to 'destroy all indiscriminately, be it jade or rock', and Luk had volunteered as go-between for Lee and Amukas, since 'Amukas held some prejudice against Lee'. The aim was to 'reopen negotiations and invite Lee to participate'. That evening he had reached Lee, who expressed his willingness to discuss things; yet the next morning, when he phoned a certain management consultant in Hong Kong, he was given the impression that Amukas might not want to see Lee. Later, when Luk reached Amukas, he agreed to meet with Lee, and even suggested that the three of them meet privately. However, the meeting materialized only after the final settlement had been reached. Luk claimed that the solution was the result of Amukas' style and personality. Despite a strong hint from the Secretary for District Administration, Leonado Du, that 'public opinion would support JWM's tough action', Amukas had feared irritating strong Japanese unions, and refused Wong Nieu-kwen's suggestion of dismissing one worker a day because he had been a 'leftist' himself when he was young. Luk concluded that, due to tremendous pressure from the business community and government, the workers would eventually be totally neutralized. The settlement, he added, was mostly the result of Amukas' judicious use of the carrot and stick.

Luk then revealed some inside stories: There were 'Trotskyists' around who were radical regardless of the outcome; Son Yan-min and Lo Man-sa became reinvolved in the last instance, after they had quit mediating on 7 June; and all but Lee Siu-ching had something to gain. Consequently, in Luk's opinion, Lee was the 'biggest' loser. He had fought for the workers' dignity, yet he was politically alienated by his previous allies and was invited to neither the signing ritual nor the banquet. The article ended by praising the journalistic contributions of the *Hong Kong Standard* and its reporter, Liang Li-an — Luk's personal secretary in the HKNRA.

Day +74: 25 August 1986 (Monday)

The director-designate agreed to postpone the union's scheduled inauguration. Most of the workers whom the directors had contacted were unenthusiastic. One of the most crucial reasons was the weakening of the leadership — a phenomenon certainly intended by management when they decided to fire the thirty-six workers.

At the Centre, the director-designate related recent developments in the factory. The management had announced improvements in the welfare provision and a reduction in fines for absences and had promised that, on Chinese New Year's Eve, long-service gratuities would be paid to those who had worked for more than five years.

On the shop-floor, the second-floor workers were 'bored' by the morning 'chat' sessions and requested that they be held every other day; on the first and seventh floors the sessions continued. The JWM factory had yet to change its name to JETCON. According to rumour, Amukas would come for the name change.

There was interesting, widespread gossip about the dismissed workers. Three of the thirty-six had successfully applied for jobs at an old JWM branch. However, one day they had run into Woo Char-hwa, and soon after all three were fired without reason. However, veteran skilled workers had been approached by intermediaries to work in a Subcontracting plant at jobs similar to those they had had at JWM. The plant turned out to be partially owned by Woo Char-hwa, and so the workers declined, not wanting to work for Woo again or to be treated as newcomers and then dismissed after they had outlasted their usefulness.

Day: +79 30 August 1986 (Saturday)

The JWM union director-designate came to the Centre at noon to report that the factory would officially change its name on 1 September. Amukas was in Hong Kong, but had failed to show up at the factory. Management had suddenly asked all workers to fill in forms stating that workers who had accumulated a certain length of service would be acknowledged by the new company. Most of the workers had already signed the form but, before they could turn them in, they were told to forget about it, and that the forms were invalid, as the personnel manager had to consult 'experts'. Most line leaders and foremen also felt uneasy about the matter. Rumours spread that Mao Si-hai had stopped the signature-collection exercise to 'prevent further possible turmoil'. When the Centre inquired into the matter, they found that CLA was aware of it and that Lo Man-sa had also advised the management not to cause any controversy. It was clear to everybody that issues leading to the sit-in were still alive.

Day +100: 20 September 1986 (Saturday)

Production had been extremely heavy since the end of August. Management had tried to push the workers to work overtime, and those who worked the hardest were encouraged by the offer of monetary reward. Afterwards, starting in November, time-off would be given not only every Saturday but also every Monday. Workers, even those who were not supporters or director-designates, suspected that it was an effort to sabotage union organization efforts. The Centre staff dismissed this suggestion for lack of concrete evidence.

In response to Luk Ga-yip's somewhat slanderous magazine article, Fu Kwon-sin published a response, under the title 'The significance of the JWM labour dispute'. Fu emphasized the anti-discriminatory nature of the dispute and confirmed that the involvement of other Japanese industrialists had inspired the workers to appeal to the Japanese consulate. The dispute was internationalized and politicized not merely because it involved a multinational offshore manufacturing unit but also because of the involvement of different levels of government(s), as well as domestic and foreign business interests. This made the workers' struggle extremely difficult. Ironically, it also legitimized the involvement of domestic and foreign labour and human rights organizations. In addition to successfully rallying international support and establishing a union, the struggle had set a precedent. The case would be studied for a long time to come. It would serve to improve the status of Hong Kong workers and deter any further effort by business interests, either domestic or foreign, to practice union-busting.

Day +110: 30 September 1986 (Tuesday)

Three members of the union directors' board managed to avoid working overtime and came to the Centre to 'catch their breath' and be 'refreshed'. It was boring and dull in the factory; work pressure was high and organizing work was not possible. More Japanese had arrived and were involved in shop-floor operations. However, some line leaders confirmed that Japanese vice-general manager Tosai was leaving Hong Kong, and that Woo Char-hwa had been moved to a smaller office. Amukas had not appeared, though he promised he would meet with the workers in two months.

October 1986

There were few developments. Follow-up reports on JWM appeared in the

English press, including a personal profile of Gu Lai-hap, 'the gung-ho unionist'. It was possible that the news reporter, who knew that Gu was under pressure from the TWLSC directors, had filed the report, hoping to strengthen Gu's position. The other article, 'Union set-up on the quiet', reported that the government had approved the union and that the first general meeting would be held soon. It also affirmed that most of the workers had lost faith in the management and that an invisible wall separated the immediate supervisors and operatives.

November 1986

It was a very relaxed month. The factory was open only four days a week. Workers, however, were paid for five days.

December 1986

Tosai left Hong Kong. The management eliminated the position of line leader: Line leaders were 'promoted' to the rank of 'foreman', and assistant line leaders to the rank of 'assistant foreman'.

By the end of the month it was announced that, for the time being, the management would not set up a 'provident fund', as they were following the debate on the setting up of a region-wide 'central provident fund' and had decided to wait for the government's decision, to avoid the confusion of possible later changes. Workers were asked to be patient.

January 1987

A few more Japanese came to work on the shop-floor. On 15 January, contrary to previous practice, the annual wage adjustment was openly announced. For the first time, every operative was given the same raise: HK$5.00. On 19 January, the newly promoted women foremen asked the workers whether they planned to continue working for JWM, telling them there would be a lot of work during the coming year, and management wanted to be sure about the workforce. This was obviously an effort to pre-empt the expected loss of workers after the Chinese New Year break. On 22 January, a year-end banquet was announced, for the first time. All workers were invited, but each had to pay HK$30 deposit to guarantee attendance, refundable at the banquet.

February 1987

Before Chinese New Year, the management warned the workers that they had learned of cases of workers' punching work cards for others. Anyone caught doing this would be dismissed without compensation. There was no mention of how whoever's cards had been punched would be handled.

It was announced that after the New Year holidays anyone bringing in a new worker would receive a HK$400 bonus. After learning that the union had offered members discounted year-end shopping, management offered workers discounts on the purchase of JWM watches.

Overtime hours were to extend from 6:30 p.m. to 8:45 p.m. After the workers protested, this was changed to 7:45. Workers who chose to leave at 6:30 could do so.

March 1987

From the beginning of the month, the activities of the union directors intensified. It was evident that management had failed to sabotage their union. However, the so-called union was still a mirage to most workers — the legal skeleton of the union had yet to take on real body and life. It was imperative to publicly adopt democratic procedures, to legitimize the status of the director-designates and have them openly identify themselves. It was decided that on the anniversary of the dispute, a general meeting would be called to elect a new board of directors and celebrate their assumption of office. Official letterhead invitations to the event were printed and sent to various unions and labour groups, including the CLA. Individuals like Mao Si-hai, Lo Man-sa and Lee Siu-ching were invited, as were representatives of the JWM management, from Amukas to local Japanese managing director Chubiki and Woo Char-hwa. The invitation of these latter was aimed for 'domestic consumption'. To enhance the union's legitimacy and fend off fear, it would be announced to the workers during the recruitment drive that management had been informed and that the top officers were invited. If management showed up, which was unlikely, they would have to behave themselves. Their presence would mean recognition of the union, and this would boost morale. If management did not appear, they would still have to respond to the invitation, and no matter how this was done, the response itself would be a recognition of the union's existence.

The 22 March union congress and directors' inauguration was an achievement. Although only about fifty workers signed up, the occasion was joyous, thanks to friendly guests, dismissed workers, Centre volunteers and newspaper reporters.

No management personnel showed up, nor did Lo Man-sa. Both Mao Si-hai and Lee Siu-ching came — although largely for extraneous reasons.

At the beginning of March, a rift had occurred in the Tung Wah Group, Hong Kong's biggest and oldest benevolent organization and hospital group, over the issue of retirement. The dispute was deadlocked for weeks and the Labour Bureau had tried to mediate. Knowing that the JWM union's invitation was a way to legitimize itself, Mao came, as he might have had a hard time justifying himself if he had not. He had his own agenda and needed a forum to express himself. There were also disputes between the middle rank and service unions of the civil service and the government over the issue of annual pay hikes, and so Lee too came, but not just to socialize with the workers. The result was that the next day more than ten newspapers reported the JWM union inauguration, but none mentioned the union in its headline. Most captioned Mao's assurance that the Tung Wah issue would be resolved in two weeks; other articles stated, under the heading of Lee's claim, that the bottom line for the civil service unions was an 8 to 10 percent raise. Only four of the ten news items reported the name of the JWM union and the nature of the occasion.

The JWM management was cautious. Both the Japanese headquarters and the local management had responded in an ambiguous manner, by posting letters apologizing for the absence of Amukas, Chubiki and Woo Char-hwa only on Friday, 19 March, too late to arrive at the Centre until after the event. The union translated Amukas' English letter into Chinese and printed it as a leaflet to be passed out to all of the workers in the factory. The letter, addressed to the JETCON (Hong Kong) Employees Union, read:

> Dear Sirs [sic]:
>
> Thank you very much for your kind invitation to attend the ceremony to mark your union's second Board of Directors assumption of office. Unfortunately, I will be unable to attend as I have a prior engagement in the United States on that day.
>
> However, I would like to take this opportunity to express my sincere hope that, based on our past experience, we will now continue to seek mutual understanding and work together towards a common goal of prosperity for both the workers and the management.
>
>
> Yours faithfully,
>
>
> Signed
> Amukas, Managing Director
> JETCON-JWM Corporation

According to plan, the union wrote to management regarding the 'gifts' it had received from influential friends: a suggestions box and a large bulletin board. The union said these needed to be displayed on the factory premises. There was no reply from the management — it was quite clear that no request of the union would be facilitated without a fight. The union, still a bare skeleton, was by no means ready to wage war.

April 1987 and Beyond

Life, jobs and the struggle for the survival of all the workers and their families, and of the precarious union, went on. There was no end to the tears and sweat involved in making ends meet and doing it with dignity. However, there must be an end to this narration.

A few final notes: Gu was fired by TWLSC and hired by CKLRS. Chu Chi-lin got married.

Fu married Gu some five years later, in March 1991, the month an earlier version of this book was accepted as a dissertation.

7

The Reflexive Narratives: Strategic Dialogues and Dialogical Strategies, Narratives of the Coming-into-Consciousness of Being Historical Agents

The Awareness of an Encroachment of Rights: A Forced Learning Process

> We were neither particularly nor extremely badly treated prior to the incident.
>
> Generally, we were not even treated as adults. As young female workers, we were regimented and disciplined arbitrarily. We came to work to make some money. We weren't able to resist. When we reached the point where we could not put up with it, we, as individuals, simply quit.
>
> We were sometimes very dissatisfied with our situation. Not everyone chose just to change jobs. We complained only when the management came down on us and oppression ran unchecked to the point we could no longer bear it. We tended to let it go after complaining and forgot about the whole thing after a while. Usually workers didn't achieve anything before they quit.

These are typical of the statements I heard when I returned to Hong Kong in September 1987 and began inquiring into the pre-event history of the JWM dispute. Step by step, as records of my conversation with workers accumulated, I was led discursively across the contested terrain of consciousness-forming and concept-making, logic and counter-logic. I will now retell the story of the strike from the problematic of consciousness-formation, to illuminate its complexity.

———————

In the middle of March 1986, eighty days prior to the sit-in, Chien Fon-yi's friend, a bookkeeper in the office, told her that the Resignation Meritorious Service Award (RMSA) had been cancelled. As far back as 1981, workers who had served JWM for five years or more were paid thirty-two days' wages upon leaving, even if they were fired. The cancellation of this benefit was one of many ways in which the management showed its discretionary power. Chien spread the news among her close associates but got no reaction, partly because the idea of leaving the company someday was too abstract for most people, and partly because it involved only a small sum of money. People soon 'forgot' about it.

About two weeks later, on 27 March, the day the monthly-rated personnel were paid, Chen Sui-guan learned that her friend Wong, who had been recently promoted to line leader, had received a lump sum of HK$7,000 in extra pay. Calculations proved that this was 6 percent of Wong's annual pay (two-thirds of a month's pay), multiplied by the number of her years of service. Was it a severance payment?

'It doesn't matter what it is', Chen and Wong decided. 'If there is extra pay for the staff, there must be similar pay for the other workers.' The same kind of reasoning was engaged in by operatives. The next day everybody was talking about the 'good deal'. Some operatives began to plan how they would spend their money — their line leaders spoke of plans to buy diamond rings or other valuables. Expectations were high and, with their leaders' assistance, the majority of workers began to figure out how much they were due.

On 1 April information leaked from above had it that JWM had been bought out by JETCON. The next day information about JETCON emerged. Workers heard that benefits for JETCON workers were less than those for

JWM workers and so listened carefully. Particularly alert were Chien's close associates. Suddenly the cancellation of the RMSA took on new significance, perhaps it was only the first step in the lowering of benefits to JETCON levels. But the workers believed they would be paid as their superiors had been — a lump sum severance payment — and hoped that JWM would 'go out of business', so that they could receive their severance pay and then decide whether to sign on with the new JETCON management.

On 3 April 1986, more news from bookkeepers in the office indicated that there would be 'extra' payments for the operatives. People were eager for the money and nobody noticed that management had again announced a reduction in the number of days for the workers' paid annual leave. They were excited when their leaders showed them newly acquired gold rings and other goodies.

After a weekend of high hopes, on 7 April the workers found nothing extra in their pay cheques. Everybody was shocked. The female line leaders, who had told the operatives what to expect two weeks previously, were frightened. They knew mistakes had been made and that the workers would not remain quiet.

Chien Fon-yi went to her bookkeeper friend and was told that the lump sum had been cancelled. It seemed to her that the decision had not been made by the Hong Kong office, but that they were following instructions. This was as much as she could say at the time.

On the seventh floor, two workers who had served JWM for more than ten years, Hon Lai-fon and Hu Hon-chi, dashed into Woo Char-hwa's office and demanded an explanation, in vain. Early next morning, Hon and Hu went down to the second floor, where almost half of the factory's operatives worked, and urged the second-floor workers to look into the 'muddy water'. There were few operatives on the sixth and seventh floors, but Hon and Hu pleaded with them to speak out. Potential leaders on the second floor were alert and apprehensive.

A gathering for an 'internal' discussion of the cancellation of RMSA was called after lunch. Some workers who had only worked for one or two years were apathetic, but were persuaded to stay and contribute to workers' solidarity by the argument that, sooner or later, everybody would become a five-year veteran and suffer a similar loss; or that such an abusive practice, if not checked, could lead to other benefits disappearing. An agreement was reached that the next day as many workers as possible should go to the office to ask for clarification.

On 10 April, during the 10:00 a.m. break, all the second-floor workers went up to the fifth-floor office. They were received by the second-floor shop manager, Yu-dan. Chien Fon-yi recalled that, at this point, most workers intended to push for lump sum severance payment but were not sure how to go about it. Severance pay had never been formally announced or even acknowledged by anyone in an official capacity; there were only rumours leaked by administrative staff. Given that the staff were now the only ones to benefit, tension erupted between them and their inferiors. Even Chien's bookkeeper friend became hesitant. She hinted that the money had been cancelled but gave no details. As she bought Chien some snacks, she sounded somewhat apologetic. 'We both know in our hearts what it was about,' said Chien, 'but I didn't push her. I was reluctant to involve her in our fight. I didn't want her to lose her job.' Afterwards, Chien did not bother her any more nor did the bookkeeper volunteer any further information. The workers understood that nobody in the upper echelons would stand behind them. If pushed, those who had leaked the news would deny it.

When the second-floor workers went to the office, they looked for an 'excuse' for doing so and decided on the issue of the cancellation of the RMSA. Yu-dan, the second-floor shop manager, was on duty in the office. He 'patted his chest' and guaranteed the workers that he could 'personally assure them that their RMSA would be available, were anyone to quit'. The workers were thus effectively silenced.

However, the discontent continued. There was a short period of calm on the shop-floors, but most workers remained unconvinced. As Chu Chi-lin described it, 'People other than us, the operatives who really produce products and work hardest, received a big sum without any reason ... Yet, given Yu-dan's guarantee, we simply couldn't insist that something was wrong. We felt suffocated and depressed. Most of us thought of quitting but we were not willing to give up the lump sum to "benefit the company"! People kept saying we should try to get the money, and then quit, as soon as possible. But could it be done? Nobody knew. Everybody wished to get laid off prior to the merger. There was nothing to do but wait.'

As the days passed, tension mounted between the 'haves' and 'have-nots'. When interrogated by the operatives, some of the monthly-rated staff admitted that they were ignorant of the nature of the payment. When pressed, most agreed it was some sort of severance pay due them, as they were asked to sign new contracts with the new company soon after they were paid.

What was meaningful to the workers was not so much the confirmation by the 'haves' of what was going on, but rather the fact that the 'haves' had participated in denial and evasion. As more and more stories were told by the 'haves', suspicion grew in the minds of the workers. Managers and leaders began to avoid mentioning the money and tried to minimize the issue and their involvement in it, and the workers' suspicions deepened.

A first theory was born, that of misappropriation. It was thought that the severance pay of the daily-rated had been given to their monthly-rated superiors. If so, it was illegal. This theory was partially supported by the behaviour of those who received a lump sum, and dictated that the way for the 'have-nots' to fight back would be to appeal to the government's anti-corruption institutions and to expose misappropriation and the differential treatment. Some authority must be able to locate the 'false document' and prove the management's guilt!

Guided by this theory, two groups of workers volunteered to approach the Government Agency Against Corruption (GAAC): One would inquire about the matter directly from the GAAC, the other would use indirect channels to find out how the GAAC operates. The first group came back with the information that the GAAC would accept the case and investigate JWM management to see whether or not corruption was involved. The workers would have to officially file the case with the GAAC, which would investigate and clarify the situation within a period of three months, but the workers would have to refrain from taking any industrial action or publicizing the issue until official investigation reports were released.

The second group found the same conditions. When the two groups got together and exchanged information, they were extremely disheartened — what was the use of having a government agency investigate if it rendered the workers inactive? If the management had cheated, they would be well prepared, and the GAAC might not find any discrepancies in JWM's official documents or, if they did, JWM might explain it away. If so, the workers would be depriving themselves of the further right to fight and would be subjecting themselves to the authority of a government agency in which they did not have confidence. The legal aspect was equally depressing: None of the laws had been drafted with workers' input and few (if any) were meant to protect their interests. So the GAAC initiative was stillborn. Yet the theory of misappropriation did not die, but lingered, to re-emerge under a different guise in future discourses.

Meanwhile, an elderly cleaning lady who had been working at JWM for more than fifteen years and could speak Japanese, complained bitterly to both Tosai and Woo that it was not fair that younger, temporary 'superiors' should get lump sum benefits while she did not. She wept and refused to leave. Tosai and Woo told her to come back the next day and promised that they would take care of the matter. Three days later, all five cleaning ladies received a small envelope of 'awards'. Though they were told to keep it secret, everybody learned about it. When workers from the seventh floor went to question management, management panicked and made awkward denials.

As this news spread, discontent mounted. Rumour had it that some foremen had told the operatives that even they, at first, had been denied the lump sum, but were paid because 'something had been done'. One foreman even commented explicitly on the operatives' action. According to Chu, he said, 'If it were us, we would definitely be fighting for the payment as well, but we would go further.'

Chu commented, 'I didn't understand what he meant, but sensed that action had been taken before the foremen were paid and that it was no use simply complaining and making a noise.' She continued, 'At an earlier stage some staff members did encourage us to fight. They changed their attitude only later.' Other workers also overheard comments, the most quoted being suggestions that 'if they are incapable of fighting efficiently, they will certainly lose their share.' The message seemed loud and clear: 'One has to fight for what one deserves.'

During those two weeks an information network developed. People who previously had only a nodding acquaintance began to consult with each other, exchange information, form alliances and co-ordinate a strategy. For the first time JWM workers began to co-operate with each other at a very basic level, thanks to management's treatment of them. They sensed they were being denied something available to their superiors, and even to their inferiors — the cleaning ladies.

Nevertheless, there would have been no story were it not for the coincidental 'Ah Si Incident', which energized the struggle and revitalized workers' strategic theorization.

Ah Si was among the first group of worker leaders to approach the Centre. At the first workers' meeting on 28 April, she made her presentation. However, immediately after the meeting, she dropped out of the scene and was not mentioned.

The role of Ah Si and the significance of her case was always a puzzle to me. My linear social scientist's mind could not understand the lack of reference to Ah Si in later actions. During various interviews I asked about it.

Ah Si used to work on the second floor as an operative. She somehow became a management favourite because she had learned Chinese folk dances and had performed a few times at JWM celebrations. For this reason she was one of the few workers sent to Japan as an 'intern', supposedly to acquire new skills and bring them back to the JWM locals. However, I was told that, as part of a plan to evade local taxation, workers were sent to Japan to work as temporary migrant workers. Because it was an opportunity to travel, this 'internship' became a manipulation — a benefit to 'lure' workers — and was a personal favour granted by particular superiors. Consequently, for most workers, 'going to Japan' was fishy. According to Chu Chi-lin, some foremen said they would never recommend 'useful' workers for 'training' in Japan, as they were usually transferred to other departments after they returned. Good workers with high skills were never recommended. Chien Fa-hin commented that some 'indecent' girls tried to 'polish the shoes' of management in order to go to Japan, but very few of them had been promoted to leader and some, upon their return, were assigned worse jobs than before. They worked hard in Japan and did not even shop, since things cost twice as much as in Hong Kong. Nevertheless, management told them they should work at least two to three years more at JWM to 'pay back' the company's investment.

Ah Si had been sent to Japan for a period of six months, after which she was asked to stay for another term, but she refused, saying she had to return to get married. The management, feeling they 'had done her a favour', was infuriated. After a few postponements and quarrels, she was finally brought back, barely in time for her wedding. Management claimed they had had to send a special envoy to fetch her, but everybody knew she had come back with a quality control foreman after his training course, and there was no special trip. Soon after her wedding, Ah Si returned to the factory to find she had been transferred to one of the worst jobs. She decided to quit.

On 15 April, Ah Si's last working day, she received her pay cheque to find that she had not been paid any RMSA. She burst into tears on the production line and her colleagues were alarmed. They urged her to check it out with management. Woo Char-hwa was in Europe on a two-week vacation and Mo Ku-sin was in charge. Mo told her she had been deprived of RMSA because she did not serve the factory for two more years after returning from Japan. She then told her co-workers that her RMSA had been flatly denied by Mo. Her case immediately reminded Chien Fon-yi of the rumour that the RMSA would be cancelled.

The news instantly spread throughout the factory. On the second floor, about fifty workers surrounded Yu-dan and questioned him. Yu-dan seemed to be unaware of what had happened. He asked the workers to elect representatives to meet with him and tried to talk the workers' representatives out of making an issue of Ah Si's case. He said Ah Si's performance 'wasn't outstanding' after her return from Japan and her RMSA was forfeited, but the workers remained unconvinced.

Yu-dan had his reasons for speaking in this manner. In Lo's words, 'Just a week before he had guaranteed that nobody could deprive us of our RMSA. After what happened to Ah Si, the whole thing blew up in his face. Not only did he not want to avoid clarifying the situation, he also spoke foolishly. Could we ever trust him?' The representatives argued with Yu-dan for more than two hours, while production on the second floor stopped.

Then Mo Ku-sin came down to deal with the situation. He rushed up the five representatives and burst out, 'Don't make trouble any more, the Japanese know what you guys are up to. I had to cover for you. If you keep making noise you'll be in big trouble.' Without allowing anyone else to talk, he continued, 'What money, what money do you want? The lump sum was only for the monthly-rated. They worked hard and accumulated it over many years. They will get paid because of the merger with JETCON. The new company will have new provisions. There will be no change in your benefits and therefore there is no need to pay you guys. There's no use for you to make noise.'

Mo's threatening statement failed to silence people like Chu. She challenged him about the discrepancies in provisions between the monthly-rated and the daily-rated. 'Who are the ones who actually produce and work like dogs?'

Mo, not allowing her to finish, replied, 'There wasn't any law or written rule dictating that the company should offer benefits at all. Don't take it for granted.' He patted his pocket, 'I have ten dollars in my pocket. If I feel like it, I may give it to you. If I don't, you don't have the right to force me to give it to you. My money, my decision. Who are you to tell me what to do? If you keep on making noise, "your tails will be cut off".'

'What do you mean cut off our tails?' Chu responded. 'You are not paying those of us who have worked over five years, nor those under five years, right? No matter what, you simply refuse to pay us the RMSA, is it right?'

'Right!' Mo shouted, as he began to walk out. 'You'd better understand what I've said.'

'Of course we do,' the representatives shouted. 'Whether you pay us or not depends upon whether you feel like it or not, right?'

'Right!' Mo screamed, and left.

Mo had vividly demonstrated how 300 or more operatives in JWM were being discriminated against. As Lo Un-pu cynically put it, 'Thanks to Mo Ku-sin's extremely revealing, nasty talk, we began to unite and to understand how much we were abused.'

Inadvertently, Mo was the founder of the 'theory of discrimination', which drew the workers together. They realized that they could not fight alone and somehow had to get external support.

The next day, management warned the foremen and leaders. They then began to talk about the 'provident fund' they had been paid or, even more ridiculously, began to deny that any money had been paid. This only supported further theorizing.

Now there were debates among the workers on how to secure external support. Hu Hon-chi had been studying in a workers' evening school run by the New Youth Society, and suggested approaching her teacher, Lin Yi-chin, a member of the District Board of Kwai Chung and the Central Kwai Chung Labour and Residents Service (CKLRS), who would help them analyse the situation. Her suggestion was not accepted; instead, it was decided to approach the Labour Bureau. Chu later said, 'Because of the name, we thought it was a bureau to protect labourers' interests. See how naive we were!'

Lo Un-pu and Hu Hon-chi were elected to go to the Labour Bureau the following Monday. They would take sick leave, and all the workers would chip in to reimburse them for their lost wages. By the evening of Friday, 18 April, more than 100 supporting signatures had been collected for Lo and Hu to take to the Bureau. The visit to the district office of the Labour Bureau was a big blow to the workers' enthusiasm. Lo and Hu were impatiently received by a clerk who, before they could present themselves adequately, interrupted and told them it was not the Bureau's policy to 'intrude into the internal affairs of a business'. They should work out the differences between themselves. In his personal opinion, they did not stand a chance, because nothing about money had been written into their employment contracts. When Lo and Hu argued that nor was it in the contracts of the monthly-rated staff, the clerk replied that there was no law telling business-owners what to do or not to do. 'You can only blame yourselves for your tough luck,' he concluded, and handed back the signature list. Lo and Hu were asked to sign the minutes of the meeting, and then were advised to 'go home and forget about the matter'.

Lo and Hu reported to the workers the next day. Most were pessimistic. However, Mo's nasty language was still in their ears, and they were indignant. 'It means we are absolutely nothing, and they (the bosses) can do anything to us! What kind of joke is this? They take us for corpses!' As emotions ran high, they decided to try anything, just to vent their anger, even if it achieved nothing. Chien Fon-yi said that some of her colleagues had already made up their minds — if worse came to worst, they would quit, with or without compensation, because it was 'not worthwhile to stay and be humiliated'.

It was then decided to have Hu arrange an appointment with district council member, Lin, at CKLRS, on Friday.

Management learned about the workers' visit to the Labour Bureau, and foremen on different production lines warned the workers that management would no longer tolerate disturbances. 'Since even the Labour Bureau has told you that you don't have a chance, be docile and keep your mouths shut.' Immediately, there were rumours that the Labour Bureau had handed over the minutes of the case to the management.

The workers became irritated, defensive and suspicious. They felt they had to battle to maintain their existing level of benefits and regain minimum dignity. As Lo Un-pu later told me, 'You might say that when we came to the Centre we were using a rather low-profile defence strategy. We were almost certain that there was little hope for the lump sum. After so many frustrations we didn't have high hopes for you guys either!'

According to Lo, the workers clearly distinguished between the RMSA and the 6 percent lump sum. They had calculated the tremendous difference between the two amounts. Ninety percent of them were interested in the six percent severance payment, not the thirty days' reward; but obtaining it would be difficult, as it was not part of anyone's stated benefits. Those who had received it had been surprised. However, the workers figured that, precisely because of its ambiguous nature, it was most likely the result of a lay-off at JWM prior to the merger, and that they still had a chance. It was not customary, in a Chinese environment, to give differential treatment within the same group of workers.

Yet Chu argued that the ultimate reason for the dispute was not the differential treatment. 'There had always been disparities between us, who earn our living by our productive capacity; and them, who get their positions through relatives, by stepping on someone or by being male. We knew that we had little in common. We didn't care what they did or got. We didn't even want to be part of them. We do a decent day's job and get a day's pay. That's it. What ignited the fury was the cancellation of the RMSA. We were forced to fight and only in fighting did we realize how badly we had been mistreated and discriminated against. It was a learning process. We had never been greedy. Many wanted to quit but decided to stay. Why? We put up with the situation for five years to protect our RMSA. How many "five years" does one have in one's life? Were it not for management's brutality, they might have been able to cover up and continue their abusive practices.'

Chien Fon-yi was convinced that even the monthly-rated staff were being discriminated against, as they had been paid only after they had discovered the provision for the payment in the merger agreement and threatened Japanese headquarters with industrial action. They had been appeased, on the condition that they would not spread the news to the daily-rated. To support her assertion, she told two stories.

An officer had commented that it was not that management wanted to save money, but that they were hesitant to pay the operatives, since they feared that they would then quit *en masse*. Chien argued otherwise — that workers might quit because of deterioration of working conditions and benefits, but not because of welfare improvement. Nevertheless, she pointed out that the officer's comment showed that there had been staff payments, and so the operatives might fight for them also.

There was also a foreman who questioned, 'Do you really think you can get what you're fighting for? There are so many of you!' The assumption behind this question was that what mattered to JWM management was not fairness, justice or principles, but rather the money itself.

Thus the workers reinterpreted the situation — there had to be some sort of fund reallocation involved, since those who got paid were virtually in zero-sum opposition to the operatives' interests. Whether such reasoning was a pretext for the workers to keep fighting or simply a theory constructed *post hoc*, it demonstrates that the workers no longer believed what their superiors said. When necessary they would also 'misunderstand' what they heard or were told.

Seen in this light, Mo's threat conveyed another message: that any disturbance in the factory frightened local management, exposing their weaknesses and errors even as they tried to keep news of the discontent from reaching their superiors in Japan. The bigger the rift, the more difficult it was for management to explain it away.

Thus, Hsiao Chia suggested an 'offensive manoeuvre': to mobilize the workers to sign an open letter demanding that management give full details of the future status of workers' benefits and an exact schedule for paying the lump sum, and threatening mass resignations if management failed to satisfy them. Surely the factory could not afford to lose all its skilled workers. Her suggestion was well received and efforts were made to solicit signatures, but the turnout was below expectations and the project fell through. In retrospect, Hsiao Chia admitted that she had overestimated the readiness of her colleagues for a showdown, but, months after the sit-in, she still believed in the logic of her proposal.

I asked Hsiao Chia where she had got her idea, and she told me of previous 'battles' with management. There had been at least three previous occasions when the workers around Hsiao Chia — mostly Hakka-speaking teenagers from the rural area of Pat Heung — had 'beaten' the management. In one case, one of the Pat Heung 'inner-circle' workers had been fired and the whole group had refused to take the company bus to work. When they arrived hours late, on public transport, the management got the message and gave in. In another case, Hsiao Chia had mobilized a whole production line on the second floor to demand personal lockers for every worker. When management refused, the workers waged an on-line strike, resuming normal production only after the matter had been settled. A third case, which concerned seating in the canteen, was also resolved to the workers' satisfaction. 'The management tended to be extremely self-serving and self-enclosing. They had to be constantly reminded, not by our words but by some kind of threat,' she concluded.

The failure of Hsiao-Chia's signature campaign reflected the workers' predicament. On the one hand, the operatives were clearly aware that they were discriminated against. While it might be true that there were two systems of wage calculation and payment, the term 'daily-rated' — at least in a Chinese context — did not mean that the operatives were ineligible for benefits. The lump sum payment — 6 percent for every year served — would have been a 'once-in-a-lifetime' windfall for some senior workers, and this is what the workers were really interested in. They were not ready to quit, but they felt it extremely unfair to be denied a severance payment acknowledging their time at JWM — a prosperous company that would no longer exist.

But the issue was also political, precisely because it was also 'moral': The workers were torn between the quantity of money and its 'colour', or possible moral taint. Chien Fa-hin explained, 'We are the kind of people who hate to be cheated. It is extremely important for us to be sure whether or not a thing is right. We won't take anything to which we are not entitled. But if we know we are mistreated we will fight to the end. Sometimes we insist on our principles even if we know we will suffer.'

To live a morally-correct life, against the unfairness of the world, means engaging in multivalent discourse, not just fitting into 'models' or complying with 'values'. Such discourse involves a dialogical contest for the appropriation of socially-available signs and meanings, in which these signs and meanings are strategically valorized. The purpose is to defend one's stance and establish one's superiority over adversaries. In this contest, adversaries may appropriate different signs and categories, or may lock themselves into a single set of signs and haggle over possible meanings. This latter situation was the one which obtained at JWM at this point.

Since the JWM management could no longer deny that monthly-rated staff had been paid a lump sum, they now emphasized that it had not been part of existing benefits, but was the result of a highly peculiar circumstance which did not concern the daily-rated. By 'marking' the situation as peculiar, they wished to legitimize the exclusion of the daily-rated. Not only was the circumstance 'marked', but the 'nature' of the money was also 'marked'; it was 'extra' money, which could not be conceptualized within any pre-existing context. Such 'marking' was designed to remove the cause of the trouble by deconceptualizing the circumstances and meaning of the payment.

However, it is generally the case that a discourse includes within itself the elements for its inversion. This reversal is by no means automatic, but is the result of a highly self-conscious struggle. The workers 'un-marked' the 'marked' and 'reconceptualized' the 'deconceptualized'. In the process, meanings were bifurcated and broadened. In particular, the sign of 'extra' was invariably transformed. The workers took 'extra' as an expression of goodwill, the equivalent of 'red packets of good-luck money'. In Chinese practice, such 'red packets' are usually awarded to younger generations by their seniors, or to subordinates by superiors. Such bestowals are ceremonial and usually take place on 'marked' occasions: New Year's Eve, birthdays, weddings, inaugurations of business and other auspicious occasions. They affirm the giver's seniority and superiority, and at the same time contribute to the joyful atmosphere. Accepting such a 'red packet' is a show of reverence and appreciation, a congratulatory gesture of the junior acknowledging the authority and seniority of the giver, and signifies a renewal of social bonds. By publicly showing respect to a junior, the senior reaffirms his/her status and gains greater reverence. Each participant thus gives the other 'face'.

However, one must be extremely careful about the implications of social ranking in giving the 'red packet'. One should avoid any situation in which the offer might be refused, as this would be a great humiliation. One should also be careful not to omit anyone of the same rank when offering 'red packets', as this would be taken as an insult. For instance, it would be unthinkable for a visiting uncle to give 'red packets' to only three of his four nephews and nieces. If he really favoured one of the children, he might put more money in the particular red packet, but he would never forget any of the others. What matters most is not how much is in a red packet but whether the act of offering the 'red packet' is publicly performed for all.

Following this cultural logic, there was ample reason for the JWM daily-rated workers to be disturbed and insulted. They had been deliberately, formally excluded. This seemed reinforced by management's repeated, assertive claims, discretional evasions and suppressive threats, which were not to be tolerated.

The workers lived at an international crossroads, bombarded daily by multiple values from all over the world, and worked in the environment of a multinational enterprise owned by Japanese, and this made the situation more complicated and confusing. The Japanese claimed they belonged to a similar 'East Asian' culture, yet remained self-defined by practices uniquely Japanese. 'Modern' Japanese asserted that they ranked at the top of modern industrial societies, yet many Japanese social relations were distinctly 'medieval'.

Hong Kong lay between East and West, both a colony and a metropolis, between existing capitalist and socialist systems. Its only resource was its labour force, whose roots remained largely rural, yet who were responsible for a two-decade-old manufacturing boom. Industrious production workers like JWM's operatives owed more to their rural, familial Chinese upbringing than to any Westernized urban modernity; yet they were not immune to the impact of government/legalist discourse and the hegemony of capitalist ideology. In sum, the moral dilemma of the JWM operatives was also influenced by Hong Kong's multifaceted confrontation of ideologies and cultural practices.

The frustrations the workers had experienced in dealing with the GAAC and the Labour Bureau, as well as with management, attested to the difficulties they felt. Chu Chi-lin told me, 'It was very painful before we came to the Centre. We knew we were being grossly mistreated, yet everybody in the establishment suggested we were fighting for something to which we were not entitled. Were we really so greedy? We did not want to be. Were we being unreasonable, or even barbaric? We were afraid that we might be and not aware of it.' In an effort to deal with this moral crisis and to act, they had to find external support. About thirty of them went to the Centre and talked to Lin, Fu and Gu. The support they got was precisely what they needed: a confirmation of their struggle and its moral legitimacy. It also helped them overcome their cultural inferiority complex — they had been told constantly, by all kinds of establishment institutions, that they were uneducated, rural, traditional, backward, parochial and pre-modern.

The institutional conditions of the Centre contributed to the achievement of this positive effect. Lin Yi-chin, founder of CKLRS and a newly-elected District Board member, was educated in England and taught in an industrial high school. His office and the CKLRS, headed by Fu and Gu respectively, were legitimate, if not prestigious, local civic organizations. Lin was acquainted with the role of organized labour in Britain. He came from a family of workers and had decided to get involved in local politics to protect working peoples' interests. Both Fu and Gu had similar family backgrounds and were college-educated labour-affairs social workers. All three were self-proclaimed 'gung-ho' unionists who worked closely with dozens of similar groups and volunteers.

The discourses typically utilized at the Centre and in other similar organizations differed from those of the JWM workers. Their working styles and principles were an offshoot of labour movements which had originated in the West decades before, which included the assumption of universal rights, values and principles — an ideology both derived from, and aimed at countering, the hegemonic act of capitalist totalization.

Despite their differences, the Centre was capable of offering precisely what the workers wanted.

On the evening of 26 April 1986, thirty-plus workers presented their case, although without all of the details. Lin's reaction was careful. He drew upon what he had learned in England, suggesting that there were not just two kinds of payment involved in management's manipulations, but at least three — the so-called RMSA, the 'mysterious lump sum' (possibly a severance payment), and the 'provident fund' management had mentioned. However, no matter what kind of money it was, the principle of fairness should apply: The benefit scheme should be equally valid for all the workers at JWM, unless special provisions had been made in individual employment contracts. This was somewhat different from the way the workers thought about it, but they could see that they had the right to be treated impartially, and that they were right, in a universally sanctioned, modern sense, to fight openly for benefits. They were overwhelmed by this unexpected positive response: that there were three payments they were entitled to, and that it was right to fight for them.

Chien Fon-yi said, 'We were so disheartened that we almost gave up. We decided to come to the Centre only because an appointment had already been made with Lin. We had nothing to lose and we just came to see what he had to say.' Chu Chi-lin also confirmed that 'management and the Labour Bureau had almost succeeded in brainwashing us and we had almost succumbed to the formula of "quit if dissatisfied". It was so disgusting to work for such a bunch of hypocrites that we'd have rather left than fought for the money. We were good workers with skills and could work anywhere. Our leaving would be their loss, and they knew it.'

On 28 April, the day the workers had their first general meeting, Woo Char-hwa returned from his vacation and realized that the discontent among workers had increased exponentially. According to Chien Fon-yi, Woo was a very sophisticated and manipulative person. Unlike Mo Ku-sin, he would never speak his mind or reveal secrets. Realizing he had to cover up the real issue and divert the workers' attention, he decided to call Ah Si to pick up her RMSA and show the workers that they had 'misunderstood' that their RMSA had been cancelled. Since he had paid Ah Si, everyone should simply forget about the matter and go back to work.

A week earlier, this would have been effective, but now it was too late. The workers were convinced that they were entitled to all three payments — the two that had been made to the monthly-rated and the one that had been promised by management. At their general meeting, the workers resolved to organize and fight. Ah Si attended the meeting and rallied behind her colleagues. She did not mention the payment from Woo, nor was it mentioned by anyone else, although it became a piece of hot gossip the next morning. The significance of this 'secret deal' was immediately obvious to everyone: It was proof that Woo and management had 'dirt on their bodies' and that they had had to pay off Ah Si to cover up their corruption. Thus began the 'dirt on the body' (they were hiding something shameful) and 'tinkering with the pot' (they were trying to explain away discrepancies) theories, which resurfaced on various occasions. Still angered by the cleaning ladies incident, the workers rallied under the banner 'no fight, no gain'; as a collective, they would be successful if they persisted, because they had convinced themselves that their rights had been encroached upon.

Afterwards, Ah Si ceased to appear and was forgotten by her struggling colleagues. This was all right — Ah Si had carried out her task and gained her share — and none of her colleagues owed her anything. At my request, some six months later, Chien Fa-hin reflected upon the matter and concluded, 'We sympathized with her situation and also appreciated her willingness to share her story and help rally support. We are certainly aware that there were personal motives and hidden agendas involved. She had always been management's pet. [That] the fight between management and their pets should have supported our cause is somewhat ironic. I'm glad she got what she wanted. We don't owe her any favours. Neither do we wish to comment on her self-interest. I think that was why she wasn't mentioned.'

The Making of a Collective Identity

By the end of April, every daily-rated operative at JWM was aware of discrimination. Every day, the enthusiastic operatives reported what happened to them and how they reacted to the Centre. In their speech, the content and meaning of the pronouns 'we', 'our' and 'us' varied daily, leaving the Centre staff puzzled. Only in retrospect, with the help of important leading figures a few months later, did it occur to me that the workers' collective self was in a constant state of making.

In the beginning, the use of 'we' by representatives and supporters usually denoted only immediate close circles of three or four workers, although one of them on the second floor included more than ten. These multiple 'we(s)' came to the Centre to relay their messages and to learn from the others. It is fair to say that each 'we' communicated with the Centre more intensively (and also extensively) than with other 'we' groups. The Centre became a practical information pool for these various circles and later, for different floors. Although workers worked together in larger contexts — workers from different floors had earlier sent delegates to the GAAC and the Labour Bureau, and had chipped in to reimburse them for their lost day's wages – this was tangential. One second-floor leader commented that 'nobody wanted any one group or floor to act alone. Everybody suspected that the others might strike a secret deal with management at any time to benefit themselves.'

The reasons for going to the GAAC were based on a theory of misappropriation: that the extra lump sum of the daily-rated had been 'swallowed up' by management and the monthly-rated. The firing of Ah Si and its justification by management — the so-called lack of 'outstanding' criteria — also supported this theory. The refusal of payment by JW management to daily-rated operatives thus made them aware of themselves as sharing a common destiny: Not until they learned that they were termed 'daily-rated' and therefore inferior, and not until they became aware of being treated arbitrarily, did workers on different floors realize the importance of the other workers' existence. The management's overreaction to the workers' preliminary discontent thus served as a catalyst to mould individual workers into a coherent body.

This coalition, however, proved to be expedient and precarious. After the GAAC and the Labour Bureau failed the workers, their morale almost collapsed. Positive reinforcement from without was needed, and this is why

The Reflexive Narratives 297

the previously abandoned idea of approaching the Centre was again picked up. There was also an intellectual aspect to this move — the theory of misappropriation had been tested and had failed. A new theory had to be established.

The response from the Centre was thus encouraging and useful. The Centre staff sympathized with their plight, and provided the workers with new munitions and brain power. However, it had been unexpected that the Centre staff should have information that would help workers construct their new theory of the 'mysterious money' — the three different kinds of payment which management might have withheld from the operatives. Lin Yi-chin's three analytic categories were appropriated by some supporters to construct their native theory of practical struggle.

The ordinary organization and mobilization procedure proposed by the Centre was adopted by the not-yet-emerged worker leaders, most of whom wanted a general meeting of operatives from different floors. None was in a position either to make such a suggestion or to initiate such a project. They needed somebody with both the prestige to summon their colleagues for a just cause and the resources to provide the necessary infrastructure. It was Lin who volunteered the former and the Centre that volunteered the latter.

The first general meeting brought more than 160 female operatives from six different floors. The eleven representatives (RPs) elected to negotiate with management were to remain the visible 'leadership' (although later the group grew to fifteen). However, other leaders who kept a low profile, working as low-echelon mobilizers and providing logistical services, were actually the 'think-tank' of the second-floor leadership; and it was only long after the sit-in had begun that the Centre staff became aware of this multilayered leadership structure. Even then we never fully appreciated the strength and resilience of this extended group of 'cadres' during the whole period of the dispute. The leaders, whom we called representatives, were actually acknowledged volunteers rather than elected leaders. This became clear to the Centre staff only after the leadership split. In retrospect, some of the most 'radical' RPs were, at least partially, motivated by personal gain. When one of them talked of 'we', it often meant either the speaker herself, or herself plus the colleagues she claimed to represent.

Still, after the general meeting the usage of 'we' did begin to denote the female daily-rated as a whole, albeit sporadically and unevenly. In most cases, 'we' was adopted in response to outsiders', especially the Centre staff's, use of 'you' (the explicitly plural form in Chinese) to mean the female workers. It is important not to discount the efforts of the supporters and leaders who were striving to build solidarity among their co-workers. When I inquired into the rationale for gathering 'struggle funds' from the workers in the first general meeting six months after the dispute, I was told, 'We were not sure whether we would need money or even how much, but we were sure monetary commitments would get people to commit themselves.'

This logic applies to more than just money. To engage someone's time, mind, work and action is to engage the person, and many worker actions can be better understood with this in mind. A series of actions after the first general meeting, including the signature campaign, were aimed at both committing the workers and displaying their solidarity to management (who responded by trying to interview representatives individually — a 'divide- and- rule tactic'). On 1 May (May Day) when the supporters and RPs at the Centre came to the conclusion that, without action on the shop-floor, management would never take them seriously and the emerging worker enthusiasm would dissipate, they decided to have 300 operatives blow whistles at the same time. They also sent a delegation with the Centre staff to a May Day rally, the JWM case received public attention, and those who were involved began to feel part of a broader social category called 'workers'.

The shrill noise of 300 whistles frightened management the next day, and the workers were delighted. Management then put up the notice of the 'improvement' of some welfare provisions, but this backfired, as it dwelt on minor points and avoided the core of the matter — the 'mysterious' money — and was interpreted as a hardening of management's position. (This 'notice war' was repeated at various intervals — an example of workers deliberately 'misunderstanding' messages issued by the management. The management frequently did the same thing. For both groups, 'misunderstanding' could serve to fulfil their needs for internal consensus.)

To counter the notice the operatives drafted a second open letter to management. For the first time, they documented management's 'discrimination' practices against daily-rated operatives and requested to be treated 'fairly' and 'cordially'. This was, again, more than a war of words: The accompanying leaflet, *Expose Cheating*, was written to educate workers and sensitize them to the issue of long-service payments. The tenor of the leaflet reflected a deep mistrust as well as and the 'conspiracy theory'.

One version of the conspiracy theory was that, owing to the imminent merger with JETCON, the management was not only attempting to deny JWM operatives their due lump sum, but was conspiring to lower the overall welfare scheme to the level of JETCON's. Thus, operatives at JWM should get in touch with workers from JETCON, exchange information and co-ordinate actions; and the decision was made to demonstrate at JETCON and pass out leaflets to JETCON workers. The existence of the JETCON workers as a critical 'they' also made the JWM operatives a more likely 'we'.

Meanwhile, management continued to attempt to 'divide and conquer', promoting fifteen operatives to the newly-created position of assistant line leader, a blatant attempt at co-optation which only embarrassed and alienated those promoted.

The march to JETCON served to link JWM operatives from different floors in their first collective show of force. It was fun, and greatly enhanced morale and confidence among the operatives. The clumsy reaction of both JETCON and JWM managements to this humiliation promoted further worker theorizing. Workers now reasoned that management feared the dispute would go public and cause the prestigious Japanese firms to 'lose face'. This understanding guided further actions.

Encouraged by the popularity of blowing whistles, leaders felt it time for further action. To allow the workers to play with the management, to show them that they were not craving negotiations, it was decided to demand twenty-four hours' notice of any negotiations.

After the JETCON incident, management became paranoid about their rebelling workers. Eager to sow discord, they instructed all foremen and line leaders to 'chat' individually with their underlings. However, some foremen and line leaders went overboard and forced their underlings to sign documents. This 'provocation', as the workers' leaders termed it, again alerted the theorists, who used these actions to strengthen their conspiracy theory and to demonstrate that there were more lessons to learn. Reports that the leaflet teams had been tailed by foremen fitted in with the leaders' warnings.

The suspension of the first round of negotiations on 9 May was no surprise to the workers, but they were surprised by management's lack of preparation and sensitivity. Tosai's anger and abrupt exit were considered undignified. Woo's branding of the Centre staff as members of the criminal underworld was considered insulting, and his insistence on keeping 'business secrets' and only partially revealing an 'official document' increased worker distrust. The meeting resulted in the workers' decision to increase the number of their RPs. Now the 'we' used by supporters who came to the Centre for daily consultations became more definite: It denoted themselves and their immediate associates.

Confrontation was brewing as each side increased pressure upon the other. Management's tailing of off-duty operatives snowballed, not only further antagonizing less-involved workers but also frightening them. Heavy-handed gestures of individual managers and foremen were understood as deliberate, planned terror tactics, and workers chose to interpret them not as signs of management weakness and panic but as the outgrowth of habitual chauvinism. Grievances expressed by operatives during small group discussions now had a cathartic effect. Listening to one another's stories of suffering led to a sense of communion. Despite differences between floors, it became clear that 'a three-foot-thick sheet of ice takes more than one cold day to form'.

Spontaneous slow-downs on various shop-floors had been going on for some time and, especially on lines where experienced operatives were in control, yield fell even as overtime was extended. But co-ordinated industrial action was still lacking. In Chu Chi-lin's words, 'Things don't just happen, they must be made to happen.' Collective action, and collective identity as well, were the results of mobilization and organization.

It was at this juncture that the Labour Bureau stepped in. Bureau personnel, unprepared and misinformed, were initially used by management as a mouthpiece. On occasion, they invited insult by repeating management clichés, offering yet another arena for ideological warfare. When the Bureau reiterated that only the monthly-rated were eligible for the lump sum payment, the story of the cleaning ladies was put forth — not to 'convince' or embarrass the Bureau people, but to valorize a historical theory, 'If you don't fight you get nothing, if you do you might — like the cleaning ladies — have a chance.'

The Bureau mistakenly attempted to excuse management's refusal to pay the lump sum by saying they were afraid workers would quit *en masse*. Generally speaking, in the past neither employees nor employers in Hong Kong had felt any commitment to one another. Employers dismissed their workforce at will to retain flexibility in the extremely volatile market; and employees, faced with this situation, tended to 'vote with their feet', often shifting jobs for better pay or working conditions. In other words, there had been no job security. However, by the end of the 1980s the situation was changing. The labour force was aging, more career-bound second-generation workers were emerging, and some of the better-established manufacturers were becoming aware of the importance of a reliable, stable workforce. The logic of existing employment practices was thus questioned by both buyers and sellers of labour power. At JWM, the workers, while fighting for a 'once-in-a-lifetime' severance payment, were yet clear-minded enough to note:
1. that they had the right not to be treated in a discriminatory fashion;
2. that finding another job was difficult, and that it meant losing whatever long-service increment they were entitled to; and
3. that it was only because they refused to quit that they had a chance to get paid, not the other way around.

The Labour Bureau thus misread the workers' psychology. Their expectation that workers would 'take the money and quit' showed the workers that the Bureau was on the side of management. As Lo Un-pu commented a year later, 'It was because of the lack of job security of any sort that we labourers constantly had to shop around to reduce our chances of being abused, sometimes without being aware of it. It was typical and exceedingly irresponsible of management, and for a government agent, to claim that it was because the workers would not sell themselves outright that they should be denied benefits.'

The intervention of the Labour Bureau heightened the workers' feelings of mistrust towards their superiors. They remembered how the Bureau's local office had denied them assistance. Now they saw the Bureau intervening at management's request. However, JWM management did not trust the Bureau any more than the workers did. Even as management constantly misinformed the Bureau, they were refused contact with the operatives. They were in a position to please neither side, yet had to pull both to the negotiating table to avoid further deterioration of relations. Thus they even turned to the Centre staff, going so far as to push them to attend the negotiations, an act tantamount to recognizing the Centre's status as the workers' legal counsel. The Centre, though aware that this was not necessarily a blessing, could not back out.

Gu and Fu were put in an extremely tenuous position when they were shown the company document during the 14 May meeting. Forced to relay what she had seen to the workers under the surveillance of both management and the Labour Bureau, Gu had resorted to body language. Circumstances like these called for stronger bonds to be built, not only between Centre staff and leaders, but also among enthusiastic operatives. Everybody became aware that tacit agreement and unspoken communication were needed in emergency situations.

The workers turned the dollar figure in the company document into evidence for their theory of severance payment. Based upon this 'evidence', they formulated a theory of management forgery, reinforcing their enmity towards management.

All these events accelerated anxiety on the production lines. There were repeated demands for organized collective action, and it was suggested that if negotiations with local management failed, workers should negotiate directly with the Japanese headquarters.

Meanwhile, the idea of a JWM operatives' union began to gather momentum. Workers were motivated to unionize because they believed that management had already decided to get rid of the leaders, and they hoped that unionization would deter a wholesale dismissal and, if a 'witch-hunt' occurred, give them more leverage to rally support and resist.

The boredom caused by going slow all day, which was experienced as self-torture, led to better co-operation among the workers. The ebb-and-flow style slow-down proposed at the 19 May general meeting helped solve this problem and showed management who was in control. To discipline the workers and co-ordinate a fixed production quota, workers authorized the RPs and ALLs to run their lines. The Centre staff saw this as a surprising leap forward for the workers thus to reinvent a sort of workers' council. 'We' now indicated a new phase of solidarity.

When the fourteen RPs went to the Labour Bureau for another negotiating session the next day, they did so with strengthened confidence, heightened morale and a new self-consciousness. Neither the Bureau nor management were aware of this; but then local Labour Relations Director Tu's opening lecture was cut short by Chen Siu-guan, and then Chu Chi-lin jumped in to accuse management of disregarding previous agreements by again forcing individual workers to fill in forms. Representatives who seldom talked in meetings spoke out, some requesting that detailed minutes be taken of the meeting, others saying it was a waste of time talking to 'small potatoes' not in a position to make decisions. Then Mo Ku-sin, the lower-level manager who could never retain his composure, shouted at the RPs, exposing the management's plot to fire workers. The meeting ended in disarray and animosity.

A 'closet-politics theory' now emerged — the dispute had not, so far, been reported to Japanese headquarters. Local management, perhaps with something to hide, had tried to cover up the dispute for fear their failure to manage it would cost them dearly. They wished to settle quietly, as soon as possible, at the local level, but lacked the resources to reward the daily-rated; middle and lower-level staff feared that they would be punished or even dismissed if the daily-rated won their battle. The 'theory of losing face' supported this: Management was afraid of publicizing the dispute and damaging JWM's name — so what could they do but continue covering up and pressing on?

Based on the above analysis, and because of the need to take the initiative, supporters decided to send the telegram, signed by 180 workers, to the managing director at Japanese headquarters. They aimed to achieve two goals: to heighten their position vis-à-vis local management and to validate their position as 'the' workers of Hong Kong JWM vis-à-vis the corporate giant, JWM.

It was this symbolic positioning that led Japanese headquarters to react ambiguously. They responded, but pretended that they had not received the telegram. As one leader put it, they 'continued to cover their ears while they were stealing the bell'. The workers, however, were prepared for this. They were familiar with the vanity and arrogance of male/patrimonial chauvinistic psychology, as they had experienced it under Japanese-style management.

Yet top JWM management in Japan had responded even more clumsily than the workers had expected. The Labour Bureau was informed of the telegram. Tu rushed to the Centre to accuse the staff of assisting them, complaining that the workers should not have done this during the agreed 'cooling-off period'. Told that the cable had been sent prior to the agreement, and that the workers believed that informing headquarters was a 'cool' thing to do, Tu was upset. He warned the Centre that, in his opinion, it would be impossible for the workers to get the money they were fighting for, no matter how hard they tried. Whether intended or not, this was a meaningful hint for the workers.

The tug of war between the JWM local authority and the workers' leadership for the workers' allegiance then reached a point of no return. It was the Japanese top management who unwittingly gave the workers' leadership a hand at this crucial moment. There was a need to discipline the rank-and-file's habit of individual 'guerrilla warfare', as more and more workers began to see their struggle as a fight for dignity. When the workers learned that their peaceful appeal for fair treatment to top management had not even been acknowledged, not even the most moderate among the workers could retain 'false hope' any more. Neither did anyone believe in the neutrality of the Labour Bureau. A bloody witch hunt was imminent, and the workers would have to fight with their backs to the wall. When the JETCON workers proved incapable of organizing, Chien Fon-yi commented later, 'We realized that we could rely only on ourselves, no one else.'

One of the reasons for inaction by the JETCON workers was that the Centre was too preoccupied to assist them. More importantly, however, it was JETCON monthly-rated staff who wished to be treated like their JWM counterparts, and who had pushed the daily-rated to approach the Centre; but for unknown reasons they dropped out after two weeks, leaving the daily-rated in limbo.

The JWM workers' leadership had never trusted their JETCON counterparts anyway. It was expedient to try to involve them, but they were nevertheless disappointed by their immobility. However, it occurred to the JWM workers' leadership that JETCON worker involvement might not be to their advantage, as the Labour Bureau's comments implied that JWM management's rigidity was caused by pressure from the Japanese business community, who feared that concessions to JWM workers might trigger similar demands in other Japanese-owned concerns. According to this theory, the fewer people and production units involved, the less the risk and fear for Japanese interests in Hong Kong, and consequently the less pressure on JWM management, who then might be more willing to settle on JWM workers' terms. None of the Bureau's other arguments had seemed particularly persuasive to the workers, but their stance concerning JETCON workers was. The JWM workers' leadership was impressed, if not convinced. Thus there was a further distancing from the JETCON workers.

JETCON workers resented this policy of keeping them at arm's length. When the fifteen JETCON workers came to the Centre on 22 May, they accused the JWM workers of being 'selfish' and 'tricky', and complained that they were 'being used'. Some suggested JWM workers were 'destroying the bridge after they had crossed the river', an insulting comment suggesting total ungratefulness.

Thus ended hope of co-operation between the 'working sisters' of JWM and JETCON. It was a blow to the Centre staff. However, for the workers and their leadership, it was a call for self-reliance, and from then on, the 'we' of the struggling JWM workers became more clearly defined. JWM workers now began to configure themselves as a collective entity within the incorporated body of Hong Kong JWM, and this facilitated the organization of their union. Long after the dispute, Chien Fa-hin explained that 'there was a need to protect our leaders against imminent dismissal. We began to feel that we could "forget" the idea of organizing a united JWM-JETCON front. Of course, the fight was ours, not theirs.'

Clearly, for the workers the evolution of the meaning of 'us' reached a critical point around 23 May (Day –8), when they began to ask the Centre to communicate with existing unions on their behalf. They had decided that management would have to pay a price if they ventured to dismiss any of them.

At this point, creative activities were initiated among the rank and file. The workers composed their 'battle song' and created a stage-play, in sharp contrast to the 'underwater' manipulations of the 'envoys' from the Japanese headquarters, which the workers did not find surprising. However, they did not expect the stealthy personal involvement of vice-general manager Woo.

The workers came up with several explanations for Woo's clandestine activities — the theory of 'dirt', the theory of 'tinkering with the pot' — and a third 'personality theory'. According to Hsiao Chia, some older workers believed that Woo, a rather cowardly and indecisive person, was being coerced and blackmailed by his long-time subordinates. A Woo faction existed at Hong Kong JWM, and it was common practice for subordinates to 'polish' Woo's shoes by frequently playing mahjong and intentionally losing. Woo patronized those who supported him and favoured them with whatever rewards were available from JWM. Now that a blunder had been made, Woo had to minimize possible damage to his supporters. 'Although I believed that this might very well be a plausible motivation,' Hsiao Chia opined, 'I agreed with Chu Chi-lin that it wasn't useful for us to think this way. For the sake of building our solidarity, I supported Chu's explanation that Woo was deliberately trying to deceive us and divert our attention.' Woo had once commented that the daily-rated workers' low wages and high turnover meant that they had themselves to blame for not receiving the lump sum award. This greatly heightened the workers' enmity. 'Such a statement enraged all of us,' Hsiao Chia recalled. 'It was even more ridiculous to say that we should be abused out of fear that we might quit. Finally, everybody agreed with us that we shouldn't pay attention to what happened within management. We should instead concentrate on preparing the inauguration meeting and boosting morale.'

The 27 May rally and union inauguration was a great morale-booster. Workers had such a good time that the occasion became near-legendary, drawing mostly favourable news coverage in more than ten daily newspapers. However, the leadership realized that a showdown was imminent. Management's silence was an ominous. As Chu later put it, 'It was the calm before the storm. We [referring to Chu and her immediate core group] all sensed and awaited it eagerly and impatiently. We were not sure how long the high emotions of the workers would last. To maintain them one must boost them. On the other hand, we were afraid we would exhaust the potential prematurely.'

'There was a strong mix of tension and laxity in the air,' recalled Fu a year later. 'Gu and I wished we could manage to buy more time to allow the workers to strengthen their organization. We were not sure, however, whether management was adopting postponement tactics to wear down the workers' solidarity. Yet we agreed with Ma that the workers were swimming upstream. If you don't advance, you back down. Something had to be done to maintain and enhance the solidarity level. Without collective action, organization and collective thinking, one can't valorize one's sense of collective identity.'

Issues such as this 'necessity to mobilize' were rather paradoxical. The sense of uncertainty and potential threat motivated and inspired the core leadership, who used it to heighten worker unity, which in turn tended to reinforce the cycle of antagonistic confrontation. The war clouds hung low, as uncertainties and threats were multiplied and magnified.

To break this vicious circle required external input — possibly a peace initiative from a third party. According to Lo Un-pu, the cable sent to the Japanese headquarters was to 'put the ball in their court and oblige top management to pick it up and respond' in the hope that they would behave in a 'civilized' fashion. But nobody was ready to bet on it. There was danger in trying to taunt the adversary into an early showdown, yet the leaders felt they had to risk it.

The move was effective in that it immediately brought a delegation to Hong Kong, yet one which ignored the workers and resorted to 'underwater' manipulations. This behaviour confirmed the workers' bias — the Japanese were habitual double-dealers — and aroused strong moral indignation among them. Gu later commented, 'The management was too ambitious and careless to plan their action rationally. There was a premature wholesale overkill. They took a chance in trying to get rid of all the "thorns in their eyes" — not one, two or even three, but thirty-six. They didn't realize that such perfunctory overbearingness would create tremendous antipathy. Such an act turned out to be a surprisingly effective catalyst in cementing different groups of workers into one collective body. The oil they poured onto the fire splashed back on themselves and they were badly burned.'

Gu was both right and wrong in her assessment of the 'slaughter' of 31 May; right in saying management was overambitious and strategically careless, but wrong in saying that their jumping the gun with dismissals had led to action. In fact, it was precisely because of *over*-deliberated execution that the dismissals led to a defeat for JWM management. Tied down by trifles and petty conventions, the management was incapable of reacting to the unexpected repercussions caused by the dismissals. The demonstration of blind faith in force, disregard for human feeling and eagerness for total victory made it apparent that management cared only about gaining immediate advantage. This gave JWM workers a moral hold over management.

The dismissals were timed perfectly. Immediately after the afternoon break, cohorts of male staff, foremen and line leaders were guarding different floors, and the big manila envelopes containing dismissal notices were ready in the fifth-floor meeting room. To prevent suspicion and communication among the workers, the dismissals were to be carried out one floor at a time, first at the workers' weakest point, the seventh floor, lastly at their strongest point, the second floor. The final attack on the second floor, with all the personnel pooled for enforcement, was to take place ten minutes before the working day ended, by which time the dismissed workers from the seventh, first, third and sixth floors would be off the premises, or in the fourth-floor canteen/locker room ready to leave. There would be absolutely no support for the second floor.

Ample evidence from various workers reveals that the plan was strictly adhered to by nervous staff members, who employed unnecessary force and coercion. Floor managers approached workers; male and female management personnel and line leaders encircled them, forced them to stop work, stand up, and leave immediately, allowing no questions or even time to gather their personal belongings. Every move of the workers, both those dismissed and those not, was videotaped.

'Who did they think they were dealing with?' 'We were handled like criminals and murderers.' 'We had never been insulted and humiliated like this.' 'We will never forget or forgive this.' 'We had no choice but to fight to the end to redress such an injustice.' This passionate language was employed again and again in my interviews, even two years later. The newly-constituted 'we' was thus born at the tip of management's advancing bayonet.

The occupation of the canteen and the sit-in on the premises that followed the protest on the fifth floor was completely unplanned and unanticipated, and it was its unplanned nature that activated the creativity of the workers and led them to join forces. Afterwards they slept and lived together like sisters on the canteen floor, shared food and drink, lamentation and laughter, and all the ups and downs of subsequent events. The grievances accumulated in their years of bitter factory life were poured out, and they sobbed and held one another in a profoundly emotional, collective catharsis and transcendence. That afternoon, when company lawyers and an army of 'company bouncers', as the workers had characterized the male staff, forcefully expelled Gu and Fu, the JWM workers' collective identity reached its zenith. On the brink of a riot, the workers as a social force, capable of struggle, had emerged. Left to struggle for themselves, they had forged, through their own actions in the complexity of circumstances, a genuine working people's collective: a *working class*.

Ironies and What-ifs in the Making of Histories

Human practice is subject to multiple forces, many of which the actors themselves create and identify with. When 'making history', participants are aware of the existence of 'others' as both co-interveners (synchrony), and as things prior or posterior in sequence (diachrony).

With historical agents-in-action, every move is anticipated. There is constant acknowledgement and denial of the efficacy of others, especially that of adversaries. Within everyone's 'existential' capacity, everyone acquires a sense of historicity. Within this existential awareness are means of transcendence, as imaginations are stretched, allies are made or discarded, hypotheses are made and recast, and answers are sorted and put on trial.

The workers keep going until they hit their heads against the wall and bounce back.

From an *omniscient* point of view, human struggles may resemble badly-performed farces or worn-out cartoons; groups representing forces of oppression and liberation may resemble guinea pigs running in the maze of history. The victory of one group over another can seem almost accidental. For the self-appointed spectators and minute-takers (i.e., historians and social researchers) who peer at history from behind a veil of disinterest and dispassion, historical ironies seem the rule, and the pursuit of a general sense of 'historicity' becomes a self-indulgent exercise in refining a delicate, cynical taste for paradox. These narrators of history are writers. But the agents of history-in-the-making are seldom concerned with the validity of general historical claims Their sense of reality is more humorous. Fighters in real life are neither wholly serious nor light-heartedly ironical. They strive to act and overcome, not to understand or transcend.

Months after the JWM sit-in, I struggled to understand what had happened through my interviews with the leaders, who were history-makers reflecting on the histories in which they had participated. I, at most, had been a semi-bystander/observer *qua* volunteer/supporter. Their spontaneous philosophies at times clashed with my own 'intellectual' ones. In referencing an act, they referred to the common stock of knowledge available from their struggle. They reflected upon hypothetical scenarios — the 'what-ifs' and 'so-whats' — that occurred as alternative possibilities both during and after their actions. In businesslike fashion, histories were constructed piece by piece through the selection of particular sets of signifying practices.

To be historical is to be theoretical. Unexpected and 'accidental' events and circumstances became comprehensible and meaningful, bit by bit, as dialogue shuttled back and forth between the interviewees and myself. This juggling of contrasting views led to a discursive articulation, transforming both interviewees and interviewer. What emerged was a common understanding that 'things good to think about' need not necessarily correspond to 'things good to do'.

Nobody knew why Lam Tu-pi, JWM's legal consultant, called the Centre on the morning of 31 May to warn of the upcoming dismissal. The Centre staff speculated that he actually wanted only to warn Lo Man-Sa, director of CLA, as both men were members of the steering committee of one of Hong Kong's first quasi-political organizations. They reasoned that since both Lam and Lo were involved with the 'democrats' and social issues, Lam was obliged to inform Lo and prepare him for the worst. Lo may have told Lam to contact the Centre directly, since Lo would look bad if he learned of the dismissal and yet failed to inform the workers. However, this guesswork was difficult to verify during my interview with Lo, who changed the subject without confirming or denying these speculations. Undoubtedly, it was out of a sense of moral obligation that he felt obliged not to do so.

What was in Lam's mind when he decided to reveal management's top secret to the Centre and hence to the workers? Did he not have any second thoughts that he might be jeopardizing his legal career? Or was he sure that there was nothing the workers could do, even if they learned about the dismissal in advance? Was he shocked when he learned that a 'riot', resulting from the dismissal, had occurred on the very day that he had secretly informed the workers? Was this why he behaved so stiffly and coldly when he represented JWM management? Was he sure that his informer's role would never be revealed? Did he think that he had gone overboard, and had to suppress the workers overtly to demonstrate his company loyalty? How did he feel about the events that followed?

Another puzzling 'accident' occurred — or, more precisely, failed to occur — immediately after Lam's telephone call: During the lunch break neither the JWM workers assigned to call to report from different floors, nor even conscientious Chi-mei, remembered to call the Centre. Why did the communication system collapse at the precise moment it was most needed? Prolonged investigation later revealed that it was because of all sorts of accidental mishaps that the most undesirable circumstances resulted. Gu was extremely anxious and worried by Lam's secret information all afternoon. Long after the dispute had ended, Centre staff continued to wonder about the incident. They reasoned that, were it not for all the other unexpected things, the workers might very well have been defeated instantly, owing to the communication breakdown. They felt that their failure to reach the workers with Lam's advance warning had left them unprepared. In my interviews with them, most of the leaders disagreed with this interpretation, but no counterargument was formulated. A 'what-if' question in my interviews revealed a rather unlikely reality. 'What if somebody had called the Centre and learned what management was going to do in the afternoon?' I asked. 'Wouldn't the situation have been more favourable for the workers if you guys knew what to expect and were prepared for it?'

'No, it wouldn't,' answered Chu Chi-lin and her core group.

'Why not? At least you would have been better prepared psychologically!'

'No, there was absolutely no way to prepare, even if we had known what was going to happen. Worse, we as leaders would not have known what to do. Knowing would have rendered us too cautious, hesitant and indecisive. Should we consult with the other floors or not? If so, how should we go about it? Would a consensus be reached? "Psychological preparedness", on the contrary, might have left the rank and file not knowing where to turn. If they had known in advance, they would have calculated their response. To wit, the last drop of our strength, our spontaneity and moral indignation would have evaporated instantly, and we would have ended up going home, one by one, in complete defeat, without a fight!'

An uprising can never be prefabricated: To learn the ultimate 'secret of heaven' only dilutes its quintessential momentum and spontaneity. The anthropologist had to learn this the hard way. The 'secret dismissal' had surprised both sets of actors and the observers as well.

According to Chien Fa-hin, a seventh-floor RP, management's dismissal of the leaders starting from the floors where social organization was weakest was not a success. 'No sooner had we resumed production after the 3:30 break than foremen and line leaders came up to five of us. We were told to drop our work and leave the shop-floor at once. We resisted. Why should we do so? The line leaders said, "Because you have been fired. You are ordered to go."

'Five of us made eye contact and decided not to comply. It was working time and we were not going anywhere. "If there are envelopes, why don't you bring them over," Hon Lai-fon demanded.

'At the same time, an argument ensued over whether or not there was any legitimate reason for management to dismiss us *en masse*. "You are all fired because you are guilty of misconduct and of intruding in the company's internal business!" one foreman shouted.

'We knew there was no use arguing, but felt we should do so in order to buy time and try to spur our colleagues to take action. There was little response. In the chaos, more management staff flooded in. Among those who dashed towards us was a raging Woo Char-hwa. Following him was a cohort of "thugs". Some of them carried video cameras and began aiming them at us.

'We were still resisting. One of the dismissed initiated a fierce quarrel with Woo. Woo, elated and proud, shut her up and shouted, "If you want to quarrel, go to the Labour Bureau, sue us in Labour Court!" At this moment, I turned to those colleagues who were still sitting on their stools lost and confused. I raised my hands and made a strong gesture, to call for an uprising. I was immediately stopped by force. Women line leaders, some of them from other floors, held me in their arms and tried to drag me out of the room. Meanwhile, I noticed "thugs", male and female, standing beside almost every worker. I caught a brief glimpse of Hon Lai-fon grabbing her big envelope and running down the stairs.

'I was surrounded by line leaders and foremen as I made my way down the stairs to the locker room to pick up my personal belongings. I also noticed that the iron-gate to the sixth-floor shop had been pulled down and locked. There were members of the staff guarding the stairs all the way down. In the locker room, I tried to stay as long as possible. Video filming teams followed my every move and management staff eagerly urged us to leave quickly. It was not until I was expelled from the factory building that I ran into Hon by the factory gate and decided to phone the Centre. Even then we were still wondering whether or not the seventh floor was the only floor chosen by management, to "kill one as a warning for a hundred".'

But on the seventh floor, management was almost 100 percent successful. Immediately afterwards, on the first, third and sixth floors, resistance was also minimal. Although discontent was widespread among the operatives, they failed to stop their leaders from being fired.

'It was extremely calm on the second floor after the 3:30 break,' recalled Hsiao Chia. 'We weren't even aware that there were "watchdogs" around and watching our every move, until somebody went to the toilet and found management staff guarding the staircase and the iron gate pulled halfway down. This news spread throughout the shop-floor in minutes and more workers decided to go to the toilet. As the gate was pushed up and again pulled down, unrest on the shop-floor began to prevail.

'Suddenly, the double doors were violently pushed open and I saw Hon Lai-fon dash forward screaming something, raising her arm and waving a big brown envelope. In a split second she was pulled out by foremen from outside, as well as inside. I was sitting facing the swing doors so I was quite sure that there was a big envelope in her hand.'

According to Chu Chi-lin, 'I didn't exactly catch sight of the brown envelope myself. But, looking at everybody else, we knew things must be happening. People who sat in the front passed the word on, as everybody kept asking and confirming, "the stage-play, the drama, the envelope, yes, yes, yes." Yet there were still some uncertainties and hesitations. "Dash out, dash out" some yelled, while others tried to get a better picture. Production ground to a halt. Foremen and line leaders became extremely nervous, expecting something yet not knowing exactly what to do.

' "There must be something of grave importance behind their hesitation," Yin-Yon, who sat beside me, suggested. We exchanged glances, and I couldn't restrain myself any more. I told myself, "What the heck, there's nothing to lose, we just dash up and find out what is happening. Otherwise, we might be too late to salvage anything." Not knowing from where I got my courage. I shouted, "Let's dash up to the office, our representatives have been fired!" Before I had finished, "Big Brother", Mui Len-shu and Siu Fen-ni had left their seats. Together, we rushed out and, using our bodies, fought our way up the staircase to the fifth-floor office. I heard screaming and yelling, but I had absolutely no idea whether or not anyone followed us.'

Chien Fon-yi — 'Big Brother' — recollected, 'The faces of our foremen and line leaders turned pale after Hon Lai-fon was forcibly pushed out. Two of them stood guard by the swinging doors, while others closely watched those of us who were most active. It was too obvious for us to miss the message. It wasn't possible that these "running dogs" would lose their heads out of fear of Hon's arrival. In my mind, Hon's waving arm and the brown thing in her hand were like flashing warning signals. A "slaughter" must be in progress on the other floors. As Chu shouted, "Let's go, it doesn't matter any more!" I pushed my way out. Unwittingly, everyone dashed out with us. We were furious. Gum Fu-yan, a line leader, tried to block my way and I brushed her away. Next, we reached a checkpoint guarded by male foremen. The foremen threatened us, "If you dare dash out, all of you will be fired!" "So what, we're quitting anyway," we shouted back as we pushed our way through.

'There were two more male staff guarding the staircase. They tried to block the stairs. Some of us pushed them aside while some more petite colleagues slipped through under their arms. Mrs Sheou, Woo's secretary, desperate and low-spirited, screamed at us. Siu Fen-ni went up to her and scolded her back. We were literally forced up the stairs by people pushing from behind. When we reached the gate leading to the fifth-floor office, there were more male staff pushing at random.

'Suddenly, the management's line of defence collapsed, probably at the sight of more than 100 of us. As the staff withdrew to the left side of the office area, we occupied the rest of the floor. The corridor was crowded and I was pushed again, into the office. It was in such chaos; I heard screaming from all directions. No sooner had I been pushed to the floor by staff who were trying desperately to hold out and defend the office than I saw Siu-guan also sitting on the floor, crying and scolding. We were locked in the office, as more and more fellow workers joined in the fifth-floor occupation.'

By the time the second-floor workers had occupied the fifth-floor office, the news of the dismissals had spread throughout the building. Workers from the other floors who had not been fired were instructed to leave after their leaders were expelled. As they converged in the canteen/locker room, they exchanged information about the insulting abuses management had heaped on their representatives. Emotions were high, but a sense of powerlessness prevailed. It seemed too late to do anything. However, when they learned that their second-floor colleagues had occupied the office floor, they were ecstatic. Without hesitation, they rushed up the stairs to (in their own words) 'gain long overdue justice'. Messengers were sent down to the street to call those who had already left back to join in the resistance. At the factory gate they met their dismissed leaders as well, who called the Centre. They were told to wait for Gu. When she arrived, all the workers, including those dismissed and those not yet dismissed, took the lift to the fifth floor and joined the occupation.

Chien Fa-hin's memories, some eight months later, reflected on the scene and its accompanying sentiments. Somewhat nostalgically, she recalled, 'We were so happy when we saw our colleagues and fellow representatives again. In less than an hour, things were so different that it seemed as if a whole lifetime had passed. We felt like hugging each other and weeping on each other's shoulders. We felt so down at being expelled. We thought the whole thing was over and we had been totally defeated. We didn't want to believe it. We refused to go home. We didn't want to give up hope, but we didn't expect anything so spectacular either!'

It had never occurred to us at the Centre that the stage-play of 27 May should ever have any real significance in their real-world struggle. Yet the image of a waving arm and a big brown envelope were invoked repeatedly in various interviewee's memories. It was this image of a shared 'has been' – the skit — which brought the workers to a common sense of the present and of 'what could be'. The image was vivid and forceful precisely because it was a recollected experience itself, not one merely mediated through words or other signs. It was this specific bodily practice that transformed the workers' ritualistic 'could be' into a real-world 'should be' situation. The compressed temporal/spatial anticipation flared into a framework for the present, and every individual had to decide whether to enact (re-enact) a ritually predestined part or to fail in her assigned role. Hon Lai-fon decided to enact the whistle blower's role by waving her arm with the big brown envelope: dramatic prefiguration, somewhat light-heartedly performed, transformed into powerful historical action. What followed rested on the complicity of other actors. The little drama constituted a mythical history, a legacy, which one could willingly engage as an agent. For those who made that choice, it was imperative to dash up to the office. This action was dictated by the pre-existing common experience — that of performing in, watching and discussing the play — which was engraved in their collective memories. There was no need for heroism or personal courage: one simply submitted to one's predestined role, which had been collectively envisaged only five days earlier in the bodily practice of a stage play.

When the question, 'What if nobody had come up with the idea of putting on a show in the first place, would it have made any difference?' was posed to Chu Chi-lin, she speculated, 'In that case, nothing would have happened, I'm sure.'

On the following day there were conflicting reports in the media concerning the number of workers dismissed. About two-thirds of the twenty or so newspapers reported thirty-six dismissals, while the other third reported nineteen, yet nobody questioned the discrepancy. This situation lasted for three days, until 3 June, when seventeen more dismissal envelopes were dispatched by management, but were stopped and held by the labour officer, Mao Si-hai. The next day some papers reported that seventeen more workers had been dismissed, bringing the total to thirty-six. Other papers claimed that the original thirty-six workers had once again been fired, but that this time the dismissals were official and final.

In the press, both reports of how the final figures were reached sounded plausible and credible, but I was interested in why and how these explanations came into being. I checked with the historical agents themselves.

First of all, how was the figure of nineteen dismissals initially arrived at? Reviewing the reports of the 31 May events, I discovered that the number nineteen occurred only in those reports adopting the management's perspective. The reporters who had filed the reports confirmed to me that they had been given the number by the management.

But where did the thirty-six come from? This was more difficult. Reporters who had not reported from management's perspective did not necessarily intend a workers' angle. They did not report the management figure only because management had been too timid to confirm or deny anything, and the reporters were not aggressive enough to push. Instead, they went to the easy source — the workers — who claimed that thirty-six had been fired.

But why did the workers claim thirty-six dismissals and management nineteen? Thirty-six is the number that has been historically verified; it was not guesswork on the workers' part. Part of the answer to this question came one weekend in December, when I happened to be at the Centre. Siu Fan-ni was visiting, and when our conversation turned to the sit-in, she recalled, 'As we dashed up to the office, everybody was excited ... however, I was also deeply troubled. We had been fighting and struggling together for months. This might very well be the last occasion we would share. What I was most afraid of was that all of our representatives would be fired and we would be left alone. What if I was not fired? It was unthinkable that I might have to stay on after all this. Fortunately, it didn't take long for me to learn that I was one of the thirty-six. It was such a relief. I was so happy that I couldn't help but jump up and down like a child ... '

'In the chaos, Ho-chie found the door of the right-hand conference room unlocked. Daringly, she sneaked into the room and found seventeen more dismissal envelopes stacked on the big conference table. She read through all the envelopes. All of them were addressed to the second-floor, die-hards, representatives and union directors. I learned from her that I was one of them. Together with the nineteen from the other floors, we figured out that the first wave of the slaughter was aimed at the thirty-six of us.'

'And based on that you guys told the Centre that thirty-six had been fired, and announced it to the press?'

'Yes, it was decided that way.'

'But when the workers claimed thirty-six had been fired, weren't you actually pushing yourself into a corner? In other words, by publicly announcing it, hadn't the workers themselves fired seventeen more of their colleagues, before management even had a chance to do so?'

'Yes,' Siu Fan-ni replied, 'we were compelled to engage in a last-ditch battle, forced by management. It would have been self-deception to pretend that we hadn't been fired simply because management hadn't had a chance to lay violent hands on us.'

A few days later, Chu Chi-lin expressed a similar sentiment, 'They had simply gone overboard on the matter. It was too much, too excessive. They had to pay for the overkill, swallow the bitter fruit. Why should we leave them any room to back down or rectify their mistakes without being punished? They had to be defeated and we were ready to beat those running dogs who oppressed us and licked their superiors' asses!'

'But what if you had fought for the nineteen who had already been fired and left the seventeen from the second floor alone? Wouldn't that have been a better way to preserve your strength and leadership? For instance, wasn't there an obvious lack of mature leadership in the union after all of you left?'

'No, it wouldn't have been possible. At whom do you think the slaughter was aimed? Those of us from the second floor — the workers' stronghold — the seventeen who constituted the real core of the struggle. The management were no fools. They knew exactly what they were doing and the minimum necessary to achieve their goal was to totally shatter the workers' leadership. If we fought only for the nineteen, they [management] would know our fight would be lukewarm and our mobilization half-hearted. Without the second-floor leaders' claim that they had also been fired, who would have been ready for a total war? How could we have mobilized all the workers so efficiently? The overkill policy adopted by management offered us a hold over them. We could not refuse their offer and throw away a golden opportunity to arm ourselves.'

According to Lo Un-pu, 'We knew we were on the right track when we learned the next morning that management only admitted to firing nineteen. It was obvious that they were trying to save the situation and hide their viciousness.'

'Wouldn't it have been possible for the workers to go along with management? I mean, it might have been a good opportunity to shift gears, so to speak, to go along with the number of nineteen and disclaim their intention to dismiss the remaining seventeen? That way, might not the core leadership — the seventeen from the second floor — have been salvaged?'

Lo responded, 'It may have been possible. In fact, we discussed the matter carefully, but we didn't think it was worth the risk. We might very well have trapped ourselves in a situation where we would fail to gain an advantage and instead incur a loss. We were not presumptuous enough to think we could outsmart anybody. On the other hand, we were also aware of the fact that we couldn't take for granted the morale of the rank and file. We were not always 100 percent sure of our mobilization capabilities. We were even less sure about how long it could be sustained. We had constraints too. We had to be realistic.'

There was yet another dimension under consideration — a moral dimension. To paraphrase Mui Len-shu, 'As far as I'm concerned, the fourteen of us who were the representatives deserved the dismissal. The other twenty-two were innocent victims. However, no matter how much or how little one had contributed to the subversion of management, we were all in the same boat and shared the same sentiments. Who were we to deny somebody who would sacrifice their jobs for the common good?'

'Big Brother' Chien Fon-yi then added, 'Of course it doesn't mean that we agreed with Siu-guan's actions at the 3 June meeting. Her challenge to Woo that we had not exactly been fired only served to remind him. Wilful and stupid, she always failed to keep her composure at crucial moments. To cause the arch enemy to totally lose face is not always a good policy. However, to be fair and put the matter into perspective, I don't think she was to blame. Things had reached the stage where what had to happen happened. I never fantasized that there was a possibility that they might give up firing us. The showdown was unavoidable, it was only a matter of time.'

I asked Ho-chie, who had discovered the seventeen envelopes, 'Why didn't you simply throw them away? It might not have prevented management from eventually firing the seventeen, but at least it could have caused them more trouble and work.'

'Well, I did think about doing that. However, I figured that those envelopes belonged to management. We were no mob.'

Hsiao Chia added, 'We were fighting against unjustifiable practices. But could we simply adopt whatever means possible, without regard for the moral implications? This question was always in our minds. We knew there was also a limit to cool-minded calculation. At a certain point in time, decisions must be made. A price must be paid. That's what we've learned from our lives. It's silly to think we can win them all, or that we can have things both ways.'

The workers' core leadership, then, was quite aware of the various pluses and minuses of claiming thirty-six dismissals. In retrospect, they showed that they were prepared for the adverse effects to which they had exposed themselves.

To paraphrase Chu Chi-lin: Dropouts and sell-outs were expected at the downturn. There is no endless banquet and there is no endless battle. They felt good about themselves, not sorry that they had not won more. They had had a good fight and had decent memories to fall back on.

To account for transformations in the various interest-constellations among the workers would be another book. Suffice to say that the workers and their leaders were convinced that it was useless to dwell on such matters, but that it was necessary to act. There are always consequences that are beyond one's immediate control. Too many 'what-ifs' would have been harmful. Engaged combatants tend to neutralize the 'what-ifs' with the practical interrogation, 'So what?'

'Yes, there were all kinds of possibilities. Most of them had occurred to us and were brushed aside by competing on-the-spot imperatives of one sort or another. To make the best of what we had at hand, was, and is, what we are,' concluded Hsiao Chia.

Thus, despite a discourse of multiple justifications, there was a strong common interest among the dismissed, the to-be-dismissed and the not-yet-dismissed. Their strategy was to utilize the animosity created by management's overkill to build greater solidarity. At this moment, the logic of mobilization dictated that the politics of generalization be adopted to prevent possible management withdrawal and the potential loss of worker unity.

Later, however, the same logic of mobilization would have to abandon this politics of generalization, or at least modify it. In order to salvage the workers' collective consciousness, the leadership was forced to particularize workers' interests to counter the claim made by some of the 'helping hands' (such as Son) that they also cared about *every single worker*. Although this policy worked to the immediate advantage of particular individuals, such as Chen Siu-guan and Hon Lai-fon, who had the highest compensation at stake, it split the common body of workers. To survive, the workers had constantly to take and then alter their positions, and valorize them through ideological interpellation. This dynamic adjustment of tactics was crucial.

Despite its seeming coherence and stability, the institutional power (management) was also fluid. About nine months after the sit-in, I managed to interview management's spokeswoman, Ms Chan Mei-fon, who, with bitterness, had quit M/S Beagos and Taylor, the US firm which had handled public relations for JWM. She was eager to talk, especially about the JWM case, because after all her work she had not even been paid a bonus at the Chinese New Year. She said I should have located her earlier, when she would have passed on her personal files on the JWM matter — hundreds of telecommunications between the JWM Japan headquarters and the Hong Kong office, and inches-thick files of conference minutes. She had worked fourteen to sixteen hours a day for ten days of the sit-in; had been in charge of all external communications, including news conferences and press releases; and had presided over every single management meeting.

Speaking somewhat sarcastically, she told me, 'There were great dogfights among the local management, as well as between the Japanese and the Hong Kong staff. Everywhere was chaos. Nobody knew what was going on or what to do. The Japanese labour-relations expert, who never showed up personally, must have been a butcher. He only knew how to make [things] worse. I think I was the only one who was relatively cool-minded. And gradually I, as a woman who would supposedly understand the female workers, was frequently consulted.'

'What kind of experience did you have dealing with industrial disputes? Were you trained in the US?'

'Are you kidding! I knew absolutely nothing about industrial disputes prior to the JWM case. My training was as a secretary here in Hong Kong.'

'So you must have worked very closely with the experts sent over from the States, right?'

'What experts? Sent by whom?'

'The crisis handling team sent over by Beagos and Taylor to help control the situation ...'

Before I finished, she burst into laughter, 'The "crisis team" is sitting in front of you. Nobody was sent in from anywhere. I am unaware of the existence of such a team at B & T at all. Our company dealt with regular public-relations matters. JWM was desperate and was so eager to secure American expertise that our firm was forced to take the case. There was no reason to push business out of the door, right? The funny thing was that our firm had to charge JWM hundreds of US dollars per hour for the "experts". Only then did JWM begin to have confidence in me. Can you imagine how much B & T made? It was a windfall! However, they didn't even appreciate my efforts. It was disgusting.'

'Did you think you had done a good job for JWM?'

'Yes, I did. I worked hard and tried everything possible to help them. I had to rely on my instincts and show them that I knew exactly what I was doing. I was all alone, nobody in my firm would even pick up the phone to talk to me — but I feel pretty bad about it now.'

'Why?'

'Why? Because I feel that I was betrayed and abused. And I regret that I was a part of the heartless efforts by the JWM management to perpetuate wicked deeds. I began to think that those working girls must be good girls and that they chose to rebel only because they were being badly abused. It was a good lesson in life for me. Maybe I do deserve bad treatment from my employer for what I've done.' She ended her narrative with this reflection, while I was still recovering from the shock of all the ironies involved.

Ms Chan's account hinted at an aspect of institutional 'power' which might constitute an area for further inquiry. I would suggest that a part of management's image of institutional coherence and stability stemmed from their capacity to absorb wasteful consumption and to keep the fact hidden.

It was both shocking and embarrassing for everybody involved in the JWM case to find, on the third morning after the dispute was formally resolved, an entire page of the English-language *Hong Kong Standard* devoted to an 'inside' story exposing 'a fear of the re-emergence of the Trotskyists' in the JWM case (Appendix, Day +3).

In Hong Kong, the label 'Trotskyist' is so serious that neither the JWM management nor the government had ever employed it. To call someone a Trotskyist was to brand her/him a public enemy — a vicious tactic considered illegitimate in any confrontation. It could only be designed to arouse ill will and sow discord among radicals, and was interpreted as a strategy that the 'left' (pro-China) forces had adopted to attack their adversaries. It was therefore surprising that such a can of worms was opened in journalistic discourse, even more so as the story had obviously been in preparation for some time. It was first published in a paper that had given the least coverage to the JWM case, making the whole business even stranger. Later, a similar report appeared in the Chinese-language *Ming Pao*. Evidently, this was a concerted effort at manipulating public opinion (Appendix, Day +5).

Some two months later, a lengthy article was published in a popular political commentary under the byline of Luk Ga-yip, the chairman of the

The whole-paged coverage on HKS devoted to the 'inside' story of 'Trotskyist' involvement in the JWM sit-in.

Hong Kong News Reporters Association. Luk renewed accusations of 'Trotskyist elements' intervening in the JWM dispute settlement. He also threw out quite a few inside stories and bad-mouthed Lee Siu-ching, calling him the biggest loser. But most enlightening was his exaggerated praise of the writer of the *Hong Kong Standard* report, Ms Liang Li-an (Appendix, Day +3).

As it turned out, Luk had been chief of the City Desk at the *Standard* during the JWM dispute. Ms Liang was not only working under him as a reporter, but was also his personal secretary in his capacity as chairman of the Hong Kong News Reporters Association. I interviewed Ms Liang.

'I had been following the JWM case from very early on. People thought I was following it as a reporter, but I was a unionist, a staff member of the News Reporters Association. But when all the labour groups interfered, I did not. I was not participating as a supporter but as an observer.

'Luk told me to keep an eye on the Trotskyists. I could identify a few who used to belong to Trotskyist organizations — I believe they still do — but they didn't know who I was. Some simply took me as a reporter, some thought I was, like them, there to help.'

'So your project was quite different from the others. Why do you think Luk wanted you to do that?'

'We decided we should monitor the Trotskyists. Luk told me that he had been badly beaten by them a few years ago. He decided to expose their destructive nature as far as Hong Kong was concerned.'

Thus private revenge turned public scandal. In this case, the interesting part was the utilizing of multiple, socially-endowed institutional identities to create a spurious but institutionally authorized and professionally authenticated 'documented truth'.

On 9 June, reporter Peter Chan published an article in the English-language *SCMP* suggesting that tougher unions might emerge from the JWM dispute (Appendix, Day +10). But although Chan was a keen observer, he was a naive analyst. There were signs of co-operation between Son and Lo in their involvement with the JWM workers, but both of them ceased 'assisting' the workers after 6 June, and when the workers refused to accept their deal, they had withdrawn to protect their respective political interests, rather than showing their hands to each other. As leaders of 'established' labour organizations, they could hardly afford to have their reputations shattered by setbacks in labour disputes. They were engaged in a repetitive game with government labour agents and management communities. To keep everybody in business, a mode of behaviour and a pattern of rules had developed, which was not designed to achieve anyone's final victory, which was, unfortunately, what the JWM workers were after. Son and Lo had a realistic assessment of the utility of a union in the political context of Hong Kong. They knew that JWM workers had false hopes for their union. They were also quite clear that unionization, as seen by the workers, was primarily of tactical value. Under the rubric of defending the workers' right to organize, both the FLU and the CLA had to claim to support the struggle — yet both Son and Lo argued against an 'excess of radicalism and militancy', in order, they said, 'to protect their future union's activities and strength'. To this end, they challenged the 'inexperience' of the JWM leaders and 'some small, unestablished local labour groups'. Son claimed it was necessary to suppress JWM militancy to protect the long-term interests of all Hong Kong workers and Hong Kong's prosperity as a whole; Lo said it was in order to counter JWM leaders' radicalism, take care of every single worker's genuine interest and minimize risk and loss, mainly in monetary terms.

However, Son and Lo's rationalizations were not merely self-serving excuses, but radiated from a self-centred point of view maintained in the absence of any understanding of how JWM workers' leadership was actually constituted.

Although seventeen of the dismissed workers came from the second floor — which, as the major shop-floor, housed more than 100 operatives — it would be misleading to assume that this was because the leadership was concentrated there, or that leaders were always visible or charismatic. In fact, the workers' leadership was but a façade for a long-existing complex of social relations.

One aspect of this story is an elaborate set of nicknames used on the second floor, known even to management: Chu Chi-lin was 'Little Wife', Chien Fon-yi was 'Big Brother', Kau-fu was 'Uncle', Siu Fen-ni was 'Daughter', Lo Un-pu was 'Wet Nurse', and so on; altogether involving more than twenty second-floor workers. This group was almost coterminous with the leadership which management decided to dismiss. Other workers explained to me that these terms were, in effect, metaphors, and were by and large accurate in symbolizing the character or image of particular individuals. But why relational terms, I wondered; and why only about twenty? In an interview with Lo Un-pu, I jokingly asked, ' "Little Wife" is a funny nickname, doesn't "Little Wife" mean that one should have a husband?'

'Of course, she certainly did.'

'She did? You mean Chu Chi-lin?'

'Yes — not a real husband, but a husband in our sense.'

'Who? Who was her husband? Why?'

'Hsiao Chia was her husband. You didn't know that?'

'Hsiao Chia doesn't even have a name (nickname)!'

'Hsiao Chia was close to Chu and they always paired together, like husband and wife. In addition, Hsiao Chia always acted more like a man.'

'Why "Little Wife", and not just "Wife"?'

'Hsiao Chia had somebody very close to her who had left the factory. She was the "big wife" and Chu was the second one, called "Little Wife".'

'Interesting. But why didn't Hsiao Chia have a name?'

'She didn't need one. Everything began with and derived from her. She was the centre of the whole "big family", if you want to call it that. For instance, to whom do you think Chien was "big brother"? She was the brother of Hsiao Chia. Siu was the daughter of Hsiao Chia. Even I, who was only a quasi member of the family, was Hsiao Chia's "wet nurse"!'

Here then was a hidden centre upon which hinged a complicated network of relations. Hsiao Chia had been overlooked by me and by every member of the Centre staff. How had the 'family' come about? I asked her. Hsiao Chia laughed at my question and answered:

'It was after a movie entitled "Family of the Great River" in which the famous female actress Hon-chie plays the husband. Some six years ago, we went to the movie together, and about ten of us who worked at JWM decided that we should organize our "family". The "family" expanded, with new members every year. At its peak, we were more than thirty.'

'Why?' I asked.

'We were very close friends, we got along very well. If we had been boys, we might very well have established a kind of blood-brotherhood. I think because we were teenage girls, we were more family-oriented, we felt a need to enhance our relationship. We felt good about making a fictitious family. The way we addressed each other, we actually felt that there were extra ties which bound us together. Those who were not members of the "family" envied us. We tried to make our life, both in and out of the factory premises, easier and gayer. However, it also caused a lot of trouble.'

'Do you think management had the "family" in mind when they tried to deal with the dispute?'

'I am 100 percent sure about it. All the staff on the second floor knew of the "family". Woo Char-hwa sometimes jokingly addressed us by our nicknames and we resented it. They knew that we were the core, the so-called troublemakers. They had experienced our ability to organize and to resist. There was no doubt in our minds that we were the target of their "slaughter". If they wanted to wipe out workers' leadership and suffocate our union, they would have to fire all of us, all the members of the family, without exception. Mr Ma once announced that I didn't deserve to be fired since I took a week off prior to the dismissal.' She couldn't help laughing again. 'He was certainly mistaken. I'm not saying that I was the "black-hand" behind it, but I do think the management was too greedy. Those who were fired on the other floors were wronged and did not deserve it, including their representatives. There was no overkill on our floor, we were all prepared for it.'

If we adjust our gaze to a different level of the constitution of 'the social' in this fictitious family, another layer emerges: Chu Chi-lin confirmed that she was very close to Hsiao Chia. She told me, 'Hsiao Chia often came to my home and stayed overnight with me. Sometimes on the weekend we chatted until morning.'

I now began to understand how advice from the Centre had been considered by the leadership. They constantly conferred with each other — on the bus, in bed, over the phone and through coded glances. 'Outside' opinions were adopted, but only after long and elaborate discussion, and only when they found them useful.

I learned that Chu Chi-lin was to marry Hsiao Chia's brother in a year and that after a few months Hsiao Chia and her brother would move to Chu's village. Like almost all the 'family members', Hsiao Chia was also a resident of the Pat Heung (eight-village) area. The 'family members' were all teenagers from Hakka-speaking farming families. After finishing their compulsory education, they had been recruited to work for JWM — their first and only job, to which they had been introduced by neighbours and relatives. They had taken the jobs mainly because JWM offered a free bus service for the hour-long ride to work. The bus ride became an important occasion, during which they built lifelong relationships.

'We were not really relatives. We were friends. Even if some of us were remotely related, we never had anything to do with that kind of familial relation. As females, we were not eligible for annual ancestor-worship ceremonies. We made our relationships out of nothing. As young girls from a rural area who had never had a job, we were deemed country bumpkins, stupid,' recalled Chien Fon-yi. 'We, however, accepted this and tried to prove ourselves by working hard. The management knew perfectly well that they would never be able to get good workers like us any more, especially among the city-dwelling teenagers of today. That's why Woo Char-hwa tried to lure some of us back, to work for his privately owned factory that subcontracts jobs from JWM.'

'We are good workers, we work hard,' added Lo Un-pu. 'And we are good fighters, we resist hard. We feel good, you may say proud, about our ability to produce, not to polish shoes or earn our bread as running dogs. We found we had a lot in common and felt that we were the same kind of people. We never imagined that the sense of oneness in us would enable us to fight for a cause.'

The sociologically-minded might wish to speculate on the meaning and nature of solidarity among the rural leadership of the industrial dispute — a solidarity of non-industrial origin transposed into a partially industrialized context. These social relations, however, did not exist for any particular teleological goal. Like anything we may label 'cultural', they were available for valorization when a position-taking situation developed — but they remained largely invisible and 'underground' during the dispute.

On the other hand, monetary aspects of the conflict were also significant. Chien Fa-hin, from Pat Heung but not a member of 'the family', was fired for being an RP. She became extremely close to Chu Chi-lin during the course of struggle and has admired her ever since. In an interview, she spoke of her experiences helping and teaching production skills and management techniques to newly recruited male foremen. They were young boys, usually just out of technical high school, who had been recruited through 'relations', and knew practically nothing about watch manufacturing; yet they were hired to supervise the female daily-rated operatives. People with skill and patience like Chien Fa-hin were assigned to 'familiarize' them, and they taught them everything they knew. Soon, the boys were 'in charge' of the workers, with monthly salaries 50 percent higher than those of their mentors, with benefits their female mentors were kept in ignorance of. Not until the sit-in did Chien discover something very wrong with this. 'The boys were treated with great favour simply because they were born male,' she said. Nevertheless, Chien failed to articulate that it had always been the operatives who controlled overall production. Analytically speaking, this was the basic 'materiality' that provided the edge for the operatives' industrial action — yet it remained unseen, as the operatives took their own skills and productivity as their *raison d'être*.

Chien explained that the workers lived with their parents. They usually did not pay rent — one of the major items in a Hong Kong family budget, but gave a portion of their income to their parents, keeping more than 50 percent for themselves. 'There was not much opportunity to spend money. Most of the time — unlike the city girls who went out and shopped a lot — we worked and went home.'

Some might ask: If the workers had not been rural and only semi-self-supporting, might things have been very different? I can give no positivistic answer, but agree that 'trade-offs' between dignity and material survival may be conceived differently as one's 'politics' differs. My experience with Mao Si-hai and Lo Man-sa suggest exactly this.

Lo Man-sa was defensive, even evasive in interview. He asserted that the JWM case was an anomaly, that management had responded more softly than was typical of Japanese employers. He attributed this solely to the personality of Mr Amukas: If it had not been for Amukas' resolution, no one would have had the guts to defy the Japanese Chamber of Commerce, which had demanded the strike be crushed and that no reward be made. Lo agreed that Amukas — chief executive of the world's biggest watch manufacturer, the biggest Japanese investor in Hong Kong — had been in a better position than others to oppose the chamber, although he refused to reveal details of how the chamber had arrived at its resolution or how it had attempted to enforce it. Lo acknowledged that the period prior to Amukas' intervention was typical of postwar Japanese union-busting. He admired Amukas and complimented him on 'having the style of a great general' and being extremely far-sighted. 'This was ironic, and rather atypical for a Japanese male of his position and power' (see van Wolferen 1990).

There was no denying that both the Japanese and the Hong Kong governments had their fingerprints all over the JWM 'incident': Lo confirmed that the Secretary for District Administration, Leonardo Du, who had studied in Japan and spoke perfect Japanese, had relayed the Governor's message to Amukas expressing support. He also confirmed that the chief UMELCO member, Wong Nieu-kwen, who had urged the JWM management to fire one worker a day to intimidate them, had close ties with Japanese banking and business interests.

Lo fiercely criticized 'inexperienced' local groups who had coloured the JWM industrial dispute with Japanese and Chinese nationalism. He reiterated statements made to the press during the latter part of the sit-in that the dispute had had absolutely nothing to do with ethnic differences or historical antagonisms. He began to blast the Centre for playing 'little tricks' on the factory premises while he was striving to negotiate with management on the workers' behalf. He was still bitter about actions that had discounted his moral authority, discredited his representation, and belittled his organization. He argued that his aim was to protect the incipient union and to keep as many workers working as possible: 'We had to preserve the workers' strength. Somebody had to stay and man the union. As we Chinese say, "To catch a big fish, one must cast a long line." Only unsophisticated and rude fellows would "force the dog into the corner and push it to jump the fence". Too many organizations were involved. If the workers had approached us first, we would have solved the problem, relying solely on ourselves. We would by no means have got whoever was interested involved, especially foreign labour organizations. To be practical, what could they do to help us? At best, they could only offer moral support, which has only symbolic value.'

Lo apparently forgot that he himself had not been invited by the workers' leadership, but he was not too dull to sense the need to defend himself against accusations that he had tried to split the workers and undermine their solidarity. He raised his voice. 'In representing an established group like the CLA, my burden was much heavier than that of the small local groups. I not only had to take care of those who were fighting, but also to take care of those who were willing to take the money and leave. I'm sure that to get such a lump sum payment was to them the chance of a lifetime. I could not forget or neglect those who were not ready or willing to fight. They might have been timid but they were also intimidated. They were even more in need of assistance from people like me. That was why I strove to find a solution that would be acceptable to everyone. I admit it was a difficult position. But I was not like some of the groups, who only took care of workers who held positions in accordance with their own subjective wishes ...'

It was amazing that an acclaimed labour leader should resort to such language. There was no mention of the workers' justice or dignity, or of living beings or subjects-in-struggle. Nor was there a trace of the logic of a social movement. Hidden behind the rhetoric was a declaration of power, gain, and dominance. I understood his statements from an institutional and institution-centred point of view: CLA was perceived — or at least perceived itself — as the establishment. Lo was up for membership of the Basic Law Consultative Committee, and he had made himself both eligible and available to the government's labour advisory board. To become a quasi-governmental institution was one of the CLA's goals. The CLA's *raison d'être* was thus transformed, and Lo's patronizing logic was deeply resented by the workers, although they lacked a specific name for it.

Ideologies that facilitate such patronizing stances as Lo's are both more and less than culturally-specific creations. They exist in many places within the less-than-culturally-specific upper echelons of a particular society, varying in the form and operations of concrete domination. They are defined by the kinds of 'politics of equivalence' (Laclau and Mouffe 1985) they invoke and valorize.

In our case, despite the non-existence of a mythologized 'East Asian Culture' shared by Chinese and Japanese, a chauvinistic dividing and pairing of dominant social categories was used to prop up the patriarchal politics of both Hong Kong and Japanese managements. It is necessary to understand this phenomenon to understand why Amukas did what he did.

Amukas had come to Hong Kong as an emissary of JWM, but he avoided any contact or communication with the workers. Instead, using JWM's banking connections in Hong Kong, he relied on Sa Mo-han, a Japanese bank employee, as his informal intermediary. Sa, the mysterious middleman, was not recruited to mediate between Japanese top management and the workers and their leaders. According to a statement he made to the Centre staff after the sit-in, he had been chosen because of his acquaintance with Lo. According to Lo, Amukas was operating under the assumption that Lo, as the guru of the independent labour movement in Hong Kong, would necessarily be involved in the case. They thus approached him with a management initiative — a secret diplomacy — in order to gain better control of the situation.

This typical Japanese behind-the-scenes manipulation, however, was aborted shortly after it began, not because Amukas misjudged Lo's obligation to co-operate, but because he believed Lo was at the top of a chain of command that, in reality, did not exist. The patriarchal social relations prevailing in Japan's corporation-controlled 'yellow unions' had left him with a rather inapplicable model (Rohlen 1979). However, while Japanese multinationals had succeeded in centralizing management control from the top down, minimizing localization in their overseas units, they had failed to patronize local unions. Because of a strict policy of union-busting, unions were not only antagonistic to management but also to any form of multinationalization, or even the slightest hint of co-optation.

Amukas, however, learned something from the JWM case, and publicly welcomed the establishment of JWM/local unions, knowing that he must give up conventional union-busting tactics and simply hope that the union might one day be 'domesticated'.

Amukas was both a flexible strategist and a quick learner. At first, he stayed behind the scenes and abstained from making comments. However, once he spoke, it was more like a cabinet minister than the CEO of a multinational corporation. He completely opposed conventional JWM rhetoric and reasoning and disavowed the view that daily-rated operatives did not deserve benefits because they might not stay long. Then he spoke as a professor, on the changing nature of Hong Kong society and industry. It was rare for the Hong Kong media to hear someone openly promulgate the 'progressive' idea that Hong Kong was no longer a society of young unemployed, that the children of first-generation labourers were more career-oriented, and that therefore society now required social welfare. It is paradoxical (if not grotesque) that such statements came from the managing director of a multinational corporation in the middle of its worst industrial crisis. After justifying the workers' right to request better benefits and security, Amukas reiterated that JWM benefits had been the best all along, both in Japan and, particularly, in Hong Kong. He then praised 'his workers' as the best in Hong Kong and repeatedly extended his appreciation for their not damaging anything on the factory premises.

The Reflexive Narratives   337

Such public statements were designed to avert pressures from the Japanese Chamber of Commerce, between whom and JWM there existed a genuine conflict of interest. From the point of view of the members of the chamber, the JWM dispute threatened their very existence. There would be terrible repercussions if JWM failed to suppress its rebelling workers and a precedent was set for workers elsewhere. Worse, it would tarnish the image of the miraculous 'Japanese system'. If this myth were discredited, could Japanese business maintain its place in Hong Kong?

Amukas, however, was most concerned with putting an end to the scandal and resuming regular production without further trouble and with minimum damage to his valuable workforce. He knew the value of JWM's Hong Kong pool of skilled workers, built over the course of a decade. The issue at stake for Amukas and JWM was quite different from the crisis and its consequences as perceived by the Japanese Chamber of Commerce. For the latter, the JWM conflict was a remote, though genuine, reality. The chamber argued that they, as foreign investors, were creating 'employment' for Hong Kong and its people. Consequently, they deserved to be served with absolute loyalty, and any transgressors had to be surgically removed. This ideology, however, leads the capital owner to forget that transactions must take place between two parties and be beneficial to both — nobody enters into transactions merely to benefit others.

In analytical terms, the contradiction between Amukas and the chamber was at least threefold: between concern for the immediate, individual predicament and a more remote, collective sense of crisis; between on-the-ground, specific minimization of loss and the abstract and general quest for a common good; and between the concrete role of the industrialist as productivity-tapper and the ideological status of job-provider/creator maintained by transnational investors.

In pragmatic terms, these contradictions manifested themselves in the concrete practices of agenda-setting and priority-fixing. For JWM to salvage Hong Kong as one of its most important productive bases, Amukas had to retain his workers. Thus the conflict was located on the fault-line separating Hong Kong as a profit-generating site from Hong Kong as a machine with genuine people and (therefore) productivity. It was along this line that Amukas struggled to resist his fellow-investors.

Amukas found himself in this struggle, however, as a result of ironies and paradoxes far exceeding his immediate predicament — those basic to the capitalist mode of employment. It is imperative that an employer have juridico-legal rights to fire his/her workers whenever and wherever it is deemed necessary. In the case of JWM, therefore, the dismissals were not simply a tactic to discipline the Sellers of Labour Power (SOLP). 'Free' labour, bought by the Purchaser of Labour Power (POLP), is 'free' precisely because it can be bought in the morning and dismissed that very evening. The POLP has the right to refuse to buy labour power from its owner and instead make profits from the dead labour (fixed capital) they own; the SOLP has the right to starve or to sell its labour power to some other POLP (Bendix 1974). This is, in theory, the essence of the capitalist mode of production and, in reality, a fact of life for millions in Hong Kong. It was touted as what had 'made' Hong Kong Hong Kong: a *laissez-faire* economy under the rule of a *laissez-faire* government (Schiffer 1983).

Now, to what extent was Amukas prepared to resist the pressure from his opponents to dismiss his delinquent workers? Not much. He certainly did not want to jeopardize the above-mentioned ideological fortress, which was not only the buttress of the prevailing 'capitalist' wage system, but also the legitimizing basis of the colonial administrative state. If Amukas wanted to retain the bulk of his productive force, he had to walk the fine line between salvaging the local JWM and avoiding open antagonism with his fellow Japanese investors, other foreign interests, and the host country's 'anxious' regime. Another reading of Leonardo Du's move thus emerges: Du may have been so worried that Amukas would give in to his workers that he could hardly restrain from volunteering his advice — a rather un-*laissez-faire* sentiment for a government functionary in a 'capitalist colony' (Polanyi 1974).

Thus the problem Amukas faced was the basic contradiction of modern political economy. An ultimate solution was not possible. He could only engage in the standard manipulation of *realpolitik* — to isolate economic aspects from their political-moral context, and then manipulate each of them separately.

One 'purely economic' solution would have been to raise the award stakes until they were high enough to appease both those who had been fired and those who wanted confrontation. Amukas thus began playing the role of a benign boss or 'benevolent parent-king' (van Wolferen 1990). I would argue that Amukas did so willingly, although he might very well have sensed that it had been the workers who had set him up in the role. And so we must take up the discussion of a patriarchal politics of equivalence.

The politics of equivalence involved in Amukas's benevolent parent-king role involved equating a series of bifurcated pairings of social categories:

manager	:	worker
parent	:	child
ruler	:	subjects
male	:	female
elder	:	youngster
intellectual	:	manual worker
educated	:	uneducated
modern	:	traditional
urban	:	rural
western	:	oriental
scientific	:	cultural

The list could obviously be expanded. In the JWM confrontation, Amukas obviously belongs in the left-hand column above, while the workers belong in the right-hand column.

The logic which enabled the practice of patronage was embedded in a sexist and orientalist discourse. With a Japanese-style twist, this was couched in the language of familial ideas. One might say that the ghosts of an ideological trinity — household-company-state — had undergone plastic surgery, yet still longed for a 'company as family' (Kondo 1990). In fact, the JWM daily-rated operatives had been precluded from the 'family' and treated as handmaids and temporary helpers (van Helvoort 1979). The company-as-family nostalgia itself might be of some aesthetic value, but the on-the-ground reality of 'paternalism' (Bennett and Iwao 1963) and 'paternalistic care' was not pleasant to look at (Gordon 1985).

The industrial ideology of 'familialism' invariably invokes government and state power. Information leaked to the media confirmed that the Governor himself had been keeping a keen eye on the development of the JWM dispute. Mao Si-hai revealed that JWM management had 'easy access' to high-ranking officers. Amukas had paid the necessary 'courtesy' calls to the relevant authorities soon after his arrival. While the Japanese-speaking Leonado Du played the role of go-between and introduced Amukas to his friends, Lo Man-sa was told that government ministers were watching the Labour Bureau. Heated debate served to further government intervention, with special attention called to the rise of anti-Japanese emotions.

It was precisely at this juncture that Mao Si-hai, the Chief Labour Relations Officer, issued a stern warning. He told the press that the JWM dispute had developed into a 'social issue' and had already fuelled grave concern among foreign investors. If it were not resolved soon, this incident would make foreign investors reluctant to invest. Only then did Amukas announce that the dispute had caused great losses for JWM and that their 'confidence' in Hong Kong had decreased. He declared a deadline for workers to return to work or to be dismissed *en masse*, and also that JWM would 'reconsider' reinvestments in Hong Kong. On the same day, JWM workers went to the Japanese consulate to demonstrate, after which some commentators accused the JWM workers of jeopardizing the 'prosperity and stability' of Hong Kong.

Interestingly, no one with the slightest sense of *real economik* would have believed threats of 'divestment' by the Japanese during this particular period. The weakening of the US dollar in the world market was at its worst and the revaluation of the Japanese yen had forced a spectacular exodus of Japanese manufacturing labour processes. Hong Kong was actually one of the few reliable places to invest. According to figures released by the Japanese Chamber of Commerce in 1987, during the first six months of 1986 Hong Kong's trade with Japan had increased some 19 percent compared to the same period in 1985. Watches and clocks had risen 101 percent — increasing from HK$91 million to HK$183 million. In reality, almost all of this 'trade' in watches and clocks between Hong Kong and Japan was between multinational subsidiaries and their principals, with JWM the dominant one. The trend continued into July 1986.

When I finally approached the Japanese consulate for interviews, it was too late to talk with those who had been involved, as they had all been transferred to other countries, so it was interesting to learn from the newly-arrived commercial attaché that he had heard that the JWM incident had been 'put off by the Hong Kong government'.

It was only after years of work on the JWM case that it occurred to me that there might be something of macro-historical significance in the time frame of the incident. Important events had occurred both immediately before and immediately after the JWM sit-in.

On 28 May, the Governor of Hong Kong, Warren Smith, returned from Japan after completing a two-day business promotion trip. He announced great expectations of increased Japanese investment in Hong Kong. On the same page of many newspapers, next to Smith's news, was the report, accompanied by pictures, that the JWM workers had organized their union and denounced the discriminatory practices of the JWM management.

On 14 June, one day after the agreement between JWM and the workers, representatives from four of Hong Kong's educational unions or associations demonstrated in front of the Japanese consulate, protesting the Japanese ministry of education's refusal to rectify distortions and denials of Second World War aggressions and atrocities. They announced that a mass demonstration would be organized, replicating the 30,000-person rally held three years earlier, if the Japanese government continued to ignore the sentiments of six million Hong Kong Chinese.

Most likely, both the government and the Japanese consulate had known of this demonstration in advance. Would they not, therefore, strive to avert the possible convergence of workers, teachers, and students in a political incident? Was it not plausible that these considerations had forced both Amukas and Mao Si-hai to push to conclude the dispute before the demonstration?

On the other hand, would the educational groups, who had refused to endorse the JWM workers some two weeks earlier, have cancelled their scheduled action to avoid benefiting the JWM workers and transforming their dispute into something more important? Why, in fact, had the JWM workers and their supporters, some of whom had close connections with educational groups, failed to take note of this upcoming social action? If the JWM workers had held out a day longer, what might have resulted from the conflation of anti-Japanese sentiments, or of a possible worker–teacher–student alliance challenging Japanese business interests in Hong Kong? Might there have been a new boycott of Japanese goods?

Regimes within Regimes, States over States

The second-floor shop at JWM was basically a service unit which repaired rejects from other production sites and from various markets. The workforce of experienced, stable, skilled female operatives were mainly single girls from the Pat Heung area, aged 18 to 25. Most of them could independently overhaul watches, rather than function as simple links in a production chain. They solved production problems themselves and used their mental capacities as well as manual skills. They might accurately be classified as individual artisans working under a common factory roof, rather than industrial workers. They possessed person-specific, rather than factory-specific, skills, which might well be similarly applied in a wholly different production setting (Braverman 1974).

We can appreciate the extent of the production setback if JWM lost these workers, and why Woo Char-hwa behaved proudly at first, but humbly later, in his dealings with Chu Chi-lin and her associates. On the last day of the sit-in, Woo had tried at length to persuade Chu and her associates to accept the compensation offered by Amukas. A few weeks later, intermediaries relayed word that dismissed JWM operatives had been offered similar jobs on the factory premises of JWM subcontractors — of which Woo was a partial owner!

From this, it is tempting for a 'social scientist' to jump to the conclusion that JWM management had been 'irrational' in handling labour discontent. However, this avoids the real issues involved, and fails to confront the issue of 'whose rationality and which battlefields?'.

Contradictions sometimes manifested themselves along ethnic lines. But more frequently, I was told, tensions arose from the arbitrariness embedded in the vertical Japanese command structure. Among the Hong Kong Chinese, patron/client relations (Scott 1976) led to collusion. However, as JWM was a Japanese multinational transplanted into a Chinese society, the patterns of collision and collusion of interest/power can also be seen as refracting differences existing in higher-level regimes (communal, societal and state) (Burawoy 1985).

For example, the way in which the female operatives' status was defined at JWM involved both racism and sexism — the daily-rated workforce was composed entirely of Chinese females. However, the contradictions involved in this fact were never adequately articulated, but were seldom mentioned, and easily brushed aside, as a result of the ways they were treated within the overall polity of Hong Kong and Japanese societies. It might be fair to say that, generally speaking, racism and sexism in Hong Kong were less rampant than in Japan. Nevertheless, in Hong Kong, contradictions concerning these issues were institutionally and habitually downplayed, most frequently being explained away and legitimized by transposing racial and sexual bias to the realm of ordinary necessity. The expected and tolerated racism and sexism of a Japanese context was superimposed onto its subsidiary in Hong Kong; and Hong Kong as the host society allowed these practices to be transplanted on its territory, as 'company culture'. Discourse on racism and sexism at JWM was thus effectively suppressed. However, the antagonism due to differential treatment between the monthly-rated and the daily-rated (general Japanese business categories) in regard to the 'mysterious money' was of another nature.

Hong Kong, a British colony, was always highly stratified, in terms both of social status and wealth, and the majority had been trained to accept fixed hierarchies and certain privileges of the powers-that-be. However, the other side of the coin of this reigning hegemonic ideology was a strong commercial-egalitarian element — an 'antidote' which serves to set limitations on the infringement of common peoples' everyday livelihood and moral dignity, and opposes unchecked abuses of power. Commercial Hong Kong is thus neither democratic nor monarchical; social issues are de-politicized in *realpolitik*, but are re-politicized in 'pre-political' arenas (Havel 1988). Money is seen as the source of everything, but it is seen as up for grabs, by choice or by chance, and within this ethos people have but themselves to blame for their respective successes or failures. Failure might follow success, or success follow failure. Ephemerality, vicissitude and precariousness are the rule — consequently, there are no permanent patrons or clients. The bonds between patron and client are chains of reciprocity constituting a shared sense of 'fairness'. What matters is that there is room for reciprocal retribution in case relations are inverted. The Hong Kong 'lifeworld' is open to entry by all parties.

For this reason, despite their acceptance of the sexist-racist nature of overall dominance, the workers — upon suddenly finding that, as daily-rated, they were excluded from the lump sum reward — were troubled. They were being denied equal entry and fair reciprocity — an unbearable, humiliating insult precisely because the money had been allotted discreetly, as an extraordinary reward, rather than as part of regular wage payments.

At this particular junction in the JWM dispute, disparities between Japanese practice and Chinese convention became explosively conspicuous, triggered by the habitual Japanese-style management practice of clandestine or deceptive manipulation of employment benefits. The contrast was seen

The Reflexive Narratives 345

as one between openness, fairness and impartiality on the one hand, and overt favouritism on the other.

However, this analytical perspective too — although valid — cannot answer certain questions. For instance, why did management and workers repeatedly fail to understand each other? Why did the Hong Kong Chinese staff fail to convey to their Japanese colleagues and superiors the cultural messages from their inferiors that they had undoubtedly understood? Why did Japanese staff members who spoke Cantonese and had been in Hong Kong for many years still fail to understand the workers in their charge? Hundreds of people other than workers and management had been involved in the case for months. If miscommunication was simply the result of cultural differences, why was there no attempt to 'translate' and explain to the contending parties?

Furthermore, why was it that standard, generally valid management techniques did not work? Why did Japanese-style manipulation skills fail to work? Might this not suggest that the common East Asian culture was mere rhetoric and myth, and that the myth was breaking down?

―――――

If there had been no naive reading of social practice, then neither would there have been any naive misunderstanding. In the JWM case, it was not that management was unwilling or incapable of comprehending what the workers wanted, but that management was *forbidden to show any understanding*. It was necessary, at times, for individuals in the management to make misunderstandings out of intended disinformation, as well as to make disinformation from intended misunderstandings. The reasons for this have never been spelled out. Management in Hong Kong had a lot to hide, and good reasons for hiding it.

First of all, we must look at employment practices prevalent in Japan. Since the war, dividing the workforce into discreet categories was common in Japanese manufacturing. Unsurprisingly, jobs were usually sexually defined. However, this was only the beginning of an overall military-style regimentation of production. The three-tiered ranking in the armed forces — officers, sergeants, and soldiers — had its parallel in the three-tiered ranking of staff, foremen, and operatives. In the military, a sergeant promoted to master sergeant reached the top of his career, as he was ineligible for promotion to officer rank; likewise, a soldier was ineligible for promotion to sergeant. Officer, sergeant, and soldier were thus mutually exclusive categories, separated by watertight boundaries. A comparable situation existed in the Japanese-style factory regime: Foremen had no opportunity for promotion to staff rank; nor were operatives eligible to become foremen. The unprecedented expansion of Japanese industry during the Korean War made this situation more rigid and more widespread. Operatives in industries like textiles and electronics were exclusively cheap, young female labourers. But I would argue that it was primarily the militaristic logic carried over to postwar industries by demobilized wartime officers that made Japanese industry 'Japan-style' as such. Practices based on sex bias were but necessary corollaries.

Japanese industry embodied a 'secondary' workforce, which, by some estimations, constituted more than half of the total workforce in Japan in the late 1980s. Members of this 'secondary' workforce were engaged mainly in direct manual production in the manufacturing sector, and were usually paid wages either in overt or disguised piece-rate form, that is, the nominally-termed hourly or daily rate was a disguise for a collective piece-wage, calculated with piece-wage logic and principles. These workers had neither job security nor prospect of advancement. Furthermore, they were never considered by management as people they 'employed', but were, ambiguously, 'temporarily employed'. One might work in the same situation for more than twenty years and yet remain 'temporary', without even the chance to become a contract worker. Japanese government legislation concerning 'contract work' only took effect in the late 1980s, but was never vigorously enforced by the Labour Department, and so very few 'contracts' ever resulted. The defining feature marking the inferiority of this secondary labour force is the fact that they were unqualified for any job security considerations or any minimum welfare provisions. It is not even accurate to say that they could be fired at any time — for, theoretically, they were fired every evening when they left the factory gate, then hired again the following morning. They were thus ineligible for compensation and without hope of seniority or retirement or even severance pay.

In a military set-up, there are two sets of labour relations in a three-tiered structure of officers, sergeants, and conscript soldiers: one among career servicemen (officers and sergeants), the other between conscripts and career servicemen. A soldier is conscripted for a term of service to fulfil a duty; he will return to his own livelihood once his obligation is fulfiled. A career serviceman, however, is hired as a professional specializing in war, and is in a position to build a lifelong career. The analogy between the military and that of Japanese secondary employment holds: Like conscript soldiers, the secondary labour force is deemed to consist of non-career workers who serve their terms, are paid their due, and are dumped back in their 'livelihood' after they have been profitably used. No consideration is given to their security and welfare because they are 'conscripts', not 'career servicemen'. While it might not be fair that a conscript, or a factory worker, should have to serve longer than normal, or that he/she should be 'sacrificed' during the term of service, there is nothing to be done about it, it is simply unfortunate. Once the term of service is over, it is a pity if a soldier or factory worker can not earn a living or has nowhere to go, but that is a 'social' problem; the military — or the industrial sector — is not to be blamed. Certainly neither the military nor the industrial sector wants to entertain illusions that they might solve problems of this nature or magnitude!

This practice of 'temporary hiring' was seldom talked about and had never been formally legalized. It remained socially tolerated, but as it became increasingly criticized and challenged in Japan, industrialists tried to avoid mentioning it — a situation of 'you can do it but you can't talk about it'. It is difficult to find any reference to it in the enormous number of documents promoting Japanese-style management. Yet, as offshore manufacturing increased, industrialists tried similar practices in their overseas subsidiaries, where working forces were ignorant of the real nature of such employment. In effect, this made for a better safety margin for management.

The industrialists were quite right in their calculations. Were it not for the dispute that erupted at JWM, the intricacies involved in the practice of temporary hiring and the creation of an 'outcast' labour force might have been buried forever.

The complete rejection of Mr Ma by the workers, at one point, is interesting. Six days after the sit-in, Ma suggested to the workers that JWM might have been treating them as some sort of 'outcast' workforce — temporary hires, Japanese-style — but even before he had had a chance to elaborate, he was violently silenced and his suggestion refuted. It became clear to me during the interviews that the workers rejected Ma because of the implications of the suggestion. It was unthinkable for Hong Kong female workers to deem themselves industrial conscripts obligated to contribute their adulthood to the creation of national wealth. Similarly, it was impossible for them to swallow their indignation once they learned that they had been relegated to secondary status and had thus been discriminated against. The society in which they had been brought up had never taught them to accept such a role. They felt they had chosen JWM as their 'employer' and had settled for something less than a career, but something they nevertheless saw as worthwhile.

However, I became convinced that the JWM management — at least the local top managers — actually shared the above analysis among themselves, and were quite clear as to its implications for the workers. As they were sure that the workers would never accept such status — that of temporary hired employees ineligible for welfare — they knew that clarification would only worsen the antagonism.

Top management thus portrayed the contradiction as a cultural misunderstanding or a problem of social relations. They thus singled out lower-level management and imputed blame on them. Since the middle of May, when the issue of the 'mysterious money' had become the focal point of the workers' struggle, conflict between operatives and foremen had intensified. But, whenever there was a chance, top management 'leaked' the secret that it was the low-ranking staff members who had blocked any management concession. The argument was that if the operatives were rewarded for rebellion, it would be impossible for foremen and line leaders to control them. This logic had been brought home to the workers through middlemen Son, Lo and Mao, as well as by Amukas himself.

Many workers accepted this interpretation. Some believed that their superiors had to suppress the workers in order to save themselves from corruption charges. Others resented the comprador/running-dog attitude of lower management. Some considered the zero-sum game between lower management and operatives inevitable — if operatives won, their superiors lost. If rebelling workers stayed on, foremen and line leaders might have to leave. After the sit-in, some workers agreed that it would be impossible for the foremen to abuse them any longer. For those foremen used to dominating others, this meant a loss of both power and face.

There was some truth to this reasoning. Animosity between operatives and their immediate superiors increased exponentially as the dispute proceeded. The superintendents gave the worst possible explanation for every move the operatives made. Similarly, every action taken by foremen and line leaders was put down to the most vicious of motives by the operatives. Tension rose to the point where physical confrontation became almost inevitable. On the afternoon of 3 June, when management tried to expel Gu and Fu, and when foreman Po Lo-du continued to make sexist remarks, there was a riot in the making.

Discussions with the workers' core leaders identified at least four layered power/interest blocs within management strata:
(1) The top layer was composed exclusively of Japanese. Even Woo, who had been educated in Japan and had a Japanese wife, was excluded from this stratum.
(2) Top-middle management included Woo and other shop-floor managers — both Hong Kong Chinese who spoke Japanese and Japanese who had been in Hong Kong long enough to be able to speak Cantonese.
(3) The middle-low layer included Japanese and Hong Kong Chinese

technicians, clerks and managerial staff, who worked in the office rather than on the shop-floor.

(4) The low layer consisted exclusively of Hong Kong Chinese stationed on different shop-floors as foremen and line leaders — the lowest level of monthly-rated personnel.

According to the workers, there were complicated relations of power/interest between and even within these four management layers. As worker-management animosity increased, tension also mounted between low-level management and their superiors. Lower-level staff felt increasingly uneasy at being sandwiched between management and workers. The longer the dispute lasted, the greater their feelings of insecurity and the greater their need to protect themselves and prove their usefulness. They were frightened by the possibility that JWM authorities might yield to the workers' demands and pay them, effectively eliminating a crucial difference between lower-level management and the operatives. They would lose nothing monetarily, but they would no longer be privileged. They also suspected that if anyone had to take the blame for the 'unfortunate misunderstanding' between JWM and its workers, it would be them.

In addition, if the operatives won they would not be grateful to lower-level management. Favours offered by JWM would instead serve to make lower-level staff redundant. Given the workers' 'corruption theory', it was likely the workers would accuse lower-level management of wrongdoing and ignore the offences of those higher up. Thus, the 'radicalism' of lower-level staff — the overreaction characteristic of those in self-conscious comprador positions — was both structural and situational.

Given the social relations of production and the concrete shop-floor dynamics in this specific case, the JWM factory regime reflects a basic thesis of Marglin (1976). The small group of top management from Japan was a political delegation (in the judiciary-legal sense) representing proprietorial rights. On-the-ground, everyday control and disciplinary responsibilities were relegated to middle-lower and lower-level staff; that is, locally-recruited male high-school graduates who were not technicians but were in fact what

O'Connor has termed 'guard labour' (O'Connor 1975), and were non-productive elements in the production environment. Their *raison d'être* was their loyalty to the interests of the proprietor of capital. They were hired to protect and police. The logic of their existence and survival had absolutely nothing in common with that of those they policed and surveyed — the operatives.

During peaceful periods of regular production, lower-level staff were usually idle. To make their presence seem less redundant to their employer they often favoured individual operatives, colluding with them for minor conveniences or petty gains. They also blocked information, to prove their indispensability as intermediaries between the proprietor and the productive forces. Some tended to throw their weight around to create difficult situations, grab more power, and remind their employer of their potential usefulness as tools for suppression. Lacking productivity to justify themselves, scheming and power-mongering were their sole means of valorizing their identity. Their position was precarious.

In the JWM crisis, lower-level management's very existence was at stake. Their strategy was two-pronged. Firstly, they sought to deepen the rift between workers and JWM management, hoping that management would then have to fall back on lower-level staff to minimize further damage and/or to regain control. In either case, management would have to fire the workers' leaders, but keep lower-level staff. This strategy was evident when Po Lo-du tried to incite a riot on the afternoon of 3 June. Secondly, they allowed management to identify lower-level staff as die-hards who insisted on overkill, thus offering JWM top authorities relief from the political and moral burdens of the crisis, in the hope that this would safeguard lower-level management's position after the dispute was over. Since everybody in management knew that lower-level staff did not play any part in the dismissals, their compliance had to be taken as partially coerced. But, by the same token, their willingness to take the blame and bear the political and moral liability would be rewarded, at least by management allowing them to retain their jobs.

The above strategy was evident in the total absence of lower-level staff as the dispute neared its end. However, their calculations had fallen short of their employers' calculations, since, although they kept their jobs, the foremen's positions were eliminated and a group of Japanese 'technicians' took their places. Most of the previous 'guard labour' thus became the subject of this new guard. To their dismay, the demoted guards were made to sit on the production lines and participate in operations, under the surveillance of the Japanese 'technicians' — an ethnic battle they had helped themselves to lose!

Top management had needed a pharisaic way out of their moral predicament, and so they had capitalized, so to speak, on the semi-willing surrender of decency on the part of local management. A new intermediate category was created to historicize, as well as mediate, the suppression.

However, top management had not been able to make permanent black sheep out of lower-level staff in operatives' eyes. Very few workers believed that foremen and line leaders had initiated the dismissals. 'What could they do?' was a common sentiment. 'They were paid to bite us! Whatever they did, they were ordered and forced to do by their superiors, the JWM company. They should not be blamed. They were not all or always bad. If they had been understanding towards those of us who worked below, it would have been okay, whether or not they were idle.' There were also particular voices, 'We pity them, they had to sacrifice so much just to keep their jobs. But that is the fate of someone who sells loyalty instead of productivity. We would not want to be like that. It's better to sweat working than to compromise your decency.'

In addition to the lower-level staff, volunteers of local labour service groups were also systematically victimized, and eventually became the ideal object of blame. However, they first had to be labelled. This task was mainly carried out by a 'third party', Chief Labour Relations Officer Mao Si-hai. The labour militants who closely supported the workers were at first labelled 'elements of the underworld' by JWM management, and then, after the sit-in began, were accused of 'intruding into JWM's internal affairs'. Later, after management had brought quite a few additional parties into the dispute, including Labour Bureau people, public relations companies and lawyers, Japanese union-busting experts, the Japanese Chamber of Commerce, foreign investors' clubs, leaders of local union establishments, government officers and an army of security guards, the 'gung-ho' unionists, especially Gu and Fu, became caught in a cross-fire. Gu and Fu were denounced as having incited and entrapped the workers, causing them to lose their jobs. In reality they had been invited to mediate the situation and assist the workers, but their status was never legitimized or even formally acknowledged. As the stalemate persisted, they were transformed into targets of legal and coercive action. By claiming that they were blocking 'direct negotiations' between the workers and management, JWM secured a court injunction and expelled them.

This, however, did not end their ordeal, but only signified the beginning of their subjection to public slander. After the failure of direct negotiations between management and workers and the expulsion of these 'third parties', Mao Si-hai announced to the press that, due to the inexperience of 'some small volunteer groups', insignificant grudges had been grossly magnified. The JWM workers were then blamed for seeking assistance from 'amateurs' and 'failing to contact the Bureau in the first place'.

This first attack was rather mild, and was aimed at defending the Bureau itself. But two days after the vote, on 8 July, the media again quoted Mao concerning the JWM case. He now claimed that the workers had flip-flopped, not knowing what they wanted, due to the 'unknown motives' of third parties who had turned a simple labour dispute into a 'social incident' and had threatened the stability and prosperity of Hong Kong as a whole. For the sake of building their political capital, Mao claimed, these local groups had adopted a policy of 'destroying all, be it jade or rock' and sowing discord for private ends.

Mao Si-hai was well known by foes and friends as a master schemer. He was too sophisticated simply to blast the weak. He immediately turned around and commented that mismanagement on JWM's part had enabled the dispute to proceed unchecked. As a labour relations expert, he now suggested that the whole misunderstanding was caused by inadequate communication between management and workers and generously proposed to JWM management that the Bureau run a management training course for them.

From the beginning of his intervention, Mao had pursued a policy of divide and rule, encouraging individual workers to 'speak out' and 'make their own choices' whenever he could. He then declared that the factory should 'recover normal production' at once, and increase rewards for those who might be willing to quit upon payment.

Mao had good reasons for his actions. It was crucial to the stability of his own job to minimize the annual stoppage rate. He had demonstrated spectacular success in previous years, but had suffered a major setback in 1986, when stoppages, calculated in days per person, were triple those of the previous year, with the JWM stoppage making up almost half of the total.

Mao's use of subtle or direct pressure, depending on the situation, was most evident when he spent hours persuading Chu Chi-lin. He was extremely friendly, understanding, candid, lucid, and open-minded with her. He claimed to know the struggling workers' point of view: that what had to be done, had to be done. Chu told me that she was not flattered that Mao had treated her as a competent adversary. She already knew that. But she admitted that his bluntness was compelling, as it signalled his acceptance of her as a high-calibre strategist of his own rank.

When I interviewed Mao, he was frank, open and impressively 'professional'. He treated me as a labour relations expert, equal to himself and his technocratic colleagues. He began by endorsing the idea that, with regard to the JWM case, ' "... an ice-sheet three feet thick takes more than one cold day to form" — the grudge and animosity between management and workers had deep roots.' He enumerated 'mistakes' committed by JWM management at various stages of the conflict, and made casual reference to the workers' poor scheming and planning. Yet he was careful and businesslike, confining his discussion to technical matters. He emphasized that no one should be blamed for the unfortunate event, neither management nor the workers. 'They were all amateurs, inexperienced in labour disputes, *especially from our point of view, right?*' [emphasis mine] Before I could respond, he went on, 'Such a mishap should not have happened at all. It could have been prevented if the managers had better communication skills. The JWM managing director knows that and agrees with me. He has requested that we run training courses for the local staff and we are about to do so.' He admitted that the Bureau staff were not perfect, but said, 'The JWM case has taught us important lessons. We are carefully compiling review materials for our internal staff to use in on-the-job training.'

Surprisingly, he levelled no criticisms at the workers. I pursued this, asking for comments on the workers besides his perceptions of their amateurism and inexperience. He replied, 'It is up to the unionists and workers themselves to carry out any self-examination or soul-searching. As far as we are concerned, the job of management, like that of the government, is to govern. The fact that JWM lost control of the situation and the workers is indicative of their lack of expertise and of the absence of labour relations professionals, like you and me. What its workers did or did not do is not important, it is of less importance or consequence. They were just young girls from the countryside ... ' In other words, the female operatives were not qualified to make mistakes affecting their own fate! Their resistance was brushed aside, their struggles lightly dismissed. The logic involved is obvious: The women were young, from the countryside, and less educated, that is, they were ideal, stereotypical objects for victimization and stigmatization.

Not sensing my disgust with his analysis, Mao continued to lecture on 'modern' management skills. He seemed knowledgeable, fluent in the jargon of existing schools of management, which he mingled with clichés from industrial psychology, all delivered with a twist typical of a British colonial administrator's self-confidence. He wound up his presentation by proposing that a management–worker consultation board, mediated by labour officers, be set up to facilitate communication in the future and to monitor the level of tension before conflict erupted.

During a later interview, Mao was relaxed and enthusiastic. He surprised me by engaging in an abstract discussion, showing flexibility in his opinions on the causal linkages between welfare provisions and job stability. He agreed that the Hong Kong reality was much too complicated for any textbook discussion, as both employers and employees had maintained a kind of hit-and-run attitude for three decades, with neither committed to long-term engagements. This fast-buck mentality of investors motivated capitalists to withhold reinvestment and to shift modes of valorization at will. Workers thus tended to 'vote with their feet', according to the valorization of market return for labour power. But the situation was changing, he went on, as the first generation of 'accidentally trapped' labour force aged and their children — a true career–worker cohort — emerged. These workers thus had to play a very different game and come up with a new hire-out policy, as well as new engagement patterns, but employers were slow to respond. Their inaction and inertia, coupled with the recent chronic short supply of labour, exacerbated tensions. According to Mao, the standard arguments used by JWM management during the dispute had grown hollow, even ridiculous.

When employers needed to stabilize their workforce, it was a serious error to ignore changing historical conditions. Nevertheless, Mao insisted that there was nothing intrinsically wrong with a situation in which workers could quit or be fired at any time, without entitlement to any benefits. The problem was simply that this was now obsolete. On this score, Mao was practical, about himself and about his job. He and his colleagues in the Labour Bureau had recently advocated a kind of 'private provident fund' for employers, to alleviate the volatile impact of a shortage of labour. Yet the Labour Bureau was the chief opponent of unions and labour groups who wanted a government-guaranteed, centrally-administered public provident fund, insisting that a private provident fund be set up between individual employers and their employees in private contractual terms, administered by the respective managements, contributed to by both management and workers, and made available to workers only after a fixed period of consecutive service. Following *laissez-faire* principles, the government was not to have any role in operating this private fund.

Mao and the Labour Bureau steadfastly opposed the official legalization of collective bargaining, and stubbornly resisted any attempt to pressure the government to legally acknowledge the status of unions and to force employers to deal with them. 'These are all private matters,' he stated, 'as we have learned from Western experience, our government had better stay out.' More philosophically, Mao claimed, 'We believe that there are a lot of things that cannot be pushed too hard. I would like to see a process of "natural" development. That's why I don't think government legislation is necessary for unionization.'

'Do you mean you believe in the natural working out of social contradictions, through contests as well as conflicts?' I queried.

'Well, our society must be functional, and we are helping to keep it functioning. To eliminate or minimize conflict is my job. For instance, all the unionists and workers talk about fairness. What fairness? How fair is fair and fair enough? Is there an absolute fairness in this world? Is it possible? Desirable? How we understand fair is important. It is extremely important to eliminate possible conflict by restoring a sense of fairness, especially among those who suspect they are being mistreated. So, there is no fairness. However, there is always a deep sense that fairness should be obtained and prevail. In a word, it isn't possible to be fair, but it is imperative to be seen as being fair. The perception of fairness is important and takes tremendous skill. By the same token, we are not supposed to govern every single minor thing, but it is of the utmost importance that we be seen as governing. So long as we are seen as fair, and we are seen as governing, it is all right ... '

Sensing that I was somewhat puzzled by this statement, Mao philosophized further, 'You see, life is just like a performance on stage. One has to play one's assigned role according to the script. There are many different dramas played on different stages, but one plays one role at a time. There is no eternal role, but one has to play to the fullest extent possible.'

Such a vision, in which real life was relegated to theatrical practice and thus miraculously transformed the world into an inconsequential and unreal setting, has actually been quite common in Chinese statist/dynastic politics. In my understanding, it is a rather peculiar cultural device enabling the escape from moral predicaments.

'Do you think cultural elements played a significant role in the unfolding of the JWM case?' I asked Mao.

'No, of course not. There was nothing cultural about the event, not a bit! ... It was nothing cultural. It was real and practical. There was logic and calculation, as well as skill and technique. Culture does not play any role in tested knowledge such as ... '

Our conversation ended on this note, as it became evident that we were talking at cross-purposes. Mao's parting words have stayed with me, however, and have been quite useful in guarding against the excesses of a wholesale cultural approach often characteristic of inquiries of an anthropological nature.

8 Opening up, by Way of an Epilogue

In concluding this ethnographic project and in initiating detailed analyses which lead beyond the scope of this monograph, some observations and provisional formulations are in order, to indicate the nature of the problematique.

The Non-Existence of 'Industrial Solidarity' and the Reproduction of Everyday Livelihood

Throughout the JWM case what was conspicuous, at least to this student of industrial sociology, was the absence of anything called 'industrial solidarity' among the struggling workers. Hidden layers of social connectedness outside the industrial context were the adhesive binding together the 300-plus young women. The forms of these linkages, which represented complicated relationships, were extremely dynamic and fluid. A number of attempts to pinpoint their existence failed.

Before the dispute, workers were divided and confined to their respective shop-floors and those from different floors had at most no more than nodding acquaintances. They were by no means 'friends'. It was the factory-wide dispute, led by the daily-rated workers, which transformed their self-identification from that of individual workers on such-and-such a floor to operatives who were paid daily wages and who faced the same humiliating denial of rewards. It was the very suppression, through which JWM management volunteered itself as a necessary and critical 'other', that built an arena where the operatives could fight. Every contest contributed to further shaping the profile of an incipient, conscious collectivity. Previously existing ties were rediscovered, redefined and transformed into elements contributing to the struggle, and new ties were formed where there had formerly been none. Yet if one conceives of this as a kind of 'solidarity', it was one which had virtually nothing to do with 'things industrial' as such.

I knew that the workers' core leadership — represented by Chu Chi-lin and her close associates — consisted mainly of second-floor Hakka-speaking operatives from the rural area of Pat Heung. Trained in anthropology and subject to its essentialistic predispositions, I tried to relate their 'pristine existence' to their present life, to use their 'primordial state of being' to account for the peculiar give-and-take among them. I was exhilarated when I found that there had been a fictive 'extended family' centred around Hsiao Chia, which, at its highest point, involved more than thirty JWM female workers.

Thanks to my interviewees' insistence and stubbornness, this attempt was defeated.

'It was a joke,' I was repeatedly told. Finally I had to learn to take a joke as a joke — a joke which helped transform the harsh shop-floor environment into a jocular liveable environment, which served to reproduce elements of an everyday *lifeworld* of the underdog in the presence of an environment-provider who reproduced a profit-extracting mechanism, with its power structure and chains of command.

'The "family" was never meant to "function", and nobody had ever thought it to be useful for advancing our cause. It did not occur to us in the struggle. And only God knows that we never had an idea there would be a struggle like the one in which we were involved.' This was Hsiao Chia's and her 'little wife', Chu Chi-lin's, final verdict on their 'extended family'.

Having said this, what about the rural area of Pat Heung? Can we say something regarding the place where the JWM workers' leadership was nurtured? If we are talking about *lifeworld* rather than primordial essentials, the answer is: 'yes'.

Concerning the perspective of the reproduction of everyday life, my interviewees had made hints about their *habitus* (Bourdieu 1977, 1990b). However, I was careful not to take their word as 'data' or positivistic proof of any sort.

For one thing, all the Pat Heung women lived in their natal homes, shared food with their families and contributed a portion of their wages to a common familial budget. They did not have to worry about housing and family chores, and relied only partially on their wages to survive. The portion of wages employed in reproducing their livelihood was smaller than that of their city-dwelling colleagues. They knew this and adopted a double standard, in terms of commitment to the struggle, for themselves on the one hand and their urban counterparts on the other, acknowledging that they could afford not to work for extended periods of time, unlike the 'city-girls'. Had they been aware of it, they might well have taken up another discourse of political economy: who subsidized whom — the rural or the urban population — in the rapid accumulation of capital in modern times (Arrighi 1973; Schiffer 1983; Wolpe 1972; Wong 1972).

However, for our Pat Heung workers the existential situation signified things of a very different order. Their existence was significant and meaningful, I would suggest, because it enabled them to take pride in themselves in a dehumanizing work situation. They valued themselves as skilled and reliable workers. For most of them, work at the JWM factory was their first job. They successfully resisted being sucked into the whirlpool of consumerism. They had no need to change jobs annually to jack up their wages. They had made themselves the backbone of the JWM service unit. In making a living at JWM they had to sell their labour, not their dignity, and their sense of dignity remained an important ingredient in the reproduction of their *lifeworld*.

In reality, they were one of the very few groups of workers who were seriously engaged with their employers. To quote Hsiao Chia, 'We had been so earnest with them that we felt doubly hurt and insulted.' In Chu Chi-lin's words, 'They must have learned by now that there's no kidding, as far as we are concerned. We work earnestly and we fight seriously.' Lo Un-pu echoed her, 'We are a good working force, not slaves. We can also be the worst enemy and the fiercest fighters.'

Analytically, then, it was the peculiar social formation and its materially-embedded power constellation that informed the Pat Heung leadership and made them a socially significant force. It was the resulting 'changing relations in the balance of social forces' (Hall 1996, 419) between workers and management that defined the struggle as an ethico-moral one, one between the owner of labour power (and its productivity) and the owner of the means of production. It is also one over the reproduction of *lifeworld* (and its dignity), on the one side, and the appropriation of surplus labour and disposal of 'spent' labourers, on the other. In this sense, the fight has always been a contestation over the nature of a very specific 'politics'.

Agents, Histories and Classes in Struggle

In sum, events manifested in a series of fights constituted moments in a total struggle of the workers, within which they, with differential modes of reproducing their everyday livelihoods, were pulled together and learned to minimize their differences, at least temporarily. This was an intersubjective process. The additive nature of *Verstehen*, in the Weberian sense, often manifested itself in static constructs of the overall situation after various actions, but it was the praxis of the movement which fused the actors into a historical bloc and thereby transformed them into historical agents.

It was largely the discourse of these actors which mediated their praxis and movement. An actor was called, by the interpellations of others, to take a position, and this led to a definition of her 'identity'. The distinctness of this definition varied with the degree of (historical) subjecthood she

Opening up, by Way of an Epilogue 363

managed to constitute, that is, the degree to which she committed herself to the making of the historical moment (Crozier 1980; Laclau and Mouffe 1985; Touraine 1981). Thus the episodes within the ethnography allow us to identify the multiple intricacies of a transforming process. This ethnographic account could also facilitate a deeper penetration into the thickness of intermingled *lifeworld* discourses and reveal to us a very different sense of historicity (Touraine 1977). For instance, our ethnographic account opens up a space to deconstruct new dimensions of social connectedness and disconnectedness. One of the spaces opened was the arena of uneven development of 'agenthood', or 'subjecthood', if you wish, in the movement.

The notions of 'actor' and 'function' do not serve us well. They impose a natural/logical link which would underwrite an objective search for supposed pre-existing objects, subjects and 'functions'. Instead, I take the formation of 'subjecthood' as a process which creates agents and their 'missions'. All the intruding elements in this process constitute the contents of the 'mediation'. Culturally informed, socially defined, economically endowed and politically conditioned, the process is still most specific and concrete, and not 'cultural', 'social', or 'economic' in any general sense. These particular conditioning factors constitute a particular historical artefact which does not simply happen, but is brought into existence by agents operating within constraints. Collectively, they create something none of them can really envisage. Histories are made, at particular conjunctions, from any number of available perspectives. As each actor makes History, some forget that what he/she is making is but one history — a part of History. These makers of histories are at once empowered and deprived, but only because of their respective subjective wishes and means–end orientations rather than because of any 'primordial structures' or 'pristine functions'. 'Men make their own history, but they do not make it just as they please' — but they also make it only from individual perspectives in specific existences, with two feet planted firmly on the ground.

To cut a long story short, my work on the JWM case has helped to convince me that most of the conventional socio-scientific modes of inquiry

— functional analysis, structural analysis or class analysis — fail to grasp the central problems involved in collective actions. Since it is true that without mediation no agent exists, it is not possible to posit structures or functions of any sort prior to the existence of an agent. Without agent both structure and function lose their anchorage either to act and to be acted upon. Structure and function are merely analytical tools, which nobody but an extreme positivist would reify. In this situation, and as an *a posteriori* recollection and a tautological exercise, positing structures and functions is no more than throwing the cognitive ball back into the agnostic horizon of a positivistic metaphysics.

The documentation of the JWM case has constructively demonstrated to what extent it is impossible to invoke, much less to assume, a notion of 'working class' in the event of an 'industrial conflict'. In other words, the JWM dispute was not a case in which a theory of 'class struggle' could easily apply. So far as the JWM ethnography supports a theoretical claim, I would suggest that it is the following: 'Class' exists only while individual workers are interpellated and involved in a process of forming a collective identity, a particular historical moment when individuals consciously formulate moral-political positions and carry them into the battlefield of concrete struggle. At such moments — not earlier and not later — one can conceive of 'class'. In other words, a class theory outside a context of the concrete battling of antagonistic social forces would be a theory lacking referential power. It would invariably be an ahistorical, context-free mental exercise. It would define a lot but explain nothing.

In contrast, it is far from cynical to conclude from the JWM case that if there were workers there was no 'class'; if there was a 'class' there were no workers. It was only at the very moment when 300 female operatives defied and denounced their conventional roles as docile workers that they transformed themselves — as a collective, not as individuals — into a class. Their struggle constituted them as a class. In struggle the class was born. The workers were dead, long live the class! (Gramsci 1989; Hall 1988)

Opening up, by Way of an Epilogue 365

The Geometry of the Construction and Sabotage of Workers' Solidarity

As outlined above, I agree with Gramsci that:

> the 'unity' of classes is necessarily complex and has to be *produced* — constructed, created — as a result of specific economic, political and ideological practices. It can never be taken as automatic or 'given' (Hall 1996, 423).

The JWM workers thus made themselves a collective entity, and we have seen the 'passage' of an 'organic' historical movement 'right through the whole social formation, from economic 'base' to the sphere of ethico-political relations' (ibid., 421). Within the process by which antagonism developed into a 'total crisis', we can distinguish scenarios in which relations of social forces were changed, confrontations between the 'rulers' and the 'ruled' (the workers) ensued, ethico-political struggle germinated, political ideologies formed, and the 'conception of the world of the masses (the workers, the rank and file)' was violently and drastically modified (ibid., 419). This has been a demonstration of counter-hegemonic forces in an exercise in bringing about their intellectual, moral, economic and political unity.

The ideology of the nascent working class, in serving to cement and to unify an entire bloc-in-the-making, must be built upon what Gramsci has termed 'common sense'. 'Common sense', according to Hall's summary:

> ... is usually 'disjointed and episodic', fragmentary and contradictory ... It represents itself as the 'traditional wisdom or truth of the ages', but in fact, it is deeply a product of history, 'part of the historical process'. Why, then, is common sense so important? Because it is the terrain of conception and categories on which *the practical consciousness of the masses of the people is actually formed* (ibid., 431, emphasis added).

The JWM case can be understood, with some qualifications, as a manifestation of this. Ever since the coming-into-consciousness of an encroachment circumstance among them, the workers strove to figure out the situations which confronted them. This 'figuring out', however, was not a one-way 'cognitive' process, but a multifaceted praxis simultaneously proceeding on different fronts, with multiple orientations open to various subversions and challenges, within which different forces and positions were constantly being juggled. Documented in my ethnography are numerous *ad hoc* theories and countertheories which were devised to account for emerging circumstances and various schemes conceived by the workers' adversaries. Different actions were taken to establish bridgeheads, to get even, and to cover withdrawals. Diverse ideological gestures were manifested and visualized through dramatized and ritualized performances. All sorts of battles were waged — with proverbs (Day –22: 9 May, Day 12: 11 June, Day +2: 14 June and after), rumours (Day 8: 7 June, Day 12: 12 June ...), moral codes as well as with 'public opinions' (The month of April, Day –33: 28 April, Day –30: 1 May, Day –23: 8 May, Day –14: 17 May ...). 'Signs' and images were appropriated and recreated from the cultural repository and 'bricolaged' into novel weaponry and ammunition.

In lieu of in-depth analysis of each and every 'relevant' detail, I suggest the following schema (Figure 8.1):

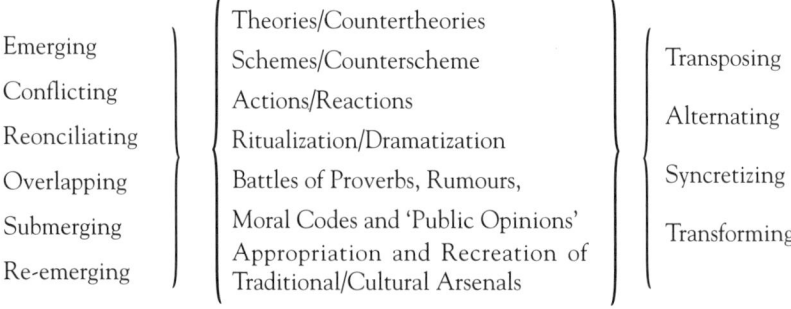

Figure 8.1 Internal Relations of Praxies

Figure 8.1 indicates the complex internal relations among sets of praxis of the workers in the course of their fights. However, it is not meant to trivialize issues or, for that matter, to suggest that every possible complication was in existence — or *in potential* — no matter what or who was acting or being acted upon. On the contrary, under conditions of a *lifeworld* struggle, possible internal complications — if not anticipated and pre-empted — were usually mitigated or simply ignored as far as possible.

These complications were invoked, magnified and utilized by nobody else but the worker contestants. For instance, what the workers had been in practice had been all along available for the management. The management could emulate all the tactics and turn them back upon the workers at any moment they deemed fit. Nevertheless, the contestants, bosses in my case, were also vulnerable to all the possible complications from which the workers might suffer. At this point, we were brought to a second observation.

If we visualize actions and discourses as creating collective identity, collective consciousness, and collective action as three nodal points of praxis, the articulation and relational interaction among them will then constitute a space in which a historical subject (workers, in our case) is constructed and valorized (see Figure 8.2).

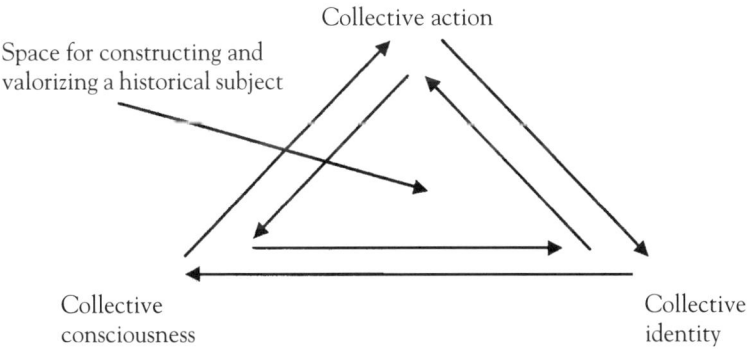

Figure 8.2 Space for formation of a historical subject

We can talk about the existence of a 'subject' of history because of the constant feedback among agents, ideologies and social movements 'in the making' (see Figure 8.3).

368   *Colours of Money, Shades of Pride*

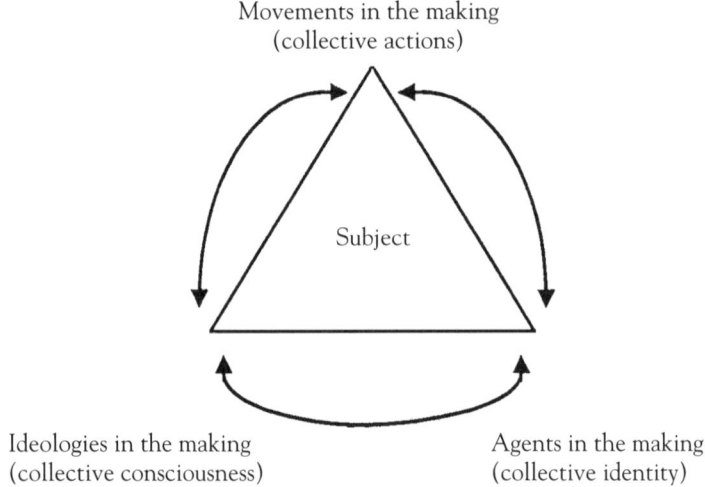

Figure 8.3 Movements, ideologies and agents in the making

Given the above schema, the workers' adversaries (that is, management and its allies) would be able to weaken the articulations and dismantle the triangle (Day –30: 1 May, Day –29: 2 May, Day –21: 10 May, Day –18: 13 May, Day –15: 16 May, Day 1: 13 May, Day 4: 3 June, Day 11: 10 June ...).

Such subversion may be illustrated by Figure 8.4:

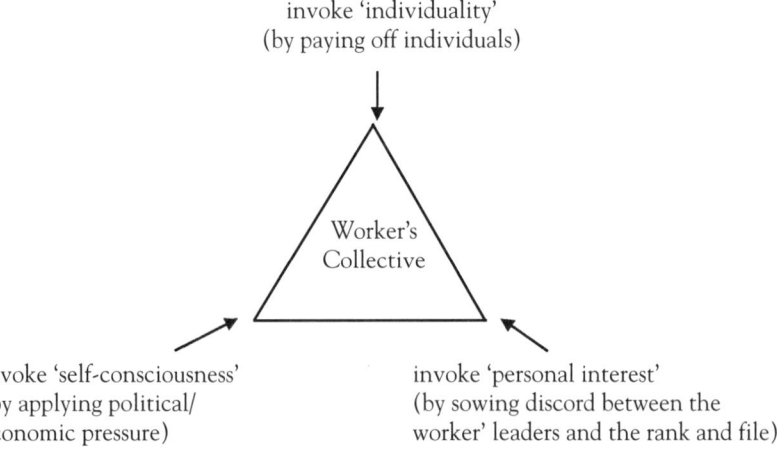

Figure 8.4 Three-pronged subversion

Opening up, by Way of an Epilogue

In the battle to subvert workers' collective action, the main tactic was to individualize the issues by increasing compensation to those who were qualified — a tactic of buying off (Day –24: 7 May, Day 5: 5 June, Day 10: 9 June). Subverting the workers' collective took the form of a continuing attempt to sow discord (Day –4: 27 May, Day 3: 2 June, Day 11: 10 June, Day 13: 12 June). Disarming the workers' counter-hegemonic forces proceeded through constant political and economic pressure, day and night, to 'soften' their position (Day –4: 27 May, Day 3: 2 June, Day 8: 7 June, Day 13: 12 June).

However, none of these tactics would be effective were they employed discretely or sporadically. They were possible precisely because they were couched in another triangle constitutive of material/institutional weight, judicial-legal privilege and a concentration of the means of coercion. This triangle is represented by Figure 8.5:

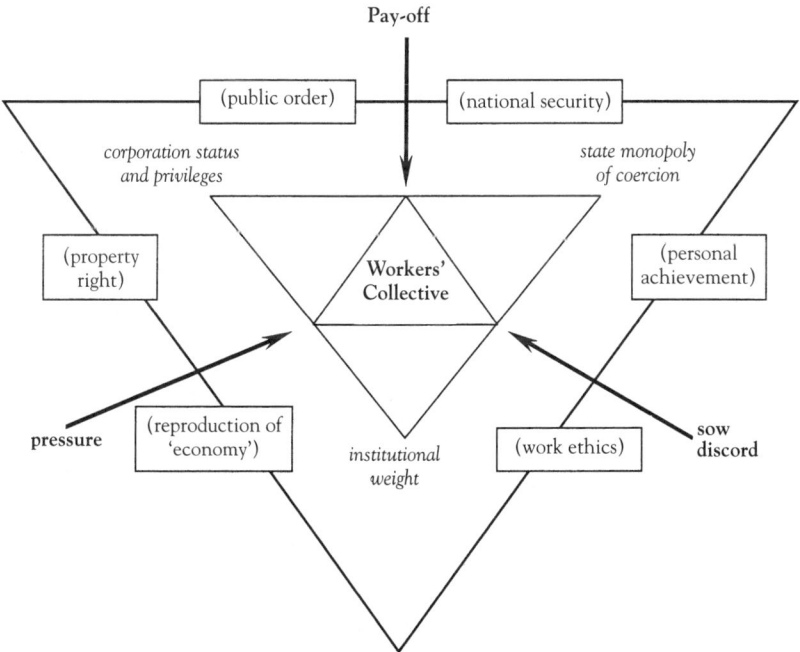

Figure 8.5 The state/corporation/institution triangle

It was the alliance of institutions, corporate interests and state apparatus which managed to encircle the workers' collective and enabled the tactics of paying-off, sowing discord and breaking solidarity. The tripartite alliance was held together by doctrines of national security and public order, notions of personal achievement and work ethic, and the imperatives of the functioning of the capitalist mode of production and of the continuation of private property rights.

What was perverse and appallingly misconceived in such a scheme was that corporate interest underwritten by rights of private ownership actually assumed priority for state protection and proclaimed itself a manifestation of the public good, to the extent of representing the public interest. That is, the interests of the workers' collective and of its hundreds of members were easily relegated to something 'personal', 'individual', and 'private'. The recreation of the livelihood and maintenance of hundreds of workers was presented as nobody else's business and therefore not the concern of the mysterious 'public' at all. This 'public' appears as a thing dehumanized, impersonalized and institutionalized, hierarchized, routinized ... a thing existing everywhere yet nowhere. 'Each household has its unique headaches' — a Chinese proverb — was the catch-phrase here, allowing no common interest among different 'households'.

Workers' 'Common Sense' and the Mapping of an Alternative Conception of the World

With the above remark we turn to yet another observation. To the extent to which the dominating doctrines, persuasions and imperatives were used to suture a hegemonic project, the JWM workers' struggle of position-making and position-taking — the making of a 'subject' (Laclau 1977) — can be seen as characteristic of an ideological interpellation countering the hegemonizing endeavour. My JWM case demonstrates that the very 'subject' is created precisely by contradictions among various forms of domination. In brief, it is the contradiction between a state-buttressed coercion and the ensemble of specific interpellations which constituted the JWM workers as an 'ideological subject'. In this sense, JWM workers had established themselves as a social agent — a class — which was the bearer of an ideological structure that in turn constituted them as subjects (Laclau 1980). At such a moment, the 'good sense' (Hall 1996, 432) of this class — 'its spontaneous, vivid but not coherent or philosophically elaborated, instinctive understanding of its basic conditions of life and the nature of the constraints and forms of exploitation to which it is commonly subjected' (ibid., 432) — was raised to the realm of an ethico-political struggle. What was at issue was never simply a matter of money, but of the 'colours' of the money, and the struggle was to preserve a sense of livelihood and its embedded dignity. What then emerged from this process of interpellation was, as Stuart Hall has suggested, an alternative 'conception of the world of the masses' (ibid., 419). In order to illustrate how the workers conceived of the world in which they struggled, I again resort to a visual illustration (see Figure 8.6).

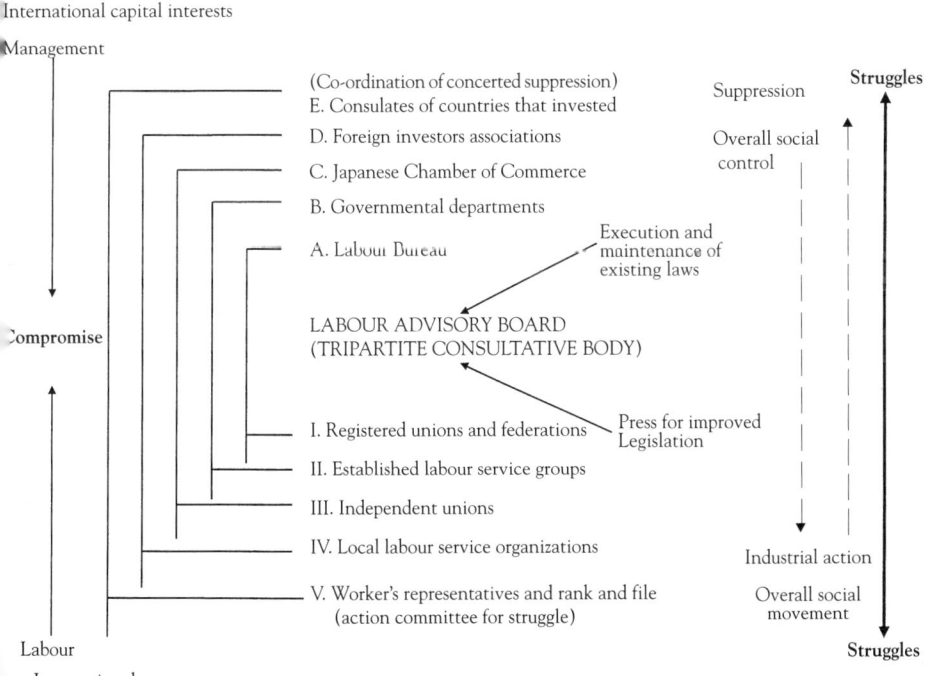

Figure 8.6 Power-Materiality constellation ('social formation' in Hong Kong)

The above representation can signify — at least for many workers and their collaborators — the structure of a microcosmic replica of the overall power-materiality constellation (social formation) in Hong Kong, as the struggling workers were able to make sense of it. This structure maintains a seemingly symmetrical institutional set-up, but it is merely a half-baked façade which serves nicely to make the domination, with all its brutality, all but invisible.

Let us begin from the middle, the 'neutral' as well as transcendental tripartite consultative body that was to 'advise the Commissioner for Labour on matters affecting labour, including legislation and international labour conventions.' (Hong Kong Government 1987) An overview of its make-up and history will be sufficient to indicate what kind of animal it was. To be 'objective', let me quote from the official report.

> In its early years the Board's membership consisted of representatives of large employers and government departments, as well as the armed services. There were no workers' representatives.
>
> In 1946, the Board became a tripartite body, with three members representing European employers, three representing Chinese employers and three representing workers of major companies. The chairman was the head of the Labour Office which was then part of the Secretariat for Chinese Affairs.
>
> In 1950, the Board was re-constituted and elected elements were introduced for the first time. Of the four members representing workers, two were elected by trade unions by secret ballot, and two were appointed by the government. Of the four members representing employers, one was nominated by the Employers' Federation of Hong Kong, one by the Chinese Manufacturers' Union (renamed Chinese Manufacturers' Association of Hong Kong in 1957), and two (chosen from European and Chinese employers respectively) appointed by the government.
>
> In 1977, the Board's membership was increased by four. The Board then comprised six representatives of employers with four nominated by employers' organisations and two appointed by the government, and six representatives of employees with three elected by trade unions and three appointed by the government.

In January 1985, the term of office of the Board was extended from one to two years and the number of elected employees' representatives was increased from three to four, offset by the reduction of appointed employee members from three to two.

The terms of reference of the Board, first adopted in November 1967, are as follows:

> To advise the Commissioner for Labour on such matters affecting labour, including legislation and conventions and recommendations of the International Labour Organisation as the Commissioner for Labour may refer to it. It may appoint such sub-committees as it may consider necessary and co-opt any person who is not a member of the Labour Advisory Board to serve on such committees.
>
> Prior to 1967, the Board's function was to advise the Commissioner on all important questions affecting the relations between employers and workers and on projected labour legislation.'

And finally I quote:

> The Committee on Labour Relations, set up in 1985, gives advice on the promotion of harmonious labour relations in Hong Kong and on the labour relations services provided by the Labour Department.

The nature of such a set-up, as instituted by an 'enlightened' colonial administration on a capitalist periphery, should now be sufficiently clear. The other institutional elements in the total make-up are nearly self-explanatory. A few notes will be enough to bring out my thesis:

(1) If we deem that A and B function to reproduce the capital establishment side of the social formation, I and II would be the equivalent in reproducing the labour establishment. They are themselves the most 'legitimatized' institutions, tinted with a thin haze of neutrality, rationality and impartiality. They are institutions tended by specialized 'professionals'. Their officials, in contact on a day-to-day basis, share a common set of values and working procedures. In other words, A and B need I and II as their counterparts and vice versa. They are engaged

in a continuously repeating game. In such a situation, the very existence of one's counterpart constitutes the very *raison d'etre* of one's own existence. This structure basically guarantees a situation in which nobody, either on the left-hand side or the right, ever attempts to eliminate his/her counterpart. I would suggest that such a 'non-antagonistic confrontation' is achieved and maintained through 'institutionalized' social conflicts — a rather effective means of social control. The corollaries of such a game are manifold. To name a few:

1a. None of the contending parties would risk their skins to reach any thorough settlement; conflicts are usually compromised and faces are usually saved under a mutually acceptable solution of false loss or false win.

1b. Both sides become 'specialists' in solving the discontent of people on the 'opposing' side. As in the legal profession, they assume the habit of dictating the whole negotiation process and become condescending vis-à-vis their clients — the workers and the management — at best, or despise them at worst.

1c. People from I and II become the easy prey of both overt (as evident in the government manifesto) and covert (as in our JWM case) co-optation and are easily turned into accomplices of the establishment and privileged interests.

2. In contrast, C, D, E are less visible. They are, however, the genuine pressure groups and lobbying powers. They tend not to participate in high-level palace politics and their position is most steadfast in case of any industrial crisis. They are, therefore, by no means soft-handed in crushing 'rebellions' or striving to reach total victory. They think they can do so precisely as they want because they lack any real contact with their archrivals — people in categories III, IV, and V.

3. Members of III, IV, V are localized grassroots organizations. They are usually small and weak, as well as numerous — typical of third-world non-government organizations (NGOs). In their respective locales, however, they are effective, vital and capable of instant grassroots

mobilization. In our JWM case, they were also worker-oriented. They renounce the working styles of both A and B as well as I and II. They insist that they are not agents or compradors of any sort and avoid playing a dictating role vis-à-vis the workers. They are, however, extremely thorough-going, especially in cases where the workers decide to fight to the very end.

Now, what are the real social consequences of such an asymmetrical institutional set-up? What did all this mean to the struggling breadwinners on the ground?

The answer is rather straightforward. To the workers and their collaborators, such an asymmetric structure, overwhelmingly biased towards capitalist interests and against their own, in effect manifestedly sanctions the necessity of their extra-legal appeal and calls for an expanded struggle at the overall societal level. Its suppressive nature legitimizes an action-oriented movement, and the coercion exemplifies a need for, and the usefulness of, employing violence if necessary. It is precisely owing to the impotence and incapacity of such a structure to restore justice or recover fairness that the terrain is left wide open for society itself to exercise self-defence and practise self-rectification. This is the rationale for a social movement, for struggle — a 'dynamic equilibrium' to check and balance — which is produced by the skewed power constellation behind the symmetric facade. Such was the 'popular philosophy' of the day, as the movement proceeds. To quote Hall, 'This "raising of popular thought" is part and parcel of the process by which a collective will is constructed, and requires extensive work of intellectual organisation — an essential part of any hegemonic political strategy.' (Hall 1996, 432)

In concluding this section on the JWM's workers' 'passage' to the creation of a collective subject for struggle, I recall Hall's identification of structure and superstructure. The JWM workers took steps resembling what Hall has suggested, and the 'objective economic crisis' developed 'via the changing relations in the balance of social forces, into crises in the state and society, and germinat(ed) in the form of ethical-political struggles and formed political ideologies, influencing the conception of the world of the masses' (ibid., 419).

However, in the JWM case, the dissolution of such a subject did not simply reverse the process. It had come much more suddenly and violently. Solidarity cracked at the height of struggle, and important representatives defected soon after substantial compensation was promised. If we look carefully, we see that minor cracks in the collective had been forming even as the collective itself was being formed. Vacillators and fence-sitters had been dropping out, although without causing any alarm. To account for all of these instances would be an extended project — but this overall scenario is anticipated by Hall:

> 'Hegemony' is a very particular, historically specific, and temporary 'moment' in the life of a society. It is rare for this degree of unity to be achieved, enabling a society to set itself a quite new historical agenda, under the leadership of a specific formation or constellation of social forces. Such periods of 'settlement' are unlikely to persist forever. There is nothing automatic about them. They have to be actively constructed and positively maintained. Crises mark the beginning of their disintegration (Hall 1996, 424).

The passage might have been written for our JWM case. Yet if the dissolution of this historical entity has been well anticipated, and is unavoidable, so is its rebirth, at some other time, under other skies. This conviction of mine found its empirical support in the follow-up researches on the body social in colonial Hong Kong which I carried out during the last decade of the twentieth century (Chiu 1996, 2000, 2002).

The HK/JWM Glocal Dynamics Revisited

In the dynamics of the JWM case, the global and local interpenetrations are mutually constitutive. The twelve perspectives suggested in Chapter 2 can be seen to have manifested themselves in the JWM case in the following manner.

The size of the 'production market' and 'available labour supply'

In our particular case, JWM International was the biggest watchmaker in the world. It occupied a major global share of the cheaper and more popular watch market. Adopting a labour process based on Fordism, JWM mass-produced millions of watches annually at various offshore sites on five continents. The Kwai Chung factory in Hong Kong, however, was not a production unit in the usual sense but a 'service' unit, which received all the call-backs to be repaired/restored by experienced, skilled operatives. In contrast to 'normal' Fordist mass production, the Kwai Chung factory labour process was akin to that of artisan production. The skilled female operatives, with a know-how acquired from many years' experience, worked individually, in a piece-by-piece manner. Many of them lived in the remote area of Pat Heung and were bused in on factory buses. Unlike female workers in garment, toy or electronic factories, who changed jobs frequently, many of these women had stayed with JWM Kwai Chung ever since they got their first jobs there through their relatives' connections. These dynamics had conditioned the basic structure of opportunities/limitations for managerial manipulation, as well as for the workers' prolonged struggle for fairness and dignity.

De-skilling and commoditization

The Kwai Chung service unit is a case to the point. We might, mistakenly, take the Kwai Chung unit as an aberrant exception to capitalist de-skilling/commoditization practices. In terms of productive activities, the operations are in fact less alienating than many: the women work like artisans, on individual pieces, with both their hands and minds. In terms of the production relationship the workers are also much less alienated than many, and many of them frequently take pride in successfully fixing up 'unfixables'.

However, if we take into consideration the labour control scheme, the remuneration system and the differential welfare as a total package, it became obvious that no matter how independent and capable these women artisans were, they were nonetheless treated as unskilled or semi-skilled manual workers, at the lowest level of the production hierarchy, who were being supervised by young male college graduates who had absolutely no knowledge of watch repair.

In the global perspective, the very *raison d'etre* of such a 'service unit' is precisely the result of a thorough de-skilling/commodification process executed in all the other Fordist mass production-lines spread around the globe. In other words, the existence of this service unit was precisely the other side of the coin. What made the whole thing perverse was not that JWM in Kwai Chung was exceptional or aberrant, but that these artisans were taken on as unskilled wage-earners (although this sowed the seeds of discontent) and were even denied severance payments, as they had been given the status of undocumented temporary jobbers. It is this, in fact, which ignited the collective resistance.

From the point of view of social movement and mass mobilization, it was precisely the artisan status and practice of the operatives that proved the most sustaining weapon in their struggle. Their skill had always been person-specific, rather than factory-specific, and so their know-how and productivity constituted their major bargaining power.

Two types of production and the dual character of an article arising from the manner of its production

The Kwai Chung case is enlightening in the sense that the plant engaged in neither assembly nor in transformation, at least not in their conventional terms. The production at Kwai Chung, for lack of a better terminology, can be called restoration production. In it, artisans and their skill constituted the major productive force, and 'bricolage' the prevailing mode of production, something similar to that of the 'cottage high-tech' which Sabel wrote about (Sabel 1984, 220–31). Yet such production was organized under a Fordist hierarchical structure. The sit-in, however, exposed the superfluous nature of the machinofactural set-up, as well as the structure of the surveillance of personnel. What was most revealing was the fact that the vice-general manager was so eager to recruit skilled workers for his own subcontracting service factory that he actually offered jobs to the striking worker's leaders even before the sit-in ended.

Organizational strategies: 'Divide and conquer' versus 'concentrate and control'

As the restoration production is highly skilled, highly labour-dependent work, and as it was the operatives (*qua* artisans) who were their own quality controllers, what relevance might the question of strategies of 'divide and conquer' or 'concentrate and control' have? In our JWM case, the style of management prior to the sit-in was one in which the operatives regulated themselves, while the line leaders, foremen and managers had virtually nothing to do — a style largely the result of habitual inertia and loose budget constraints. After the sit-in, however, the top Japanese management intervened and tried to reform and initiate a rigid system of central control. This change was obviously not production-induced, but was, rather, a measure based on the 'political' decision to replace local mid-range management with Japanese shop-floor managers, and might very well have been dictated by a misrepresented 'cultural' conviction of the superiority of a 'Japanese' style of management. What we witness here is an instance in which power operates in the guise of culture (van Wolferen 1990, 245–72) and in a situation where real putting-out is in operation.

Labour engagement and disengagement

In the JWM case, the management adopted a double-track strategy, engaging a monthly-paid staff, from whom loyalty might be expected, but refusing to engage the daily-waged operatives who were the sole force of productivity. I compare this to a military system, with officers engaged for a lifetime at one extreme; conscripts, who can be dismissed after use, at the other; and sergeants in the middle. It is important to know that the so-called Japanese-style lifelong employment, if it does exist in Japanese enterprises, applies only to the strata of managers ('officers') and foremen ('sergeants'), but never to the industrial conscripts (direct operatives and females). We can thus understand what otherwise might appear to be the irrationality of the ways the management discriminated against their most valuable labour force, the women artisans.

Buying and selling labour power

The JWM case makes it evident that the theoretical construction and objective representation of POLP and SOLP fail to address what happens on the ground. The JWM case, in fact, exposes the limitations inherent in both liberal economics and Marxist political economy. The struggle over severance payments by the female operatives became a battle for the abused to engage the multinational. They wanted to be treated as equal (*yishitongren*) human beings. They had been treated as industrial conscripts, although they had dedicated the best decade of their lives to JWM. Their severance pay represented the one and only opportunity for the value of their youth to be acknowledged and properly appreciated. Is this only a matter of economics or political economy?

Informality in economic sector relations

Insofar as Pat Heung is a rural suburban area of Hong Kong, the livelihood practices in the locale can be seen as a partial economy of the system. There were still farming activities in many households, mostly commercial farming of vegetables and flowers. In addition, these households usually had relatives overseas and received monetary remittances regularly. Also, living space — the scarcest commodity in Hong Kong — was made available for local people who engaged in various informal income activities and so-called 'ambulatory labour'. These factors enhanced the 'competitiveness' of the rural employment seekers and, at the same time, reduced their need to change jobs frequently in order to jack up wages. In other words, rural residential areas like Pat Heung became the most reliable bases for providing a stable and diligent working force. Yet this working force was also the most forceful opponent during industrial conflicts.

Opening up, by Way of an Epilogue 381

Constant internal movement and overall stability

The JWM case presents a somewhat disjunctive story. In the previous decade, the management had taken Pat Heung workers' stability for granted, while very few of the operatives had quit their jobs for higher wages. No measure of any sort was adopted to consolidate their engagement with the company. When severance payments became an issue, the management had to do whatever possible to retain the majority of the working force, and was even 'forced' to fire their leaders, the best of their best workers. This time, in the midst of JWM's merging with JETCON, it was the workers who opted for security.

And an uncommitted multinational, again, planned to adopt a 'hit and run' strategy, even while production was booming as a result of market expansion — greed had overtaken the need for stability.

The generality and/or ethnicity of knowledge systems: Analytical rationale and native rationale

In the JWM case, both the workers and management strongly warned against essentializing either the analytical rationale or the so-called native ones. In highly literate circumstances like this one, cultural repertoires as well as 'theoretical' arsenals are all opened for appropriation by either parties. In effect, this discursive warfare was waged by various supporting agents who volunteered their services either to the workers or to the management.

Social body constitution and intervention of existing social groups

During the JWM sit-in period, there were as many supporting agents on the management side as on the workers' side. Without bothering to co-ordinate among themselves, they offered their know-how and expertise in an expanding societal contestation. The battle was waged with proverbs, public opinions, judicio-legal provisions, rituals, public relations and rumours.

Civic-self formation and public image configuration

The collective of striking JWM workers was engaged in competing for legitimacy. In addition to organizing their union and registering it with the government, they were engulfed in constant actions to figure out their exact 'public' and in adjusting themselves to better appeal to it; or, conversely, trying to define a more tangible civic-self in order to solicit support from its potential 'public'. The dynamics — and dialectics — involved here were complex, and prompted me to initiate a research project on the formation of social bodies in circumstances of colonial modernity in Hong Kong (Chiu 2000, 101–49; 2002).

Collective action, collective consciousness and collective identification

In the JWM case, the managerial sabotage of the workers' solidarity took effect long before the outbreak of the strike. Organizational measures, collective representations, mass demonstrations, and ideological teach-ins were mobilized by the workers' leadership to undo or to minimize the damages caused by these schemes (which included pay-offs, the sowing of discord and the application of various pressures). In this regard, an in-depth analysis had been presented, in the guise of a sort of 'pseudo-geometry', following the extensively-detailed ethnographic account.

To Win or Not to Win, That Is Not the Question

Events have consequences. In the JWM dispute, six years after the end of the 'sit-in', discussion of the case has yet to subside; nor has the final score been settled. I do not expect any 'final' conclusion in the near future, especially regarding the question of who 'won' the battle — the management or the workers. I doubt that any such conclusion will ever be reached; the concept of a 'final stitch' in any story is fundamentally unhistorical.

However, such problems do not really seem to matter to our workers. Their lives have gone on as usual — the reproduction of everyday life is life itself. They know that business as usual has gone on without them at JWM — the reproduction of domination and control has always been the defining feature of capitalist enterprise, as it appropriates surplus and generates profits. As far as the spring of 1986 is concerned, the management did not claim victory. They knew they had not won. A suppressive profession managed to hold on to its business of suppression; there was no winning. Nor did the workers claim victory, but they knew they had won. The suppressed had managed to rise up — that was the winning.

Yet I suspect that such conclusions did not form in our workers and their leaders' minds during the last days of their struggle. What was at issue was not winning or not winning, or whether to claim victory or not to claim it. The question was whether they would win and be able to claim victory with dignity and pride, for without dignity there would be no victory and nothing to be claimed.

It was precisely at this point that Chu Chi-lin and her core group decided to give up their tactic of refusing monetary compensation from Amukas. They chose to take the 'dirty money' and 'squander it like dirt'! None of them rushed to look for jobs immediately after the end of the sit-in. Instead, they took a two-week trip through China.

'It was too lavish and unjustifiable [a thing] for us [to do]. But that was precisely what we wanted to do. That was precisely the way that kind of money should have been spent,' concluded Chu.

'That was precisely the victory,' I said.

And thus I conclude my book.

Appendix:
Selected Reports from the Press —
the Journalistic Construction of Reality
as Discursive Practice

Prologue: A Users' Manual

This appendix represents a reality constructed by multiple subjectivities, all in the same mode: that of journalistic inquiry. I will keep my re-presentation as close as possible to the journalistic texts. But to do so is by no means as easy as it sounds. The sheer quantity and repetition of the press accounts, together with current limitations of space, call for considerable selection and editing. In the process of selecting and editing, an 'I' exists, along with processes of both 'reading-in' and 'reading-out'. The texts do not talk but talk through me, and for that matter, my reader sees nothing except as he sees through me. And this 'I' who plays the role of a transmitter actually operates not only as a receiver but also as a rectifier; the sensitivity of its tuner is neither unlimited nor unbiased.

In this prologue, no attempt is made to claim that I have a marvellous or innovative 'technology' which has enabled my reproduction to approach anything close to live performance. Reproductions cannot but be things re-presented. In this sense they cannot be taken as original. Yet, in this appendix the decision whether or not to re-present them at all is based purely upon formal considerations, and does not imply any judgement about the substance of information carried therein.

In the original chapter on Journalistic Narratives, seventeen Chinese-language newspapers covered the industrial dispute. Two of them — *Sing Tao Man Pao* (STM) and *The New Evening Post* (NEP) — were evening papers which were released at noon on their issuing date. I quoted and translated almost every single entry. Some seemingly repetitive entries are meant to show subtle nuances between and among different constructions. Even so, identical information has been eliminated. The content of the evening papers were also re-presented, as they usually have information more up to date, by at least eight hours, than that of the morning papers. In effect, 'the date' of the evening paper is quite different from 'the date' of the morning paper.

Two English-language newspapers (SCMP and HKS) also covered the dispute. They aimed at a readership different from that of the Chinese papers.

Day 1 to Day 13 indicates the period of the sit-in. Days after the sit-in have similarly been prefixed with the plus sign (+); i.e., Day +1 means one day after the sit-in, etc.

However, these voluminous press narratives, for reasons of space, cannot constitute a separate chapter in the book. Instead, only a sampling of the most crucial social discourses from the journalistic world explicitly referred to in other genres of narrative are presented here.

Day 10: 9 June 1986 (Monday)
SCMP

TOUGHER UNIONS MAY EMERGE FROM BIG RIFT
by Peter Chan

Hong Kong's labour movement, which suffered a severe blow after a split nine months ago between 'left-wing' unions and influential independent unionists, may soon emerge stronger than ever. Both sides, each enjoying strong support, have recently floated the idea of renewed co-operation. The question now is who will take the first step to start a dialogue. The split occurred in October when the Joint Conference of Labour Groups on the Basic Law held an election to return labour representatives to the Basic Law Consultative Committee. Mr Lo Man-sa, director of the Christian Labour Association, was one of the nominees but was rejected at the last minute by 'leftwingers' who held most of the votes. Independent unionists then claimed Mr Lo was being discriminated against by the 170,000-member Federation of Labour Unions (FLU) which was influential among 'leftwingers'. Mr Lo walked out of the election, immediately followed by other independent unionists. Among the first was Mr Lee Siu-ching, chairman of the prominent Federation of Civil Service Unions, with 170,000 members. As both Mr Lo and Mr Lee are regarded as key leaders of independent unions, their departure was seen as a breakdown of the relationship between unions of the 'left' and independent blocs. In the past few months, contacts between the two have resumed, but the profile has been low with both sides inviting each other's officers to formal functions. Both sides acknowledge a reunion would enhance their bargaining power on issues such as a central provident fund and better worker protection. Both sides have indicated interest in normalizing relations, but neither has been willing to make the first move. Unexpectedly, the lingering labour dispute at JWM (Hong Kong) in Kwai Chung has offered a good opportunity for fresh co-operation. The dispute has drawn the Federation of Labour Unions (FLU) and the Christian Labour Association (CLA) together. For Mr Son Yan-min, a legislative councillor and a vice-chairman of the FLU, is joining with a Mr Lo in mediation efforts between workers and management. Officers of both the CLA and FLU told the *South China Morning Post* in separate interviews they were keen for a new alliance.

Mr Ku Han-yim, chairman of the FLU, said the federation had always held an open attitude towards other labour organizations. He said co-operation could be achieved on the basis of a common goal of improving labour benefits, with respect being given to each other's views. On the other side, Mr Lo said his willingness to co-operate with the FLU was not hampered by the latter's political affiliation, nor by last year's Basic Law election row.

Mr Lo said all unionists — leftwing, independent and rightwing —

should 'join hands' if they were to succeed with important proposals such as establishing a central provident fund.

Day +3: 15 June 1986 (Sunday)

CD

(special feature)

LABOUR DISPUTES INVOLVE MANY LEVELS
MANAGEMENT OFTEN NEGLECTS EXISTENCE OF
ORDINANCE AGAINST DISCRIMINATION OF TRADE UNIONS

LABOUR BUREAU AND LABOUR GROUPS FAIL TO TAKE THE
INITIATIVE IN CONCILIATING DISPUTES

Among recent labour disputes, the one at Japan Watch Multinational (JWM) is the most complicated. Besides revealing problems of communication between management and labour, the dispute also involved problems of unreasonable dismissal, the right of workers to organize labour unions, and the role of the Labour Bureau and labour groups.

Lin Yi-ching, the District Board member of Kwai Chung and Tsing Yi Districts, pointed out that the Labour Bureau mediated the dispute only after the management asked them to. Yet after the third round of negotiations between workers and management, the Labour Bureau failed to take the initiative to understand the situation of the workers. This made the workers question the Labour Bureau's role as a mediator. He pointed out that the Bureau ignored public opinion and the demands of the workers.

Earlier, Chief Labour Officer Mao Si-hai told the workers at the JWM factory that, when the strike was over, he would openly clarify the calumny he had made on workers — that the workers kept on imposing new demands during the negotiations.

Mao told the press that what he had said was based on facts and, now that the dispute was resolved, people should stop quibbling over petty matters. He told the *Central Daily* that the turning point of this strike was the early morning on the day of the Dragon Boat Festival when both parties reached an agreement in an unofficial meeting. The thirteen-day strike drew to an end the next day.

Lee Siu-ching, chairman of the Federation of Civil Service Unions, who helped with the mediation in its later stage, made a satirical remark, pointing out that certain 'VIPs' who claimed to show concern for labour's interests had failed to support the rights of JWM workers.

District Board Member Lin Yi-chin, who had been investigating the need of laid-off workers to find new jobs, also questioned the role of the currently established labour unions and labour organizations. He believes that some labour organizations are confined to a parochial outlook and often neglect grassroots interests.

A source close to the labour sector disclosed that although legislative councillor Son Yan-min and director of the Christian Labour Association Lo Man-sa aided the negotiations, few other labour leaders stood up for the JWM workers. Ouyang Chung, legislative councillor and chairman of the biggest union (the Professional Teachers' Union), and Hui Bei-kwong, executive member of the Basic Law Consultative Committee, who were also asked to intervene, refused to contact JWM workers. The staff of the Hong Kong and Kowloon Electronics Workers' Federation sent observers to the JWM factory but failed to give any assistance to the female workers there.

Lee Siu-ching said that this incident was relatively complicated but he and all the supporting groups stood firm behind the JWM workers' interests. They were not afraid to be labelled 'third parties' and they had tried to understand every detail in the development of the incident.

Lin Yi-chin said that he did not care if his intervention in the JWM strike adversely affected his political career. The Kwai Chung Residents and Workers Service Centre, to which he is affiliated, serves the rights and interests of workers and not the government or the bosses.

Fu Kwon-sin, who was expelled from the factory by the management with a court injunction order, is an executive member of the Kwai Chung Residents and Workers Services Centre. Another person who was served with an injunction was Gu Lai-hap, executive member of the Tsuen Wan Workers Service Centre. These two groups were considered by leaders of the labour establishment as lacking in experience. They were blamed for prolonging the strike and the deadlock in the negotiations.

However, those who influenced the negotiations were not the above Kwai Chung district local labour groups, but rather influential individuals and their established labour organizations who intervened at the invitation of JWM management.

Other sources pointed out that more than a dozen civil service unions and labour groups, who were independent and neutral, had won the trust of the JWM workers. They supported the thirty-six dismissed workers' demands for reinstatement and protested JWM management's discrimination against their union activities. They had also raised about US$5,000 to support the workers.

The JWM workers' representatives, who tried to form a trade union, pointed out that this strike 'had been brewing for some time'. The workers' representatives started to voice their discontent concerning the management's discrimination against daily-rated workers on April 28th. They fought for equal benefits with the monthly-rated workers. The workers sought assistance from the Labour Bureau in early May but lost confidence in it immediately. They therefore sought help from the staff of the two local labour services groups.

Lin Yi-Chin, who attended the unofficial meeting, said that he greatly admired the heroism of the five workers representatives who were present at the meeting. They demanded an increase in benefits for daily-rated workers and urged them (management) to allow their 180 colleagues to return to work with dignity.

Regarding the possible aftermath for the remaining JWM workers, Lee Siu-ching said that he would keep on reminding JWM's management that they should respect the workers' right to organize their labour union and not to breach the 'Prevention of Discrimination against Trade Unions ordinance'.

Lin Yi-chin also said that the workers' representatives had no alternative but to accept dismissal. It was simply impossible, after such a bitter dispute, for the thirty-six of them to work for JWM any longer.

After the JWM strike, workers were given a lump sum equalling 20 days' wages, which will be paid after the merger with JETCON. The daily-rated workers were also promised participation in a provident fund system by the management. This showed that workers were better respected, and that the company also acknowledged there were problems with their management style.

HKDN

(feature interview)

JWM DIRECTOR DISCUSSES RELATIONSHIP BETWEEN EMPLOYERS AND EMPLOYEES BEFORE 1997 IN HONG KONG
by Lee Kum Fung

Mr Amukas, the managing director of JWM Corporation, came specially from Japan to handle the JWM labour dispute. As an entrepreneur, he said that there would be more labour disputes as Hong Kong approaches 1997 and workers became more aware of their long-term interests.

Mr Amukas claimed that old management concepts cannot keep up with our ever-changing world. Both local and international investors in Hong Kong should draw a lesson from the JWM strike and apply advanced management concepts to provide their employees with the best possible long-term benefits. Workers will then work harder, strengthening the company's competitiveness.

At the end of last month, JWM dismissed 36 workers for 'misbehaviour', while the workers were organizing a trade union. This led to a strike by 200 employees, demanding reinstatement of the 36 leaders and recovery of their benefits. The 12-day strike ended with an agreement between the employers and employees. Both sides agreed that the service of the 36 workers would be terminated upon payment of severance pay, the workers receive their wages for the strike period, a provident fund be established, etc.

It is said that almost all the demands of the workers were realized, except the reinstatement of dismissed workers. It is said that such an agreement was criticized by certain experienced local entrepreneurs, who felt that the attitude of the Japanese employer, JWM, was too timid, and would upset the existing relationship between employers and employees in Hong Kong, as the employees now consider themselves more powerful.

Some days ago, Mr Amukas and his colleague Mr Nafuko, the personnel manager, were interviewed. They talked about the background and the development of the strike, the relationship between the employers and the employees before 1997, and the key to modern management. Their precise and perceptive ideas are worthy of consideration by Hong Kong employers and government officials. The major points of the interview are summarized as follows ('A' represents Mr Amukas ,'N' represents Mr Nafuko, 'Q' represents the interviewer):

Q: How does your company evaluate this strike?

A: Our company (early in April) announced that JWM Ltd. would merge with JETCON Technology company. This made the workers worry about their future and they sought advice from their team leaders. Since neither the team leaders nor the middle management knew anything about the new arrangement, they gave erroneous information, but they are not to blame, because the management was late in announcing benefit arrangements, causing a problem in communication. At this time, unfortunately, workers invited outside aid which incited their hostility towards the company. I feel sorry that our company has had to dismiss 36 workers. In fact, they were forced to leave due to intervention by third parties. To compensate them, we paid them a great deal of money.

Q: Some local entrepreneurs think that your company was too lenient with the striking workers and bent too much to their demands. What do you think?

A: It is just a matter of view. I am willing to accept criticism but, frankly speaking, there was no other alternative. We might have taken a stronger position if our company were not so big and so renowned. JWM is a big group with a total of five subsidiaries, including the JWM-JETCON Corporation in Hong Kong. The present solution avoids bringing trouble in our other companies by members of the labour sector or extremists making use of this to penetrate the company. I trust that our workers are so well treated that they will not be instigated to cause trouble. That's why I think this is the best solution, and most beneficial for the future.

Q: Have you consulted the Japanese consulate in Hong Kong?

A: Yes, we're reporting developments to the consulate. We also discussed the case with the Japanese General Chamber of Commerce in Hong Kong. Before the workers went to petition the Japanese consulate, we had warned the consulate and asked for advice. The consulate gave no advice, for it considered this to be a purely private issue. However, there was concern that this issue would adversely affect new investors. We were in a very difficult position. The day before the agreement was reached, we claimed that we would not contact the striking workers any more and that we would dismiss all of them. If this had happened, the strike would have lasted for one or two more weeks. If so, news of this kind would definitely have alarmed Japanese investors. Fortunately, up to now news of the strike has not reached Japan.

Q: Will this incident affect the confidence of the Japanese or other foreign investors in Hong Kong ?

A: At the beginning, Japanese expatriates treated this as a single business's concern. They read of the progress of the sit-in from the local daily news. They did not transmit the message back to Japan. Nevertheless, when third parties took part in this strike, they became worried and began to consider it a political issue.

Q: In resolving the dispute, did you employ the Japanese method of personnel management? Is Japanese-style management different from that in Hong Kong?

N: I am a newcomer to Hong Kong. I don't know anything about Hong Kong management. Although management styles may differ from place to place to meet specific domestic needs, the basic principles remain the same. The solution this time was not 'Japanese style'. In Japan, strikes usually last between eight and twenty-four hours. A strike persisting for more than 48 hours is rare. Before my visit to Hong Kong, some Hong Kong people told me that it is easy for anyone to find a new job here. If the management is firm in its stand, the workers are ready to quit and change their jobs rather than stay and fight. We considered this to be something beneficial to us. But this sit-in proved to be different.

A: We have factories in many Southeast Asian countries, such as Malaysia, Taiwan and Singapore. Nationalist movements there can sometimes affect labour conditions. We feel that there is no nationalist movement in Hong Kong. Hong Kong people enjoy freedom and have enormous flexibility in changing jobs. This used to be a way for them to compensate for whatever unfavourable working conditions existed. Thus, we used to believe the environment in Hong Kong to be advantageous for employers. However it may be that as we approach 1997, there will be more labour disputes. Hong Kong used to be a young city. The problem of retirement for the elderly has been by and large ignored, both by the business community and the authorities. It is time, nevertheless, for Hong Kong to address the question of the elderly and retirement. Under such circumstances, both trade unions and government will be concerned more about labour conditions, particularly in the area of provident fund and long-term service awards. Labour conditions have nonetheless changed over the years. I think international investors could learn from the JWM experience. It would be helpful for them in case of a labour crisis in the future.

Q: Do you believe that advanced personnel management is more suitable for Hong Kong?

A: Yes, but the question should not be confined to Hong Kong. Our management philosophy is mainly aimed at the satisfaction of the worker. The JWM group has been around more than a century. Its 4,000 overseas employees are spread all over Europe, the USA and Asia. The three factories in Hong Kong, which employ more than 900 workers, are the largest offshore units in Southeast Asia. Although the influence of trade unions is strong in Japan, we've never come upon such a thorny strike before.

N: Our management philosophy contains two basic policies: in whatever country we operate, we insist on providing better working conditions than our competitors. Secondly, we hold to the principle of respecting local culture and history.

A: We employ local people in the management strata in Europe and America. The Hong Kong JWM factory has also been localized and this will remain the same after it merges with JETCON Company. We have learnt from this incident, such as how to use local people on our management team when we are not familiar with the feelings and attitudes of the local workers and clients.

Q: Could you please sum up your future management strategy in Hong Kong?

A: We will recruit more experienced people who are familiar with the Hong Kong labour movement and the workers' conditions as our management advisers. The Chief Labour Officer of the Labour Department, Mr Mao Si-hai, has given us much useful advice. He pointed out that the management method of the 1970s would invite misunderstanding today in the 1980s. On Tuesday, a consultative body will be established. It will be composed of workers and management staff at the JWM factory. Owing to the slowdown of the import of spare parts to the US and Europe, we originally planned to slow down production here. But this incident has made us change our mind. We will transfer portions of the orders from neighbouring countries to Hong Kong in order to maintain the confidence of the Hong Kong workers.

A final note: Mr Amukas and Mr Nafuko have achieved the goals of their trip, and they will return to Japan today and tomorrow respectively.

HKS

(special feature)

JAPANESE FACTORY HAD BACKING OF GOVT. OFFICIALS

Top level Hong Kong government officials voiced support for the management last week when sit-in workers at a Japanese-owned factory stepped up their action, the *Sunday Standard* learnt.

The Governor, Sir Warren Smith, relayed a message last Tuesday through Mr Leonardo Du, the Secretary for District Administration, to the company's head.

The message stated that if the strike developed into a political issue, then the company would have the support of the government, according to several sources close to the management.

The sit-in workers at JWM (Hong Kong) Ltd. staged a demonstration on that day at the Japanese Consulate, and threatened to step up their action by urging the Hong Kong people to boycott JWM watches if the management did not give in.

The sit-in at JWM ended last Thursday after 13 days.

Approached by the *Sunday Standard*, Mr Amukas, the managing director of JWM Corporation, gave a milder version of the government backing.

'I approached Mr Leonardo Du on the phone to seek advice. He said he appreciated the company's patience.

'If the company believed it should take stronger action, public opinion would be on the company's side,' said Mr Amukas, who came from Japan specially to handle the sit-in of about 150 workers.

Mr Amukas said Mr Du spoke to him in fluent Japanese but insisted he was not sure whether Mr Du was speaking in his capacity as a Hong Kong government official.

Mr Amukas admitted that Mr Du was introduced to him by some friends after he had come to Hong Kong to inquire into the strike. Mr Amukas did not elabourate.

Mr Du was not available for comment.

Mr S. H. Mao of the Labour Department, who was involved in mediating in the dispute, admitted that the incident involved many top Hong Kong government officials and said it was not surprising that Mr Amukas could get into touch with Mr Du. No special introduction arrangement was needed, he added.

'Multinational companies nowadays can have easy direct access to senior government officials in most places, as every country is trying hard to attract foreign investment that can bring both employment opportunities and new technology,' explained Mr Mao.

HKS

CONCESSIONS CAME AS A SURPRISE

The 13-day sit-in at JWM (Hong Kong) Ltd finally came to an end last Thursday.

Although the company refused to reinstate 36 workers it had earlier dismissed, it withdrew its dismissal notice and each worker was given a reference letter stating that the company very much appreciated their performance, and they left the company of their own accord.

The sit-in workers were given their basic salary for the whole strike period.

Such an offer by the company surprised many, including the workers and the labour organizations involved.

The company threatened earlier that if the workers would not return to work, they would all be sacked. And the number of workers returning to work had increased to 104 out of the 150-odd strikers on the day of the settlement.

It seemed that the company was offering too much at a time when it was on the brink of complete victory.

'We are still trying to find out why the company made such a concession,' said Mr Fu Kwon-sin, the executive secretary of the neighbourhood and

Workers Service Centre in Kwai Chung Central, who helped the workers from the outset and was barred from entering the factory by an injunction during the strike period.

'But we guess the company is under pressure. More and more trade unions and overseas organizations were supporting us.

'I think the issue of Japanese textbook protests in Hong Kong also contributed. We don't know if the company was under pressure from the Japanese consulate general.

"Moreover, the top management from Japan discovered that the row arose from incompetent communication by the middle management of the company,' Mr Fu added.

'In retrospect, going to the Japanese consulate general may have helped,' said a worker who preferred more peaceful action and did not join the demonstration at the consulate.

'The company cannot do without all of us. It takes a training period of three months for newcomers to reach our skill and speed,' another worker said.

Mr Lo Man-sa, the director of the Christian Labour Association who has handled hundreds of labour disputes, said: 'The workers had no cards in their hand; they got such a good settlement through sheer good luck. It has to do with the personality of Mr Amukas.

'If the case was being dealt with by some other employers, all the workers would have been sacked.'

Mr S. H. Mao of the Labour Department agreed with Mr Lo.

Mr Mao praised the far-sightedness of Mr Amukas, the managing director who came from Japan to settle the dispute, and described the solution as a master stroke.

'In the long term interests of the company, the dispute had to be settled amicably. The company could have taken the opportunity to teach the workers a lesson but this would have been an empty victory, at the price of substantial good will.

HKS

WORKERS RETURN, BUT WITH 'TROTSKY' FEARS
By Liang Li-An

Workers at JWM (Hong Kong) Ltd will return to normal duties tomorrow after a sit-in of 13 days, but amid widespread fears that they will come under the influence of 'Trotskyists'.

A Labour Department official privately spelt out the fear, and was echoed by both the management and various labour organisations involved.

They hope to prevent further influence on the workers from the people they label as Trotskyist, and at the same time accuse this group of meddling and prolonging the issue.

No organisation or individual actively involved in the strike admits to being Trotskyist. The group attacked has in turn accused the parties mentioned above of 'slandering them', and accuses both the Labour Department and the various labour organisations of backing the management.

The 13-day sit-in (occurred) at JWM, a Japanese factory. All the workers involved in earlier negotiations with the company about changes in welfare arrangements were among the 36 sacked.

The company is to merge with another sister company in the near future. Daily wage workers discovered that the monthly paid employees were receiving a lump sum to transfer to the new factory. The daily staff were very dissatisfied and demanded explanations.

The workers also sought clarification of changes in long service gratuities. They were expecting to get 32 days' pay if they left the company after serving for five years, but they discovered a worker who left the company in March did not get this.

Workers went to the Labour Department for help, but in vain.

They then went for help to a local district board member's office, where they got in touch with two locally based labour organisations, the TWLSC and the CKRLS.

They were also introduced to a Kwun Tong-based LRC.

After negotiating for more than a month, workers and management were unable to come to any agreement. Some workers began a go-slow, trying to force the company to concede.

On the other hand, workers were encouraged by the three labour organisations to form a formal trade union in view of the company's unwillingness to recognise their representatives.

With the help of these organisations the workers held a press conference in late May, announcing their dispute with the company and their preparations to form a trade union.

On May 31, 36 workers were sacked. All the other workers in the factory refused to resume work and staged a sit-in.

Negotiations on the reinstatement of the 36 then began.

On the very next day, the company agreed to re-employ the 36 on condition that the daily workers would not raise the issue of the lump sum received by their monthly-paid colleagues. No settlement was reached.

Legislative Councillor Mr So Yan-min and the director of the CLA, Mr Lo Man-sa, were invited by various parties — including the management — to mediate.

Mr Son and Mr Lo failed to persuade the management to re-employ the workers, but came out with an agreement that the company would provide full severance pay to the 36.

Workers rejected this offer and stepped up their action by calling in more labour organisations and unions to help, including Mr Lee Siu-ching of the Civil Servants' Association.

Some workers accepted the money offered by the company and pulled out of the strike, while others tried to seek help from the Japanese Consulate General.

The management then declared that if the workers did not return to work in two days, all of them would be sacked. The number of workers resuming duties increased.

Eventually the company and its workers came to an agreement to end the sit-in last Thursday.

Although the company would not re-employ the 36, it withdrew its dismissal notice and gave each a reference letter stating they had left the company of their own accord.

Mr Amukas, managing director of the factory's Japanese parent company, blamed outside interference for the fact that the sit-in took 13 days to settle.

'The girls agreed to the terms and promised to come back in ten minutes' time. But they did not come back after three hours,' he said.

The labour dispute was not a complicated one, but it came to involve nearly all the major labour organisations.

One unionist pointed out that workers in local labour groups were very inexperienced, and whenever they had trouble they sought help from outside.

However, he also complained that they would accuse the unionists coming to help them of siding with the management if they did not agree with them.

A social worker said the workers were so inexperienced that they were manoeuvred to some extent by Trotskyists.

'I know at least one Trotskyist girl was able to get into the dining hall where the workers met,' said Mr Amukas. The company sought an injunction to bar outsiders from the premises.

Sources said the reason why the management refused to re-employ the dismissed 36 was because they feared those who preferred staying to taking severance pay would be much influenced by the Troskyists and might cause trouble.

A veteran social worker in the district complained bitterly about the interference of Trotskyists in the incident.

'They are very militant and try to cause as many disputes as possible. They do not think of the possible results that workers might have to suffer.

'You have to warn them of the possible effect of a go-slow, and that representatives cannot be protected from sacking during the preparation of a union,' he added.

Mr Lo said if the issue had been in more experienced hands, it might have been settled much earlier. He also complained that the workers were not informed of the possible consequences before choosing their next moves.

Even Mr Lee, who joined the dispute only at the last stage, did not agree with some of the workers' actions. He pointed out that it was no use the workers staying overnight outside the consulate general.

Talking to some workers, the *Sunday Standard* found them divided into two groups. One favoured Mr Son and Mr Lo while the other preferred the local labour groups.

Day +5: 17 June 1986 (Tuesday)

MP

(feature story)

LOW TAX RATE, FREE TRADE, SKILFUL WORKERS
HONG KONG IS NO LONGER A LOW BENEFIT REGION
JAPANESE BUSINESSMEN SAY STILL WORTH INVESTING

There have been worries that the deadlock of the strike at the Japan Watch Multinational (JWM) might stop new foreign investments from entering Hong Kong. Mr Amukas, a Japanese director who represented the management in the negotiations, thought that foreign investors should be well prepared, since seeking better benefits is a definite trend among Hong Kong workers. Although production costs are bound to rise, other favourable factors in Hong Kong would still make it a worthwhile place for investment, he emphasized.

Mr Amukas flew to Hong Kong from JWM's headquarters in Japan to handle the strike. He claimed that the company had about 4,000 overseas employees in 20 sites all over the world. According to him, strikes were unprecedented at the headquarters in Japan or at any other overseas branch.

He had been worried that clashes between workers and managerial staff would easily be provoked in countries like Malaysia and Singapore where there is a strong sense of nationalism. It never occurred to him that Hong Kong, which is a free port where employers can employ and dismiss workers at will, would have labour problems.

However, he has learnt from this incident that there is a new tendency in Hong Kong, and foreign investors should no longer treat it as a low-benefits region, as they did before. He said that provident fund and retirement pay have growing importance to workers in Hong Kong. In fact, workers in other countries already enjoy such benefits.

He reminded foreign investors that they should be aware of the reasonable tendency of workers to strive for better benefits and be fully prepared before investing. The management should also respect workers and help them to better their living standards. He said that production costs would undoubtedly increase when better welfare benefits were given to workers. However, Hong Kong has other important factors to attract investment, such as a low tax rate, a free trade system, highly-skill workers, etc., which are unmatched in other regions. According to him, Hong Kong, after weighing all factors, is still a good place for investment.

MP

WEAKNESS IN JWM MANAGEMENT
36 WOMEN WORKERS WHO SUFFER MUCH
HOPE FOR COMPENSATION

Looking at the resolution of the strike, some think the employer has won. However, others point out that the employees gained the upper hand at the last stage of the strike, for there was no need for the employer to give such high compensation to the workers.

Mr Amukas said that he did not like to be regarded as the winner and had no intention of blaming anyone. He admitted that problems did exist in the management. The ones who lost most were the 36 dismissed workers who eventually agreed to resign — which is why the company agreed to give them maximum compensation.

He explained that the factory could not reemploy these workers because of the interference of third parties. Continuous publicity of the labour dispute has caused it to become a social issue. Every sector, especially those involving foreign investors, is greatly concerned over the development of this incident. Due to great pressure, he could not keep on the dismissed female workers, otherwise other people would look down on the management and take it as a sign of indecision and weakness.

Mr Amukas said that he handled this incident with a view for the future.

As the strike has already taken place, the most important thing to do now is to restore the confidence of the workers and the management staff. Since there is a great surplus created from offshore manufacturing units for JWM, the factory does not intend to move out of Hong Kong. On the contrary, the company is preparing to disperse its production to Japan's neighbouring countries. For JWM, Hong Kong remains the major area of production, which is why JWM decided to merge with the other company and strengthen its management. He did not want the dispute to cause the resignation of the majority of workers. He also ordered the management not to be nostalgic about the past 14 peaceful years. They should, instead, take this unhappy incident as a lesson and improve the relationship between the employer and the employees. He has also invited the Labour Department as a third party to analyse the gains and losses from this incident.

He also told us that he has made many verbal promises to the workers, and so will come back in two months to check on the factory's progress.

He claimed that he does not object to the Hong Kong workers' setting up a workers' union. Once it is set up, it will be the first overseas workers' union in the company. This can also be considered something to be happy about!

MP

(feature story)

INTERVENING IN THE WATCH FACTORY STRIKE
INCITING SLEEP OUT IN FRONT OF CONSULATE
THE 'TROTSKYITES' ARE COMING BACK
ALERT PEOPLE OF THE LABOUR SECTOR

The JWM factory, which had been on strike, resumed normal production yesterday. According to figures released by the management, apart from the 36 workers who agreed to leave, the remaining 180 workers have all returned to work and this incident can be considered satisfactorily settled. Such crises abound in small and medium factories. In addition, the 'Trotskyites,' who have long been silent, intervened in this matter. Thus, both workers and management should remain vigilant.

In this incident, the Labour Department said interference by third parties led to many missed opportunities for a resolution. The 'third parties' referred to here are people who were not present at the negotiations but only incited the workers from behind the scenes, not the labour movement leaders who mediated in this incident.

A person from the labour sector warned that people pursuing the 'Trotskyite' line intervened in the JWM incident. This indicates that the 'Trotskyites' have come back on the scene.

This labour sector person pointed out that 'Trotskyites' act in a radical way. For example, this strike need not have taken such a long time to resolve, but the 'Trotskyite' intervention complicated matters. Fortunately, the matter was settled satisfactorily, and no other workers apart from the 36 were dismissed. Some people from the labour sector had wanted to help mediate in the dispute, but they maintained a low profile because they found 'Trotskyites' lurking behind the scenes.

People from various organizations who had participated in the negotiations pointed out that the 'Trotskyites' had been quiet for quite a long time in Hong Kong. Only rarely have they intervened in labour disputes in recent years. Their activity this time is astounding. Their most conspicuous move was instigating some women workers to sleep outside the Japanese Consulate in protest.

DISPUTES ARISE EASILY IN MANUFACTURING SECTOR COULD BE HOTBED FOR THE RISE OF TROTSKYITES

Some experienced labou-sector people pointed out that the 'Trotskyites' can most easily interfere in the manufacturing sector, for that is where trade union membership is weakest. Management in many small and medium-sized factories in this sector are backward and labour disputes can easily arise.

As to whether the 'Trotskyite' influence can grow in the future, in other spheres, it also depends on whether political and economic development in Hong Kong will exacerbate class differences.

One person involved in the mediation this time thought that, after this incident, many labour organizations will heighten their vigilance. These labour organizations will by no means co-operate with the 'Trotskyites'. Any action initiated by the latter will most probably be taken by them alone.

However, the staff of the Central Kwai Chung Labour and Residents Service Centre (CKLRS), who were the first to respond to a request of the workers to help resolve this incident, strongly object to the claim that there was 'Trotskyite' intervention.

CENTRAL KWAI CHUNG LABOUR AND RESIDENTS SERVICE DENY TROTSKYITE INTERVENTION IN THE STRIKE

The staff at CKLRS pointed out that the workers decided to adopt an open attitude to organizations which were willing to offer assistance. They said that throughout the strike, many labour organizations of different backgrounds had assisted in mediation or shown support for the workers. They wondered why there was no outcry against the pro-China 'leftists' or the 'independents,' but only the 'Trotskyites'. Such accusations were deliberately misleading.

They admitted however that there was at least one woman considered to be a 'Trotskyite' who was present at a workers' rally. But she only spoke briefly with the workers; it was doubtful that she had influenced them much.

What is most unjust is that, because of accusations of intervention by 'Trotskyites', CKLRS has also been accused of being connected with them.

Nevertheless, some mediators pointed out that since the 'Trotskyites' showed enthusiasm, the workers had thought highly of them. They had considerable influence with some workers in the later stages of the strike.

Some other labour sector people believed that it was only accidental that the 'Trotskyites' appeared this time, the development of the issue having created favourable conditions for their intervention.

KNOWING THE TROTSKYITES ARE RADICAL, LABOUR ORGANIZATIONS MOSTLY AVOID THEM

In general, when a dispute arises and the 'Trotskyites' want to intervene, prominent labour organization assisting the workers refuse to be involved, because they know well that the radical actions of the 'Trotskyites' can make matters worse.

The 'Trotskyites' were able to intervene this time perhaps because the labour organization which initially handled this dispute was inexperienced. They therefore needed to seek assistance from other organizations. Also, the 'Trotskyites' who intervened had disguised their real nature. They did not appear in their usual manner. If the labour organization handling this issue had been an established trade union with experience, there would have been little chance for 'Trotskyite' intervention. In addition, the management did not strictly apply the injunction order and so the strike was delayed for two weeks. This was one more reason why the 'Trotskyites' were able to intervene.

MP

(feature article)

MAO SI-HAI POINTS OUT WAYS TO AVOID LABOUR DISPUTES: IMPROVEMENT OF STAFF BENEFITS AND PERSONNEL MANAGEMENT

Mr Mao Si-hai, Senior Labour Relations Officer of the Labour Department, pointed out that the underlying factors which caused the JWM strike are actually a latent crisis for many factories in Hong Kong. If employers do not change their concept of workers welfare and personnel management, similar incidents may occur in other factories.

Mr Mao pointed out that there is a general misconception that labour disputes arise because one of the two parties makes a wrong decision or troublemakers incite the workers. But in fact, many disputes arise because a correct policy of the employer is misunderstood in the course of transmission, causing a sense of insecurity among the workers. If such a situation is handled inappropriately, things can worsen and possibly get out of control. The JWM strike is a typical case of such a labour dispute. Four intrinsic factors caused this incident, and these factors exist in many factories in Hong Kong.

First of all, the employer often does not explicitly set forth the workers' benefits. The managerial strata may think that this allows for maximum flexibility, allowing them to reward good workers. This traditional method of management in fact turns benefits into personal favours. In an institution with a large staff, the problem of unequal distribution will arise, and misunderstandings can easily develop.

Mr Mao stressed that when an institution reaches a certain size, it should institutionalize the benefits for the staff and publish them in an employee's manual. This practice can encourage the workers and, more importantly, prevent misunderstandings between the management and the workers.

Secondly, the managerial strata tends not to give a detailed and consistent explanation of certain significant policies to the workers.

This strike arose because the daily-rated workers had a misunderstanding that the management gave an extra bonus to monthly-rated workers, which was unjust. The management in the beginning did not explain clearly the source of this 'mysterious money', which led to conjecture and intensified the doubts of the workers.

EQUALITY AND COOPERATION BETWEEN EMPLOYER AND WORKERS ARE INDISPENSABLE FOR A MODERN MANAGEMENT SYSTEM

Thirdly, in factories with more than 100 workers, there must be channels for direct communication between workers' representatives and the top layer of management.

Mr Mao suggested that a labour-management consultative system could serve as a sort of 'safety valve'. Such a system has been in place for many years in public utility institutions, and has operated well. However, such a system does not exist extensively in the private sector. When problems arise, the management simply blames troublemakers and overlooks the fact that there is no normal channel through which workers may lodge complaints.

He further pointed out that the management is often worried about workers forming trade unions. In fact, they do not understand that workers seek help from trade unions only when they have no channel for making complaints. If there already exists an effective channel for communication, many problems can be settled immediately, instead of developing into labour disputes, and there need not be any fear of third-party intervention.

Lastly, the general managerial staff in Hong Kong is concerned only with raising production and overlooks the question of personnel management. Employers seldom train their managerial staff in this. Hence, when problems arise, the management lacks specialized knowledge and can only handle the matter with their personal experience and common sense, and this often reduces the chance for resolving problems.

When the level of specialized personnel management skills is low in the management strata, class differences between them and the workers also become acute and conflicts are more easily aggravated.

Mr Mao pointed out that the spirit of modern management is co-operation and equality between labour and management. There should not be water-tight classification of senior and junior ranks. In 1968, the government amended the previous 'Master and Servant Ordinance' and re-named it the 'Employment Ordinance' to reflect this trend.

He revealed that in the coming years, the work of the Labour and Employer Relations Section will help institutions in Hong Kong to improve their personnel management system.

Mr Mao said that the Labour Department will investigate the causes and development of the JWM dispute as well as review the role of the Labour Department for future reference. The managerial strata of other factories should also draw lessons from this case. They should check to see if they also have similar weaknesses, so that improvements be made as soon as possible.

MP

(feature article)

STRIKE MEDIATOR SUGGESTS LABOUR DEPARTMENT HAVE EXECUTIVE OFFICER INTERVIEW WORKERS SEEKING HELP

A person who had mediated in the JWM strike suggested that the Labour Department should assign executive officers to be the first persons interviewing workers who seek assistance instead of clerical staff, who are likely to overlook crucial points and might cause workers to lose confidence in the Labour Department.

This person pointed out that the JWM strike exposes a weak link in the present structure of the Labour Department. The staff interviewing workers in the branch offices are clerks or assistant clerks. In contrast, many years ago, the District Office, after re-evaluating previous practice, decided to have executive officers interview citizens seeking assistance, and this led to great improvement in the public's impression of the government.

He pointed out that long before this strike broke out, workers from the factory had sought help from the branch office of the Labour Department. Since they did not receive appropriate assistance from the interviewer, the confidence of the workers in the Labour Department dissipated and they turned to their local labour service groups for assistance. Later, when the dispute deteriorated, senior staff of the Labour Department got involved but were not trusted by the workers.

This mediator pointed out that the District Offices had executive officers interview citizens. In contrast, workers who seek help from the Labour Department are usually much more agitated emotionally and need specialized personnel to offer assistance. He thus appealed to the Labour Department to review the present structure.

CD

(commentary)

BY-PRODUCT OF JWM STRIKE: LABOUR-MANAGEMENT CONSULTATIVE COMMITTEE FORMED TO HELP COMMUNICATION AND RESOLUTION OF DISPUTES

The strike at JWM (Hong Kong) Ltd lasted for 13 days and ended with the mediation of members of the Legislative Council, the District Board, the Labour Department and dozens of labour organizations. The company withdrew 'misbehaviour' as the reason for dismissing 36 female workers. Instead, they received compensation and resigned voluntarily. The remaining 180 striking workers will resume work next Monday.

The strike, which has attracted much public attention, arose when JWM merged with another company, only the monthly-rated workers got severance pay, and daily-rated workers felt discriminated against. Just as the daily-rated workers were forming a trade union, most of the unions' executive members were dismissed for 'misbehaviour'. This led to a strike of over ten days.

Mr S. H. Mao, the Chief Labour Relations Officer of the Labour Department, was involved in mediating the dispute. He claimed that this dispute was mainly caused by the merger of two companies and a misunderstanding between the employer and the employees. The Labour Department will help JWM set up a labour-management consultative committee in order to prevent similar events in the future.

Mr Amukas, the managing director of JWM Headquarters in Japan, said that after this strike, the newly merged company will improve management methods and allow the workers to form their trade union.

What is the difference between a trade union and a labour-management consultation committee? Which is better?

The Labour Department has encouraged companies to form consultative systems since the late 1960s. It suggested that this was one of the most successful ways of gaining the confidence of the workers. Such procedures can also help progressive employers improve their relationship with employees as well as solve daily problems.

Mr Dai Yu-si, a legislative councillor who has had more than 40 years' experience in dealing with strikes, said, 'The Labour Department should not lay down any rules or force companies to form consultative committees; nor should it compel the companies to recognize the status of the trade unions. There are obvious differences between consultative committees and trade unions. In meetings of the consultative committee, employers and employees can discuss such matters as working conditions and improvements to the factory. But they cannot negotiate wages. Mr Dai also pointed out that employers can only talk about the question of wages during a recession. However, a trade union is quite different. It has the right to ask the employer to ameliorate unreasonable treatment, discuss questions of wages and even go on strike.

Concerning the JWM strike, Mr Dai said that when workers desire to form a trade union, the employer should not interfere. If the workers had formed the union before the strike, the union executive members could have concentrated their strength on gaining their rights. But the union had not been formed, so the different opinions of the workers could not come into agreement, making the strike more difficult to solve.

Mr Lo Man-sa, director of the Christian Labour Association, who mediated in this incident, emphasized that this strike was only a dispute between the employer and employees, and was in no way a Sino-Japanese racial confrontation.

On the labour-management consultative system, Miss Chou Mei-ying, member of the Christian Labour Association, said that the forming of consultative committees can provide a channel for the workers to voice their grievances, but the committee may not be able to solve difficult problems. The Mass Transit Railway (MTR) had a consultative committee before the 1984 strike, but the employer could still dictate every decision. Consequently, the failure of the consultative committee led to the decision to strike by the MTR drivers.

Miss Chou said that usually the consultative committee was set up only by the employer. Workers cannot speak for their rights. The workers' ability to speak up for their rights in the consultative committee is even less than that in the 'yellow workers' unions' formed by the government or the employers. Now that JWM is allowing workers to form a trade union, how the consultative committee and the trade union are to co-exist in the same company and whether this will lead to another confrontation is an open question.

WKY

(feature article)

DIFFICULTIES STILL EXIST IN ORGANIZING TRADE UNIONS
CHIEF LABOUR OFFICER SAYS LACK OF COMMUNICATION MAIN CAUSE
SCHOLAR PROPOSES SETTING UP THIRD-PARTY ORGANIZATION TO REDUCE LABOUR-EMPLOYER CONFRONTATIONS

Though the workers in Hong Kong have certain safeguards, there are still difficulties involved in organizing trade unions.

Articles 87 and 98 of the International Labour Pact safeguard the rights of workers to organize and join a trade union freely without being discriminated against by the employer. Since 1974, there have been no court cases involving discrimination against workers for organizing a trade union.

However, Mr Hui Bei-kwong, Secretary of the Federation of Hong Kong and Kowloon Labour Associations, said that in the past decade there have been cases of employees being dismissed for organizing a trade union in the workplace. Employers often use other excuses to dismiss them. Even in cases where the employer breaches the Labour Ordinance, the maximum fine is $5,000. Under these circumstances it is understandable that in general, the workers' desire to set up a trade union is not great, and their response to others wishing to do so is not enthusiastic.

Mr Mao Si-hai, the Chief Labour Relations Officer, said that the main obstacle to setting up a trade union is lack of communication. Labour and management tend to confront each other and both resort to radical action, instead of co-operating.

Dr Luk Sa-bien of the Management Department of the University of Hong Kong, said that Hong Kong could follow Britain's example in setting up a third party organization to help workers who wish to set up a trade union reach an agreement with their employer and reduce confrontations.

Day +10: 22 June 1986 (Sunday)
SP

(Feature article)

MORE FRUSTRATION FOR THE LABOUR MOVEMENT VANGUARDS AGAIN SACRIFICE HEROICALLY

Vanguards organizing labour movements in public and private institutions are always a mote in the eye of the capitalists — like the group of MTR vanguards who were all dismissed. Lately, over 30 blue collar leaders in a factory had to resign voluntarily at the insistence of the capitalists. Though their action brought better welfare for other workers, they themselves lost their jobs.

Hong Kong society does not tolerate militant labour movements, and the majority of — indeed, all — capitalists disdain labour movements once away from the negotiating table. Hence, vanguards of the labour movement sacrifice themselves heroically one after the other. The most conspicuous example was the government's dismissal of a trade union leader in 1982. What that vanguard gained was higher wages, but his action was not accepted by the authorities, and eventually he was dismissed for 'unsatisfactory conduct and work, and a uncompromising attitude'. The intervention of over 20 civil service unions could not force the authorities to concede.

A similar case was the dismissal of militant trade union leaders by the MTR company, which sought to get rid of trade union leaders who refused to sit down at the negotiating table, even at the cost of affecting its service to the public. This case dealt a hard blow to the labour movement. When the MTR got rid of its hostile opponents, the welfare of other staff members improved at once.

Last year, the MTR company further implemented some new ideas and plans, and conducted a survey of the entire staff in order to heighten the understanding of the managerial layer of the staff's opinion on matters affecting their work. It found that the staff had a very good impression of the company, were interested and devoted to their work, and had only minor criticisms on matters such as wages, internal communication, and channels of consultation.

It is generally bad for either labour or management when they adopt a stance of confrontation, especially when communication channels are lacking. Militant workers are never tolerated by employers. In the JWM case, a strike broke out in the factory and the employer was firm in dismissing trade union leaders who devoted themselves to fighting for the benefit of all workers. The employer even accused other trade unions of intervention as 'third parties', which led to a deterioration in the situation. As soon as labour movement vanguards were swept away, the management immediately announced that the company would consider setting up a labour-management consultative committee to strengthen communication between the two parties. The management promised to consider setting up a provident fund in six months, a significant breakthrough in the industrial district of Kwai Chung. The improved benefits for the remaining workers were brought about by the labour movement vanguard who 'sacrificed heroically'. They received an insignificant severance payment while their rice bowl was broken.

Leaders of labour movements, consequently, must adopt a calm and peaceful attitude toward their personal loss. For, without legal protection, they will never be able to enjoy the benefits they fight for on behalf of their fellow workers. If possible, they should avoid confrontation. Many benefits can be gradually achieved at the negotiating table. If an industrial action is abruptly called, the employer often over-reacts, and the workers' leaders are often forced to quit or are fired. It will take time for Hong Kong to accept British or American-style labour movements. Pushing too hard can only hurt the movement.

Last year, there were only three labour disputes leading to a total of 1160 hours of work stoppage. This reflects the constraints on Hong Kong's labour movement, even if the labour management relationship is by no means harmonious! [sic]

Day +15: 27 June 1986 (Friday)
WKY

(Feature article)

FROM AN ORDINARY WORKER TO A SOCIAL WORKER
AH LAN LAMENTS THE COST OF A STRIKE
WORKERS' RIGHTS HAVE TO BE FOUGHT FOR
BUT THOSE WHO SUFFER ARE ALWAYS THE WORKERS

by Shan

The JWM strike, which had lasted two weeks, ended a week ago. The group of strong and unbending young women workers' representatives must have left a deep impression on people. What do they feel about the days of resistance now that they have returned to ordinary life? Our reporter interviewed one of the workers' representatives, Ah Lan.

Ah-lan said: ' If I had been given time to think matters over calmly, maybe I would not have favoured using such radical means to fight the employer.'

She sighed and said that in a strike, whatever the outcome, the workers themselves are always the ones who suffer most.

The JWM strike was, for her, an unforgettable event. It was also a turning point in her life. She had never before thought herself capable of dealing with such complicated matters and had never imagined that she would hold meetings with officers. She had never dreamt that she would meet with the director of the parent company, the chief labour officer of the Labour Department, and television and newspaper reporters.

With the strike, her life was totally changed. She has been transformed into another person. Before the strike, her life was no different from that of thousands of other women workers. During lunch or break time, she was a devoted paper mahjong player and had a zest for small-scale gambling. She would also go shopping or to the cinema after work. Looking back now on her past, she feels that it was futile and meaningless. In those days, she felt that she was useless, unable to contribute anything to society. Apart from doing simple work in the factory, she was like a crippled person.

She had never imagined that she could represent the workers in negotiations with the employer and fight for their rights. It was a difficult period for her, physically and emotionally. But, with the thought that she could do something for the others, she discarded all worries and dealt with all obstacles fearlessly. She did not think of what she herself could gain, but only of what all the workers wanted to gain.

Eventually she was dismissed and had to search for a new job, meeting with even greater difficulties as all factories in the district refused to employ JWM women workers. It was only after many difficulties that she found her present job outside the neighbourhood.

Nevertheless, she regrets nothing. Although she herself never enjoyed the benefits she had fought for, yet, seeing her former fellow workers return to their posts and receive better remuneration, she experiences a sense of achievement and joy. Her efforts were not in vain.

This spirit of service and sacrifice prevailed during the whole strike. After the strike, Ah-lan became a volunteer at the Tsuen Wan Workers Service Centre. She frequently participates in various social activities. She said that her life became more meaningful, and she learned to be concerned for society and to understand it and though her ability was small, she could still contribute a little. In addition, she was also one of the volunteers in the recent signature campaign against the building of the Daya Bay nuclear plant.

Commenting on her relationship with various local labour groups, she said that throughout the strike, she received assistance from them and learned about labourers' rights. Yet, all the help she got was of an advisory nature. All the decisions were made by the workers themselves. As for the so-called 'Trotskyites', she said that she knew nothing of them. As far as she is concerned, all such reports were fabricated.

She also felt that the strike had taught the workers that they cannot be deprived of their rights as long as they stand up and fight for justice. They must not be timid or give up struggling. But she stressed that in the process of fighting for their rights, they must adopt peaceful means and must not bring the situation to a stalemate, or the workers would be the ones to suffer.

She said that the final success in negotiating with the director of the Japanese headquarters was due to the following consideration: although the workers' representatives themselves did not have financial problems and had nothing to worry about, some of their fellow workers who supported them had financial difficulties and the strike further affected their income. The situation was very unfavourable for them. Hence, in consideration of the whole group, the representatives decided to resolve the strike as early as possible.

Day +18: 30 June 1986 (Monday)

CD

(Feature article)

ORDINARY STRIKE BUT MULTIPLE INTERVENTIONS
INCLUDING OFFICIAL AND UNOFFICIAL ORGANIZATIONS
STRONGMEN OF LABOUR MOVEMENT ALSO INVOLVED
JWM ISSUE BELONGS TO THE PAST BUT WARRANTS STUDY
by reporter Chan Kwok-lam

The JWM issue belongs to the past but it is believed that the strike will attract more attention in the near future because of the number of people who were involved and the complicated nature of the affair.

Apart from the workers, the employer and the Labour Department, those involved included Son Yan-min, Legislative Councillor and Deputy Executive Director of the Hong Kong Federation of Labour Unions; Lo Man-sa, Director of the Christian Labour Association Industrial Committee; and Lee Siu-ching, Chairman of the Federation of Civil Service Unions, all strongmen in the labour movement. There was also an incident in which the workers petitioned the Japanese Consulate in Hong Kong. In addition, there was the so-called Trotskyite controversy and the third-party intervention which allegedly obstructed negotiations between workers and employer. Two staff members of local associations were forbidden to enter the factory by a court injunction order. On top of all this, the appearance of both Lo Man-sa and Son Yan-min in the same strike was not only rare, but historical.

WOMEN WORKERS DENY THAT THEY WERE MANIPULATED BY OTHERS

Some commented that there were many thorny issues involved, mainly because the workers, who lacked experience, were manipulated by third parties; their demands were so capricious that the employer could not do anything until very late. Do the workers who participated in the strike agree with this assessment? Our reporter interviewed some women workers who 'resigned voluntarily'.

One woman worker said that the strike was spontaneous and not influenced by any third party. Their demands were unequivocal. From start to finish, they had only demanded that JWM's management clarify the question of the workers' benefits. Long before the strike started, they had telexed the head office in Japan to enquire about the situation because the factory in Hong Kong did not offer a satisfactory explanation. They were told that the Japanese headquarters had entrusted someone who knew the Hong Kong situation to look into their situation and enquire into some political organizations and labour associations, but no formal contact of any sort resulted. The workers said that they did not know why the Japanese company investigated the matter indirectly.

Later, when the workers organized a trade union, they again telexed the Japanese company. There was no excuse for the headquarters' not being informed of their difficulties.

As for the intervention of the Trotskyites and the third parties, the worker said that there were no Trotskyites among the groups that came to their assistance. Only once did a young person from the Revolutionary Marxist League appear at the staircase of the factory. When they went to petition the Japanese Consulate, there was an elderly man from the *October Review* who gave a letter with donations to the workers. The old man stayed for a little while and then left. Neither of them appeared again, and no workers contacted them.

In the course of negotiations, the workers said that Fu Kwon-sin, an executive of CKLRS, and Gu Lai-hap, an executive of TWLSC, were served with an injunction order by the employer and forbidden entry to the factory. At the negotiating table, the workers 'fought alone'. Nevertheless, they encountered some labour-association representatives who were not invited by them. These representatives stood firm behind the management and tried to persuade the workers to give up their demands. If one claims that there were outsiders intervening and manipulating the workers, they were surely not from the groups supporting the workers, but from those called in by the management.

The workers said that they got the inspiration to petition the Japanese Consulate when they heard Chief Labour Officer Mao Si-hai repeatedly say that JWM was under pressure from other Japanese investors. Based on this, they went to the consulate to petition. As a matter of fact, after the petition was delivered JWM's attitude suddenly softened.

The workers thought that the turning point in resolving the strike was the day of the Dragon Boat Festival at the Shangri La Hotel when workers' representatives, accompanied by Lin Yi-chin, member of the Kwai Chung and Tsing Yi District Board, met with Mr Amukas, director of the Japanese headquarters' office. Amukas attempted to understand the situation of the workers. He said to the workers that much about the strike at the Hong Kong factory had not been reported to the Japanese company.

THOSE WHO SUFFER ARE EVENTUALLY THE WORKERS

A worker who quit said that they decided to leave 'voluntarily' mainly because they did not want the strike to drag on and affect those workers with financial problems. They did not admit defeat. During the strike, some people from outside believed that the workers could not persist and fight to the end. The workers believe their actions belied this judgement. This incident also taught the workers that they had the strength to fight for their rights on their own. One worker even said that she was no longer afraid to face difficulties.

The workers thought that, besides local associations, it was Lee Siu-ching who had given them the greatest support. He not only gave them spiritual support, but also raised money for the workers.

Mr Amukas, director of JWM, said after the strike that the 36 workers 'leaving voluntarily' were victims of inappropriate management by the middle strata.

However, had Mr Amukas ever pondered on the question: Why is it always the workers who are the ones sacrificed? We tried to contact Woo Char-hwa, director of JWM in Hong Kong, and Mao Si-hai, the chief labour relations officer, concerning the question of why there were labour association representatives not invited by the workers at the negotiating table, but they were unavailable for comment.

Works Cited

Althusser, L. *Lenin and Philosophy, and Other Essays*. New York: Monthly Review Press, 1971.

Arrighi, Giovanni. 'Labor Supplies in Historical Perspective: A Study of the Proletarianization of the African Peasantry in Rhodesia.' In *Essay on The Political Economy of Africa*, edited by Giovanni Arrighi and John S. Saul, 180–232. New York: Monthly Review Press, 1973.

Babbage, Charles. *On the Economy of Machinery and Manufactures*. London, Fairfield, NY: A. M. Kelly, 1986.

Bendix, Reinhard. *Work and Authority in Industry: Ideologies of Management in the Course of Industrialization*. Berkeley: University of California Press, 1974.

Bennett, John W. and Iwao Ishino. *Paternalism in the Japanese Economy*. Minneapolis: University of Minnesota Press, 1963.

Block, Maurice. 'The Long Term and the Short Term: The Economic and Political Significance of the Morality of Kinship.' In *The Character of Kinships*, edited by Jack Goody, 75–87. Cambridge, England: Cambridge University Press, 1973.

Bourdieu, Pierre. *Outline of a Theory of Practice*. Cambridge, England: Cambridge University Press, 1977.

———. *In Other Words: Essays Towards a Reflexive Sociology*. Stanford: Stanford University Press, 1990a.

———. *The Logic of Practice*. Cambridge: Polity Press, 1990b.

Braverman, Harry. *Labor and Monopoly Capital: The Degradation of Work in the Twentieth Century*. New York: Monthly Review Press, 1974.

Burawoy, Michael. 'The Anthropology of Industrial Work.' *Annual Review of Anthropology* 8 (1979): 231–66.

———. 'The Changing Face of Factory Regimes Under Advanced Capitalism.' Paper presented to the Center for the study of Advanced Industrial Societies, University of Chicago, 1983.

———. *The Politics of Production*. London: Vereo, 1985.

Chakrabarty, D. *Provincializing Europe: Postcolonial Thought and Historical Difference*. Princeton: Princeton University Press, 2000.

Cheval, K. *Social Conditions, Hong Kong: Britain's Last Stronghold*. London: Association for Radical East Asian Studies, 1972.

Chiu, Fred Y. L. 'The Specificity of the Political on Tiananmen Square, or a Poetic of the Popular Resistance in Beijing'. *Dialectical Anthropology* 16 (1991): 333–47.

———. 'Popular Democracy versus Class Struggle — A 1987 Chicago Debate.' In *Politics of Post-modernity — on Social Movements and their Discourses* (in Chinese), 1–45. Taipei: Tonsan publications, 1995.

———. 'Politics and the Body Social in Colonial Hong Kong.' *Positions: East Asia Cultures Critique* 4, no. 2 (1996): 185–215.

———. 'Suborientalism and the Subimperialist Predicament: Aboriginal Discourse and the Poverty of State-Nation Imagery.' *Positions: East Asia Cultures Critique* 8, no. 1 (2000): 101–49.

———. 'Combating the Double Processes of Decolonization/Re-colonization in Hong Kong or, "Postcoloniality" as Double-Pronged Moral Politics.' *Cultural Studies Review* 8, no. 2 (November 2002): 33–61.

———. 'De-class-ifying from the Proletariat — An Epistemological Critique of Lingering Class-ism.' *Economic and Political Weekly* (in press).

Cohn, Bernard. *An Anthropologist Among the Historians and Other Essays*. Delhi and New York: Oxford University Press, 1987.

Cooper, Eugene. 'Karl Marx's Other Island: The Evolution of Peripheral Capitalism in Hong Kong.' *Bulletin of Concerned Asian Scholars* 14, no. 1 (1982): 25–31.

Crapanzano, V. *Waiting: The Whites of South Africa*. New York: Random House, 1985.

Crozier, Michel. *Actors and Systems: The Politics of Collective Action*. Chicago: University of Chicago Press, 1980.

de Certeau, M. *The Practice of Everyday Life*. Berkeley: University of California Press, 1984.

Dening, Greg. *Performances*. Chicago: University of Chicago Press, 1996.

Elvin, Mark. *The Pattern of the Chinese Past*. Stanford: Stanford University Press, 1973.

England, Joe, and John Rear. *Chinese Labour Under British Rule*. London and Hong Kong: Oxford University Press, 1975.

Feuerbach, Ludwig. *The Essence of Christianity*. New York: Harper and Row, 1957.

———. *Lectures on the Essence of Religion*. New York: Harper and Row, 1967.

Foucault, Michel. *The Archaeology of Knowledge*. New York: Harper and Row, 1976.

Fröebel, F. *The New International Division of Labour*. Cambridge and New York: Cambridge University Press, 1980.

Fröebel, F., J. Heinrichs and O. Kreye. 'Export-Oriented Industrialization of Underdeveloped Countries.' *Monthly Review* (November 1978): 23–4.

Giddens, Anthony. *Capitalism and Modern Social Theory*, Cambridge: Cambridge University Press, 1971.

———. *Central Problems in Social Theory*. London: McMillan, 1979.

Gordon, Andrew. *The Evolution of Labor Relations in Japan's Heavy Industry, 1853–1955*. Cambridge, MA: Council on East Asian Studies, Harvard University, 1985.

———. *Theories of Poverty and Underemployment: Orthodox, Radical and Dual Labor Market Perspectives*. Lexington, MA: DC Heath, 1972.

Gramsci, Antonio. *Selections From The Prison Notebooks of Antonio Gramsci*. New York: International Publishers, 1989.

Hall, Stuart. *The Hard Road to Renewal: Thatcherism and the Crisis of the Left*. London: Verso, 1988.

———. 'Gramsci's Relevance for the Study of Race and Ethnicity.' In *Stuart Hall*, edited by B. Morley and K. H. Chen, 411–40. London and New York: Routledge, 1996.

———. 'The Problem of Ideology — Marxism Without Guarantees.' In *Stuart Hall*, edited by B. Morley and K. H. Chen, 25–46. London and New York: Routledge, 1996.

Hall, Stuart and M. Jaques. *The Politics of Thatcherism*. London: Lawrence and Wishart, 1983.

———. *New Times: the Changing Face of Politics in the 1990s*. London: Lawrence and Wishart, 1989.

Halliday, Jon. 'Hong Kong: Britain's Chinese Colony.' *New Left Review* 87–88: 91–113.

Harootunian, Harry D. *Things Seen and Unseen: Discourse and Ideology in Tokugawa Nativism*. Chicago: University of Chicago Press, 1988.

Harris, Peter Bernard. *Hong Kong: A Study in Bureaucratic Politics*. Hong Kong: Heinemann Asia, 1978.

Havel, Vaclav. 'Anti-Political Politics.' In *Civil Society and the State*, edited by John Keane, 381–98. London: Verso, 1988.

Hershfield, David C. *The Multinational Union Challenges the Multinational Company*. New York: The Conference Board, Inc., 1975.

Hong Kong Government. *Labour Advisory Board: Report For 1985 and 1986*. Hong Kong: Hong Kong Government, 1987.

Hopkins, Keith. *Hong Kong: The Industrial Colony*. Oxford: Oxford University Press, 1971.

Kondo, Dorinne K. *Crafting Selves: Power, Gender, and Discourses of Identity in a Japanese Workplace*. Chicago: University of Chicago Press, 1990.

Laclau, Ernesto. *Politics and Ideology in Marxist Theory*. London: Verso, 1977.

———. 'Democratic Antagonism and the Capitalist State.' In *The Frontiers of Political Theory*, edited by Michael Freeman and David Robertson. New York: St. Martin's Press, 1980.

Laclau, Ernesto and Chantal Mouffe. *Hegemony and Socialist Strategy: Towards and Radical Democratic Politics*. London: Verso, 1985.

Lewis, Arthur W. 'Economic Development with Unlimited Supplies of Labour.' *The Manchester School of Economic and Social Studies* XXII (1954): 139–91.

———. 'Unlimited Labour: Further Notes.' *The Manchester School of Economic and Social Studies* XXVI (1958): 1–32.

Long, Norman and Paul Richardson. 'Informal Sector, Petty Commodity Production & the Social Relations of Small-Scale Enterprise.' In *The New Economic Anthropology*, edited by J. Clammer. New York: St. Martin's, 1978.

Marglin, Stephen A. 'What Do Bosses Do?' In *The Division of Labour: The Labour Process and Class-Struggle in Modern Capitalism*, edited by Andre Gorz, 13–54. Hassocks: Harvester Press, 1976.

Marx, Karl. *Capital*. New York: International Publishers, 1967.

Mkandawire, P. T. 'Employment Strategies in the Third World: A Critique.' *Journal of Contemporary Asia* 7, No. 1 (1977): 27–43.

Moeran, M. *Okubo Diary: Portrait of a Japanese Valley*. Stanford: Stanford University Press, 1985.

Morley, B. and K. H. Chen, eds. *Stuart Hall*. London & New York: Routledge, 1996.

O'Connor, James. 'Productive and Unproductive Labor'. *Politics and Society* 5, No. 3 (1975): 297–336.

Polanyi, Karl. *The Great Transformation*. Boston: Beacon Press, 1974.

Portes, Alejandro and John Walton. *Labor, Class and the International System*. New York: Academic Press, 1981.

Przeworski, Adam. 'Proletariat into a Class: The Process of Class Formation.' In *Capitalism and Social Democrcy*, 47–97. Cambridge: Cambridge University Press, 1989.

Rabushka, Alvin. *Value for Money: The Hong Kong Budgetary Process*. Stanford: Hoover Institute Press, 1976.

———. *Hong Kong: A Study in Economic Freedom*. Chicago: University of Chicago Press, 1979.

Rohlen, Thomas P. *For Harmony and Strength*. Berkeley: University of California Press, 1979.

Rowe, William T. *Hankow: Conflict and Community in a Chinese City, 1796–1895*. Stanford: Stanford University Press, 1984.

Sabel, Charles F. *Work and Politics: The Division of Labour in Industry*. Cambridge: Cambridge University Press, 1984.

Sahlins, Marchall. *Islands of History*. Chicago: University of Chicago Press, 1985.

Sassen-Koob, S. 'Recomposition and Peripheralization at the Core.' *Contemporary Marxism* 5 (Summer 1982): 88–100.
Schiffer, J. R. 'Anatomy of a Laissez-Faire Government: The Hong Kong Growth Model Reconsidered.' Unpublished Paper (November 1983). Hong Kong: The University of Hong Kong.
Scott, James C. *The Moral Economy of the Peasant*. New Haven: Yale University Press, 1976.
Sit, Victor F. S. and H. Ng. 'Ambulatory Labour in Hong Kong.' *International Labour Review* 119, No. 4. 1980 n.p.
Smith, Henry. *John Stuart Mill's Other Island: A Study of the Economic Development of Hong Kong*. London: Institute of Economic Affair Limited, 1966.
Thomson, E. P. 'Time, Work-Discipline, and Industrial Capitalism.' *Past and Present* 38 (1967): 56–97.
Touraine, Alain. *The Self-production of Society*. Chicago: University of Chicago Press, 1977.
———. *The Voice and the Eye: An Analysis of Social Movements*. Cambridge: Cambridge University Press, 1981.
———. *Return of the Actor: Social Theory in Postindustrial Society*. Minneapolis: University of Minnesota Press, 1988.
———. *Can We Live Together?* Cambridge: Polity Press, 2000.
———. *Beyond Neoliberalism*, Cambridge: Polity Press, 2001.
Touraine, A., M. Wieviorka and F. Dubet. *The Workers' Movement*. Cambridge: Cambridge University Press, 1987.
Tsing, A. L. *In the Realm of the Diamond Queen: Marginality in an Out-Of-The-Way Place*. Princeton: Princeton University Press, 1993.
van Helvoort, Ernest. *The Japanese Working Man: What Choice? What Reward?* Vancouver: University of British Columbia Press, 1979.
van Wolferen, Karel. *The Enigma of Japanese Power*. New York: Vintage Books, 1990.
Voloshinov, V. N. *Marxism and the Philosophy of Language*. New York: Seminar Press Inc., 1973.
———. *Freudianism: A Critical Sketch*. Bloomington: Indiana University Press, 1987.
Watson, Tony J. *Sociology, Work and Industry*. London & Boston: Routledge & Kegan Paul, 1980.
Willis, Paul. *Learning to Labour: How Working Class Kids Get Working Class Jobs*. Farnborough: Saxon House, 1977.
Wolpe, Harold. 'Capitalism & Cheap Labour-Power in South Africa: From Segregation to Apartheid.' *Economy and Society* 1, no. 4 (1972): 425–56.
Wong, John. 'Hong Kong's Food Supply from China: Dependence or Interdependence?' *Economics Journal/Economic Society* (1972): 49–57. Hong Kong: The University of Hong Kong.
Woronoff, Jon. *Hong Kong: Capitalist Paradise*. Hong Kong: Heinemann, 1980.